CHRISTIAN FAITH
AND THE ENVIRONMENT

ECOLOGY AND JUSTICE
An Orbis Series on Global Ecology

Advisory Board Members
Mary Evelyn Tucker
John A. Grim
Leonardo Boff
Sean McDonagh

The Orbis Series *Ecology and Justice* publishes books that seek to integrate an understanding of the Earth as an interconnected life system with concerns for just and sustainable systems that benefit the entire Earth. Books in the Series concentrate on ways to:

• reexamine the human-Earth relationship in the light of contemporary cosmological thought
• develop visions of common life marked by ecological integrity and social justice
• expand on the work of those who are developing such fields as eco-social ecology, bioregionalism, and animal rights
• promote inclusive participative strategies that enhance the struggle of the Earth's voiceless poor for justice
• deepen appreciation for and expand dialogue among religious traditions on the issue of ecology
• encourage spiritual discipline, social engagement, and the reform of religion and society toward these ends.

Viewing the present moment as a time for responsible creativity, the Series seeks authors who speak to ecojustice concerns and who bring into dialogue perspectives from the Christian community, from the world's other religions, from secular and scientific circles, and from new paradigms of thought and action.

Ecology and Justice Series

CHRISTIAN FAITH AND THE ENVIRONMENT

Making Vital Connections

Brennan R. Hill

ORBIS BOOKS

Maryknoll, New York 10545

The Catholic Foreign Mission Society of America (Maryknoll) recruits and trains people for overseas missionary service. Through Orbis Books, Maryknoll aims to foster the international dialogue that is essential to mission. The books published, however, reflect the opinions of their authors and are not meant to represent the official position of the society.

Library of Congress Cataloging-in-Publication Data
Hill, Brennan.
    Christian faith and the environment : making vital connections / Brennan R. Hill.
       p.   cm. – (Ecology and justice series)
    Includes bibliographical references and index.
    ISBN 1-57075-210-9
    1. Human ecology–Religious aspects–Christianity.   I. Title.
II. Series: Ecology and justice.
BT695.5.H55   1998
261.8'362–dc21

                                   98-26654
                                     CIP

To my beloved wife, Marie,
and to those who will inherit the earth,
especially my daughter, Ami, my son, B.J.,
my future grandchildren, and all my students.

Those of us who love the sea, who recognize the blood relationship of all earth's beings, who see on this Water Planet a growing threat to our most fundamental biological machinery, do not command the money and power of even a single major multinational corporation. But we can wield the formidable power of our numbers, the strength of a great unified crowd of citizens of the planet . . . and the most effective weapon we have as citizens—as parents—is the sheer force of our numbers. It is the weaponry of the peacemakers and the common people throughout history.

For all the darkness that presently confronts us and our descendants, there is no reason to give up. There is every reason to take up the fight, because we have within our grasp the power of the people to force the right decisions. The more people, the more power, the more hope.

–Jacques-Yves Cousteau

Contents

Acknowledgments

I wish to thank Xavier University for providing me with a sabbatical semester to finish this book. Special gratitude goes to Dr. William Burrows of Orbis Books for his many helpful suggestions and for guiding this book toward publication; to my wife, Marie, for all her splendid editing and proofreading; to Darleen Frickman for all the assistance she rendered; to Matthew Hogan for helping me with the case studies; and to Sr. Debbie Harmeling, the librarian at the Athenaeum, for all her generous help.

Introduction

Concern for the conservation of our environment is relatively recent. Since the beginning of the industrial revolution in the nineteenth century and the many advances in technology in the twentieth century, the Western world has been focused on production and consumption and has been largely optimistic about future progress in these areas. The environmental hazards of polluted air and water were simply accepted as the necessary evils one had to tolerate in order to have jobs and economic security.

Those who were oppressed by unfavorable environments in the past had to accept their situations. James Nash, a pioneer in the area of environmental theology, writes about how his family put up with pollution for the sake of jobs:

> The steel mills in the lower Monongahela Valley of western Pennsylvania in the 1940s and 1950s were an environmental catastrophe. Thick putrid clouds of pollutants bellowed almost continuously from the McKeesport Works across the river to our row houses on the bluffs in West Mifflin and Duquesne. "Dirt" and "soot" from the mills were ubiquitous; snow sometimes seemed to fall gray and always turned dirty early. Chemical particles from the clouds sometimes penetrated the paint on cars and rare wooden houses; we wondered about their effects on our lungs and burning eyes. The persistent noises, day and night, from the blast furnaces and the freight trains were often deafening. . . . The trees in the woods along the steep hillside were stunted, but we did not know why. The Monongahela River, a sewer for the mills, was biologically dead for maybe twenty miles. . . . Even the sun was unusually hazy and the humidity abnormally high in summer.[1]

Nash goes on to say that employment was so important to his family that leaving the area was out of the question. He laments the fact that generations of his family put up with all this and kept quiet about the environmental degradation because "we didn't know any better."[2]

EARLY VOICES OF PROTEST

One of the first voices of alarm and protest toward the deterioration in the environment came in 1962. In that year Rachel Carson published her much acclaimed book, *The Silent Spring,* a study of the poisoning of the land and the killing of its life-systems. In the same year Aldo Leopold published *A Sand County Almanac,* a seminal book on the beauty and interconnection of living things and "land ethic." In the 1970s Wendell Berry and others had significant influence on the growing public awareness with regard to the degrading of the environment.

By the 1980s the environmental movement was well underway. In 1984 The Worldwatch Institute began publishing its annual *State of the World,* and in 1987 the United Nations World Commission published its important study on the relationship of environment and development.[3] Today there seems to be an ever-growing consciousness among people around the world and in the United States. Since the first Earth Day in this country in the 1970s until the second in 1990, there has been a tremendous growth in response to environmental concerns.

CHRISTIAN CONCERNS

The awakening of the Christian churches toward the environment is also of recent vintage. Lynn White's well-known charge that Christianity should bear an immense burden of the guilt for the ecological crisis came in 1967. White maintained that Western technology, science, and commitment to progress were largely conditioned by the Christian belief that God created the world to be ruled and used by human beings. White charged that Western Christianity placed humans at the center of life and believed that God had given them "dominion" over creation. Furthermore, White predicted that the degradation of the earth would worsen unless Christian beliefs were reformed and an equality recognized among God's creatures.[4]

White's accusation provoked an avalanche of reaction. Many agreed with White's thesis and carried the charges even further, maintaining that it was necessary to jettison the Christian tradition in order to save the earth. Some suggested a return to the ancient and indigenous religions in which nature was reverenced. As result, the environmental movement has often been characterized by hostility toward the Christian tradition.[5]

Naturally there was a defensive response to the charges of White from religious thinkers, mostly from the Protestant and Evangelical communities. In fact, a significant religious environmental movement has grown out of this response, and authors from many denominations have made substantial contributions to the integration of religion and ecology.[6] The World Council of Churches published a significant statement in 1991, and individual denominations began to issue their own statements, most notably the American Baptists, the Presbyterians, and the Evangelical Lutherans. In 1991 an important statement was issued by religious leaders who attended the Summit on Environment.[7]

A NEW CATHOLIC AWARENESS

Among the Christian churches, the Catholic church has been slow to address environmental issues. The church remained quite aloof from the debate that swirled around White's charges and gave little attention to environmental issues. The Second Vatican Council (1962-65), the most significant church council in modern times, was concerned primarily with church reform, and although it did turn its attention to world issues, the council did not deal with ecology. Although there have been mentions of ecology scattered in modern papal statements, the only substantial document is that by John Paul II, issued in 1990.[8] Even the new *Catechism of the Catholic Church* deals only obliquely with environmental concerns under its treatment of "creation."[9]

Bishops' conferences throughout the world have also begun to address environmental issues and the grave concerns they have over the rapid deterioration of their own local areas. These include bishops of the Dominican Republic (1987), Guatemala (1988), Northern Italy (1988), Philippines (1988), Australia (1990), and the United States (1991).[10] The Council of European Bishops issued a joint statement with leaders from European Protestant churches in 1995 and in 1997.[11]

Catholic theologians are just beginning to address environmental issues.[12] Much of this interest has grown out of Catholic theology's contemporary concern with public issues, peace and justice, and liberation. Since environmental concerns are closely related to social, political, economic, and gender issues, ecology is now beginning to receive some theological attention. However, there is still little urgency among many Catholic biblical scholars, systematic theologians, and moralists to address the present environmental crisis. Convincing Catholics on the grassroots level will be another level of challenge. One needs only attend Mass to become aware of how seldom environmental concerns are mentioned in homilies or eucharistic liturgical prayers. A considerable number of Catholics are still private, otherworldly, and traditional in their beliefs and their spirituality. Even those concerned about the environment as citizens are often not accustomed to connecting their religious beliefs with such "secular" issues. A good number of younger Christians (many of whom are concerned about ecology) are not familiar enough with the intricacies of the tradition to be able to make the needed connections with ecology.

MAKING VITAL CONNECTIONS

In this book I have set out to link many areas of Christian belief with the environment. I begin by establishing a theological framework, showing how the methods of such contemporary theologians as Rahner, Lonergan, Tillich,

Teilhard, and Tracy have taught Christians how to build bridges between the Christian tradition and current issues. Working within such a context of connection, I explore the scriptures, both Hebrew and Christian, searching for ways to integrate their wisdom with our concerns for the earth. Next, I examine threads within Christology and sacramental theology that might be woven into an environmental theology.

Midway through the book I examine some of the growing number of church documents on ecology. These documents originated in Protestant, Catholic, and Evangelical churches and congregations and are representative of both first- and third-world countries. They reveal the global as well as ecumenical dimensions of the environmental crisis. They also provide a road map for how Christian scriptures, beliefs, and ethical teachings are to be reinterpreted and carefully applied to the task of conserving the earth and sharing its resources.

In chapter 7 I turn my attention to the God question and discuss how atheism, as well as various notions and images of God, can affect attitudes toward the environment. In chapter 8 I provide an overview of the ever-increasing writings by feminist theologians on the environment. In chapter 9 I consider how some of the rich traditions of Christian spirituality might be useful in developing a spirituality for caring for the earth. Finally, in the concluding chapter I deal with Christian values and moral teachings and suggest how these might be helpful in developing an environmental ethic.

I consider this work to be a beginning, a modest pioneering effort to join Christian scripture, doctrines, spirituality, and ethical values with our contemporary concerns for the earth. It is my hope that this book will stimulate many other such efforts, so that the Christian churches can take their place in the vanguard of those determined to provide future generations with a healthy and beautiful world in which to live.

1.

Toward an Environmental Theology

My favorite poet, Li Po, wrote about our beautiful area, Three Gorges, which is along Yangtze River. He said: "You ask me: why do I live on this green mountain? I smile, no answer, my heart serene." Now the government has decided to flood our whole area and build a dam. They will destroy 13 cities, 140 towns and 1352 villages in the process. My family has been here for many generations: it is all we know. And it will be hard to watch our homes, our sacred pagodas and monuments, even the graves of our ancestors covered over forever in the muddy waters of the Yangtze. A million of us will have to move on and start again—who knows where. Some complain, but they are quickly silenced. One courageous woman wrote on how many of our top scientists oppose the dam and say it will ruin the environment, but she was imprisoned. My heart is not serene.

—Yu-Lan Wu, Three Gorges, China

It seems evident that the earth's environment is facing a crisis. In response, the global community is calling upon scientists, economists, politicians, and experts in many areas for solutions to this complex and multifaceted crisis. World religions are also being asked to reach into their rich traditions of beliefs and values for ways to conserve the earth. Christians, who number well over a billion people, are being urgently requested to recognize a relationship between their faith and the future of the planet.

There will be a need for new theological approaches if the Christian tradition is to be linked with environmental issues. In part, these approaches might borrow from the now classical methods and insights of twentieth-century systematic theologians, such as Karl Rahner, Bernard Lonergan, Paul Tillich, and David Tracy, all of whom have shown how to link doctrine with human experience, culture, and the world. The work of Pierre Teilhard de Chardin, which is a benchmark for connecting the Christian tradition with science and the earth, might also be useful. Throughout this chapter I will suggest how the insights of such theologians might provide the foundation for the eventual formulation of an environmental theology.

This entire theological endeavor—and it has only just begun—will involve a complete rereading and revisioning of the Christian tradition in light of modern ecology. In my view an environmental theology should include the following components: (1) a sound foundation in scripture, using contemporary biblical criticism for its interpretations; (2) a Christian approach to anthropology and human experience; (3) an emphasis on the transforming role of theology; and (4) an ongoing correlation of Catholic doctrinal and moral beliefs with the ecological concerns of today's world.

THE SCRIPTURES AS FOUNDATIONAL

One of the most significant moves of the Second Vatican Council was to call its people back to the Bible. The council moved away from the past bifurcation of scripture and tradition and viewed them as integrally connected, coming from the same wellspring, and deserving of equal esteem.[1]

Much of systematic theology in the centuries just prior to Vatican II had focused on the official definitions of councils and popes and had used scripture mostly as "proof texts" to further strengthen the authority of the church's doctrinal pronouncements. The post–Reformation church had become preoccupied with defending its dogmatic positions, and thus theology gradually lost the deep richness it had had in ancient and medieval times. The so-called manual theology of the eighteenth and nineteenth centuries focused on explaining doctrinal texts. Scripture was no longer the primary resource it had been in past centuries.

Contemporary theology views both scripture and tradition as much more integrally related; it sees them as having developed over time both in interpretation and in application. It is in scripture that God's self-revelation to countless peoples unfolds over a span of thousands of years. It is in biblical revelation where God gradually unfolds the mysterious plan to create and to save the world. This self-revelation of God we now realize is not given literally by dictation but is mysteriously hidden in the myths, stories, prayers, and searchings of God's people. Biblical stories tell of the origins of the world from the Creator's power, as well as God's calling of the great leaders of Israel and Christianity. Scripture narrates God's unfailing, saving presence and power in the world. It gives an inspired account of God coming to people as a saving God, as a God who at one point becomes incarnate in the world and is personified in the person of Jesus Christ. The Bible tells of the beginnings of Christ's church, gives accounts of this church's memories of Jesus and his teachings, and vividly recounts the deepest searchings of God's people. It is this divine revelation with regard to the nature of God, creation, incarnation, and salvation that needs to be linked with our environmental concerns. There is unlimited richness in the Bible that needs to be studied and contemplated in light of our concerns for the earth.

Scripture is interpretive and theological in that it presents a diverse and yet inspired account of how people over thousands of years wrestled with many interpretations of God's movements in their lives. The diversity of views produces multiple theologies in the Bible. The theologies of the Hebrew scriptures reflect thousands of years of vigorous and prayerful seeking to understand the self-revelation of God. The Christian theologies of the New Testament evolved over a half-century as different communities grappled with the significance of Jesus and his teachings. The Bible is indeed a library of ancient Hebrew and Christian theologies. These are the theologies that need to be explored and then carefully applied to the ecological issues of today. Yet these applications have to be made carefully. Whimsical, strained, or overly pious connections will not effectively motivate thinking people to get involved in environmental issues.

The Shift from the Literal Approach

Contemporary theology has moved away from a literalist or fundamentalist view of scripture. The literalist approach tends to view scripture as history and biography, a divinely inspired account of what happened and what was said in ancient times. This approach tends to lock the scriptural teaching in the past, often giving it little or no relevance to contemporary problems. At the same time, the literal approach can nurture a piety that is otherworldly and private, a spirituality that is concerned primarily with personal salvation. Here one would not expect many connections to be made between scripture and public affairs, including ecology.

Since the 1940s Catholic biblical scholarship has studied the Bible in its cultural, linguistic, and historical settings. Scripture is now studied in all the complexities of its sources, literary forms, ongoing editing, interpretations, and multiple theologies. Over the last fifty years much effort has been given to locating the original meaning of scriptural passages, that is, the initial intent of the authors. Biblical research, however, cannot be content with locating the original meaning of scriptural texts, for to stop there is to risk seeing the scriptures as archaic and irrelevant. Instead, biblical criticism needs to consider scripture as a living word from a dynamic God, a revelation that is pertinent to the concerns of each age. The original meaning is important, but it is also crucial that there be an openness to fresh meanings and new applications that are germane to today's issues. Such openness in the past paved the way for a dialogue between scripture and science, and between scripture and contemporary social problems. Today such expansiveness is needed to establish a dialogue between our biblical tradition and our modern environmental concerns. As Catholic biblical scholarship approaches the half-century mark, many of its findings are now relevant to contemporary environmental issues.

Biblical scholarship comes to us from experts. It is "from above," and though invaluable, such scholarship offers only a partial view of the scriptures. There is also a need to understand scriptures "from below," that is, filtered through the life experience of the faithful. This approach has been taken in recent times by the poor and oppressed in the Third World. Ordinary people struggling for justice have been able to integrate the scriptural passages into their own present context and discern new meanings. For many, the Jesus of the gospels has become a liberator who stands with them as they are victimized. Gospel teachings have come to life again and given oppressed peoples the courage to stand against injustice. Similarly, we now see how scripture can awaken people to see how their earth is being debased and to take action against those who are responsible.

Applying Scripture to Ecology

Both the Hebrew and Christian scriptures can provide us with a wealth of resources to help us better understand and care for our environment. As we shall see in detail in the next chapter, the Hebrew scriptures have much to tell us about how all reality comes from the creative hand of God and is therefore good and worth sustaining. Many rich veins of creation theology point to how humans are called to share responsibly in the creative powers of God and to represent God in the care of creation.

The scriptures portray humans in their highest dignity as well as in their lowest disgrace. Throughout scripture there exists a sacred covenant between God, the earth, and every living creature, as well as a constant divine availability of forgiveness and salvation from a gracious God. In the scriptures God's children celebrate the glory of God along with all of creation, and at the same time they debase creation with slavery, violence, and greed. The scriptures leave little doubt that human beings are responsible for sin and corruption yet maintain that humans never lose their status as "images of God" or their responsibility to cultivate and to care for creation.

The dignity of the earth and all living things is clearly revealed throughout the Hebrew scriptures. God is revealed as the source, owner, sustainer, and destiny of all creation. Creation itself can teach us how to care for and preserve all things. Creation is also the context in which the saving God brings redemption to all of creation. There is a past for creation, a dynamic present, and a new creation that can be hoped for in the future.

The magnificent creation theologies of the Hebrew scriptures are carried over into the Christian scriptures. We shall see in chapter 3 how, through the incarnation, God enters creation and becomes flesh. The Son of God leads an authentic human life and reveals the presence and power of God's reign in the world. Jesus uses nature to instruct on the creativity and care that God exerts in creation. Human beings, especially the poor and oppressed, are raised to their proper dignity. In Jesus, God reveals the divine will to be provider, healer, and savior of the world.

God as the Center

The scriptures, while clearly revealing the dignity of both the human and the earth, are God-centered. The central figure of the drama of creation and redemption is the Creator God. Sometimes hidden and at other times an imposing presence, the divinity is an ever-acting presence in history. In the Hebrew scriptures rock, shepherd, mother, father, spouse, and many other images are used to describe the manifold dimensions of this mysterious God.

In the Christian scriptures Jesus calls this God "Abba" (loving Dad); during his life, death, and resurrection Jesus is gradually revealed to be the Son of God, the incarnation of this creating and saving God. Jesus' entire life is presented as a search for the will of his God, a prayerful reflection on how his God must be honored and praised. Jesus reveals through the Hebrew image of kingdom the loving and saving presence and power of Abba God. Abba creates, cares for, and constantly saves the world.

The Bible with its God-centered perspective provides us with grounds for recognizing the dignity of both humans and earth. Here all have their source, sustenance, and goal from the Creator. Here all of reality reflects the goodness, beauty, and love of God. God is perceived not as a distant force, but as a personal power present in all things. Through this biblical perspective scriptures can assist in developing an environmental theology that connects both humans and the earth with the ground and center of their existence, the Creator-God.

A CHRISTIAN ANTHROPOLOGY

An environmental theology will recognize the dignity of the human person and see humans as uniquely singular and yet integral to creation. Humans are creatures who have the capacity to search for meaning and ultimacy, not only through reason but also through other God-given capacities. In the following we will examine this view of the human person from the point of view of contemporary theology.

Human Dignity

The dignity of the human person is at the very heart of the Christian tradition. The Hebrew scriptures highlight this dignity in their descriptions of humans being created in the "image and likeness of God." Human life is described as precious in that it comes from the very breath of God, and humans are commissioned to reproduce this life in their children. Moreover, God solemnly forbids the taking of life in the Mosaic law. Those who have lost their freedom will be liberated by God; those who have degraded their lives with sin can be forgiven and saved. Gradually the Hebrew people came to understand that human life does not end in death but will rise into new life.

The dignity of human life is also at the heart of Jesus' gospel. In the person of Jesus Christ, God reveals the "godliness" of human life. Jesus describes himself as "the way, the truth, and the life," as "the resurrection and the life." His entire life is dedicated to extending love, forgiveness, compassion, and healing to other persons, especially the poorest of the poor. Moreover, Jesus promises those who believe in him "eternal life." We will look at the biblical views on human dignity in more detail in later chapters.

Environmental theology will require an anthropology that reclaims the dignity of human life. This dignity does not give humans claim to superiority or domination over other peoples or the rest of creation. Rather, it confers on each person a unique responsibility to care for people who share the same dignity and to care for all of creation. In this perspective all things are linked, so that respect for human life implies regard for all life and for the earth itself. As the bishops of the United States point out: "Our tradition calls us to protect the life and dignity of the human person, and it is increasingly clear that this task cannot be separated from the care and defense of all of creation."[2]

Environmentalists often point out that many of our ecological crises today are a result of placing the human at the center of the world and all life. Humanism, secularism, and capitalism have all stressed that the human person reigns supreme in the world, and that the earth and its resources are here to satisfy, to be used, and to be manipulated for profit. Our present-day consumer society, with all its superfluous goods and waste, is a product of such a mentality. Nature has become a commodity to be controlled and exploited for the benefits of people. Nature is denied an integrity of its own; it exists only for human consumption, recreation, or aesthetic pleasure.

The Human in Context

Christianity itself has often been human-centered. The hierarchical mentality so prevalent in the Christian tradition has viewed humans at the apex of creation, the ones who have dominion over all things. Even the most recent *Catechism of the Catholic Church* asserts that "God created everything for man."[3] The catechism goes on to advocate responsible stewardship, but nonetheless places everything on the earth for human purposes and thus ignores the fact that each thing has its own distinctive purpose, meaning, and integrity.

Some scholars urge a shift to an earth-centered perspective, wherein the earth and its resources are seen to have an integral worth and dignity of their own. The human person is then seen to be part of and not greater than the environment. Thomas Berry, a scholar who is centered on the earth and calls himself a "geologian," writes: "So too there is need to remember that the human is a component member of the earth and its life systems. The earth and its well-being are our basic referents as regards reality and value. The earth can exist without us. We cannot exist without the earth."[4]

Placing the earth at the center can have its own problems if carried to the extreme. In the so-called deep ecology movement humans are viewed as creatures on a par with all other creatures. In conflict situations humans have no more right to preferential consideration than any other creatures.[5] This is an attempt to topple past hierarchical thinking, but in so doing humans lose their uniqueness and indeed even their given responsibility to sustain nature. The earth-centered approach can also lead to the sacralization of nature that was common in "pagan" religions. The Judeo-Christian tradition has recognized the goodness of creation but has not raised it to the level of the divine. All things are good, but they are not God. If creation is to be considered "holy" at all, it is because its holiness is derived from the Creator.

Humanity Linked with the Earth

An effective environmental theology will require a contemporary Christian anthropology, one that values the dignity and distinctiveness of the human person and yet does not thereby give humans the right to dominate the rest of reality. Humans are part of nature, and therefore there is an interconnectedness between humanity and the rest of creation. If there is to be a hierarchy of existence at all, it should follow Jesus' teachings that the last shall be first and that the higher will serve the lower.

Edward Schillebeeckx has observed that it is impossible to define the reality we call humanity. Not only is human nature such a complex reality, it also is a reality that is still "on the way" in its development. Human nature has been derived from nature itself, is part of it, and continues to evolve along with the universe and the earth. Matter, as well as spirit, comes from the Creator. Our destiny, then, is linked irrevocably with that of our world. As Rahner points out, the human person "achieves his transcendence precisely by means of the material of the world, of its bodily corporeality and history."[6]

It has been said that our bodies are made out of stardust, derivatives from the original Big Bang explosion. This also means that our bodies are related to all the other products of the original event, including stars, plants, animals, and rocks. (Even the primitive creation myth in Genesis 2 describes us as "mud people," made from the earth and destined to return to the earth.) Since we are so closely related to nature, we can learn about ourselves by studying nature. We can also become aware that to destroy anything of the earth is in a way to destroy ourselves. Modern notions that we are "masters of the universe," here to dominate and use our surroundings as autonomous individuals, do not authentically reflect how we are related to the world in which we live.

Not only do humans share in the materiality of the universe, they share also in its history. Creation is ongoing, and as the world changes and develops, human life is shaped and molded. Conversely, as human life and culture change, the world is profoundly affected. The futures of the world and of humanity are intimately connected.

Humans are indeed singular within creation. They are the only creatures who can reflectively reason, give meaning to reality, choose freely, and act responsibly. This singularity does not make the human superior to other creatures, however, nor does it give humans the right to dominate or oppress the rest of creation. Rather, the uniqueness of humans gives them a responsibility to care for all of creation and to share in the creative and sustaining power of the Creator.

For people of faith the future of humankind and the world is ultimately in the hands of the Creator. As Schillebeeckx points out, the God of Christianity is God of the future, drawing all creation to a "new creation."[7] God has freely chosen to express divinity outwardly in creation and then actually enter creation even more intimately in the person of Jesus. The world is now the setting whereby God continues to communicate God's self to us. Humans, then, are called to listen and give meaning to this revelation and to assist creation in coming to the end time, when knowing and being become one.

The environmental implications are clear. To endanger and even to destroy our world are to do harm to ourselves and to reject our call to help bring creation to its rightful fulfillment. Sustaining our earth is integral to human destiny. We cannot be mere observers, users, or even researchers of the world. Most certainly we are not justified in being dominators or manipulators of our world. We are neither the center of our world nor its master. Rather, we are called to be servants to our world and co-creators with our God.

The Human Person as Searcher

Theology often places a great deal of emphasis on the cognitive. The classic definition of theology by Anselm is "faith seeking understanding." Theology is investigative, analytical, interpretive. Theology studies the history of the Christian tradition, interprets its beliefs, and applies them to contemporary issues.

Karl Rahner, perhaps more than any other theologian of our time, has been able to move theology beyond mere abstraction and theoretical explanation of doctrine to a searching endeavor that plumbs the very depths of being. He has been able to link the doing of theology to the way humans were created by God. Rahner pointed out that we are questioners, constantly seeking to understand.[8] He taught that the path of questioning leads us to investigate and search out the meaning of all of reality. Of all creatures we are the ones who have been gifted with the powers of self-reflection, analysis, and synthesis. We are capable of discovering the truth, beauty, unity, and harmony of creation. No other creature is capable of grasping the meaning and purpose of our world. Thus we are the only creature who can exert major influences on the world in which we live.

Rahner also observed that God can be found as the horizon of our questioning. God's revelation can come to us in the midst of our struggle to learn, understand, and reflect on our world. According to Rahner, humans have the capacity to reach out for the transcendent. People have an unlimited openness to reality and ultimately can open themselves to God. As "beings," people by necessity are involved with the "being" of the world and have the capacity to go beyond finite beings to the infinite Being. Knowledge of the world can be linked to the Creator of our world. Even the constant human experience of limitations in understanding and awareness of the inadequacies of concepts can be used by God to help us to reach out beyond what we see.[9]

Rahner pointed out in his earliest work that humans are "spirits in the world." People are part spirit and part world, and thus are in a unique position to bridge the gap between spirit and materiality. Humans are knowing subjects who have a "being with the world" and have been gifted with the extraordinary capacity to transcend the world and come into contact with the divine source, sustainer, and goal of all reality. They are uniquely capable of looking at the world, discovering God's purpose and goal in creating it, and discerning the roles to play in destroying or sustaining it.

Rahner's anthropology stands in contrast to that of other modern influential thinkers like Marx, Feuerbach, Nietzsche, and Freud. All of these men denied the existence of the spiritual dimension of reality and held that ultimate reality (God) was a mere illusion or human projection. These latter views have helped produce a materialism and secularism that have proved most destructive of the environment. In contrast Rahner and others have proffered an anthropology that recognizes the existence of God and the spiritual. Moreover, this anthropology holds that the Creator and the spiritual dimension of life are accessible to human reason. Reason is not locked into the material world and need not be satisfied with mere measuring and analysis. Reason can transcend the boundaries of observable phenomena and go beyond the boundaries of everyday life. Reason can go beyond being to the Divine Being present in all. Bernard Lonergan has written: "The question of God, then, lies within man's reason."[10] Thus reason can serve as a bridge between the world in which we live and the God who created it.

The human capacity to search has many implications for an environmental theology. There is a need to question, to probe, and to search for a better understanding of the world in which we live. Environmental theology will have to be familiar with science and have a clear and accurate grasp of the state of the environment and a realistic understanding of pressing ecological issues globally and locally.

At the same time this very search for understanding nature and our experience of it can be a path to better understand God's presence and power in our world, as well as more clearly to discern our responsibilities toward care of our environment. Our openness to the beauty of nature can lead to an openness to God in nature. Our scientific questioning can lead us to encounters with the Creator. Commitment to the earth can lead to new insights into our religious traditions.

As "spirits in the world," we are the only creatures equipped to recognize the spiritual dimension in all of reality, the presence of the divine in all of creation. Such awareness obviously has significant environmental implications. One who is touched with the presence of God's beauty, power, and love in the world will no doubt take seriously the care and enrichment of the earth and its resources.

Even with a clear understanding of our environment and a readiness to apply our religious beliefs, the solutions will not be simple. Piety or an overly sentimental appreciation of nature will not be enough. Solutions to environmental problems involve a vigorous application of economics, politics, and science, as well as a revisioning of religious beliefs and moral values. Such cooperation among the disciplines was noted at a historic gathering of religious leaders and scientists in Washington, D.C., in 1992: "We believe that science and religion, working together, have an essential contribution to make toward any significant mitigation and resolution of the world environmental crisis. What good are the most fervent moral imperatives if we do not understand the dangers and how to avoid them? What good is all the data in the world without a steadfast moral compass?"[11]

Beyond the Rational

An environmental theology must go beyond the cognitive and be linked holistically to other human capacities. Once again it was Rahner who insightfully linked theology with human experience. He situated his theology in the context of human anthropology and asserted that humans were actually created as beings with the capacity to receive divine revelation through experience in the world. In his view humans have a potential to know and love the absolute Being who is the source of all creation. God is a Creator who has called all things into being and has uniquely linked the divine self with being, first through the process of creation and then even more dramatically through the incarnation.[12] Rahner saw human persons as knowing, imagining, feeling, deciding, and acting persons. In their own environments they have the capacity to receive, understand, and relate to God's self-disclosure.

Bernard Lonergan often wrote about the mind's capacity to undergo conversion. By this he meant that the mind has the power to see beyond what seems to be and to perceive reality as it is. The mind also has the capacity to move on to love, and eventually on to action.[13] Lonergan indicated that human consciousness has experiences; after inquiring in order to understand these experiences, it can move toward judgments and decisions to act. Thus each person is called to a meaningful conscious life, one gained through careful knowing, loving, and doing. For Lonergan, human knowledge properly leads to love and ultimately to the experience of God's love, the highest level of human consciousness. In love, the transcendent enters the heart and becomes real. Faith, then, is achieved when knowledge is born into love. Lonergan puts it this way: "Faith, accordingly, is such further knowledge when the love is God's love flooding our hearts."[14]

A Holistic Search

The environmental theologian needs to go beyond mere knowledge of the Christian tradition and the environment. This knowledge has be translated into a genuine love of all human beings and nature as well. There must also be a resolve to act against those who seek to bring degradation to the world and to resist those who relegate the poor to the most hazardous areas and deprive them of resources. In approaching the environment we need to experience our surroundings, come to understand them, make judgments on what needs to be done to sustain them, and then decide to act on behalf of them. Such conversion is indeed of the whole person and is the road to faith and the experience of the love of God through nature.[15]

This holistic approach to human reaction identifies other feelings toward environmental issues.The religious thinker also can be driven to act on behalf of the environment by feelings of anger toward those who wantonly destroy the environment; compassion for the people, animals, and other living things that suffer from ecological poisoning; hope for sustaining the earth in spite of all the vast destruction; concern for the future generations; and many other feelings that easily can be stirred once one understands the growing list of environmental problems that faces us today.

Finally, what Bernard Meland calls an "appreciative awareness" of our world is important here. This is the enjoyment we gain from looking at a beautiful piece of art, watching a graceful ballet, listening to a lovely piece of music, or simply taking a walk along the ocean. The human aesthetic sense is unique and can provoke strong feelings and deep resolve. It is in such experiences that the person of faith can encounter the Creator.[16]

Environmental theology needs to approach the earth with a deep appreciation for the beauty and integrity of all things. Such appreciation, as well as the desire to preserve such beauty for future generations, can be a strong motive for acting on behalf of sustaining the environment.

HUMAN EXPERIENCE AS RESOURCE

Human experience has been retrieved as a valuable resource in theology. Traditional manual theology often departed from the richness of patristic and medieval theology. Manual theology generally supported a dualism, sharply separating the natural from the supernatural, the "worldly" experience from the spiritual experience. Thinkers such as Maurice Blondel and John Henry Newman stressed the importance of human experience in theology in the nineteenth century, but this notion did not become part of the mainstream until the work of Rahner and Lonergan. Both of these theologians demonstrated that the study of the human is the study of God because there is a created continuity between the two. God has built a bridge between the human and the divine within humanity itself, and then used human experience of the world as the means for revealing the divine self. The grace of God is actually within the reach of human experience. Thus, as Schillebeeckx points out, in our human experiences we have access to "glimpses of an ultimate total meaning of human life."[17] Indeed, the revelation in scripture seems to be the result of such human reflection on life experience.

From this perspective one can encounter God as the horizon of human experience. The wide spectrum of human reality–ranging from watching a full moon at night, falling in love, or watching the birth of a baby, to being abused or unjustly oppressed–can be occasions where one can meet God. The Christian, then, can listen to the world and discover the revelation of God. In the everyday struggles of work, raising a family, doing the many tasks connected with life, one can meet the "holy." This experience of God in everyday life is open to everyone. Obviously there will be need for careful discernment, because *experience* is a slippery term and is open to a wide variety of interpretations.

This approach to theology, of course, is most suited to our needs here. It assumes that the universe is filled with mystery, and that by appreciating the intricacies of storms, land, air, water, and other aspects of our world, a person can grow closer to the Creator. A theology grounded in the human experience of the beauty and power of nature provides strong motivation to recognize the integrity of all things. Here the world is not a place for use and abuse, but the place where people meet their God. This approach to theology works within a "friendly universe" that somehow has come from the hand of God and that reveals the grandeur of the Creator. Here one does not experience the world rationally and disengaged, merely observing and measuring a mechanical world. Rather, the world is experienced as a living and dynamic reality that opens to transcendence and ultimately to God. Human beings are thinkers and actors in a world that has a sacred dimension, a world that deserves respect and care.

The Diversity of Human Experience

Too often when scholars speak of human experience as a resource for theology they limit the experience to that of white, middle-class Europeans or Americans. There are many other voices that need to be heard. We live in a world church, where the experience of women and men of many nations and ethnic backgrounds is viewed as a valuable resource for theological reflection. The church—and its theologians—turns a serious and compassionate ear to those who experience oppression of any kind.

The pleas of environmental distress come from a wide range of contexts: from the people of Newfoundland, whose lives and cultural traditions have been disrupted by the over-fishing by factory ships, to the people of North Carolina, whose waterways and aquifers are being degraded by the growing number of pig farms; from those in areas of Australia where children cannot be allowed outside for school recess because of the intensity of harmful rays due to ozone depletion, to the coastline of El Salvador, where the Pacific beaches and coastal waters have been blackened by the run-off of sewage. People from all over the world cry out for clean air and water, for land on which to grow food, and for a place to live that is fresh, clean, and healthy. These are the voices that must be heard in doing environmental theology, so that a moral conscience and action plans for solutions may be developed.

This is not to say that all those who live in environmentally depressed areas want to improve their situation. In many areas of poverty the concern is for financial security, and little attention is given to ecology. As one of my students, Tomas, an exchange student from the Czech Republic observed: "You know, Americans can afford to be environmentalists. You have had your industrial revolution and now get many of your goods manufactured elsewhere. We in the Czech Republic have just gained our freedom from communism and the Soviet Union. We are just starting to recover from years of domination, and we need a new economy and new factories. Ecological problems are not our concern right now. And I never heard of any theological work in this area. It was certainly never mentioned in my schools." Environmental theology will not only have to listen, but it will also have to be capable of enlightening those who do not understand the hazards that surround them.

Human Experience as Revelatory

Pre–Vatican II theology often emphasized God's transcendence and thus viewed divine revelation as coming "from above" to God's people. In so doing this theology tended to lose touch with the mystical and spiritual dimensions of reality that were stressed in earlier theology. In the nineteenth- and twentieth-century perspectives, revelation often seemed to enter from another world and carried instructions on how to leave this world and go to heaven. The "world" itself was often perceived as "fallen," or as a "vale of tears" that was to be endured until one received a heavenly reward in another life. The world was often more a temptation to be avoided than a place to receive God's revelation or a milieu in which to serve.

Contemporary theology reclaims earlier emphases on God's immanence, and thus it also recognizes revelation as coming more "from below." In this perspective revelation includes the experience of God in human life, and then demonstrates how these experiences play a role in the formulation of doctrines. For example, the doctrine of the divinity of Jesus Christ was in part derived from the disciples' experience of God's power in Jesus' everyday teaching and healing. Likewise, early disciples' experiences of Jesus as risen served as the basis for later reinterpretation of Jesus as the gospel accounts of his ministry were written. Later doctrines about Jesus as savior were also in part affected by earlier experiences of the saving power of God that was operative in Jesus of Nazareth.

Another example of revelation "from below" can be drawn from the doctrine of creation. Most likely early Jewish experiences of God present with them in their gardens and farms led to later creation stories in Genesis 2. Centuries later Jews experienced God on a much more cosmic scale and had been influenced by pagan creation stories. With this background the Hebrew authors wrote the creation story in Genesis 1. Likewise, real life experience of conscience situations and moral issues most likely led to the Hebrew formulations of their laws as "the laws of God."

A more contemporary example of theology "from below" comes from violence and oppression. Such experiences have led marginal and oppressed people to reinterpret the gospels and discover Jesus to be in solidarity with them as their liberator. Moreover, their consciousness of Jesus' saving presence and power in their lives has given many the courage to develop a theology of liberation. This view of the faith has enabled them to stand up to oppressors and to struggle for peace and justice. Previously they might have accepted their situation as "the will of God" while awaiting escape from life into a supernatural realm. For Christians, human experience has always been a rich trove of meaning and purpose, a place to discover traces of the Creator.

Viewing revelation as coming through experience does not imply, however, that theology is simply deduced from experience. Otherwise liberal theologians would be correct in their position that culture sets the norms for religious beliefs. Only God reveals, and thus revelation comes in the context of experience and culture but is not dictated to by cultural experience. Revelation is the self-revelation of God in the midst of the world. Theology must always be a servant and interpreter of God's revelation, not the discoverer or source of God's truth. Tradition is a living reality and is linked to experience, but at the same time tradition transcends human experience.[18]

Experience as a Stimulant to Reflection

Experience can often stimulate significant theological insights. The devastating experience of the Holocaust has brought many to newer understanding of sin, providence, and forgiveness. Hiroshima and Nagasaki sent theologians back to the drawing board with regard to the so-called just-war theory. The mass deaths of David Koresh and his Branch Davidians in Texas, as well as the group suicide of the Heaven's Gate community in California, have stimulated much theological reflection on apocalyptic beliefs. Science's new powers over birth and death have moved theologians to reconsider what role people can be allowed to play in manipulating life. Recent findings in astrophysics about the immensity of the universe and about the possibility of some form of life on Mars or other planets have moved theologians to reconsider traditional beliefs on creation and redemption. Women's experiences of being suppressed in society as well as in religion have moved many to reexamine carefully the scriptures as well as Christian tradition from the feminine perspective.

An approach to theology that requires listening to the experience of others puts new demands on theologians. Here the only theology that is given credibility is one that reflects a careful hearing as well as a diligent theological reflection on the experience. Credibility is given only to theologians who are present to those who suffer or are oppressed and who are competent to reinterpret and connect Christian beliefs with the needs of individuals and communities. [19]

Environmental theology needs to draw from people's experience of the degradation of the earth and its resources and suggest beliefs and values that might offer solutions. If faithful people listen closely enough to the anguish of living things and the veritable "crying out" of the earth, they will have the beliefs and the conscience to put an end to the abuse and destruction. Conversely, believers can use their own religious traditions as invaluable resources for learning how to sustain creation.

THE SECULAR EXPERIENCE

Theology faces a unique challenge in modern times in that experience has become extremely secularized, that is, lacking any link with God or religion. Modern science has its own autonomy and proceeds to discover many of the causes of events that in earlier times were attributed to divine action. Modern education often proceeds without any reference to religious beliefs. The disciplines of history, mathematics, language, art, psychology, and so on, generally proceed in their work without reference to God.

In some ways such secularization is good, in that it enables us to set aside superstitions and myths and analyze reality and the world with objectivity and precision. This objective approach eventually can become a pathway into mystery. Science often comes to its own limits and opens up into areas of mystery that only revelation can address. Astrophysics now reveals a cosmos so infinite in design and scope that many are moved to deeper faith in the One who is ultimately the source for such a world. Technology has made such advances in areas touching on life and death that it now often needs religious beliefs and moral values for direction. History uncovers the facts of the past and moves to ultimate questions, such as why there is so much destruction and violence in our world. Secularization, which cuts the ultimate away, can lead to a deeper appreciation for religious beliefs and values.

Theology can help secular culture better understand levels of meaning and purpose beyond the scope of research. Theology can offer moral and spiritual values that can prevent society from destroying itself. It can provide many people in our society who hunger for spirituality with hope and courage. It can assist people who encounter suffering, disabilities, or death by offering them purpose and meaning. As one theologian puts it, the secular world can be the grammar through which God reveals.[20]

The Experience of an Endangered Environment

The threats to our environment have always been with us, but they never before have reached the hazardous conditions of today. Since the industrial revolution and the invention of chemicals, environmental problems have become so severe that some predict dire results in the not-too-distant future.

The experience of environmental deterioration now is obvious and intense throughout the planet. Ozone depletion threatens the very existence of healthy life and the food chain. The constant elimination of species severs connections in the web of life, without our realizing what the future consequences will be. The pollution of waterways, land, and air threatens both health and the delicate balance of weather patterns.

We have come to a profound limit experience in our environment. This experience seems to be moving many to look for ways in which religious beliefs and values might help us. For many, it appears that the forces of greed, power, and apathy have become so overwhelming that only faith and trust in the Creator offer a solution.

On the positive side, there is still much beauty and richness in our environment, enough to motivate us to resist further destruction and to begin the process of sustaining the earth. There are those who believe that the world itself holds the key to how we might better appreciate and sustain the earth. This is the position of geologian Thomas Berry, who writes: "The universe, the solar system, and the planet earth in themselves and in their evolutionary emergence constitute for the human community the primary revelation of that ultimate mystery whence all things emerge into being."[21]

Experience in the World

We have seen how contemporary Catholic theology has shifted from centering on the church and its teachings to the human person as a hearer of revelation and an actor in the world. From this perspective the human being is an embodied spirit in the world, called to understand, love, and act in a responsible manner. This approach is helpful to an environmental theology, but there is need to go further and link the human to earth in ways beyond consciousness and being.

Pierre Teilhard de Chardin, a priest-scientist who helped Catholics link their tradition with modern views of evolution, saw a unity in all of reality. He taught that matter has been and will remain always "on the way" to spirit. He believed that there was a kind of cohesive force, a "love" that holds the universe together.[22] Moreover, it was his conviction that there was an "innerness" in all of reality, even in the rocks and other so-called inanimate objects. Modern analysis of the nuclear activity within all things supports his views.

Teilhard offered a vision of the world, which he called the "divine milieu." He saw creation as a process wherein matter has gradually evolved toward life and then toward spirit. For him, humans are the ultimate in that development, and Christ was the epitome of what evolution could accomplish. Teilhard's vision, both scientifically and theologically, is of a universe progressing and developing upward toward ultimate fulfillment in Christ, a process he called "Christogenesis."[23] While some of Teilhard's thought is today scientifically outdated, his vision is still influential and the benchmark for integrating creation with evolution.

Teilhard's vision revealed the inwardness, dignity, and ultimate destiny of material things. Yet it was still a vision committed to progress without critique of the ecological damage that has accompanied it. Environmental theology can make good use of Teilhard's views on the great depth and dignity that is in all of matter, as well as his insights on how all things are linked together. At the same time, Teilhard's vision embraced the kind of progress that has been achieved at the expense of the earth. We live in an era different from Teilhard's, and we have an awareness regarding the dangers to our environment which was not available to him or others of his generation. Still, his mystical appreciation for the inwardness of all things and his link between Christian beliefs and the earth, with proper critique, still can be invaluable to environmental theology.

A TRANSFORMING THEOLOGY

Authentic theology is not only interpretive but also transformative. Theology can deeply change people's lives and move them to struggle "to make a difference."[24] As David Tracy observes, for theology to be effective today, it must have an interest in the issues of the day and play a transforming role in the world.[25] An isolated theology that is afraid to take risks cannot lead people to freedom.

In the past, Christian beliefs have often changed people's lives and moved them toward action. Think of how certain understandings of the tradition moved people like Harriet Tubman, Martin Luther King Jr., Dorothy Day, Thomas Merton, and Oscar Romero to dedicate themselves to freedom and justice. The gospel message of repentance can turn people's lives around and move them in new directions.

The awakening of Catholics toward environmental concerns is most certainly a historic move in a new direction. Any appropriate theology will have the task of transforming the conscience of believers and moving them actively to engage in ecological issues.

A Theology Concerned about Justice

Ecological concerns are often issues of justice, both toward the earth itself and toward the many people who are forced to live in unhealthy and undesirable conditions. Environmental theology will have to be connected to justice issues. It will have to include, along with the recent integration of faith and justice, a concern for the injustices connected with the unequal distribution of resources, the abuse of living things, and the pollution of our water, land, and air. Let us look briefly at how faith and justice have been linked and consider the implications for ecology.

As we know, the Catholic church has been gradually integrating justice into its theological framework. In modern times this process began when Pope Leo XIII addressed the horrible working conditions of the industrial revolution and condemned the dehumanizing effects of both socialism and liberal capitalism. He called for all to listen to the unchanging truths of the "deposit of faith" so that social justice could be achieved. He challenged the secularists, who held that religion had no place in matters of economics or politics. Leo insisted that Christ's message of compassion and justice had direct bearing on such mundane issues as fair salaries, decent working conditions, and even on the formation of labor organizations.[26]

In the twentieth century Pius XI issued a similar document, once again asserting the church's right to struggle for social justice and condemning the greed and oppression of liberal capitalism, communism, and fascism. Likewise, Pius XII, who was pope during World War II, reiterated the church's social teachings and often decried the tragic loss of life and the destruction that went on during the war. The pope supported economic relief for those impoverished by the war and urged that the postwar recovery be brought about democratically and with justice. In his teaching Pius XII represents a more worldly theology, one that did not look for facile solutions by following ancient traditions but that urged a secular world to pursue its own solutions to peace and justice.[27]

In the same tradition John XXIII gained the attention of both the world and the church with his strong positions on peace, justice, and church reform. He began the process of helping the church find its place in the context of modernity. Pope John championed individual and communal freedoms, the interdependence of people's solidarity in the struggle for freedom, and the rights of all people to participate in the political process. He brought the same enthusiasm to bringing freedom, change and new life into the church itself, and he initiated an astounding period of renewal.[28]

The Second Vatican Council continued linking the Catholic tradition with a concern for justice. The council proclaimed that the church is primarily a community of people that offers gospel service to the world. The council recognized the movement of God's Spirit throughout the world and called for a discernment of how God's revelation can be mediated through the "signs of the times." In a now classic statement the council declared the church in solidarity with contemporary society: "The joys and the hopes, the griefs and the anxieties of the [people] of this age, especially those who are poor or in any way afflicted, these too are the joys and hopes, the griefs and anxieties of the followers of Christ."[29]

Paul VI issued a powerful letter on social justice in 1967 *(On Promoting the Development of Peoples)*. He also was the first pope to be a world traveler and to carry his message of peace and justice to a global audience. In 1971 a world synod of bishops focused on world justice, reiterated the church's solidarity with victims of oppression, and proclaimed that action for justice was "a constitutive dimension" of the church's mission.

John Paul II has been an indefatigable advocate for peace and justice. In his unparalleled papal trips around the world, his many addresses, and particularly in his 1988 encyclical, *The Social Concern of the Church,* John Paul has solidly supported the oppressed and their struggle for human rights. He has spoken out repeatedly on human dignity, called for all systems of government to evaluate themselves in the light of gospel values, and challenged all people to a radical conversion toward a more simple lifestyle. He is the first pope in history to speak extensively on environmental issues.

A Liberating Theology

Catholic concern for social justice found attentive ears with the bishops of Latin America, a continent where violence and oppression against the poor had prevailed for centuries. At two historic meetings the bishops began to use the language of liberation and pledged that the church would be in solidarity with the poor. A movement of liberation theologies ensued, which valued theology "from below," from the experience of the marginalized and oppressed. This theology promoted small base communities of Christians, nurtured a spirituality of praxis and resistance, and called for a "preferential option for the poor." Liberation theology is a "listening" theology; it hears the cries of the poor and accepts them as a valid resource for doing theology. From such listening new understandings of Jesus Christ, the church, and the sacraments entered the tradition. Archbishop Romero, who became a staunch supporter of the poor in his country—and paid for his commitment with his life—has become a key symbol of this theology. Liberation theology became prominent in the 1980s and spread to Africa and Asia. At present it is in a transitional stage, yet its principles still seem to be in force in many parts of the world.

Justice and Ecology

The church's teachings on social justice, as well as the many liberation theologies that have developed from it, now need to be turned to environmental concerns. Pillaging the environment is closely related to poverty, hunger, poor health conditions, unequal distribution of resources, and violence. Moreover, the values in the social-justice tradition—justice, human dignity, the protection of women and children, the common good, the rights to own property, health care, shelter, and food—are closely connected with sustaining the earth and its resources.

A "listening" theology "from below" can teach us how to listen to the earth, to learn of its beauty, dignity, and needs. It can teach us how to attend to the countless numbers who are deprived of the basic necessities because their environment is being destroyed. A liberating theology can teach us how to look "below" to the nature from which we arose and how to discover our links with the earth and all living things. It can assist us in reaching out to the lowest people on the social ladder and in seeing how they are being deprived of clean water, air, good health, and adequate food and shelter as a result of environmental neglect.

Environmental theology will have be concerned with oppression and the abuse of rights. It will recognize the rights of all species to exist, the rights of animals to be treated with respect and care. People's rights to own fertile land, enjoy clean air and water, and have decent, healthy living conditions will be of concern to such theology. There will even be new struggles for the earth's rights to be honored and sustained. There is a crucial need today for a theology that addresses ecological justice. People are being subjected to unhealthy environments by greedy developers; auto and oil industries, which resist alternative fuels and rapid transit; and industries that illegally pollute air, land, and water. Massive degradation to the environment continues to cause drought, freakish weather conditions, famine, and human deprivation. Catholic theology is called to be prophetic and concerned with praxis on behalf of the earth.

The environmental crisis has reached global proportions. Depletion of the ozone, pollution of waterways and oceans, the "greenhouse effect," over-fishing, the destruction of the rainforests, and the extinction of species affect the peoples of all nations. They are global problems. Diverse and complicated issues of peace and justice call for a theology that links every appropriate area of the Catholic tradition with ecology.

A CORRELATIVE THEOLOGY

As we have seen, contemporary theologians view human persons as created with an openness to the transcendent. Theological methods enable people to relate their religious beliefs to the everyday problems in our world. Rahner once said, "I envisage a theology which is in dialogue with its time and lives courageously with it and in it."[30] Especially since the Second Vatican Council, theologians have been attuned to the "signs of the times" and have engaged in efforts to reinterpret the tradition so that it might interconnect with world issues. The role of the theologian here becomes one of a mediator between religion and the world, between the world and God's grace. We will now discuss some specific efforts to connect theology with the world, and then see how these might relate to environmental theology.

Tillich's Approach

Paul Tillich was one of the pioneers in demonstrating the relationship between religion and culture. Tillich actually described himself as the "theologian of culture."[31] It was his conviction that religion arises from the cultures that people develop, so he recognized an intimate relationship between religion and culture. Tillich believed that God is the ultimate ground of all existence and hence of all culture. Therefore it was his conviction that our most ultimate questions arise out of our cultural experiences. The role of religion in Tillich's view is to attempt to provide answers to these ultimate questions. He called his theological method "co-relative," because it strives to relate religious tradition with cultural questions.

Tillich believed that the drive for autonomy—independence and freedom—
is basic to human nature. Influenced by the dialectic model of Hegel, Tillich
observed that all human cultures shift back and forth between two extremes.
At one extreme people seek complete autonomy or freedom. In so doing
they cut themselves off from ultimacy, from the infinite ground of their existence. Their cultures then become isolated, empty, meaningless. People without meaning and hope are then inclined to turn to absolute authority for
solutions. In such "heteronomous" cultures, the "nomos" or law comes from
another. Such cultures are subject to tyrants, who attempt to gain ultimate
control; people gradually lose their freedom and can be led to destruction.
The rise of Nazism in Germany, which drove Tillich from his homeland,
demonstrated convincingly how deadly such a cultural process could be. He
watched his fellow Germans hand over much of their personal freedom to
Hitler, watched as the Nazi war machine crushed the freedom of many peoples,
and then saw the tragic devastation that came to Germany in the end.

Tillich proposed that cultures strive to be "theonomous"; that is, committed to the belief that God is the true and ultimate ground of all existence.
Tillich observed that only in theonomous cultures can authentic freedom and
authority thrive. Such cultures live by faith, which for Tillich was the ultimate
concern for the ground of being.

Since Tillich's correlative method for theology can be helpful in developing an environmental theology, it might be useful to examine some of its
tenets in more detail and then to show how these might be useful to an environmental theology.

Autonomous Culture

According to Tillich, autonomy is the human drive to make free and independent choices. Cultures, which are human creations, are created out of
choices, and thus cultures reflect the individuality and uniqueness of the people.
Since human beings are finite and limited, they can easily become estranged
from the true source and purpose that gives authentic meaning to their lives.
People are thus quite capable of creating cultural forms that are cut off from
God and ultimate meaning. Tillich describes cultures that are secularized,
materialistic, or hedonistic as "purely autonomous." Such cultures are based
on self-centered choices, cut off from the laws of God.[32]

In purely autonomous cultures, cultural forms can become "frozen" and
"empty," devoid of substantial meaning. Those who live in such cultures often
get caught up in feelings of purposelessness and anxiety. Tillich pointed to the
existential feelings of "absurdity" that characterized many after World War II.
In our times widespread spiritual hunger and anxieties over the future might be
considered indications of cultures that have become autonomous and thus cut
off from ultimate meaning. Tillich held that there was a "depth of reason,"
whereby reason could be in touch with the divine.[33] Cultures cut off from this
"depth of reason," according to Tillich, are doomed to failure.

Tillich analyzed various periods of history to demonstrate his theology of culture. He cited the medieval period as a culture that properly linked reason with the Christian tradition. Following the Middle Ages a number of factors led to the separation of reason from religion: reaction to church authority during the Reformation; nominalism, which put God out of reach of reason; the privatization of faith and religion; the Enlightenment, which often gave reason ultimate authority; and the industrial revolution.

In the modern era, according to Tillich, an ideal was produced whereby humans thought they could control nature and society through an exercise of complete freedom. Human logic and inventiveness could devise economic, political, social, and even religious structures that would bring about harmony and success in the human community. In the process the notion of reason was transformed from a power whereby humans could be in touch with the mysteries of nature and ultimacy, to a tool to be used in the service of an industrial and technological society. A process of secularization set in which denied or at best ignored divine ultimacy.

Tillich maintained that modern capitalism grew out of this drive for autonomy. Capitalism is characterized by an extreme drive for economic independence and self-sufficiency. The economic system becomes a law unto itself, while profit-making and the accumulation of goods become the ultimate goals. Production and economics are placed above nature.

In our own time we can see how these trends endure. The process of secularization continues. For many people religious beliefs and values have little relevance to modern progress in economics, politics, industry, and technology. Profit is often the driving force and can overshadow the need for religious considerations or moral values. For many, God is simply not relevant to contemporary concerns. For others, God is a private matter, part of one's personal life, but not relevant to social or political issues.

Secularization cuts us away from depth and ultimacy and reduces nature to a commodity that can be exploited. Material things become mere objects to sell or acquire. Accumulation takes on the aspect of a goal in life. Utopias, like the "American Dream," are proffered by politicians in their campaigns for office. Economies are driven by creating and then fulfilling needs. Guns and armaments are needed to protect individual and national possessions from those who might protest their oppression. As a result, people lose contact with the true center of life, God, and drift from their authentic meaning and purpose. Chaos, meaninglessness, emptiness, and violence soon characterize such a culture.

Autonomy and the Environment

It is ironic that most of the great theologians of the twentieth century failed to observe that the secularization process not only led our culture into an abyss of meaninglessness but also contributed to the degradation of our environment. Little if anything is said on this crucial issue by theological giants like Rahner, Barth, Tillich, Lonergan, or Bonhoeffer. Each in his own way attempted to relate the Christian tradition to our contemporary world, but none of them included the crucial area of the environment.

With our present awareness of how endangered the environment is, it becomes clear that a false autonomy can affect the way we look at our environment. Reason cut away from its depth, its link to God, can move easily to the position that the "good" is whatever works, whatever brings financial gain. The yardstick for progress then can be measured in terms of what sells, what is useful, or even what gives one power over another. We can easily view the resources of the earth, living creatures, even people, as mere objects for our use.

From this perspective the environment is a "commodity field" to be used for profit. Huge fishing factories cruise the oceans, gorging their holds with the "catch of the day," with little thought to giving the fish time to replenish or to the waste that occurs as unsuitable fish are cast aside. Forests are denuded for development with little consideration of the indigenous people who have lived there for centuries or of replanting what has been taken. Rivers are dammed with no care for the damage to surrounding ecosystems. Nuclear plants are constructed with little concern for long-term dangers to the environment.

Separated from beliefs in the Creator, the value of life, and the dignity of the human person, society can be in danger of destroying itself as well as the world in which it lives. Without an ultimate center or depth, there is a loss of meaning, purpose, and goal. Human culture is set adrift and often reaches for drugs, chemicals, and other distractions.

Heteronomous Cultures

Tillich uses the word *heteronomous* (meaning "other than self") to refer to cultures that are led by absolute authorities and laws that take away personal freedom.[34] It seems that often when people lose meaning and purpose as a result of a false autonomy, they are vulnerable to absolute authorities or even tyrants. Such authorities even can be in the religious realm, wherein certain figures clothe themselves with divine authority and grace. Tillich uses for his examples the "divine right" of kings and certain forms of church leadership.[35] It is said that Hitler viewed himself as a prophet sent by God to purify the human race of undesirables and to establish the rule of the super race for a thousand years. In such a heteronomous culture, doctrines, laws, offices, and individuals can take on a level of ultimacy that properly belongs only to God.

The dominance of such alien and absolute authority inevitably negates freedom and creativity. It offers simple solutions to life's mysteries, solutions that supposedly can be obtained by blind acceptance of a given ideology or set of laws. "You will be happy and successful if you follow my commands" is the position of the tyrant. In religion, heteronomous authority generally encourages unquestioning faith and obedience. Beliefs and laws are static and time-less, and salvation is promised to those who adhere to them. Quite often such salvation is personal, cut off from the world, and unconcerned about "secular issues."

Heteronomy and the Environment

Absolute authority is seldom concerned about social issues. Its energies are generally spent preserving its own tradition and authority. Power and domi-nance are the watchwords, whether over people, resources, or even over the environment itself. Whether "captains of industry," "lords of the Manor," or the "high priests" of religion, the major concern is for power and control.

For autocratic leadership the resources of the earth are simply means to an end. The earth, living things, and even people are commodities to be used. One thinks of the Conquistadors and the devastation they brought on the people and the environment of the West Indies and parts of Latin America; the destruction of peoples and ecosystems that was inflicted on Africa by colonialists; the vast areas of India that the British stripped of resources, plung-ing the native people into squalor. In this country the Native Americans were decimated and their lands confiscated and often devastated by people de-luded by an ideology of "manifest destiny."

More recently, one thinks of the immense destruction done to Vietnam by constant bombing and releasing of Agent Orange over the magnificent for-ests, farming areas, and people. Another example is the extensive "carpet-bombing" by U.S. forces during Desert Storm. Then, dictator Saddam Hussein, after his defeat, set oil wells aflame and severed oil lines so that oil flowed openly into the Persian Gulf. Throughout history wars have devastated the earth's ecosystems.

The dismantling of the Berlin Wall and the collapse of the Soviet Union led to other frightening revelations of ways autocratic regimes had ravaged their environments. In Eastern Europe the damage to land and seaways through pollution has been devastating. Communism in its "will to power" over peoples and nations viewed the environment merely as a resource to be used in its feverish arms race. In this ideology there was no ultimacy, no value for the spiritual depths of things, no notion of creation or Creator. Sustaining the earth was not a value for the totalitarian leaders of the Soviet Union. Those who did object to the pollution and wanton destruction were quickly dis-patched to mental institutions or far-off gulags in Siberia.

Theonomy

Tillich's theology of culture works toward a *theonomy,* a cultural situation in which God is believed to be the ultimate ground of human existence and of cultural forms. Here theology carefully critiques cultures that represent either extreme autonomy or absolute authority. Theology uncovers and promotes the "holy" in cultural forms ranging from politics to art.

In Tillich's theonomous culture, ultimacy in being and meaning are highly valued. In such a culture both reasoning and authority are rooted in the ultimate and thus produce cultural creations that convey the experience of the sacred. Reason in its depths is in touch with the transcendent and can thus express ultimacy in what it creates. Authority here is rooted in the divine and is guided by its norms.

One finds in such a culture a concern for ultimacy, a "faith-full" approach to all reality that guides decisions and action. Faith linked with reason approaches reality with a regard for ultimacy. There is always the conviction that the divine is the ground of all reality. Thus the thinking and believing subject is not the "bearer of all power," as in a secular and purely technological culture, but is dedicated to honoring ultimacy in all things.[36] The "really real," for Tillich, is that which is the ground of all reality, the divine. Thus Tillich proposes a "belief-ful realism" that accepts the modern world and yet at the same time integrates faith with reason. At all times there is the effort to indicate to people the presence of ultimacy in their world.

Theonomy and Ecology

Tillich's notion of a theonomous culture can be useful in reminding contemporary society of the need to integrate religious beliefs and values with decisions that affect the environment. It is a perspective that recognizes the ultimate ground of all things, the Creator, and therefore deals with the earth with respect and care. It can stand in critique of the extreme individualism in this country and also resist autocratic authority. The twentieth century has had convincing evidence of the vast destruction that can result from liberal capitalism, fascism, and communism. Theonomy stands in opposition to these extremes and can provide useful norms for the kind of theology we are here constructing.

Some Possibilities and Limitations

There are certain aspects of theology of culture that could be useful to the environmental theologian. First of all, this approach does try to link religion with culture and connect tradition with the real world. It is a prophetic theology that stands in criticism of the demonic, which can arise out of a false autonomy or absolute authority. The notion of God is one that stresses the immanence of the divine in culture. Such an approach to life can help the ecological movement locate and witness to the presence of God in the world. This method of theology also provides a critique for political or social structures that are either secularized or have been taken over by absolute authority. In either case serious damage is usually inflicted on the environment.

There are limitations to Tillich's approach, however. First, the focus is on culture, which is humanly constructed; very little is said about the universe or the earth. Moreover, Tillich's theology of culture is human-centered. It gives little attention to the importance of other living things and the earth. In addition, the notion of God and even of Jesus in the theology of Tillich is quite philosophical and often vague. Even though Tillich stresses immanence, the presence and power of God in his theology lacks personal intimacy and vividness. Nor is Tillich comfortable with the teaching authority of the church.

An environmental theology can gain much insight from Tillich's correlative method but would need to place more emphasis on scripture and biblical criticism. An environmental theology looks to scripture as a primary source, both in its context and its applicability to ecology.

The Revisionist Method

In his now classic work, *Blessed Rage for Order*, David Tracy, a highly influential Catholic theologian, proposed a method of theology that would not only be connected to modern culture but could also be enriched by it. This approach to theology recognizes the truth claims of both the Catholic tradition and the present times. It rejects both secularism's break from religion and the otherworldly approach of so many theologies "from above."[37]

Tracy agreed with Tillich that the totally autonomous thinker lives in an illusion of individualism. As a student of Lonergan, Tracy recognized that humans are capable of authentic self-transcendence and can move from experience to understanding, and then from judgment to action.

Tracy contrasts his revisionist approach to theology with "orthodox theology," which focuses on the preservation of static doctrine and generally has little interest in worldly issues. His method also departs from so-called liberal theology, which too easily gives way to the pragmatism and materialism of modern culture.

Revisionist theology has two sources, the Christian texts and the culture. Its goal is to put both the questions and answers of each in dialogue with the other. In this method revelation can come through human experience and at times stand in critique of the Christian tradition. Conversely, the tradition can be constantly reinterpreted and serve to both critique and transform culture. The revisionist method of theology can thus help uncover the religious dimension of everyday life and connect revised interpretations of the tradition with issues of the day.

Tracy has shown how Christian doctrines have arisen from experience and how each doctrine has its own history of development and interpretation. Revisionist theology attempts to discover the truth claims of the religious texts of the Christian tradition as well as the truth of culture, and places each in dialogue with the other. Thus a process of mutual enrichment and correction begins that enhances both the tradition and the culture.

Since revisionist theology is so closely linked to human culture, it is diverse and reflects the various "levels of consciousness" that Lonergan wrote about when he described the psychology of human conversion.[38] This dynamic approach to theology accepts the possibility of growth and development in both society and religion. It is open to the new and the pluralistic in both religion and culture. It is also open to interfaith dialogue and allows the product of such dialogue to address cultural issues.

Revisionist theology sets out to transform society. It is thus a public theology, which can be supportive as well as confrontational. Tracy has commented that our culture today is having a difficult time "naming" itself.[39] He observes that there are so many movements going on concurrently that it is often quite difficult to locate and name even the major shifts that are taking place. Often it seems as though there is no center—and few universal norms. Tracy points out that the twentieth century began with great hopes and then saw some of the greatest horrors of all times with two world wars, a depression, the Holocaust, Hiroshima, and Nagasaki. We could add the shocking horrors of Rwanda, Bosnia, Oklahoma City, and the spread of AIDS through the world like some medieval plague. At the same time, there have been great advances toward peace: the Berlin Wall came down, Western communism collapsed and the Soviet Union was dismantled, Apartheid ended in South Africa, and a fragile peace struggles to survive in Ireland and Israel. With all this complexity even our best minds are hard-pressed to make projections as to where our culture is going.

Revisionist theology participates in the world and listens to its successes and failures, its cries for peace and justice, its celebration over successful accomplishments. Yet revisionist theology is positioned to critique the excesses of consumerism; the monopoly of megastores; the hedonism of some of our youth culture, and the inequality among classes, races, ethnic groups, and genders. It recognizes that a "new self" is emerging in an age of cybernetics, miracle drugs, and ever-advancing technology, and it attempts to discern the meaning of that new self.[40]

This method of theology also takes a critical approach to religious thought. It rejects the antimodernists in the church, who since the beginning of the twentieth century have condemned change and progress in the church, and who stubbornly have remained aloof from the world. It also rejects those among the postmoderns who call for the "death of the subject," abandon the subjective pursuit of truth as futile, and propose deconstruction of tradition. Tracy and many other theologians fear that these positions represent the revival of a new brand of nihilism.

The revisionist model seems to move beyond Tillich's correlation approach in that the revisionists recognize that culture not only raises ultimate questions but also is a resource for ultimate answers. Revisionists, in other words, recognize the possibility of theology "from below," as do liberation theologians. This means that theology has to come down from its ivory tower and listen to and share in the sufferings of the present age.[41]

The revisionist approach to theology can be of value to the development of an environmental theology. The revisionists are open to new interpretations of tradition and accept that religious tradition can be influenced and even enriched by culture. At the same time, revisionists insist that religious tradition should be a prophetic and freeing force in culture. Clearly this is a perspective that offers much potential for a mutually beneficial dialogue among the Catholic tradition, the environmental movement, and the many industries that deeply affect the earth and its resources.

The revisionist model of theology also has some limitations. It moves beyond Tillich in seeing culture not only as a source for ultimate questions but also as a place to discover correctives to religion. But revisionist theology gives considerable attention to culture and thus unduly focuses on the human. A theology suitable for dealing with ecological concerns must go beyond humans and their culture and focus on nature itself. It will be a theology that draws revelation not only from religious tradition and culture but also from the earth.

Earth-centered Theology

This needed move beyond culture to the material world is suggested by Thomas Berry. Berry maintains that we are moving into a new era wherein humans must connect with the earth and see their world as the source of the primary revelation about ultimate mystery.[42] While I do not agree with Berry's devaluation of the role the Catholic tradition can play in environmental theology, I do think that his pointing to our world as a source for religious revelation is important. Berry goes beyond the correlative method of Tillich and the revisionist model of Tracy as he looks beyond culture to the earth and the universe for ecological answers. Yet Berry does not seem to have enough regard for modern progress to be able to dialogue productively with either religion or culture on ecological matters.

Environmental theology can take a page from correlational, revisionist, and earth-centered approaches. Its thrust must be to interconnect, to link together, to reveal the web-like ties that exist among all realities. Its concern here is to proceed with an anthropology that is open to the world, not only in its cultural context but in the larger natural framework.

SUMMARY

Catholic environmental theology is still under construction. As it is developed it will continue to draw from the Hebrew and Christian scriptures as its primary sources. It will use the best of contemporary biblical criticism for context, the original meanings, authentic interpretations, and appropriate applications to ecological issues. At the same time, it will be honest in its critique of where biblical views either fall short or even can be detrimental to sustaining the earth.

This new theological approach promotes the human capacity to be open to the transcendent, and yet it need not be "human-centered." It acknowledges the presence of God's grace in the world and endeavors to open minds and hearts to participate fully in the divine life in the world. Its hope is to give a new awareness of the beauty, dignity, and indeed "holiness" that is intrinsic to creation, and thus motivate people to relate to creation with more sensitivity and care.

Most important, environmental theology acknowledges the interconnection among human life, other living things, and the earth itself. It holds the conviction that God the Creator has extended the divine self to all things and can be experienced in all things. Environmental theology encourages Christians to see themselves as part of, but not greater than, the world in which they live. It is a prophetic theology that stands in confrontation to the position of dominance over nature that has for so long prevailed in the West.

The urgency of the environmental crisis calls for a theology that is transformative; a theology that calls for conversion of minds and hearts to see the value and integrity of creation and motivates people to honor and sustain it. This theology must demand just treatment of living things and a fair distribution of the earth's resources, and be a strong advocate for the poor and oppressed of the world. Environmental theology is deeply concerned with the liberation of living things and resources from abuse as well as freeing people from deprivation. It is a dynamic theology that struggles to honor the rights of each human being to clean air and water; it promotes the universal right to own land on which to live and work; and it is an advocate for an earth that is healthy for all to live on, a world safe from destructive forces.

This newly emerging theology is correlational, linking Christian beliefs and moral values with environmental issues. It will retrieve areas of the tradition that connect with ecology and provide legitimate new interpretations of the tradition that can be applied to environmental issues. It calls for a revisioning of the Christian doctrinal and moral tradition in light of contemporary environmental concerns. At the same time, this theology is serious about having accurate scientific data on these ecological issues. It also recognizes a world church and is open to the beliefs and values of other churches and religions in this regard.

Environmental theology is inclusive; it listens to the voices of different genders, races, ethnic backgrounds, and national concerns. It is capable of listening to the earth and even the universe itself for guidance in relating to and caring for all that surrounds us.

2.

The Hebrew Scriptures

Almost every day in Mexico City is a bad air day. The smog seems to come from all directions. There are many new factories belching black smoke all day and night, and I drive to work in the heavy traffic through a blue haze. Other day I saw a young mother and her baby riding in the back of a panel truck and the thick exhaust was blowing right in their faces.

Twenty million people live in this city and most of them use propane gas for heating water and cooking. Many of our propane tanks leak gas into the air. When I go to work in the morning I have to wear a mask so I won't choke. And now that we can't use our cars one day a week. How am I supposed to get to work? To make things worse, the city is using groundwater at twice the rate of natural recharge. Yet 14 million in our city don't have running water. Our water mains leak badly and the sewage system is so antiquated that it is causing the city to gradually sink a bit each year. I fear for the future of our great city.

                                        –José Gastaldi, Mexico City

Hebrew scripture is a library of ancient theologies, wherein one can listen to the perennial human struggle to comprehend the mysteries of God and life on the earth. This unique and inspired literature often uses myths that echo the searching questions and theological insights of other peoples: Canaanites, Egyptians, Babylonians, and others who at one point or another influenced the Hebrew people. The authors of the Hebrew scriptures use many of the literary forms of ancient times, and often creatively formulate their own forms. Encased in this library of poetry, song, story, prayer, history, law, and many other kinds of literature is an enormous treasure of Hebrew faith and wisdom. This resource, of course, has provided the foundation for Christian thought and belief; it has been a key factor in shaping many world cultures. Even today, its perceptions, beliefs, and values bear application to the struggles facing the contemporary world.

The application of the scriptures to today's problems must not be done arbitrarily. Hebrew scripture is a complex collection, gathered, edited, and interpreted throughout many centuries of Israel's ongoing history. Each piece has its own original context and meaning, a *historical sense,* which modern biblical criticism has endeavored to unearth.This historical sense, however, does not exhaust the meaning of scriptural texts. Scripture is a "living word" that has been constantly interpreted and applied to many historical and cultural situations throughout history. The history of both Jewish and Christian interpretation indicates that these texts were introduced to new communities, and that many other levels of meaning were subsequently uncovered.[1] As long as one recognizes the intricate complexity of scripture, and endeavors to be true to the original context and meaning, it seems legitimate to cautiously apply these scriptures also to the events of our own day.

In this chapter I will attempt to connect some of the Hebrew creation theologies with contemporary environmental concerns. It is my conviction that these theologies of creation can assist us in gaining the religious vision and values we need to address and act upon the many environmental challenges of today. I will examine some of the Hebrew perspectives on human life, the nature of the earth, and God, and suggest along the way some connections between these ancient beliefs and the environment.

HEBREW ANTHROPOLOGY

The Hebrew library explores a number of anthropological questions and offers a wide spectrum of insights. The Book of Genesis explores the beginnings of human life and the origin of sin, and celebrates God's covenant with the earth. The Book of Job explores the question of "why bad things happen to good people" and ends with some profound observations by the Creator. Psalms, which includes some of the great liturgical hymns of the Temple, covers a whole range of human feelings with regard to life on earth and celebrates along with all of creation the glories of God. Proverbs offers many insights from the sages with regard to human living and gives voice to "Lady Wisdom." Qoheleth, the preacher, expounds on his somewhat skeptical view of life and then gives his own fatalistic advice for enjoying the gifts of this mysterious God before we face the end in death. The Song of Songs celebrates the sensuality and joy of human love in the context of God's beautiful creation. Throughout this Hebrew library we are told about both the nobility and the depravity of human beings. Let's look more closely into the library to see what it tells us about humanity.

The Hebrews seemed to derive their anthropology "from below," that is, from their experience of everyday life. Life experience told them that people could display great virtue and yet were also capable of horrible evil. There is both a light side and a dark side to human nature, and throughout the Hebrew scriptures these contrasts are explored. The description of human beings can range from "images of God" to the lowly "worm." They are portrayed as having royal dominion and at the same time as being the authors of wanton destruction and injustice. Humans can join the stars in praising the Creator and yet betray their sacred trust with God in many grievous ways. They can sing of love and then moan in desperate abandonment. We will explore some of these elements of Hebrew anthropology and then see what implications they might have with regard to environmental concerns.

Made in the Image of God

Upon opening the Hebrew bible one first encounters the "in the beginning" story in Genesis 1. This is actually a very sophisticated story written in the sixth century B.C.E., following the Babylonian exile. Composed by the "Priestly author," and echoing a Babylonian myth called *Enuma Elish,* this is a cosmic, highly artistic, and liturgical account of creation, which paints the whole process on a large canvas.[2] Humans are created as the last and climactic creatures on the sixth and final day of a long week of creating. After commanding the earth to "bring forth" cattle, creeping things, and wild animals, God gathers his heavenly consorts and says: "Let us make humankind in our image" (Gn 1:26). The Priestly writer then tells us:

> So God created humankind in his image,
> in the image of God he created them;
> male and female he created them.
> —Genesis 1:27

Then this cosmic Creator of "good things" blessed his god-like creatures, told them to multiply and "subdue" the earth, and gave them "dominion" over the fish, the birds, and all living things on earth. The Creator was pleased with his creation and took a well-earned rest on the Sabbath.

The depiction of human beings as being made in "the image and likeness of God" is perhaps the most widely known and discussed element of Hebrew anthropology. This image has had a profound influence on Jewish and Christian moral teaching on the sacredness of human life. It has also been used by various races and nations to claim superiority over others. For instance, the Conquistadors of the sixteenth century decided that the indigenous people of the New World were not made in the image of God. These "natives" were thus considered to be subhuman and could be enslaved and deprived of their rich resources. Slavery and even the Holocaust were justified by saying that certain peoples were not fully human, not truly created in the image of God.

Surprisingly, this notion that humans are images of God is not common in the Hebrew scriptures. Other than the Priestly passages in Genesis (1:26-27; 5:3; 9:6) it appears only one other time. In Psalm 8 the human being is described as crowned with glory, "a little lower than God" (v. 5) and having dominion over creation.[3] The actual meaning of this belief has received a great deal of attention from scholars over the centuries, whether humans resemble God by virtue of their reason, freedom, spiritual makeup, or even gender.

The Hebrew word used for "image" is *selem.* It is a concrete word, which elsewhere in scripture is used to mean a "statue" or an "icon." This biblical image echoes Egyptian texts that describe the pharaoh as the image of the deity.[4] Von Rad has suggested that biblical use of this image might also have been influenced by the custom of great kings and pharaohs to place images of themselves throughout their empires in order to symbolize their presence and authority. Anderson suggests that the image conveys the notion that humans gain their worth and dignity from being "crowned," in the manner of kings and queens, and assigned to represent God in creation. Hence we might say that humans in the Genesis 1 creation story are created to function as commissioned viceroys of the Creator.[5]

Authentic kings and queens in the Hebrew scriptures were expected to represent God's powerful leadership justly and honorably. They were fully responsible for the welfare of the people and country entrusted to them. In the Psalms the good king is described as one who "trusts in the LORD"; one who loves beauty and brings justice and peace to the afflicted and the poor (Pss 21; 45; 72). Deuteronomy says that the king should not acquire many things for himself; neither should he be one who is "exalting himself above other members of the community" (Dt 17:20). Whenever the rulers are not capable of guaranteeing the welfare of those entrusted to them, they are no longer authentic leaders and must forfeit dominion.[6] It is for this reason that the prophetic literature so often condemned royal abuses of justice and benevolence, and predicted that tyrannical oppressors will be struck down by the Lord (Is 10; 14; 32).

As "images of God" then, humans were created to act nobly in the place of the Creator. They were commissioned to stand for God and represent the caring and creative will of God.[7] Since Yahweh was a God of constant love, compassionate care, and saving power, this was to be the role of humans toward all of creation. Individually and corporately, humans of all nations, races, and religions possess this same unique dignity and mirror God's presence in the world. It seems clear that this leaves no room for "lording over" or "mastering" humans or any other living things.[8] Tragically, the passage has all too often been distorted and used to justify the domination of both human beings and nature.

The notion that humans are images of God also seems to indicate that God created human beings to be companions for the Creator. God created someone who could relate to and communicate with God as a friend, who could be articulate in the praise and worship of the deity.[9] The "I" of God made a "thou" who could name the animals and act freely and responsibly in partnership with God in the creative process. This companion of God was also empowered "to multiply," to produce other "images of God" through procreation. All humans, regardless of race, religion, nationality, or worldview, would thus be children of God, and by this very fact they would possess a unique dignity.

Humbler Images

Elsewhere through the Hebrew scriptures humans are described in a more "earthy" fashion, with all their limitations, weaknesses, and sins. The human person is at times described as a "fool," a "worm," and a "sinner." Humans are creatures of the "dust," whose lives last for a brief moment, and who often can make little sense of the meaning of life.

We are perhaps most familiar with the depiction of the human being offered in Genesis 2. This is an earlier myth; it seems to have been composed around the ninth century B.C.E. The story begins on a barren stretch of soil, with a stream welling up out of the earth and watering the ground. The Creator, a more rural and homey figure than the cosmic God of the first story, fashions a human being out of mud and then makes the figure into a living being by giving it the breath of life.

The word *Adamah* in Hebrew means "earth," and thus Adam is an "earth man," who is forever linked to the other creatures of the earth, and like them is destined to die and return to the soil from which he is made. This is an ancient anthropology, with roots in Babylonian and Egyptian literature. It shows that the human race belongs both to the gods and the earth. Humans take their origins from the Creator, and yet the elements of the human body are the same as those of the earth from which they are derived. This is a more "humble" (*humus*-earth) image of the human and helps puts the notion of "dominion" into its proper perspective.

It is the "breath of life" (Gn 2:7) that makes the human a living being. Scholars are quick to point out this image does not refer to the traditional notion that a "soul" is given to a body. As Westermann points out: "The Bible does not say that a human being is made up of body and soul, or of body, soul, and spirit. God's creation is this man in the totality of his being. Therefore God is concerned not only with the 'soul,' but equally with the body. A higher regard for the spiritual ideal than for the corporeal or material has no basis in the creation faith of Genesis."[10] There is no question here of a dichotomy between the material and spiritual, of the spiritual being higher than the material, or of the soul being superior to the flesh.

Then this "potter God" plants an exotic garden and places the "mud man" in it, asking him to cultivate it and to care for it. The Lord God also sets down his first law: "You are free to eat from any of the trees of the garden except the tree of knowledge of good and bad." This God is portrayed as caring and thoughtful, a divinity concerned about the loneliness of the new creature.

God makes a stab at finding a suitable companion for the first human by making animals and birds out of the same mud. God's first effort misses the mark, so he tries again. He puts the man to sleep, removes one of his ribs, and finally "gets it right" when he forms a woman to be the suitable companion and spouse for the first human.

This "Yahwist" creation tradition continues with the account of how the woman is deceived by the serpent and eats the fruit of the forbidden tree. She believes the serpent rather than her Creator about what will happen should they eat the fruit; she eats the fruit and then persuades her mate to do the same. In this story, which finds some parallels in the Babylonian Gilgamesh poem, the first humans lose their innocence. The woman must now experience pain in childbirth and mastery from her mate. The man must sweat and toil amid the difficulties of nature, and then return to the earth from which he was made. The Creator clothes his shameful creatures in leather garments and then banishes them from the garden.

The creation theology of Genesis 1 links humans and animals in that both are described as "living beings" and are blessed with the capacity to multiply. Psalm 104 goes even further and proclaims that all living beings are provided for by God and share the breath of life (*ruah*). This breath of life that God shares will sustain and constantly renew all of creation:

> These all look to you
> to give them their food in due season;
> when you give to them, they gather it up;
>   when you open your hand, they are filled with good
>   things.
> When you hide your face, they are dismayed;
>   when you take away their breath, they die
>   and return to their dust.
> When you send forth your spirit, they are created;
>   and you renew the face of the ground.
>   —Psalm 104:27-30

Dominion

The notion of humans having dominion over "all the living things that move on the earth" has been a subject of extensive debate, especially since the much-discussed article by Lynn White, in which the author charged that this notion led to a Western dualism of humans over nature and resulted in extensive exploitation of the environment.[11] The White thesis is broadly recognized as an oversimplified account of the development of the modern environmental crisis. Nonetheless, it started a debate that has forced many scholars to look more closely at the real meaning of "dominion" in Genesis.

The original meaning of the dominion given to humans over all living things on earth does not seem to carry any connotation of exploitation or abuse. As mentioned earlier, this royal prerogative that humans share with God, as divine representatives, is that of being co-creators who act out of justice and care. Humans are created to share a personal relationship with God and, by reason of this relationship, are called to represent the Creator in sustaining order, peace, and harmony on the earth. Such healing and peacemaking was God's way of dealing with people throughout the history of Israel, and it is God's law that those made in the divine image do the same. As Bernard Anderson puts it: "Thus the special status of human kind as the image of God is a call to responsibility, not only in relation to other humans, but also to all of nature. Human dominion is not to be exercised wantonly but wisely and benevolently so that it may be, in some degree, the sign of God's rule over the creation."[12] One can see this notion of stewardship reflected in the laws of Deuteronomy, which forbid the careless and wanton destruction of nature (Dt 20:19; 22:6; 25:4). This theme also comes through clearly in God's command to Adam to be the caretaker of God's garden by working and protecting the garden (Gn 2:16). Israel's creation theology never indicates that the earth was created to be exploited by humans. Rather, humans are commissioned to sustain creation with Yahweh's ultimate purpose in mind, and in such a way that creation will give glory to the Creator.

Neither does to "subdue" the earth (Gn 1:28) imply either a command or permission to exploit or misuse nature. Instead, it is a blessing.[13] For the Hebrew, it seemed to indicate a divine commissioning to deal properly with nature in a way that would help bring forth food and resources. Certainly the Creator's commissioning does not justify the exploitation of the earth's resources or the enslavement of other humans. In fact, in the Book of Job, Yahweh makes it clear that humans have neither the knowledge nor power over God's creatures (Jb 38:39–39:30).

Biblical scholar Claus Westermann maintains that "dominion" in Genesis 1 refers to the responsible care that a leader would be expected to exercise over those in his charge. He writes: "'Dominion' is not meant here in the sense of arbitrary employment of power. That would be a fateful misunderstanding of this commission for dominion. It is meant rather in the sense of the other classic form of dominion, that of kingship. It means the full responsibility of the ruler for the welfare of the people and country entrusted to him."[14]

It seems clear, then, there is no textual basis in Genesis 1 for the exploitation of creation. Any form of such violence toward creation would be viewed by the Hebrew as contempt of God's commission. Desire to gain mastery over nature was not a value for ancient Israelites. Nature was viewed as beyond their control, and in fact, they often felt subjugated and even punished by nature. Indeed, the earth was the Lord's, and the Hebrews seemed to see themselves as creatures who were called to care for the earth in God's name. In contrast to the Sumerian myths–in which the God Enki creates human beings to be surrogate laborers for the gods, who are unwilling to do the arduous tasks on earth–the Hebrew God commissions humans to share in his ongoing process of creating.[15]

There is no evidence that subsequent Christian teachings on creation, which developed out of Hebrew creation theology, took the notion of dominion to mean "domination." Early Christians, desert fathers, Celtic saints, Francis, medieval theologians–none used this notion as permission to exploit the environment.[16] In fact, the divine image and dominion notions were often used as a basis for defending human dignity against discrimination and social injustice. If anything, these beliefs denoted a calling to deal with all of creation sensitively and responsibly.

Exploitative interpretations of "dominion" seem to be largely a modern phenomenon, prevalent since the discovery of the New World, the Enlightenment, and the development of modern science and technology. In part, the ecological crisis can be attributed to these movements, as well as to such modern developments as colonialism, secularization, nationalism, industrialization, fascism, and communism. Seldom were these movements driven by interpretations of the Hebrew scriptures! And if creation theology has been used as justification for "mastering the world," it has been done only by distorting the original meaning of the Hebrew texts.

Human Limitations

Though humans, as we have seen, have been described in Hebrew theology as "images of God," "a little lower than God," and as creatures having "dominion," the Hebrew scriptures more often view human limitations and failings. Qoheleth, for instance, laments that we humans are quite powerless:

> Indeed, they do not know what is to be, for who can tell them how it will be? No one has power over the wind to restrain the wind, or power over the day of death.   –Ecclesiastes 8:7-8

The Preacher (Qoheleth) here characterizes the human search for meaning to be futile. He challenges the traditional views that the good are rewarded and the bad punished, and he denies that there is any apparent divine justice or providence. There is, therefore, no future upon which humans can depend, no real hope for purpose or meaning. One cannot have much confidence in the next generation, for they don't learn from those who came before them. He detests the fruits of his labors because he must leave them to someone who will come after him, and "who knows whether they will be wise or foolish" (Eccl 2:19).[17] Ultimately, all that humans can look forward to is death, so

Qoheleth maintains that we have no other choice than to seize the day and enjoy the gifts that God has given us. The Preacher does in fact choose to obey the commands of God but with little apparent reason other than a certain fear of God.

Other sections of the Hebrew library also deal with human limitations. The writer of Sirach points out that we often feel insignificant—individuals among countless people who simply don't know us. At times we feel lost in a boundless creation where we are unable to comprehend the foundations of things or the ways of God. Proverbs tell us that in our confusion only God "directs the steps" (Prv 16:9); "it is the purpose of the LORD that will be established" (Prv 19:21). The psalmist at times seems overwhelmed at how weighty and vast are the thoughts of God, thoughts so countless as to be compared to the sands of the desert (Ps 139:17-18). Though humans are crowned with glory and honor, the psalmist wonders why God could possibly be mindful of and care for us (Ps 8:3-4). We are weak and vulnerable, and the lives of some are "but a breath," while others live out a mere delusion (Ps 62:9). Psalm 103 reflects upon the transitoriness of life and concludes that the only constant is the love of God:

> As for mortals, their days are like grass;
> they flourish like a flower of the field;
> for the wind passes over it, and it is gone,
> and its place knows it no more.
> But the steadfast love of the LORD is from everlasting to
> everlasting.
> —Psalm 103:15-17

The Book of Job explores human shortcomings in some depth. Like Qoheleth, Job challenges the traditional wisdom that the good receive rewards and the evil are punished. In this dramatic story a good man's life is reduced to rubble, and rather than being "patient," as Job is often characterized, he rebels and challenges God for such injustice. The Lord comes out of the whirlwind and puts Job through an extremely intimidating interrogation. Where was he when the foundations of the earth were laid, or when the stars and heavenly beings shouted out for joy? Where was he when the sea rushed from the womb of the earth and was wrapped in garments of clouds and swaddling clothes of darkness? (These images will be echoed in Luke's nativity story.) Where was he when the dawn of morning, the snow, hail, and thunder came forth for the first time? What does Job know of deserts and grasslands, of the habits of lions or ravens? (Jb 38:1-41).

Job comes to realize how insignificant a role humans play in creation. He learns that humans cannot challenge or debate with God, and he finds out that human standards are not adequate to deal with the mysteries of creation.

All he can do in the face of life's mysteries is abandon himself to the Lord. In this story humans seem puny, helpless. They are at times comparable to maggots and worms (Jb 25:6). (They certainly are not the marvels of creation that they often seem to be in Genesis or Psalms!)

Humans as the Source of Sin

The Hebrews were clear in their belief that the source of evil in the world was the abuse of human freedom rather than the cruelty or capriciousness of the gods, as pagan mythology would often have it. Disobedience, pride, jealousy, greed, and lust lay at the base of sin. This is clearly demonstrated in the account of the forbidden fruit in Genesis 2. Though Genesis does not speak of a "fall," or degradation of human into an inferior state of being (as in Augustine's notion of original sin), it concerns itself with the origin of the human limitations of death, pain, toil, and sin.

The creation stories continue on for seven more chapters, tracking the development of evil with an account of the first murder—Cain kills his brother Abel—and the story of Noah's family and the flood. Chapter 6 opens with further echoes of pagan myths, as the mysterious "sons of heaven" come to earth and take as many wives as they wish from the beautiful daughters of the tribes. The Lord is outraged at human wickedness, regrets that he ever made living creatures, and decides to start all over again. God instructs Noah to build an ark and take his family and two of every living creature aboard. A great flood destroys all life on land, but when the waters recede, Noah is able to take his family and his entire entourage ashore to begin creation once again.

God then makes a covenant with Noah, his descendants, and every living creature that was with Noah. The Creator vows never again to devastate the earth: "This is the sign of the covenant that I make between me and you and every living creature that is with you, for all future generations: I have set my bow in the clouds, and it shall be a sign of the covenant between me and the earth" (Gn 9:12-13). The myth then describes the beginning of new clans and nations. When humans begin to build a tower to the heavens, God punishes them by confusing their languages and scattering them all over the earth. The story then recounts the birth of the great patriarch Abram.

This human capacity to sin is also explored in the psalms. The psalmist points out that transgression exists deep within the heart of the wicked because of self-flattery and lack of fear of God. The wicked are filled with deceit, and they are preoccupied with plotting evil (Ps 36). Sins affect humans down to their very bones and weigh heavily on them as a burden (Ps 38:3-4). Personal sin is described by Amos in terms of afflicting the righteous, taking bribes, and pushing aside the needy (Am 5:12). Sirach speaks of anger toward neighbor and acts of insolence, arrogance, and injustice (Sir 10:6-7). Hosea observes that sinful self-destruction can come from lack of knowledge. "My people are destroyed for lack of knowledge" (Hos 4:6). Particularly serious is ignorance of the fact that our Creator is the one responsible for all we have. Sin consists in forgetting that God is our maker[18]: "Israel has forgotten his Maker" (Hos 8:14). Earlier Yahweh complained of Israel:

> "She did not know
>   that it was I who gave her
>   the grain, the wine, and the oil,
> and who lavished upon her silver and gold."
>   —Hosea 2:8

Although humans never cease to be images of God, as we read on through the Hebrew scriptures we see that they do bring upon themselves shame, guilt, pain, enslavement, violence, oppression and corruption as a result of their limitations and sinfulness. Their greed and selfishness often move them to oppress others and to take more than their share of God's gifts, thereby depriving others of sustenance.

Israel is often portrayed as a sinful nation, unfaithful to God's covenant and God's law. Sinfulness involves the disturbance of the natural order and harmony that the Creator has placed in the universe. Idolatry, disobedience, and corruption often infected God's people and alienated them from their Creator. Yet God's constant love and forgiveness repeatedly call them back and restore them to the peace and harmony that is the will of the Creator. The psalmist recalls that both his community and its ancestors have repeatedly sinned. He speaks to Yahweh, saying his ancient ancestors in Egypt

> did not consider your wonderful works;
> they did not remember the abundance of your steadfast
>   love,
> but rebelled against the Most High at the Red Sea.
>   —Psalm 106:7

Yet God saves the people, not because of any merits of their own, but out of pure love and graciousness.

On a More Positive Note

The Song of Songs sets aside the negative views of the human person. In this magnificently sensual poetry we do not find Eden's shame about nakedness or fear of nature or of the Creator. In the Song of Songs we have lovers who are comfortable with nature and see it "as musical accompaniment to the inner stirrings of the human heart."[19] Woman here is neither helper nor seducer, as depicted in other portions of the Hebrew scriptures. Rather, the woman is an openhearted and tender lover, one who views human sexual love as something beautiful and desirable in itself and not merely as a way to "increase and multiply." The lovers liken each other to many of the most beautiful sights of nature, and declare their love for each other.

> My beloved speaks and says to me;
> "Arise, my love, my fair one,
>   and come away;
> for now the winter is past,
>   the rain is over and gone.
> The flowers appear on the earth;
>   the time of singing has come,
> and the voice of the turtledove
>   is heard in our land."
>   —Song of Songs 2:10-14

In this magnificent love poetry there is no mention of the dark side of humanity, which is often emphasized in the Hebrew scripture. Here there is gender equality, with no sense of dominance or submission. Once again creation is viewed as becoming whole again, and human love mirrors the divine love that brought it forth. As Roland Murphy comments: "The experience of love not only draws upon the textures of nature for its metaphors, it opens the eyes of the lovers themselves to the beauty of the world around them . . . a vision of God's creation become whole again."[20]

Hebrew Anthropology and the Environment

Our survey of the Hebrew understanding of humanity allows for many applications to the environmental issues of today. I will signal just a few. First, human persons have been made in the image and likeness of God, meaning that they are to be representatives of God. They "stand in" for a creative God, whose constant love and healing power are present in the world. As images of such a God, human beings carry the responsibility of being trustees, caretakers, and sustainers of the earth and its resources. As John Paul II puts it: "God entrusted the whole of creation to the man and woman, and only then—as we read—could he rest."[21]

God's creation is good; each and every element of it has a purpose and contributes to the success of the whole. Each species needs to be seen as important, protected and preserved so that it can carry out its own unique function in the web of life. Each area of creation needs to be respected as having value in itself, not just valued according to its use to humans. We are commissioned by God to preserve and sustain the web of life, to maintain the beauty and bounty of the earth's resources.[22] We are blessed with resources that we need, but they must be used without jeopardizing future generations.

As people who come from the earth and return to it, we need to be part of and not greater than the world. We are made from the same elements of the earth and share the same breath of life as other living creatures. We are connected integrally with our environment; there is a mutual interdependence among ourselves and all the living things and resources on earth. Therefore, "dominion" in no way justifies abuse or exploitation of our environment. We are caretakers, trustees of many precious "gifts," and this sacred trust is to be carried out conscientiously and responsibly. If we do have any nobility among living things, it obliges us to act toward our environment with compassion, love, and justice. As the renowned Hebrew scripture scholar Bernard Anderson puts it: "Humans, for their part, are called to an ecological task: to be faithful managers of God's estate. . . . Human responsibility, however, is grounded in God's covenant, which is universal and ecological. Its sign is the rainbow after the storm: a phenomenon of the natural order known to all human beings."[23]

It is clear from the Hebrew scriptures that although humans have a unique dignity they also are limited. Even with all our technological and scientific advances, there is much about the workings of the environment that we don't know and perhaps never will understand. Astrophysics, microbiology, and many other sciences have raised more questions than given answers. Such limitations indicate that we should proceed cautiously with our commitment to "progress." So much that was deemed advancement and development in the past has seriously damaged our environment. Now that we understand this, future decisions need to be made with much more long-term considerations.

The sciences will continue to uncover more of the "what" of reality but will always fall short on the "how" and the "why" of things. As great scientists like Einstein and Hawking have recognized, even with our great advances in knowledge we stand before a mystery that is beyond our comprehension. For people of faith, only God is the source of the ultimate meaning of creation. Religious beliefs and values, therefore, must play a vital role in any decisions that we make regarding our environment. A purely secular approach to ecological matters is too often driven by utilitarian or even greedy motives. Without a religious perspective we can easily lose touch with the sacred dimension of the world. As one of my students put it in an essay: "I have never before made any connection between my Christian beliefs and ecological questions. I now think that to be a Christian is to belong to a community of faith in which each is connected to one another and to God. This interconnection parallels the interconnection of all of God's creation. In the web of life, every organism from the smallest insect to the largest tree is important in the overall balance of life on the earth. We are responsible for each other—to all people and to all of nature."

Sins against the Earth

Human sinfulness becomes abundantly apparent as we begin to learn of the severe damage that has been inflicted upon God's creation. Human ignorance, greed, and deceit have from the beginning been destructive to the earth. Humans have consistently disturbed the harmony and integrity of the world around them, but much of the most serious devastation has been done in modern times, especially in the last two hundred years. With modern science, industry, and technology, we are now, far more than ever before, capable of doing irreparable harm to our ecosystems. Our air, water, and soil have been severely depleted. The world's resources, given us to share, are now extremely inequitably distributed, are often shamefully wasted, and are being rapidly exhausted. We have disturbed the natural harmony of many ecosystems, destroyed countless species, and brought many others to the brink of extinction. We have seriously damaged the delicate layers in the outer atmosphere, which affect our weather and filter out deadly ultraviolet rays. We have "morally offended" the earth as well as many of its occupants by forcing large populations into refugee areas, where they proceed to devastate the small areas in which they are forced to struggle for survival.

Hebrew creation theology can bring us back to the "giftedness" of nature, to the sacredness of life. Through the magnificent literature of Psalms and the Song of Songs, God calls us to wholeness, to harmony with nature, to oneness among humans and our environment. A new creation spirituality is emerging among Christians, a spirituality that views the material and the physical as integrally linked with the spiritual. It is an "earthy" spirituality that values all aspects of nature and is committed to sustaining the environment. Peace, harmony, simplicity, and concern for others are hallmarks of this emerging spirituality.

HEBREW THEOLOGY OF THE WORLD

Westermann points out that the notion that the world was created by God came to the Hebrews rather late in their belief system. Apparently their experience and celebration of redemption from slavery in Egypt came first, and then belief in "creation" developed as a logical context for such salvation to take place.[24] The celebration of Sabbath also seems to have been foundational to the Hebrew conception of God's creative process. The Israelites first celebrated the saving acts of Yahweh in history and then gradually began to appreciate the sacred space (creation) in which these saving acts took place.

Creation out of Chaos

Chaos is commonly experienced in life, whether the disarray following natural disasters or the many upheavals in social and human life. Yet when we have faith, God can help us rise above chaos. It is possibly the experience of God constantly saving them from this dark side of life that influenced Hebrew thinking on creation. For the Israelites, the creative process came to be identified with God constantly overcoming chaos and bringing creation to fulfillment. It has been suggested that even Hebrew eschatology arose out of the experience of chaotic situations and the hope that God would ultimately bring about harmony and peace in some future end time.[25]

The creation story in Genesis 1 mythologizes this process of God overcoming chaos. Here the earth is originally a formless wasteland, an abyss covered with darkness *(tohu va-bohu)*. Suddenly, a mighty wind *(ruah)* sweeps over the chaos, and with a mere "word" God begins the creative process by bringing forth light. In this creation story we hear the echoes of the Babylonian myth of Marduk, the god of order, overcoming Tiamat, the goddess of chaos, or the struggle of the Canaanite god Baal to overcome Yamm (sea), the god of chaos. In Genesis, however, there is no struggle; there is not even an opponent. With mere wind and word God begins the process of ordering. The struggle with chaos, however, does appear in other passages of the Hebrew scriptures, where God is described as a warrior who conquers the sea monsters Rahab and Leviathan (Pss 74:14; 89:10; Is 27:1; 51:9; Jb 9:13; 26:12).

Though chaos is overcome in the creative act, it always seems to remain in the wings, threatening to engulf creation again. Chaos breaks out of its boundaries in the fall, in the great flood, and at devastating times such as the enslavement in Egypt or the captivity in Babylon. Often the prophets warn of chaos should the Hebrews continue to rebel and reject the protection of their God. Jeremiah describes his vision of such devastation:

> I looked on the earth, and lo, it was waste and void;
>   and to the heavens, and they had no light.
> I looked on the mountains, and lo, they were quaking,
>   and all the hills moved to and fro.
> I looked, and lo, there was no one at all,
>   and all the birds of the air had fled.
> I looked, and lo, the fruitful land was a desert,
>   and all its cities were laid in ruins
>   before the LORD, before his fierce anger.
>   –Jeremiah 4:23-26

While the prophets don't speak of a fallen creation, they do describe history as fallen, as repeatedly corrupted by the misuse of human freedom.[26] Constantly, throughout the Hebrew scriptures, God calls his creation back from the brink of disaster and brings it renewal. The creative wind, the *ruah* of God, returns to bring about a "new creation." The prophetic voice is always dedicated to call God's people to be open to such renewal. The psalmist prays:

> When you send forth your spirit, they are created;
>   and you renew the face of the ground.
>   —Psalm 104:30

Hebrew faith is committed to the belief that without God's presence and power the world will fall back into the darkness of chaos. At the same time, there is a conviction that divine power will ultimately prevail over chaos, and a time of great fulfillment will come about. Ultimately, creation is an ongoing process moving toward such a final "new creation."

The World in Perspective

The Hebrew world was much smaller and self-contained than our contemporary world with its billions of galaxies extending into limitless space. The oldest creation story (Genesis 2) limits the world to a garden, and even the cosmic story in Genesis 1 views the world as self-contained within the boundaries of a solid, light-filled dome above and the underworld below.

Even from such a limited perspective the world seemed vast to the Hebrews, and they used it as a measure of their Creator. The vastness of creation is at times used by the Hebrew as a measure of God's love and forgiveness:

> For as the heavens are high above the earth,
>   so great is his steadfast love toward those who fear
>   him;
> as far as the east is from the west,
>   so far he removes our transgressions from us.
>   —Psalm 103:11-12

At other times, the enormity of God seems to have humbled the sages. They are then moved to remark that before the divine grandeur the entire world looked as though it were a mere speck of dust or a drop of morning dew (Wis 11:22).

Creation Is Good

For the Hebrew, all of creation was from the hand of the Creator and was therefore "good." The liturgical refrain in Genesis 1 repeatedly proclaims: "God saw that it was good." This goodness is not only aesthetic goodness by virtue of beauty, or a goodness arising out of usefulness. Primarily, this goodness is a result of things serving the divine purpose and plan. The author of Sirach puts it this way:

> All the works of the Lord are very good,
>> and whatever he commands will be done at the
>>> appointed time. . . .
> Everything has been created for its own purpose. . . .
> From the beginning good things were created for the
>> good,
>> but for sinners good things and bad.
>>> —Sirach 39:16, 21, 25

In this theology of creation every creature is assigned a place in God's plan in order that it might perform "its appointed role in serving and glorifying the Creator. Thus God calls each by name, and with sovereignty gives each creature its unique nature and function."[27] In Psalm 104 all creatures, including human beings, carry out their respective roles on a plane of equality. Psalm 148 actually recognizes nature as being able to pay homage to the Creator.

> Praise him, sun and moon;
>> praise him, all you shining stars!
> Praise him, you highest heavens,
>> and you waters above the heavens!
> Let them praise the name of the LORD.
>> —Psalm 148:3-5 (see also Psalm 89)

From this perspective there is no place for a dualism that would place humanity over nature.

Belief in the goodness of creation, of course, does not deny that there is evil in the world. That is obvious from the many accounts of sin in the Hebrew scriptures. Yet for the Jew, as we pointed out earlier, sin always finds its origin in humans; it arises from their rebellion and disobedience. And as Augustine pointed out, sin is the absence of goodness. Sin is not of God, and thus from God's all-knowing point of view, creation maintains its course toward the purpose and goal given to it by the Creator God. Westermann puts it this way: "In God's eyes it [creation] is good in a way not immediately apparent from the works themselves. In human eyes there is much in these works which is not good; much of it is incomprehensible, much that is dreadful. But his [the writer of Genesis 1] sentence—that creation was good in God's eyes—relieves the individual of the judgment of the whole. A creature cannot oversee the entirety of the whole and thus cannot evaluate it."[28] God's plan is solely for harmony, goodness, and interrelatedness. Disharmony and destruction come only from the human attempt to be greater than, rather than part of. Ultimately, it is God's plan for wholeness and goodness to prevail.[29]

The Earth Is the Lord's

The creation theology of the Hebrews stands in contrast to that of its neighboring religions. In other ancient religions the creatures of earth, and even the earth itself, are often identified with the gods or considered to be gods in their own right. In addition, ancient religions frequently saw the gods struggling among each other to manipulate and control the world and its creatures.

In contrast, the Hebrews viewed the world and its creatures as separate from the Creator, who made and indeed transcends all things. Moreover, this one God, Yahweh, is not the capricious manipulator that we see in other ancient religions. Rather, the Creator God is a loving and caring "maker" who shares creative powers with human beings. At the same time, it is quite clear in the Hebrew scriptures that all of creation belongs solely to the Creator. In several psalms the biblical writer proclaims this divine ownership of the world:

> The earth is the LORD's and all that is in it,
>> the world, and those who live in it.
>>> —Psalm 24:1

> The heavens are yours, the earth also is yours;
>> the world and all that is in it—you have founded
>>> them.
>>> —Psalm 89:11

The House of the Lord

Creation is also described by the ancient Jews as the dwelling place of God, the "house of God" (Ps 52:8; 55:14). In fact, the great Hebrew Temples of Jerusalem seem to have been built to represent a microcosm of creation, a place where God would dwell and remind all worshipers of the divine omnipresence in the universe.[30] The Temple was a place to come and remember that humans are children of God, who enjoy an eternal covenant with the Creator. Thus the author of Exodus has God say: "Indeed, the whole earth is mine, but you shall be for me a priestly kingdom and a holy nation" (Ex 19:5-6).

Coupled with the belief that the world belongs to the Creator is the Hebrew acknowledgment that God is actually present in the world. The writer of the Wisdom of Solomon observes:

> The spirit of the Lord has filled the world,
>> and that which holds all things together knows what is
>>> said.
>>> —Wisdom 1:7

In a delightfully poetic flourish the psalmist conveys this divine indwelling by dressing Yahweh in nature and describing the deity as a kind of "volcanic figure." God emerges with the smoke of the mountains coming from his nostrils, fire coming from his mouth, glowing coals around him, and darkness under his feet. Yahweh rides a cherub and flies swiftly on the wings of the wind under a dark canopy thick with clouds and water. God thunders through the heavens, flashing lightning as arrows upon his enemies, and then God lays bare the seas and the earth with the mere breath of his nostrils (Ps 18:7-15). Here is the grandeur and power of the Creator, dressed in creation. At the same time it is clear in Hebrew faith that nature is not to be identified with creation. Yahweh always transcends nature and yet graciously allows nature to witness to the glory of the Creator. The presence of the Divine within creation does not have the concreteness for the Hebrew that it has in Babylonian or Egyptian mythology. Thus the Hebrews would not allow images for God.

Nature Can Instruct

The literature of the Native Americans reveals how they learned about life from the eagle, the buffalo, the rushing waters, or the sun. There is a similar point of view in Hebrew creation theology. Psalm 65 relates that we can learn of God's blessings from the rushing waters, harvests of grain, soft showers, overflowing pastures, and meadows filled with flocks. All of these "shout and sing together for joy" and teach us of the love and generosity of God (Ps 65:9-13). The psalmist learns of God's care and intimacy from the natural process of birth. In Psalm 139 the poet sees God "knitting" him together in the womb of his mother. He learns from watching midwives attending births that we can depend on God for safety and warmth.

> Yet it was you who took me from the womb;
>   you kept me safe on my mother's breast.
> On you I was cast from my birth,
>   and since my mother bore me you have been my
>   God.
> –Psalm 22:9-10

From watching a mother nursing her baby, Isaiah is able to meditate on God's constant care and the tenderness and compassion with which the Creator cares for all human beings (Is 49). He could look to life experience as a medium of revelation.

The Hebrews believed that their God disclosed the divine self through nature. In Job, God comes in the whirlwind, and through the story of nature reveals the mystery and the power of the Creator. Winds and gentle breezes can teach us of both the power and gentleness of God. Famines can teach us of God's ultimate power over fertility. We can learn from the olive tree, the fig tree, or the bramble about foolish ambition (Jgs 9:8-15). We can learn from the animals about the ironies of life and the nature of genuine authority and leadership:

> Four things on earth are small,
>   yet they are exceedingly wise:
> the ants are a people without strength,
>   yet they provide their food in the summer;
> the badgers are a people without power,
>   yet they make their homes in the rocks;
> the locusts have no king,
>   yet all of them march in rank;
> the lizard can be grasped in the hand,
>   yet it is found in kings' palaces.
> Three things are stately in their stride;
>   four are stately in their gait:
> the lion, which is mightiest among wild animals
>   and does not turn back before any;
> the strutting rooster, the he-goat,
>   and a king striding before his people.
>   —Proverbs 30:24-31

The sage observes that even the tiny ant can show us the way to wisdom (Prv 6:6). And the Book of Maccabees points out that observing animals can teach mothers to love and feel for their children and even to risk their lives to protect them. The lowly bee can teach us about courage, "since even bees at the time for making honeycombs defend themselves against intruders and, as though with an iron dart, sting those who approach their hive and defend it even to the death" (4 Mc 14:19).

Psalm 19 is a classic celebration of such divine disclosure through nature:

> The heavens are telling the glory of God;
>   and the firmament proclaims his handiwork.
> Day to day pours forth speech,
>   and night to night declares knowledge.
> There is no speech, nor are there words;
>   their voice is not heard;
> yet their voice goes out through all the earth,
>   and their words to the end of the world.
>   —Psalm 19:1-4

Anderson points out that in studying the behavior of animals, trees, and insects, the sages are not trying to use clever figures of speech to teach moral lessons. Rather, they are attempting to fathom the meaning of human existence by getting in touch with all things that have come from the hands of the Creator.[31] As we observed earlier, the answers of God to Job demonstrate that much can be learned about life and our own inadequacies if we carefully reflect on nature.

Wisdom as a Teacher in Nature

The creative and self-revealing principle in God is at times personified in Hebrew literature as Wisdom. This notion of a personified Wisdom seems to have been influenced by Egyptian mythology.[32] Wisdom here seems to be an approach to reality, a way to understand the mysteries of life, a perspective on life from the point of view of God. For the Hebrew, "the LORD by wisdom founded the earth" (Prv 3:19), so it is through that earth that wisdom can be found. Wisdom is the basis for order in nature, and it is *through nature* that wisdom calls us to learn of the self-revelation of God.

Strikingly, the Hebrews personified Wisdom as a woman. Murphy points out how unique this notion is: "There is nothing quite like the personification of Wisdom. She is personified as a woman and in a unique way."[33] Proverbs tells us that this wonderful feminine power was created "before the beginning of the earth" (v. 23) and stood beside the Creator, serving as a link between the divine and human.

> Then I was beside him, like a master worker;
> and I was daily his delight,
>   rejoicing before him always,
> rejoicing in his inhabited world
>   and delighting in the human race.
>   —Proverbs 8:30-31

Lady Wisdom belongs both to God and to the earth; thus she can show us our connection with creation. The sages observe that Lady Wisdom can help us find life because she originates from the Most High. At times the sages even give her traits that seem to identify her with Almighty God. She is holy, all-powerful, and penetrates all things. She is "the breath of the power of God," "a pure emanation of the glory of the Almighty." Lady Wisdom is a reflection of eternal light and an image of God's goodness. She can do all things and renew all things; she can make people into the friends of God and prophets (Wis 7:23-27). Like the Creator, she too dresses herself in the mists, the clouds, and can traverse the oceans and the earth to be with every people and learn from every nation (Sir 24:3-6). She can teach us of the mysteries of creation because she was there from the beginning. She can teach humans about God's many blessings, about the goodness of all creation and the eternal order of things. She can reveal the glory and obedience of God's plan in nature, the purpose of each creature, and the things hidden in God (Sir 42). The sages speak of falling in love with her and of having a sensual intimacy with her:

> Happy is the person who meditates on wisdom
>   and reasons intelligently,
> who reflects in his heart on her ways
>   and ponders her secrets,
> pursuing her like a hunter,
>   and lying in wait on her paths;
> who peers through her windows
>   and listens at her doors;
> who camps near her house
>   and fastens his tent peg to her walls;
> who pitches his tent near her,
>   and so occupies an excellent lodging place;
> who places his children under her shelter,
>   and lodges under her boughs;
> who is sheltered by her from the heat,
>   and dwells in the midst of her glory.
>   –Sirach 14:22-27

As Crenshaw points out: "The sages never tired of speaking about the self-revealing universe. Ever wooing men and women, the universe never fully discloses her mystery."[34] In contrast, both Job and Qoheleth represent a "minimalist" position with regard to how much we can learn about the mysteries of life.[35]

Creation as the Context for Salvation

The Judeo-Christian tradition has often stressed salvation at the expense of creation. Catholicism in particular has been so concerned about salvation, especially personal salvation, that it has lacked a coherent theology of creation. Perhaps this is at the heart of why Catholicism has been so slow in connecting its tradition, its liturgy, and its ethical system to ecology. For many, creation represents an idyllic time in the past, a period that came to an abrupt halt with the fall, which corrupted the earth as well as all of humankind. Concern for redemption from sin, both original sin and personal sin, has often been the centerpiece of theology. The challenge today, then, is to reclaim the rich creation theology of both Hebrew and Christian scriptures, to see creation as the proper context for redemption, and once again to link saving the earth with the process of redemption.

The Hebrews only gradually linked creation with salvation. As Von Rad points out, the old cultic creeds were concerned with God's saving acts; there was no mention of creation. "Israel only discovered the correct theological relationship of the two when she learned to see Creation too as connected theologically with the saving history."[36] Eventually in Hebrew thought creation became the stage upon which salvation is worked out. As J. C. Rylaarsdam points out, creation in the larger sense was "an inference from the experience of redemption."[37]

Lohfink maintains that the so-called Priestly writer closely linked salvation with creation: "Any concern for a salvation that is not identical with responsible concern for the success of God's creation is therefore, as far as we have seen to this point, unthinkable within the framework of the theology of the priestly writing."[38] The joining of the two is apparent also in the Exodus stories. A great deal of natural phenomena is displayed to move Pharaoh to free the Hebrews. The "salvation" of the Hebrews takes place in a "sea," and then they are led by a pillar of smoke, fed with manna, and given water from a rock as they wander in the ever-symbolic "desert" on their way to the land of "milk and honey." Ultimately the Hebrews cross the Jordan River and enter into the "promised land" that had been pledged to them in the ancient days of Abraham and Moses.[39] Creation becomes the context for the events of salvation. Westermann points out that the two notions of God as Creator and Savior come together quite effectively in the psalms.[40]

The New Creation

Hebrew creation theology is a theology of hope and promise. It comes from a fundamental belief that God will always be faithful to the covenant and thus will continually renew creation. In the Wisdom of Solomon the sage teaches that God renews the whole of creation, bringing it into compliance with the divine commands and preventing God's children from being harmed (Wis 19:6). The psalmist points out that God constantly sends forth the Spirit to renew creation (Ps 104:30). The "little creed" in Deuteronomy shows how God displayed great power over nature and brought God's people to a new land. Isaiah encourages his people with the word that the Creator will never tire of helping the powerless and weary to regain their energy. God's people are precious in his sight; he loves them and is with them. He created them for his glory, bears them up on eagles' wings, and will give them birth as does a mother, gasping and panting in labor (Is 40:31; 42:14).[41]

Amos poetically described God's promise constantly to re-create the earth:

> The time is surely coming, says the LORD,
>   when the one who plows shall overtake the one who
>   reaps,
>   and the treader of grapes the one who sows the seed;
> the mountains shall drip sweet wine,
>   and all the hills shall flow with it.
> I will restore the fortunes of my people Israel,
>   and they shall rebuild the ruined cities and inhabit them.
>   —Amos 9:13-14

Ezekiel speaks of new creation in terms of the classic image of the valley of the dry bones:

> Thus says the Lord GOD to these bones: I will cause breath to enter you, and you shall live. I will lay sinews on you, and will cause flesh to come upon you, and cover you with skin, and put breath in you, and you shall live; and you shall know that I am the LORD.   —Ezekiel 37:5-6

Isaiah speaks for Yahweh and proclaims that the "new creation" will bring about peace and justice for the oppressed and the outcast (a theme with which Jesus identified himself). The blind will see, prisoners will be released,

> and new things I now declare;
> before they spring forth.
>   —Isaiah 42:9

The prophets of Israel constantly call for a restoration of harmony, order, and justice to God's creation. Isaiah and Jeremiah especially condemn the oppression and injustice that is done to the poor and warn oppressors that they will bring judgment and destruction upon themselves. They prophesy that God will bring justice and peace to all the nations of the earth. There is in this prophetic literature a messianic hope for the future, when God's people will carry out the divine plan. Micah proclaims:

> He has told you, O mortal, what is good;
>   and what does the LORD require of you
> but to do justice, and to love kindness,
>   and to walk humbly with your God?
>   —Micah 6:8

The Creator has made all things for divine glory and purpose. Hope for the earth lies in carrying out this plan. Only the Creator can restore and bring all of creation to salvation.

The prophets represent what Brueggemann calls an "alternate conscious-ness," a new vision that will confront exploitation, inequality, and injustice. The prophets call for a "new creation," where freedom, justice, and compassion will reign. They challenge some of the idealism of Psalms, where creation seems to be in order, and reveal the dark side of life. The prophets listen not only to God but to the cries of the poor and oppressed. They call God's people to a future that will be in compliance with the Creator's will and power. The prophets energize with a new vision that can be possible only with God's help.[42] Ultimately, God's spirit and purpose will prevail in creation. Ezekiel speaks for Yahweh on this:

> A new heart I will give you, and a new spirit I will put within you; and I will remove from your body the heart of stone and give you a heart of flesh. I will put my spirit within you, and make you follow my statutes and be careful to observe my ordinances. Then you shall live in the land that I gave to your ancestors; and you shall be my people, and I will be your God. —Ezekiel 36:26-28

In this theology of "re-creation," God constantly makes new beginnings, gives the people a renewed covenant with creation. All creatures are embraced with this renewal as creation moves toward the vision of the "new heavens and the new earth" (Is 66:22). This image is prominent in the apocalyptic theology of the postexilic period.

Psalm 65 celebrates God's visitation to the earth with constant gifts of water, rich harvests, animals, oil, and wine. Through the renewal of these gifts the earth tells of the glory of God and proclaims God's love and care. This is indeed an "earthy" spirituality. Roland Murphy observes that the Old Testament "does not spiritualize the realities of life; it accepts them in all their materiality as gifts, blessings. Such is a sacramental view of the universe."[43]

Earth Theology and Ecology

We have seen that the Hebrews believed all of creation belonged to God. From this perspective we are clearly caretakers of a sacred gift on loan, one that needs to be cherished, cared for, and then passed on to future generations. One thinks of Chief Seattle's well-known answer to the president of the United States when the latter asked to "purchase" the Northwest. Chief Seattle was obviously perplexed and wrote: "The land does not belong to us. We belong to the land." And, of course, Chief Seattle, like the ancient Hebrews, believed that it all belonged to the Great Spirit.

The Hebrew notion that God dwells in nature is obviously valuable for anyone concerned about the environment. Nature is in a way a sanctuary, where we have access to the power of the Creator's beauty and power. This notion is captured marvelously in the following reflection from the churches of Appalachia:

> the mountain forests are sacred cathedrals,
> the holy dwelling of abundant life-forms
> which all need each other,
> including us humans,
> with all revealing God's awesome majesty
> and tender embrace.[44]

To harm nature, then, becomes a desecration, an offense against the Creator. Environmental issues thus become moral issues. Pollution of the air with deadly gases, dumping toxic waste materials in the oceans, slashing and burning of our rainforests are not only offenses against nature, they indeed should be viewed as moral offenses against the Creator.

We have seen how the Hebrew God creates order out of chaos. Certainly many areas of our environment are in a chaotic state. Weather patterns seem to have been disrupted by global warming, and we have witnessed extremes in heat and cold as well as numerous incidents of severe storms, floods, and brush fires. Our oceans have become dumping grounds for garbage and toxic waste. The ecosystems along many of the earth's waterways have been disturbed and even destroyed by dams, shoreline landscaping, and development. Fishing areas that were once rich with abundant catch are now sparse with fish because of over-fishing. Young students in parts of Australia cannot go outside their schools for recess, and must cover their skin when outside because of ozone depletion in those areas. Students in Mexico City go to school wearing masks to filter out air pollution. There is indeed an urgent need to involve ourselves with the Creator in efforts to "renew the face of the earth." People of faith realize that attempts to do things on their own often result in frustration and feelings of helplessness. With the power of God–the strength that can be gained from prayer and solidarity with other people of faith–concrete results can be achieved and the earth can be repaired.

New Perspectives

The creation theology of the Hebrew Bible can provide us with new perspectives with regard to the environment. First of all, we see that creation is much more than human life, that we are not the center of it all. There is a vastness in creation that transcends human life and that seems quite capable of going on without us. Moreover, each human life is but a brief moment within creation's long history. Each person leaves a mark and then moves on. As the one "free" creature on earth, we can choose to destroy or to sustain the place we have been given for the short period of our lives. Then we pass it all on to the next generation, for better or for worse. People of faith take this latter responsibility seriously, and the love they have for their children and for future generations moves them to live and act with care and respect for the earth.

Nature can teach us how to live our lives in a creative manner. We can learn from the forests, the oceans, the mountains, and from living things about the intricacies, the grandeur, and the tragedies of life. Nature can teach us how to value its laws and can show us how to preserve its beauty, appreciate its bounty, and sustain it in its fragility.

The Importance of Education

Education is essential, both for understanding the environment itself and for connecting our religious tradition with our concerns about ecology. Much destruction of the environment has been done out of ignorance. When refrigeration and air-conditioning were developed, most people had no idea how much damage chlorofluorocarbons (CFCs) could do to the protective ozone layer. When oil was discovered and the automobile invented, there was little understanding of how devastating the exhausts could be to our air quality or how accumulations of carbon dioxide could affect our weather patterns and water levels in the ocean. And, of course, who could have anticipated the tremendous havoc we would bring to our environment through oil spills? When huge factory-fishing ships were designed, it was not clearly understood that this would cause over-fishing and not allow time for the fish population to replenish itself.

Many of us are brought up in urban or suburban areas, where we have little contact with nature. Few of us have the opportunities to study nature, the habits of animals, the intricacies of plant and tree life, or the patterns of stars and planets in the night sky. If we do not understand our environment, it is easy to be oblivious to the damage that we and others are doing to it. Most people who understand how ecosystems work, and how essential they are to healthy living, are sensitive to environmental issues.

Education in our religious tradition is also a key to dealing with environmental issues. Religions are the source of our beliefs and values. For the Christian, the understanding of scripture and the church's doctrinal and moral tradition can be of enormous value in dealing with ecology. We have seen already the richness of the Hebrew creation tradition. Much of this tradition can provide strong motivation for getting involved in environmental issues.

Contemplating Nature

Many of my students tell me that their deepest religious experiences happen when they are in nature. For some, it might be a camping or ski trip in the mountains, a walk on a sunny beach, plowing a field for spring planting, or just sitting on the porch on a starry night. God does seem to be revealed to many people when they connect with nature. There is a spiritual dimension in all of us, and it hungers for nourishment. Nature often can bring us the inner peace, the depth of reflection, and the wholeness that we lose touch with in our busy everyday lives. The prayer and reflection that we can enjoy in nature can bring us to a whole new awareness that this is indeed God's world and that God can come to us in mysterious ways through the wonders of creation.

Saving Our Earth as well as Ourselves

Christians in the past often were preoccupied with their own personal salvation. Moreover, emphasis commonly was placed on the salvation of the soul. Scant attention was paid to including the earth, material things, or the "body" in concerns about salvation. For many, their "true home" was in heaven, and they viewed life on earth as a journey in a "valley of tears," a time to be endured while waiting to go to heaven.

Hebrew creation theology has shown us that such dualistic thinking, which separates souls from bodies, the material from the spiritual, and the natural from the supernatural, is not the biblical perspective. All of creation comes from God, and it is all good. There is in scripture a sacramental perspective. The visible is linked to the invisible, the material to the spiritual.

The noble Masai tribe of Africa seem to have such a sacramental mentality. In one of their prayers, for example, they reflect on fire:

> Thank you, Father, for your free gift of fire.
> Because it is through fire that you draw near to us
>   every day.
> It is with fire that you constantly bless us.
> Our Father, bless this fire today.
> With your power enter into it.
> Make this fire a worthy thing.
> A thing that carries your blessing.
> Let it become a reminder of your love.
> A reminder of life without end.[45]

The biblical perspective is not soul-centered or even human-centered. For the Hebrew, God is at the center of all reality, and God's covenant is made with all creation. Consequently, there is an interdependence in creation, a mutuality, that makes it all worth saving. The eternal reward is not heaven detached from earth, or a soul disembodied, but creation transformed, creation brought to fulfillment. The entire creation was made to be saved, to be redeemed.

There can and will be a new creation. The environmental crisis we find ourselves in can be turned around. Much progress has already been made in many areas because we are aware of the problems and have taken steps to remedy them. For the person of faith, the new creation can come about only through the power of the Creator. We are not helpless or hopeless in the face of what often appear to be overwhelming environmental problems. The wisdom of God, the power of God, the love of God are available to us, both individually and as communities, to repair the earth and to help restore it to God's purpose.

THE CREATOR

The central figure in the creation theology of the Hebrews is Yahweh, the Creator and Savior of all. Throughout the Old Testament this notion evolves, and in Hebrew mythology God moves from being multiple to being one; from a local garden potter to a cosmic Creator. God is at times portrayed as a great warrior, defending his people and destroying their enemies; or again, he is an avenging Creator, who floods the earth to punish sinners or sends plagues, storms, and devastation to those who break his laws. The Hebrew God is pictured as a rock, a shepherd, a father or mother, a midwife, even an eagle. But ultimately, the Hebrew God remains Mystery, a reality beyond name or description.

At times the Hebrew God is perceived as hidden. The psalmist often feels forsaken and cries out and groans in the night (Ps 22). When God hides from his people, they are dismayed; and if God takes away their breath, they die and return to the earth (Ps 104:29). God is even portrayed as being "asleep," and the psalmist calls upon God to wake up and save the people (Ps 44:23-24).

Though God's absence is at times reported in the Hebrew scriptures, more prominent is the experience of God's abiding, powerful, and "acting" presence, a presence that one can feel through prayer. The psalmist looks upon God "in the sanctuary" and beholds the divine "power and glory" (Ps 63:2). This all-present God of history and creation rules creation, sustains it, and is the very source of holiness (Wis 12:15-16). God's power ranges from feeding and caring for all creatures to determining and knowing the stars of the heavens (Ps 147). All creatures do the will of this God, and God's wisdom can search out everything from the darkest abyss to the workings of the human heart (Ps 64).

God's presence in nature is celebrated as a great lord who wraps himself in a garment of light and rides on a chariot of clouds on the wings of the wind (Ps 97:2-4). Yahweh's caring presence is seen as a pouring out of the divine spirit "on all flesh," so that

> your sons and your daughters shall prophesy,
>> your old men shall dream dreams,
>> and your young men shall see visions.
>>> –Joel 2:28

Indeed, God's spirit fills the world and holds all things together (Wis 1:7). The psalmist stands in awe of this caring presence:

> Where can I go from your spirit?
>> Or where can I flee from your presence?
> If I ascend to heaven, you are there;
>> if I make my bed in Sheol, you are there.
> If I take the wings of the morning
>> and settle at the farthest limits of the sea,
> even there your hand shall lead me,
>> and your right hand shall hold me fast.
>>> –Psalm 139:7-10

The Hebrews trusted in their God and believed that they could always take refuge in the divine protection. The Lord was their shepherd, who led them, restored them, and placed them on the right paths. They did not need to fear evil because God was always there to comfort them (Ps 23:1-4). The Hebrews often spoke of God's "steadfast love" and indeed looked upon God as their friend:

> The friendship of the LORD is for those who fear him,
>> and he makes his covenant known to them.
>>> –Psalm 25:14

God as Parent

It is commonly thought that father is a major Hebrew image for God. On the contrary, even though Israel was a patriarchal nation, the image of father is used for God only a handful of times in Hebrew scripture. And even at that, the image is not developed at much depth. Psalm 68 describes Yahweh as a "father of orphans and protector of widows," and cries out "you are my Father, my God" (Pss 68:5; 89:26). In Sirach there is a prayer to God as father, asking God to remove evil desires and passions from his heart (Sir 23:4-6). (This prayer is echoed in the gospel Our Father in the phrase "lead us not into temptation.")

The image of mother is also used in Hebrew theology and is more developed than the father image. Isaiah is especially fond of this image and uses it with great tenderness and sensitivity. Israel, as the children of God, are told:

> You shall nurse and be carried on her arm,
>> and dandled on her knees.
> As a mother comforts her child,
>> so I will comfort you;
>> you shall be comforted in Jerusalem.
>> —Isaiah 66:12-13

The Lord Creator formed Israel as child in her womb and will help her children (Is 44:2). As mother, God will remain with her children to their old age, always carrying them and saving them (Is 46:4). In another extremely touching passage, the Mother God promises always to remember her child:

> Can a woman forget her nursing child,
>> or show no compassion for the child of her womb?
> Even these may forget,
>> yet I will not forget you.
> See, I have inscribed you on the palms of my hands;
>> your walls are continually before me.
>> —Isaiah 49:15-16

Hosea too speaks of God as a mother, teaching her toddler to walk and taking the little one in her arms. Here the Mother God says:

> I led them with cords of human kindness,
>> with bands of love.
> I was to them like those
>> who lift infants to their cheeks.
> I bent down to them and fed them.
>> —Hosea 11:4-5

God is also described as a mother eagle, hovering over her young and taking them out to learn to fly. As they falter, she swoops down and catches them on her wings. This marvelous image demonstrates how the Mother God cares for her children with both tenderness and power.

> As an eagle stirs up its nest,
>> and hovers over its young;
> as it spreads its wings, takes them up,
>> and bears them aloft on its pinions.
>> —Deuteronomy 32:11

God as Provider

The God of the Hebrews is praised and thanked as the provider of all things. This gracious Creator bestows upon all creatures the rain, grass, and food that they need. Psalm 147 proclaims a belief that will also be echoed by Jesus:

> He gives to the animals their food,
>   and to the young ravens when they cry.
>   —Psalm 147:9

Yahweh blesses the land and visits it, coming with water, grain, bountiful harvests, and rich meadows to feed the flocks (Ps 65:9-13). If anyone should be deprived of food and water, it can only be blamed on human failings. It is greed and selfishness that cause many to be deprived unjustly of the resources of creation. This is pointed out often in the prophetic tradition, which cries out for justice and a new creation where the poor will be served. In Isaiah the Lord says,

> For I am about to create new heavens
>   and a new earth;
> the former things shall not be remembered
>   or come to mind.
> But be glad and rejoice forever
>   in what I am creating;
> for I am about to create Jerusalem as a joy,
>   and its people as a delight.
> I will rejoice in Jerusalem,
>   and delight in my people;
> no more shall the sound of weeping be heard in it,
>   or the cry of distress.
>   —Isaiah 65:17-19

God the Savior

Closely linked with God's role as Creator is the divine commitment to salvation. Isaiah puts it clearly, as Yahweh proclaims:

> But now thus says the LORD,
>   he who created you, O Jacob,
>   he who formed you, O Israel:
> Do not fear, for I have redeemed you;
>   I have called you by name, you are mine.
>   —Isaiah 43:1

God's people are precious in the divine eyes, and therefore God will gather his people to the ends of the earth. People were created for God's glory and will be constantly restored so that they can proclaim this glory with dignity (Is 43:4-7). The psalmist declares that God's "steadfast love endures forever" (Ps 136:1). The children of God, as well as the earth on which they live, receive healing from their God. Deserts and parched lands are given water, and wasted lands are restored (Ps 107:35). God constantly brings his people back from enslavement and oppression: God forgives them for their infidelities and restores them to new life.

The God of the Poor

God especially brings salvation to the poor. The Creator is indeed on the side of the needy and raises them up out of their grief and distress (Ps 113). The Creator provides the poor with water and with rich resources. God constantly reaches out to provide for the poor. The prayers of the poor will be heard (Sir 21:5); and those who reach out to them in his name will themselves be blessed. Tobit puts this in a moving way: "Do not turn your face away from anyone who is poor, and the face of God will not be turned away from you" (Tb 4:7).

God's concern for the poor brings judgment upon those who hoard the products of the earth for themselves and deprive the poor. In Isaiah, Yahweh severely chastises the greedy who deprive others:

> What do you mean by crushing my people,
>   by grinding the face of the poor? says the Lord GOD
>   of hosts.
>   —Isaiah 3:15

In Sirach, the people of God are urged to take care of the needy in God's name:

> My child, do not cheat the poor of their living,
>   and do not keep needy eyes waiting.
> Do not grieve the hungry,
>   or anger one in need.
> Do not add to the troubles of the desperate,
>   or delay giving to the needy.
> Do not reject a suppliant in distress,
>   or turn your face away from the poor.
> Do not avert your eye from the needy.
>   —Sirach 4:1-5

The Creator and the Environment

Going over the litany of environmental problems can be discouraging and even bring us to the point of feeling helpless or despairing. It might seem that the Creator is indeed asleep or has abandoned creation. Very often it seems as though the ecological crisis is getting worse, rather than better, and yet religions seem quite removed from it all. One seldom hears these matters brought up in church, and many of our religious thinkers seem quite unconcerned about ecology.

At the same time, there are so many reasons to have hope. There is a growing awareness today, especially among the young, that the earth needs to be saved. Many people of faith are waking up to the fact that their faith in the Creator's presence and power has relevance to ecology. Some people are beginning to engage in prayer and action to show appreciation for the gifts of creation and to do something to sustain the earth.

There is a shift among many faithful from seeing the Creator as a distant figure in the heavens to believing that God is a fellow sufferer, one who is intimately involved in the world and willing to empower those who want to make efforts to deal with some of our problems in this area. There is a renewed awareness that God is still the presence and power who continues to design and sustain all things. In the midst of so much chaos and destruction, many turn to God as a friend and companion, one who can be trusted to inspire them in the difficult struggles against all the devastation that is going on.

Some are suggesting that we alter our images of God. Perhaps images of the warrior God or the patriarchal God only serve to perpetuate notions of dominance and mastery. These images might well represent human projections upon God, images that have been used throughout history to rationalize oppression and domination. For many feminine theologians, it is patriarchy in society and religion that have been mainly responsible for male domination, as well as for much of the competitive and militant forces that have been so destructive in the modern era. Sallie McFague has suggested that other images, such as lover, friend, or mother, might be more helpful in matters of peace, justice, and ecology. She also suggests that the earth might be more revered if imaged as "the body of God."[46] Jay McDaniel proffers the image of heart for God, since the heart stands for the core or inner center.[47] Others are exploring some of the ancient goddess religions in efforts to restore feminine perspectives on the sacredness of the earth. Geologian Thomas Berry indicates the traditional images of God have been too much a part of the ecological problem and that we must move beyond them and listen to the universe for new understandings of the Creator. Here we would find experiences of God in the world of life, in the dawn, the sunset, soil, trees, animals, and rivers. This is the understanding of the Creator, according to Berry, that we need to deal with the ecological challenges of today.[48]

Some theologians indicate that the Creator God of the Hebrew scriptures has been used to set up hierarchical thinking in society as well as in the church, and they suggest that in the modern era the theology of the Creator should move in more egalitarian and holistic directions. Creator as purely "Other" can be too remote from the political, social, and environment challenges of today. A divinity too spiritualized can perhaps be set over and against the material or earthy, which more often than not is identified with the feminine.[49] Some hold that the word *God* itself is too tainted with masculine and dominant images to be useful in this "post-patriarchal" age.[50]

Many theologians have been influenced by Karl Rahner's approach to God as a Mystery to be discovered in human experience. This can be a useful approach to finding the link between one's experience of the environment and the Creator. Others have been more attracted to a *process theology* notion of God, because it seems more compatible with modern science, evolution, and thus environmental science. Some theologians propose a *panentheism*, whereby the universe is permeated with the presence of God. This notion of God has obvious attractions for environmentalists because of its emphasis on the immanence of God. As John Haught comments: "In this cosmology, it is not possible to be a worshipper of God without simultaneously loving and caring for our natural environment."[51]

Liberation theologians have been influential in offering images of God that are useful in the struggles against oppression. Theirs is often the God of the poor, the Liberator who frees the poor and the outcast from injustice. *Liberation theology* is a "listening theology"; it holds its ear to the whispers of the poor in order to learn from them God's self-revelation. Liberation theology, however, has not usually turned its attention either to the plight of poor women or to ecological issues. Jon Sobrino and others rejected white middle-class, North American views and maintained that liberation theology's main resource should be the suffering and oppressed. Yet many liberation theologians, though listening to the poor, are still too much influenced by European theology and its traditional notions of God. *Post-liberation theology* will perhaps not reject anyone and will truly listen to many voices and resources, especially those of the indigenous peoples around the world. Environmental concerns are global and demand that theologians be open to wherever the Spirit of God might blow.[52]

It is clear that we are in a state of flux. Many are dissatisfied with the traditional notions of God, since these so often seem to be tied in with attitudes that have been destructive of the environment. It is my position that the Hebrew scriptures offer a wide variety of God images, and that within these images there is much authentic self-revelation on the part of this Mystery we call God. Many of the reflections on God that we find in the Hebrew scriptures can be quite helpful in leading us to an appreciation of the sacredness of our environment and in moving us to be more effective partners with the Creator.

SUMMARY

We have looked at some of the Hebrew notions of human nature, the earth, and God. Obviously, there is much here that can be connected to our environmental concerns. For people of faith, we are all children of God, intimately linked to God's creation, and charged with responsibly caring for the gifts God has given us, the home that the Lord has made for us. If we can see ourselves in covenant with God as friend and partner, enormous wisdom and power are accessible to us in this task of saving the earth and all living things.

3.

The Christian Scriptures

I guess I fear for my two little ones more than anyone else. We live in the Barents Sea region in the northwest corner of Russia. We have become a dumping ground for radioactive waste. The nuclear subs are towed into the bay here and their nuclear reactors are stored in old dumps or just sunk into the sea. They say that our waters will gradually contain large quantities of uranium and plutonium. They also tow in nuclear missiles with their warheads and just dump them outside the city. From the nearby nickel smelter plant in Nikel a green mushroom floats over our city from time to time. I hope my children can get out of here before it is too late.
—Lyudmila Yaksokov, Murmansk, Russia

The New Testament is a treasured collection of Christian faith documents. Based on memories of the life, death, and resurrection of Jesus, the Christian scriptures bear witness to the earliest faith that Jesus is the messiah and savior of the world. These beliefs and values have inspired countless multitudes in their daily struggles for two millennia. Most certainly these biblical beliefs can help Christians face the challenging environmental problems of our day.

Jesus was a Jew, and therefore he held fervently to Hebrew beliefs regarding creation. He deeply valued human life, carried himself with self-regard and dignity, and insisted that each person be treated with the respect due to a child of God. Jesus was a man of the earth, who spent most of his life working with his hands. He regarded his world as coming from and indeed belonging to the Lord God. Jesus recognized the goodness of creation, saw that it was the context for God's kingdom, and freely used the things of life and nature to teach his lessons about the kingdom. Jesus faithfully followed his God-given mission to show through his life and miracles that God is a loving and saving Abba. Through his life, death, and resurrection, Jesus transformed the world into a new creation.

This chapter will focus on the New Testament and examine Jesus' gospel teachings on creation. We will then consider some of the creation themes contained in the gospel accounts of the mysteries of Jesus' life, as well as in the writings of the apostle Paul. Along the way, I will point out applications to environmental issues.

THE TEACHINGS OF JESUS

Jesus was a Jewish teacher whose insights are drawn from his own tradition. His unique contribution to this tradition seems to have its origin in his singular experience of the Creator. This experience gave Jesus extraordinary insights into the divine, the value of human life, and how to achieve blessedness through a life dedicated to the reign of God. As we shall see, Jesus' parables and miracles were often effective instruments to convey these teachings.

God as Abba

Jesus taught that God is a loving and caring Abba, who attends all creation with concern and provides for the needs of all.[1] He once said that his followers could learn of the providence of God by studying the birds of the air:

> "I tell you, my friends, do not fear those who kill the body, and after that can do nothing more. But I will warn you whom to fear: fear him who, after he has killed, has authority to cast into hell. Yes, I tell you, fear him! Are not five sparrows sold for two pennies? Yet not one of them is forgotten in God's sight. But even the hairs of your head are all counted. Do not be afraid; you are of more value than many sparrows."
> –Luke 12:4-7

Jesus had learned from his own faith and intimacy with the divine that the wonders of creation are gifts to be shared by all. The love of the Creator is inclusive and unconditional, and Jesus called his followers to share in this love and extend it even to their enemies. This is perhaps one of the most radical and difficult lessons that Jesus preached:

> "You have heard that it was said, 'You shall love your neighbor and hate your enemy.' But I say to you, Love your enemies and pray for those who persecute you, so that you may be children of your Father in heaven; for he makes his sun rise on the evil and on the good, and sends rain on the righteous and on the unrighteous." –Matthew 5:43-45

We saw in the last chapter that the Hebrews believed their God was a caring provider, supplying them with the protection and resources they needed.

Jesus proclaimed this belief in his own teaching. He taught his disciples to pray confidently for their daily bread, as well as for all their needs:

> "Ask, and it will be given you; search, and you will find; knock, and the door will be opened for you. For everyone who asks receives, and everyone who searches finds, and for everyone who knocks, the door will be opened. Is there anyone among you who, if your child asks for bread, will give a stone? Or if the child asks for a fish, will give a snake? If you then, who are evil, know how to give good gifts to your children, how much more will your Father in heaven give good things to those who ask him!"
>
> —Matthew 7:7-11

At times the kind of faith to which Jesus called his followers is startling. He told them they had no need for anxiety in their lives because the Creator Abba would provide for them in the same way in which the birds of the air, the lilies, and the grasses of the field are provided for (Mt 6:26). Jesus calls them to a detachment, a simplicity that enables them to focus on the one thing that is all important—their righteousness with God:

> "Therefore do not worry, saying, 'What will we eat?' or 'What will we drink?' or 'What will we wear?' For it is the Gentiles who strive for all these things; and indeed your heavenly Father knows that you need all these things. But strive first for the kingdom of God and his righteousness, and all these things will be given to you as well."
>
> —Matthew 6:31-33[2]

In an era of mounting consumer debt, when people are often driven to work several jobs just to keep up with the bills, are these not useful lessons? Is it possible for people to be freed from the drive to accumulate, from wasteful habits, and from the spending sprees that ultimately bring them so much anxiety and tension? We know that these habits drive production and the economies so often responsible for much of the depletion of the world's resources and pollution of its air, land, and water. Can the gospel call to simplicity and detachment from material things be the answer? John Paul II indicates that serious changes in lifestyle are essential to solve what he sees as a "moral crisis":

> In many parts of the world society is given to instant gratification and consumerism while remaining indifferent to the damage which these cause. . . . If an appreciation of the value of the human person and of human life is lacking, we will also lose interest in others and in the earth itself. Simplicity, moderation, and discipline, as well as a spirit of sacri-

fice, must become a part of everyday life, lest all suffer the negative consequences of the careless habits of a few.[3]

Human Dignity

The gospels reflect Jesus' Hebrew faith that human beings are images of God. In the Sermon on the Mount Jesus preaches the blessedness of a wide range of human experience, including poverty, mercy, and persecution. He tells the crowds that they are "the salt of the earth" and "the light of the world" (Mt 5:13-16). On another occasion Jesus teaches that people can confidently look toward their own human expectations as a basis for morality. He says: "In everything do to others as you would have them do to you" (Mt 7:12). He professes the Hebrew ethic that the love of self can be the standard for loving God and others.[4]

For Jesus, all people, whether rich or poor, good or bad, were worthy of love. Lepers, centurions, outcasts of all kinds, even enemies, were worthy of love because they were all children of God. He looked with compassion on the troubled and abandoned masses, and he urged his disciples to be laborers of the harvest and fishers of men (Mt 9:38; 4:19). Jesus particularly showed love for those just beginning their lives. He blessed and embraced the children who were brought to him and said that it is "to such as these that the kingdom of God belongs" (Mk 10:14). Jesus was the good shepherd (Jn 10:11). He loved people intensely, said they could call him "friend," and was willing to lay down his life for them.

While Jesus believed in the goodness and dignity of humans, he was at the same time realistic about our limitations. He knew the dark side of the human heart, our capacity for hatred, violence, hypocrisy, betrayal, and greed. He realized that sin is companion to humans, sapping our life like weeds, choking our strength like thorns, and poisoning us like vipers. Jesus, like all of us, was surrounded by evil and corruption, and yet he called us to the light, to a conversion to our true identity as children of God (Jn 12:35; Mt 4:16). He called people to a life of love, sacrifice, and prayer; he promised that this way, though narrow, is the true way to eternal life. In his own life Jesus consistently met hatred and rejection with love and forgiveness.[5] In his death he faced treachery and rejection with compassion. In Luke's version of the passion story Jesus died calling for forgiveness for the very enemies who had brought his life to an end: "Father, forgive them; for they know not what they are doing" (Lk 23:34). He offered his life for others and promised to be with his followers always (Mt 28:20).

Jesus' life has served as a model for each age. At this time of environmental crisis his disciples can look to him to rediscover the dignity of all peoples and to learn compassion for the millions who suffer from deprivation and injustice. His Way realistically faces the many evils inflicted on the earth and its peoples with hope, courage, and persistent efforts to bring justice and wholeness to the world. The Spirit of Jesus inspires people to take risks, undergo suffering, and even face persecution so that the world might be saved.

Achieving Blessedness

Jesus reminded his people that their God was blessed, but that they could share in this gift of holiness if they followed his Way. Union with the Creator and creation would come to those who were poor in spirit, mournful, meek, eager to be righteous, merciful, clean of heart, peaceful, and willing to suffer persecution for righteousness. These would receive the kingdom, be called children of God, and inherit the earth (Mt 5:3-11). He further instructed them that the way to righteousness was through feeding the hungry, giving drink to the thirsty, extending hospitality to the stranger, clothing the naked, and caring for the imprisoned. Such service extended to others would in fact be service to the Creator, for "just as you did it to one of the least of these who are members of my family, you did it to me" (Mt 25:40).

Concern for others, especially the poor, was at the heart of Jesus' mission. When he publicly read the scriptures in his hometown of Nazareth, he identified himself with the prophet Isaiah and acknowledged that he had been anointed "to bring good news to the poor," "to proclaim release to the captives," and "to give sight to the blind" in the Jubilee year (Lk 4:16-19). Jesus insisted that his disciples not lord it over others, but rather always be of service: "Whoever wishes to be first among you must be slave of all. For the Son of Man came not to be served but to serve, and to give his life a ransom for many" (Mk 10:44-45).

A Simple Lifestyle

Jesus himself lived simply. He once remarked to a person who asked to be his follower: "Foxes have holes, and birds of the air have nests; but the Son of Man has nowhere to lay his head" (Lk 9:58). He expected the same detachment from those who followed him, and when he sent them out on mission he instructed them: "Take nothing for your journey, no staff, nor bag, nor bread, nor money—not even an extra tunic. Whatever house you enter, stay there, and leave from there" (Lk 9:3-4). It was by following his instructions that they were able to bring the good news and healing to others (Lk 9:6).[6]

In the Acts of the Apostles we see the early community in Jerusalem still following the Master's example:

Now the whole group of those who believed were of one heart and soul, and no one claimed private ownership of any possessions, but everything they owned was held in common. With great power the apostles gave their testimony to the resurrection of the Lord Jesus, and great grace was upon them all. There was not a needy person among them, for as many as owned lands or houses sold them and brought the proceeds of what was sold.   —Acts 4:32-34

The Danger of Riches

Jesus had harsh words for those whose lives were driven by desires to accumulate. He once answered a person who wanted him to intercede in a family feud over an inheritance: "Take care! Be on your guard against all kinds of greed; for one's life does not consist in the abundance of possessions" (Lk 12:15). Jesus warned again against the futility of hoarding material and not spiritual treasures:

> "Do not store up for yourselves treasures on earth, where moth and rust consume and where thieves break in and steal; but store up for yourselves treasures in heaven, where neither moth nor rust consumes and where thieves do not break in and steal. For where your treasure is, there your heart will be also."   —Matthew 6:19-21

In one of the most touching of the gospel stories, a rich young man had to pass up the privilege of personally being with Jesus because he was unable to set aside his possessions (Lk 18:18-25). Tragically, it was too difficult for him to follow Jesus because he could not accept the conditions of discipleship. Jesus had been clear on this: "For those who want to save their life will lose it, and those who lose their life for my sake will save it. What does it profit them if they gain the whole world, but lose or forfeit themselves?" (Lk 9:24-25)

It is clear from the gospels—and this has been exemplified in the lives of the great saints—that gospel living entails detachment from material things, a sharing of one's possessions, and dedication to sacrifice for others. The gospel lifestyle stands dramatically as countercultural in our time of extraordinary materialism, greed, and isolated individualism. The lifestyle laid out by Jesus prophetically challenges the luxurious lifestyle of the privileged, which often threatens the environment and the very existence of the many millions of the poor throughout the world.

The Reign of God

The notion of the reign of God is central to Jesus' teaching and quite applicable to today's concern for the condition of the earth. Jesus ascribed to the Hebrew notion that the earth is the Lord's, and his many teachings on the reign of God are in continuity with the Hebrew notion that Yahweh is the

Creator and sustainer of all reality. Divine power not only creates, it also protects and liberates all things. God's will is that the divine power of love and creativity should prevail over evil, injustice, oppression, and destruction. God's unconditional and liberating love reveals itself "in the lives of men and women who do God's will."[7]

Jesus' teaching with regard to the reign of God rebuked those who used the notion to justify their domination over people and the earth. "Power for" can easily translate into "power over," and those in authority have perennially used the reign of God concept to justify oppression and destruction. Jesus confronted such an interpretation and clearly indicated in his teachings and actions that God's power prevails (or reigns) as a power that heals and saves. Jesus exercised this power by serving rather than controlling, by being last rather than first, and by standing in solidarity with outcasts. In his personal life, as well as in his miracles and teachings, Jesus of Nazareth gave many people an extraordinary experience of this unique power of God. He taught his disciples that they too could be instruments of this creative power in the world.[8]

The reign of God was preached by Jesus with unique intensity. The gospel accounts of his baptism and transfiguration reveal that Jesus experienced a unique intimacy with and approval from God, whom he called Abba. As a result, Jesus seemed to be convinced that his words and deeds were ushering in a new phase of God's power. Jesus saw that his message and his power were especially touching outcasts and the poor. Perhaps this led Jesus to proclaim that the poor are uniquely blessed in the eyes of God. His mission, which continued through his disciples, was in large part to restore dignity and equality to the marginal. To achieve this, Jesus called both oppressed and oppressor to conversion and urged them to live in peace and harmony as the children of God.[9]

Already but Not Yet

Jesus seems to have identified with Jews who thought that God's ultimate salvation of the world would come in the near future, although he admitted that he did not know the exact time. At the same time Jesus taught that there was a unique immediacy–a present dimension–to the reign of God. Jesus' teaching was often concerned both with alerting people to the immediacy of God's presence and power and with admonishing them to prepare for the final days.

Evil and corruption were acknowledged by Jesus to be real obstacles to the power of the reign of God. Yet, Jesus' profound faith convinced him that ultimately the saving power of God would prevail. During his lifetime Jesus constantly demonstrated this inexorable power, and in his death promised to send his Spirit to help people to continue the struggle against evil in the world.

The Reign of God and Creation

The reign of God is dealt with extensively in the gospel of Matthew. Matthew chooses a natural or "creation" setting for the presentation of his reign-of-God theology. When John the Baptist begins preaching, he is in the desert of Judea, the same "wilderness" through which Yahweh called his people toward the promised land. The desert was a stark area, thought by ancients to be filled with evil spirits. It was a barren place where one had to face one's own vulnerabilities in the hope of encountering the Creator, who overcomes chaos with order and brings new life. John came forth dressed in the austere clothing of a hermit-prophet: camel's hair tied with a leather belt. The Baptist was a man close to nature, one who could survive in the wilderness, eating only the simple natural fare of locusts and honey. John stands starkly before his listeners, his feet planted in the flow of the Jordan River, a symbolic place through which the Hebrews crossed into the land that had been promised them.

John begins by condemning the "vipers," the corrupted religious leaders who show no signs of genuine repentance. He uses natural images to demonstrate that those who do not do good will be destroyed and that the one "coming after" will bring judgment upon evil:

> "Even now the ax is lying at the root of the trees; every tree therefore that does not bear good fruit is cut down and thrown into the fire. . . . His winnowing fork is in his hand, and he will clear his threshing floor and will gather his wheat into the granary; but the chaff he will burn with unquenchable fire."   —Matthew 3:10, 12

It is into this context of creation images that Jesus steps, asking to be baptized. After Jesus' baptism in the Jordan River, creation itself responds. The dome of the sky opens and like the great hovering Spirit of Genesis, God descends upon Jesus and a voice is heard to say: "This is my Son, the Beloved, with whom I am well pleased" (Mt 3:17). In Matthew's framework a new creation breaks in with the ministry of Jesus. Out of the wilderness and the rushing waters of the Jordan new life appears and a new future opens up for all of creation.

Matthew describes Jesus' baptism as a new creation story, but then he immediately returns the reader to the wilderness, where Jesus faces his temptations from the devil. In testing scenes reminiscent of the trials of Israel in the desert, Jesus faces temptations to be presumptuous, idolatrous, and in league with evil. Unlike so many of his ancestors, Jesus remains faithful to his God and submissive to the Lord's will. He is now ready to begin his mission of calling his people to conversion: "Repent, for the kingdom of heaven has come near" (Mt 4:17).

The notion of the reign of God and some of the contexts in which it is used in the gospels offer much that is applicable to our interests in ecology. The reign of God reiterates the Hebrew belief that creation ultimately belongs to God and is offered as gift to those who dwell here at any given time. All of creation is a gift to be shared by all. This belief also reveals that God's power and presence will ultimately prevail, a source of hope for those who are tempted to dissolve into fatalism or hopelessness in the face of so many environmental dangers. The "not yet" of the reign of God is quite apparent, but it is "already" here if God's power can be a source of courage and tenacious resistance to abuse of the earth. Moreover, this creative and all-prevailing power is accessible to those who wish to participate in the divine creative process. The reign of God points to a "power with," a "power for," rather than a "power over." This serving posture confronts those who would monopolize land and resources and who seek to dominate the poor of the world. It stands prophetically against those who simply use the earth for their own profit and power.[10]

Finally, the temptation and baptism scenes reveal that Jesus is the center of creation. He has conquered the powers of evil, and powerful though they may be, they cannot prevail. He stands in the midst of creation as the beloved Son, in solidarity with sinners, and prepared to empower those who would join him in the mission to bring salvation to the earth.

Discipleship and the "World"

There is an ambiguity in the use of *the world* in the New Testament. The word *cosmos* is used throughout, with various levels of meaning. At some points the world is the context for ministry. In Matthew, Jesus tells his disciples that they are the light of the world and are to shine before others giving glory to God (Mt 5:14-16). Jesus tells his disciples: "Go into all the world and proclaim the good news" (Mk 16:15). In Jesus' prayer at his last meal with his followers he remarks that he teaches "in the world" so that they may have joy, and then he sends them "into the world" on mission (Jn 17:13-18).

At other times *the world* denotes sinfulness and the lure of material things.[11] Jesus teaches that it is not profitable to gain the whole world and yet lose one's life (Mt 16:26). In the parable of the sower he teaches that the cares of the world choke the Word (Mt 13:22). Jesus points out that the world hates him, cannot receive the Spirit of truth, and that he came into the world for judgment (Jn 9:39). He speaks of Satan as the ruler of this world, and he warns his followers that they do not belong to this world (Jn 17:14). He tells Pilate that his kingdom is not from this world (Jn 18:36).

"The world" in some instances refers to God's creation. John points out that "God so loved the world that he gave his only Son" (Jn 3:16). The Samaritans proclaim that Jesus is the savior of the world (Jn 4:42). At one point

Jesus proclaims that his flesh is "the life of the world" (Jn 6:51). At times Jesus uses the word *world* on various levels at the same time. This gospel says of Jesus: "He was in the world, and the world came into being through him; yet the world did not know him" (Jn 1:10). Here the term seems to mean "context," "creation," and "sinfulness" in one sweeping statement.

There also seems to be a dualism in John's gospel; the world can be viewed both as God's sovereign creation and a place where forces oppose the will of God. For the author of John's gospel, this dualism has cosmic dimensions, as light struggles against darkness, spirit against flesh, life against death, and God against Satan. Such dualism seems to have existed at times in first-century Judaism and even more strongly among the Gnostic Christian communities.[12]

For those committed to the environmental movement, there is a similar ambiguity with regard to the world in which they live. For people of faith, this is God's world, a place of beauty, purpose, and richness to be shared with others and to be passed on to future generations. (The Iroquois held that in every decision consideration should be given to its impact on the next seven generations.) The world emanates from a Creator who loves it and who sent his Son to save it. At the same time, the forces of ignorance, greed, and violence seem constantly to conspire to destroy the world. Jesus teaches that his Spirit will remain in the world for all time, and that his creative power will ultimately prevail in the world. His followers, then, are sustained by this belief and can live in hope that their efforts to save the earth will ultimately prevail.

TEACHING IN PARABLES

Jesus lived close to nature all his life, for he was a rustic who grew up amid the lush harvests of Galilee. The reign of his Abba had been revealed to him in the Mediterranean winds as well as in the soft night breezes from the desert. He had learned of the Creator's love and care from cycles of the fruit trees, from observing the birds and flowers, and from watching the fishermen cast their nets into the Sea of Galilee. When it came time to teach his message, Jesus used many parables to pass on to others what he had learned of the Creator from his intimacy with creation.[13]

The earliest parable recorded in Mark's gospel is that of the sower. Here Jesus links the common practice of scattering seed during planting time to the breakthrough of the reign of God. God's rule is received in different fashions. At times it cannot take root because it falls on the path, on rocky ground, or among thorns. Jesus makes it clear that in order for God's rule to take root, there must be the openness and receptivity of rich soil (Mk 4:3-9). Jesus later goes on in the same vein, observing that seeds grow and the land yields harvest without us having much to do with the process. He teaches that God's reign is mysterious, and it has much more to do with the power of God than with our efforts (Mk 4:26-29). To further explain the miraculous growth that comes from God's power, Jesus uses the example of the mustard seed, tiny in size and yet enormous in growth (Mk 4:30-32).

Scattered throughout the gospels there are other parables that use nature to teach about the reign of God. Matthew's gospel tells of a landowner who hired laborers throughout the day and at the end of the day paid them all the same. When those hired first complained of being cheated, the landowner reminded them that it was his money and that he was free to be as generous with it as he wished (Mt 20:1-15). Jesus has shown the gratuity of God's salvation, and he ends with one of his famous one-liners: "Thus, the last will be first, and the first will be last" (Mt 20:16).

Jesus at times uses the vineyard to show how both he and his message about God's rule are being rejected. He tells a parable about a landowner who leased his fine vineyard to some tenants. When it came time for him to send his servants to claim his rightful share, his envoys are abused and one is killed. He sends others, and then his own son, but they are abused and his son killed. The owner puts the tenants to death and leases his vineyard to others (Mt 21:33-41). The lesson is clear. Those who are violent and unjust bring destruction upon themselves. No doubt the Matthean community is also reflecting on how some Jewish leaders rejected Jesus in his day, and were persecuting Christians.

Luke's gospel includes a parable in which Jesus uses nature to instruct against greed. He tells of a rich man who has had a wonderful harvest. The man tears down his barns and builds larger ones so that he can hoard his crops for himself. Feeling quite secure with his full barns, he plans to "eat, drink, and be merry." Ironically, the rich man dies that very night, so all his efforts were for naught. Jesus reminds his followers that God is the Creator Provider and that they should not be so focused on material needs that they neglect their faith. Faith calls for submission to the will of the Creator, who cares for all things. Jesus concludes:

> Therefore I tell you, do not worry about your life, what you will eat, or about your body, what you will wear. For life is more than food, and the body more than clothing. Consider the ravens: they neither sow nor reap, they have neither storehouse nor barn, and yet God feeds them. Of how much more value are you than the birds! And can any of you by worrying add a single hour to your span of life? If then you are not able to do so small a thing as that, why do you worry about the rest? Consider the lilies, how they grow: they neither toil nor spin; yet I tell you, even Solomon in all his glory was not clothed like one of these. But if God so clothes the grass of the field, which is alive today and tomorrow is thrown into the oven, how much more will he clothe you—you of little faith!
>
> —Luke 12:22-28

Luke also includes a parable in which Jesus teaches that the Creator looks after all his creatures with intense love and protection. The parable is told at a time when Jesus' enemies are pressing him because of his custom of welcoming and eating with sinners. Jesus draws on the lessons he learned from the shepherds on the hillsides of Galilee, He tells of a shepherd who leaves his flock of a hundred sheep to seek out a lost sheep, and he goes on to explain that the shepherd celebrates when he returns with the lost one on his shoulders. Jesus' lesson to those who oppose his befriending sinners is clear: "Just so, I tell you, there will be more joy in heaven over one sinner who repents than over ninety-nine righteous persons who need no repentance" (Lk 15:7).

It is plain from these parables that Jesus learned much about life from observing nature. He uses these insights to convey his message. Just as many of our Native Americans learned about the Great Spirit and how to live nobly from observing the buffalo, the eagle, the bear, the running waters, and many other natural phenomena, Jesus learned from the natural world around him. His parables enabled his listeners to take hold of his stories and put them "in parallel" (the meaning of *parable*) with their own search for meaning in life.

Jesus' parables reveal that God can be encountered in nature and that nature can show us much about ourselves. All reality in some way participates in God. As Thomas Clarke puts it: "We are not to conceive of divine transcendence as indicating that God is distinct from the universe and far off, but that every created reality, every human reality, participates in the reality of God."[14]

The parables demonstrate that the workings of God are mysterious yet can be identified by those who are attentive in faith and prayer. They also teach that God's favorites are the poor and outcasts. It is the "little ones" who will ultimately prevail: the homeless, the terrorized, the dispossessed. These stories clearly indicate that those who greedily and violently abuse God's children and creation will bring judgment upon themselves. They teach that those who stand up for justice for the oppressed earth can expect to be persecuted. Finally, these parables teach us that we are all called to repentance for the destruction that we have brought upon our earth. Like the good shepherd, the Lord seeks out those who have strayed and calls them to change their ways and begin caring for the earth and all living things.

MIRACLES AND JESUS' POWER OVER CHAOS

A number of the gospel miracle stories also reflect the creation theology of the Hebrews. As we observed in chapter 2, the Priestly account of creation in Genesis depicts creation coming out of chaos and the Creator God as having the power to bring order and harmony out of turmoil and confusion.

The natural miracle stories in particular dramatize how the gospels parallel Jesus' own power with the power of the Creator over chaos. The first is the calming of the storm. The setting here is the darkness of the evening. Jesus has asked his disciples to leave the crowds and cross to the other side of the Sea of Galilee. As the boats move along, a violent squall kicks up and the boats begin to fill up. The disciples panic and seek out Jesus, who quietly sleeps on a cushion in the stern of the boat. Jesus awakes and unceremoniously stops the wind and quiets the storm. When all is quiet, Jesus chides his followers for their lack of faith (Mk 4:35-41). The meaning of the parable, of course, is multi-leveled. It speaks of the need for faith and reveals Jesus as the Lord of nature, the Creator-Savior who has power over nature.[15]

In Mark's gospel the community seems to rely on Jesus to carry it through the hard times of rejection and persecution. To show the power of Jesus, as well as their need to rely on him in faith, the early disciples portray Jesus as the master of the sea, able to calm the waves, much as Yahweh parted the Red Sea for the people of the Exodus. Here Christ seems to be identified with the Creator who can bring order out chaos.

The healing miracles often carry forth the creation motif. Once again Jesus encounters in disease and disabilities the chaos present in creation. Rather than accepting traditional beliefs–that those who suffer such afflictions should be cast out as persons cursed by God–Jesus proclaims a God of creativity and wholeness. Jesus heals those whose lives have been chaotic as a result of disease or some disability.

The gospels are filled with healing miracles, in which Jesus exhibits the compassionate and creative powers of God. Mark's gospel tells of a woman who had been hemorrhaging for twelve years and who had spent all of her money on doctors to no avail. This woman was considered to be constantly unclean, and therefore she was not allowed to appear in public. She secretly reached out to Jesus, hoping to touch his cloak. Jesus felt power go out of him, and he asked who touched him. When he looked at the woman, she fell before him in tears and told him the whole story. Jesus commended her faith and sent her in peace (Mk 5:25-34). Once again the compassion and creative power of God had come face to face with disorder and suffering in the world, and had brought wholeness and peace to a suffering person.[16]

Mark tells the story of a leper who knelt down and begged Jesus to make him clean. Jesus was not repelled by the man, nor did he seem to fear being made unclean for associating with or touching such an outcast. Instead, Jesus had pity on the man, stretched out his hand and healed him (Mk 1:40-45). Once again the gospels show the power of God over that which is chaotic and disruptive in the world. In this and other miracle stories the early Christians saw Christ as constantly with them, actively healing the turmoil and suffering in their lives.

THE MASTERY OF JESUS

The temptation to sin in Eden is paralleled in some of the miracle stories. Throughout his ministry Jesus struggles with the forces of evil; he casts out demons in some of the miracle stories. Matthew points out that "with a word" Jesus drove out demonic spirits, and that he sent forth his disciples with the same powers (Mt 8:16; 10:8). Indeed, Jesus pointed to his power to overcome evil as a sign that the reign of God had arrived. He said: "But if it is by the Spirit of God that I cast out demons, then the kingdom of God has come to you" (Mt 12:28).[17]

Jesus' feeding stories also symbolize how the Creator provides all with nourishment, both material and spiritual. Luke's gospel tells of a wondrous event where a huge crowd had followed Jesus to listen to him and have their sick healed. At the end of the day Jesus' disciples told him to dismiss the people and send them into the surrounding villages and farms for lodging and provisions. Instead, Jesus decides to feed the multitude himself with just five loaves and two fish. Amazingly, all eat their fill and leave enough to fill twelve baskets (Lk 9:12-17). The story dramatically teaches how God bountifully provides for and nurtures his creatures.[18] The story of the wedding feast at Cana, where Jesus provides the guests with bountiful wine teaches the same lesson (Jn 2:1-12).

Paul echoed this belief that God was the providing Creator when he wrote to the communities in Corinth, reminding them they were part of God's creation. He reminded them that they were God's "field," and that though they could assist in God's work, ultimately it was God who brought forth the harvest.

> I planted, Apollos watered, but God gave the growth. So neither the one who plants nor the one who waters is anything, but only God who gives the growth. The one who plants and the one who waters have a common purpose, and each will receive wages according to the labor of each. For we are God's servants, working together; you are God's field, God's building.   —1 Corinthians 3:6-9

Two miracle stories in John's gospel demonstrate God's mastery over creation. In one, Jesus comes to his disciples walking on the sea and calms their fears amid strong winds and darkness (Jn 6:16-21). In another, Jesus meets his disciples after a long night fishing without a catch and shows them how to fill their nets (Jn 21:4-8).

The miracles stories are useful resources for those who struggle to awaken the public to the seriousness of environmental problems as well as those who struggle to combat those who bring so much devastation to the planet. The miracle stories reveal a Creator who wants the earth and its inhabitants to be healed, to be whole. It is not God's will that innocent children die of dehydration or malnutrition. Nor is it the divine will that pollution, which brings disease to so many, proliferate. The Creator God does not approve of all the damage that is done daily to creation, and therefore God calls us all to conversion. This is a Creator with the power to overcome the environmental chaos that exists throughout the world. Through Christ and his disciples this healing power can be effective in restoring the earth. These stories teach us the indomitable power of faith; they reveal a loving, saving, and providing God, who has given the earth more than enough for all, if people would but share.

THE MYSTERIES OF CHRIST'S LIFE

The gospel accounts of the mysteries of Christ's life—his birth, death, and resurrection—contain extensive theological reflections. In many ways each of these accounts is a "gospel in miniature," encapsulating the beliefs of the early communities. We will look now at the accounts of these mysteries and suggest how some of their insights might assist us in our concerns for the earth.

The Birth Stories

John's gospel has no formal nativity story. Instead, the author goes back "in the beginning" and describes Jesus as the Word through whom all things came into being. Jesus is identified with the Word, the creative principle within God, and is acknowledged for his central role in the creation of all things. As creative force, Christ is the source of life and light in a whole "new creation." John writes:

> In the beginning was the Word, and the Word was with God, and the Word was God. He was in the beginning with God. All things came into being through him, and without him not one thing came into being. What has come into being in him was life, and the life was the light of all people. The light shines in the darkness, and the darkness did not overcome it.
> —John 1:1-5

Matthew's nativity story (Mt 1:18–2:18) attempts to be more historical, yet it is highly symbolic and theological. This story echoes the creation story in Genesis 1, in that Jesus' conception is through the Holy Spirit.[19] The virginal conception of the child is to be brought about by the Creator, whose power transcends the laws of nature. The announcement of the angel to Joseph also establishes the larger context of creation for Jesus' birth. The heavenly context is further accentuated by the inclusion of the Magi, mysterious astrologers from the East who are led to the Messiah by a star, a light placed by God in the heavens to guide them. The star echoes the heavenly lights that the Creator placed in the sky on the fourth day of creation (Gn 1:14-19).[20] The star also provides a cosmic dimension to the event of Jesus' birth.[21] The gifts brought by the Magi likewise contribute to the creation motif. They bring him precious gold from the mines of the East; frankincense, a fragrant gum resin from an exotic Arabian tree; and myrrh, another rare gum resin often used for embalming. Each of these earthly resources has rich symbolism, linking the birth of Christ to other contexts in which God and the human are linked: kingship (gold), worship (incense), and death (myrrh). The Magi story also introduces the powers of evil and destruction, as Herod sets out to destroy the child and kills many innocent children in his murderous attempt.[22]

In Luke's nativity story, the overshadowing of the Spirit in Jesus' conception is once again reminiscent of the Priestly account of creation, in which the Spirit of God hovers over the waters (Lk 1:35; Gn 1:1-2). The conception of Jesus is proclaimed as a new and unique creation of God. As Raymond Brown remarks: "The child is totally God's work—a new creation."[23] Likewise, the barrenness of Elizabeth being overcome by the Creator of all life reminds us of how this same creative power brought new life from the aged Sarah and reveals that "nothing will be impossible with God" (Lk 1:37).

Luke also describes the birth of Jesus with the earthy images of an animal manger and lowly shepherds tending their flocks on the hillsides. In the story the shepherds are linked with higher creation as the angels proclaim to them the birth of the savior, and sing heavenly praises of God.[24] Their song announces that this birth joins the glory of God to the earth where peace comes to those "whom he favors" (Lk 2:14). Here, again, creation becomes both the means and the context for proclaiming the salvation of God.

Paul Minear has done a great deal of reflection on the relationship between the Genesis stories and the nativity stories. He shows how their themes appear in other places in the New Testament. He points out parallels between the blessing of the shepherds in Luke's nativity story and the murder of the first shepherd, Abel; between the reaction of the earth to the murder of Abel and Revelation's account of the earth's reaction to the murder of Christian martyrs; and the more familiar contrasts between the obedience and fidelity of Jesus and Mary over and against the rebellion of Adam and Eve. 1 John 3:8 clearly points out that Christ has destroyed the power of sin: "The Son of God was revealed for this purpose, to destroy the works of the devil." And in his letter to the Corinthians, Paul contrasts Adam, the man from earth, and Jesus, the man from heaven, and preaches the restorative power of the resurrection, wherein Jesus is the "first fruits" of a restored creation (1 Cor 15:20-28).[25]

Minear also compares blessings of earth in Genesis with Luke's accounts of angels praising God for granting peace on earth at Jesus' birth. In addition, Minear looks to the gospel of John, which links Christ with the Creator and parallels the coming of the light in creation with the coming of Jesus (Jn 1:6-9). He traces this theme into the Book of Revelation, where Jesus Christ is portrayed as the Alpha and Omega of creation, the one who will bring us a new earth.[26]

Apparently the early Christian Jews took seriously the curses leveled at Adam, Eve, and Cain. Adam is told that the ground is cursed because of him and that he will have to toil all his life among thorns and thistles to get food. Then he will return to the dirt from which he came. Adam was banished from the garden and required to till the soil from which he is taken. Here indeed work and the efforts to gain food are seen as a curse. Cain is also cursed for spilling his brother's blood on the earth. This blood cries out and the earth will no longer produce for Cain (Gn 4:10-12).

In contrast, Jesus comes into the world to bless work. He uses the harvest as a symbol of God's care and mercy. In his teaching Jesus relieves his disciples from the anxiety of what they are to eat and wear, and teaches them to rely on the care and mercy of God. He reveals Abba to be a God who provides and heals; a Creator who brings light to the eyes of the blind, food to the hungry crowds on a hillside, hope to those lost in the darkness of sin, and blessings to the poor and oppressed.

The early Christians thus looked to Christ to remove these curses and bless them. Paul says to the Corinthians: "If anyone is in Christ, there is a new creation" (2 Cor 5:17). Minear sees the messages of the angels to Mary, Joseph, and the shepherds in the nativity stories as heralds of these blessings.[27] A theme in the nativity stories is that there is now good news from the Creator. In Luke, Zechariah is told that he will have "joy and gladness and that many will rejoice at his [his son's] birth" (Lk 1:14). Mary is told by Gabriel that she has found favor with God and that her Son "will be great and will be called Son of the Most High" and that his kingdom will "have no end" (Lk 1:32-33). In her canticle Mary proclaims a new age wherein the arrogant will be dispersed and the mighty will be thrown down, while the humble will be lifted up and the hungry fed (Lk 1:51-53).

Some of the Fathers of the Church—notably Justin Martyr, Tertullian, and Irenaeus—elaborated on the parallels between Mary and Eve, and Newman wrote extensively on the contrasts between the "mother of the living" and the New Eve. Whereas Eve trusts the lies of evil, is unfaithful to God, and helps usher sin and death into the world, Mary puts her faith in God, accepts the divine will, and brings forgiveness and life into the world in the person of her son.[28] Mary is free of being "ruled over," as was the case with Eve. In Luke's story she has no need of Joseph for the conception. Instead of curse, she has found favor with God and will usher in a new creation by the power of the Holy Spirit.[29]

In Luke's nativity story the canticle of Zechariah proclaims that the Lord Creator has brought redemption to his people. He uses creation imagery to point out:

> By the tender mercy of our God
>   the dawn from on high will break upon us,
> to give light to those who sit in darkness and in the
>   shadow of death,
>   to guide our feet into the way of peace.
>   –Luke 1:78-79

In the same vein, the angel of the Lord proclaims to the shepherds: "I am bringing you good news of great joy for all the people: to you is born this day in the city of David a Savior, who is the Messiah, the Lord" (Lk 2:10-11). The angels then sing out in celebration over the new creation:

> "Glory to God in the highest heaven
>   and on earth peace among those whom he favors."
>   –Luke 2:14

Blessings now replace the tragic results of the infidelity of Eden. This new creation is proclaimed by Paul to the Corinthians: "So if anyone is in Christ, there is a new creation: everything old has passed away; see, everything has become new!" (2 Cor 5:17). And to the Athenians he vividly described, quoting a Greek author, how intimately we are now linked with God: "In him we live and move and have our being" (Acts 17:28).

In these nativity stories there are many relevant applications to our concerns for the earth. Let me highlight just a few. For example, there are rich creation theologies in these nativity stories. In the high theology of John's gospel, Jesus' preexistence is proclaimed, and he is described as intimately involved in the creative process. This, of course, applies to the creative process that still goes on, and which can be for Jesus' followers a source of hope and courage in their work for sustaining the earth. The low theology of Luke and Matthew tells of the birth of a baby, and yet there can be no doubt that the birth comes from the divine power of the Creator. It is God's world, and all is gift, especially this child who is marked to be the savior of all. His followers are called to praise the Creator for these gifts and to be dedicated to sustaining and sharing them with others.

The figures of Mary, Joseph, the Magi, and others demonstrate that humans are called to be instruments of God's creative powers. All of them faithfully answered God's call and now serve as models for those who are called today to be co-creators. On the other hand, the stories clearly demonstrate that the forces of evil are operative in the world. The Cains and the Herods bring death and destruction into the world. Environmental devastation is part of this destructive process and is an offense against the Creator. Yet God will provide for the poor and bring about a "new creation" through the work of the Son and through those who faithfully carry on the Lord's life-giving mission.

The Passion Stories

Each of the four gospels includes a passion story, a highly dramatized "play" that reflects on the meaning of Jesus' suffering and death. Each of these narratives contains rich symbolism and theological themes that are relevant to the unjust "suffering" and "death" that have been inflicted on living things and on the earth itself.

Mark's account of the passion and death is the earliest. His use of natural symbolism influences the gospels that follow. Mark sets the place of Jesus' agony on the Mount of Olives, a mountain charged with religious symbolism. The mountains around the Kedron Valley were often used in the Hebrew scriptures for significant events in Jewish history. It was here that Abraham was called to offer the sacrifice of his son; it was here that David chose to build the great Temple of Jerusalem. In Zechariah 14 this mountain is the context for the great battle on the apocalyptic day of the Lord.

It is highly significant that this is one of the places Jesus went to pray, and that it served as the site where he prophesied the destruction of Jerusalem (Mk 13:3). It is the location where Jesus began his triumphant entry into Jerusalem on a colt; as well as the scene of his ascension (Mk 11:1-10; Acts 1:9, 12). Jesus' agony took place in a garden in one of the valleys of this mountain. Some scholars see a parallel between the scene in this garden and the scene in Eden; a stark contrast exists between Jesus' fidelity to God's will and the infidelity of Adam and Eve.[30] It is in this garden and in these mountains that a new creation is beginning.

Mark's passion story is one of betrayal, desolation, abandonment, and injustice. Nature's gifts are demeaned as a crown of thorns is used as an instrument of torture. And at the time of Jesus' death, creation itself provides a background of protest with "darkness over the whole land" as Jesus is crucified on a rock shaped like a skull and dies with the words "My God, my God, why have you forsaken me?" (Mk 15:34). His body is then placed in a tomb hewn out of rock.[31] Clearly, the gospels link Jesus' death with creation.

So many of the impoverished and oppressed throughout the world can relate to the abandonment and betrayal that is so profoundly described in Mark's account of Jesus' passion. They are familiar with the thorns, the rocks, and the darkness of life. They often live in desolate surroundings and feel forsaken and rejected. The injustice and oppression to which Jesus was subjected are familiar to them. And yet, faith in the Lord assures them that the stone of their "tombs" can be rolled back through God's power and that new life will be given them. Their agony—the sweat and blood they give to their lands and gardens, the betrayals they have known from their own leaders—need not end in despair. New life and a new creation are promised them by the Lord. The mountains and the valleys around them are the Lord's gifts, places they can meet their Creator. The Lord calls them to continue their struggle to preserve these places of nature and to protect them from those who bring degradation and destruction.

Matthew's passion story is similar to Mark's. The themes of betrayal, desertion, isolation, and cruelty are in his account as well. The natural symbol of darkness here relates Jesus' death to creation itself.[32] The author adds an even more powerful, stark natural symbol to Jesus' death when he writes: "The earth shook and the rocks were split. The tombs also were opened" (Mt 27:51-52). These are all traditional signs of the final age; here they signify the passing away of an old era and the opening of one that is new.[33] This apocalyptic theme is most certainly applicable to the frightening possibilities of destruction that are associated with environmental problems such as global warming or ozone depletion.

Luke's portrayal of Jesus' passion and death is different. He replaces desolation and abandonment with compassion, fidelity, and forgiveness. Jesus is a unifier, even able to broker a friendship between two old enemies, Herod and Pilate. Jesus' disciples do not desert him, and Jesus is accompanied to his cross by companions and women in tears. Jesus remains the healer as he mends the ear of the servant of the high priest, which had been cut off by a disciple. Jesus is the reconciler as he answers the plea of the criminal hanging beside him: "Today you will be with me in paradise" (Lk 23:43). And here the Master is one who forgives. He looked upon his persecutors and said: "Father, forgive them; for they know not what they are doing" (Lk 23:34).

Many of the themes in Luke's passion story are applicable to our concerns for the future of our planet. Responsible behavior toward the earth and its resources calls for a compassionate sensitivity toward all living things, fidelity to the will of God with regard to creation, and forgiveness for those who have destroyed so many of our ecosystems. It is true that much damage is done out of ignorance, but much is also done out of greed and selfishness. Yet bitterness, hatred, or condemnation will never be effective in awakening people to the harm they are inflicting on the environment. Understanding, forgiveness, and love, as exemplified by Jesus on the cross, are the "saving graces" needed to deal with these challenges. In addition, there will also have to be unity among nations, as well as great efforts at healing and reconciliation in order to deal with an environmental crisis that now has reached global proportions.

Luke's theme of reconciliation is appropriate to our concerns here. The struggle for reconciliation in South Africa is a case in point. A Truth and Reconciliation Committee has been established there, and those who have committed horrible crimes in the past are asked to confess and show signs of repentance. Only then will a people divided by hatred and oppression be able to walk with each other. There is much to forgive. The white minority has devastated many areas of this country in the search for gold and other resources. Whites have abused and subjugated the black majority for many years, isolating them in barren "homelands" and subjecting those who protested to torture, imprisonment, or even death. South Africa today stands as a symbol for the many lands devastated by colonial expansion; it calls for the same process of repentance and reconciliation throughout the world.

John's story of Jesus' suffering and death is quite singular. Jesus here is kingly and majestic, and he goes to his death with a certain nobility. Natural symbols, however, are used here as well in linking the event with creation and other saving events. It is in John's gospel that the soldiers pierced Jesus' side to make sure that he was dead, and both blood and water came forth (Jn 19:34). Scholars have given many interpretations to this passage.[34] Water is, of course, always a primal symbol, and its use links the death of Jesus with creation and the Exodus, as well as his promise to be the source of living waters (Jn 7:38). Water will subsequently become the central symbol in Christian baptism. Blood also is rich in biblical significance, often symbolizing sacrifice as well as new life. As Jesus was buried in the garden, again linking his death with Genesis, his body was wrapped with a hundred pounds of myrrh and aloes. This links the death and burial with the gifts of the Magi in Matthew's gospel.[35]

John's passion story appears to connect Jesus with the majesty and glory of the Creator. Natural symbols link his death with creation and are perhaps symbolic of the "new creation" that Jesus' death is bringing to fruition. At his arrest, trial, and crucifixion the forces of evil and destruction are powerful, yet it is clear in this gospel that Jesus will triumph over evil. While on the cross he continues to build his community, committing Mary and the beloved disciple to each other's care.

This account of Jesus' passion and death witnesses to the power and divinity of Jesus Christ. The natural symbols provide a backdrop of creation for the violence and destruction. Triumphing over all this evil is the Christ, the savior of the world. Like the other gospel accounts of the passion, John's gospel can provide hope to those engaged in conflict with the violent and destructive elements in the world. This gospel proclaims that Jesus has been and always will be part of the creative and sustaining forces in the world, and that he will ultimately bring wholeness to the earth.

The Resurrection Stories

Creation motifs also play a part in the resurrection stories. Light is used as a symbol in Matthew, Mark, and Luke, with the story of the women coming to the tomb at sunrise. John chooses to open the scene in darkness, perhaps to emphasize that the risen Lord is the new light. Luke's story also describes an earthquake as part of the scene, and he links heaven and earth by having an angel appear to the women to tell them that Jesus has been raised from the dead. The risen Lord's appearance is described to be like "lightning" and his garments like "snow" (Mt 28:3). These natural symbols place the resurrection in the context of creation and demonstrate that indeed the Lord's being raised is a new creation.

The physicality of Jesus' risen body is stressed by Luke's description of the "flesh and bones" of the risen Lord (Lk 24:39). Other material references to the body of the risen Lord include the instances when the disciples embrace his feet and when Jesus eats fish at one time and breaks bread with his disciples at another. Mary of Magdala's embrace of the Lord and Jesus' invitation to Thomas to touch his wounds emphasize that the risen Lord is somehow really present and "tangible."[36] The integration of the divine and the material in the world is shown to prevail in the resurrection.

In spite of the emphasis on physicality in the resurrection stories, it is obvious that Jesus' material body has been transformed. He is often not recognized, walks through locked doors, and can suddenly disappear from sight. The risen Lord is no longer subject to time or space. Jesus' resurrection seems to proclaim that materiality ultimately will be changed into a new creation. The material world, therefore, has not been created for destruction but for transformation and fulfillment.

Paul comments on how the new creation came about in the risen Christ.[37] He preached to the Romans that just as Adam brought sin into the world, Christ brought favor with God (Rom 5:12). Jesus Christ has replaced death with the life of grace through his death and resurrection. He is the "first fruits" of the new creation, and will ultimately hand the entire creation over to the Creator:

> But in fact Christ has been raised from the dead, the first fruits of those who have died. For since death came through a human being, the resurrection of the dead has also come through a human being; for as all die in Adam, so all will be made alive in Christ. But each in his own order: Christ the first fruits, then at his coming those who belong to Christ. Then comes the end, when he hands over the kingdom to God the Father.　　　　　　　　　　　　　　　　　　　　−1 Corinthians 15:20-24

For Paul, the resurrection is central, and through Christ's being raised materiality is brought to its fulfillment. While he distinguishes among the flesh of human beings, animals, birds, and fish, Paul points out that all have "glory," including the sun, moon, and stars. In resurrection the perishable is made imperishable, dishonor is glorified, weakness becomes power, the physical is transformed into the spiritual, and Christ becomes the new Adam. Paul sees redemption in the context of creation:

> The first man was from the earth, a man of dust; the second man is from heaven. As was the man of dust, so are those who are of the dust; and as is the man of heaven, so are those who are of heaven. Just as we have borne the image of the man of dust, we will also bear the image of the man of heaven.   −1 Corinthians 15:47-49

To become part of Christ is to become part of a "new creation," where everything is new, and all is reconciled with God. The Creator who gives seed and bread to the people will also bring about the "harvest of your righteousness" (2 Cor 9:10-11).

The resurrection is central to the Christian faith. Through raising Jesus from the dead, God has validated Jesus' life and mission, verified his teaching, and confirmed his promise of eternal life. The resurrection also reveals that the ultimate destiny of all of creation is to be transformed into a new creation. The resurrection acknowledges the dignity of the physical world and offers motivation for caring for and sustaining all things. All of nature is part of the kingdom, which in the end will be handed over to the Creator. This belief that all things have been given their own dignity, purpose, and ultimate goal by the Creator offers ample reason to reverence and preserve all of reality.

CREATION MOTIFS IN PAUL

In Paul's theology, Jesus Christ is at the center of all creation, the ultimate source and goal of all things.[38] Paul writes to the Corinthians:

> Indeed, even though there may be so-called gods in heaven or on earth—as in fact there are many gods and many lords—yet for us there is one God, the Father, from whom are all things and for whom we exist, and one Lord, Jesus Christ, through whom are all things and through whom we exist.   −1 Corinthians 8:5-6

In a similar vein he writes to the community at Colossae that Jesus Christ is the image of God who is integral to the process of creation (Col 1:15-17). These are extremely strong statements on the integrity of all things and of Christ's close association with all the things of earth. Most certainly these are valuable resources for anyone attempting to demonstrate that followers of Jesus have an obligation toward all of nature.

Paul often writes of the extraordinary dignity that has been given human life by the coming of the Christ.[39] He reminds the Christians in Rome that God has chosen them to conform to the image of Jesus Christ, who was "the firstborn" among many sisters and brothers (Rom 9:29). He preaches to the Corinthians that though death can come through a human being, Christ's resurrection reveals that a human life can also bring about eternal life (1 Cor 15:21). The letter to the Philippians reminds the disciples that Christ so valued humanity that he was willing to disregard his equality with God and empty himself into human likeness:

> Let the same mind be in you that was in Christ Jesus, who, though he was in the form of God, did not regard equality with God as something to be exploited, but emptied himself, taking the form of a slave, being born in human likeness. And being found in human form, he humbled himself and became obedient to the point of death–even death on a cross.   –Philippians 2:5-8

Paul also insists on unity among peoples. He writes the community at Colossae that to be their true selves and authentic images of their Creator, they must free themselves of the distinctions that separate them:

> You have stripped off the old self with its practices and have clothed yourselves with the new self, which is being renewed in knowledge according to the image of its creator. In that renewal there is no longer Greek and Jew, circumcised and uncircumcised, barbarian, Scythian, slave and free; but Christ is all and in all!   –Colossians 3:9-11

Paul comments also on the sinful side of humanity. Paul reminds the Roman Christians that it was through humans that sin came into the world, and that the "wages of sin is death" itself (Rom 5:12; 6:23). In a classical statement he reflects on the conflicts which sin causes in human nature:

> For we know that the law is spiritual; but I am of the flesh, sold into slavery under sin. I do not understand my own actions. For I do not do what I want, but I do the very thing I hate. Now if I do what I do not want, I agree that the law is good. But in fact it is no longer I that do it, but sin that dwells within me. For I know that nothing good dwells within me, that is, in my flesh. I can will what is right, but I cannot do it. For I do not do the good I want, but the evil I do not want is what I do. Now if I do what I do not want, it is no longer I that do it, but sin that dwells within me.   –Romans 7:14-20

When Christians lose sight of human dignity, enormous devastation comes both to human lives and the earth. In many instances humans have been reduced to the subhuman level in order to justify their annihilation. It has happened in the ancient world, during the European conquest of the New World, and in recent times in the Holocaust and in places like Cambodia, Uganda, Bosnia, and Rwanda. The drive toward domination, violence, and greed is deep within the human psyche. This drive often has brought slaughter of life, and pollution and depletion of the earth's resources. Reclaiming and acknowledging the dignity of human life are essential if the nations of the world are to carry our their responsibilities of preserving the earth.[40]

A Sacramental World

In his letters to the Christian communities Paul reflects the Hebrew belief that God reveals God's self through creation. In his letter to the Romans, Paul professes this "sacramental" perspective that God can be found in the created world: "Ever since the creation of the world his eternal power and divine nature, invisible though they are, have been understood and seen through the things he has made" (Rom 1:20). Paul recognizes the ancient Hebrew tradition that creation belongs to the Lord and is used by God to communicate to human beings.

In the same letter Paul writes magnificently of how the whole of creation awaits the fulfillment of redemption:

> For the creation waits with eager longing for the revealing of the children of God; for the creation was subjected to futility, not of its own will but by the will of the one who subjected it, in hope that the creation itself will be set free from its bondage to decay and will obtain the freedom of the glory of the children of God. We know that the whole creation has been groaning in labor pains until now; and not only the creation, but we ourselves, who have the first fruits of the Spirit, groan inwardly while we wait for adoption, the redemption of our bodies.
>
> —Romans 8:19-23[41]

Paul maintains that, for those who participate in God's love, all things will work together for the good. Creation is now being re-done, as it were, with Christ's followers being conformed to a new image of God, the image of God's Son. Christ is indeed "the firstborn within a large family" (Rom 8:28-29). Paul constantly reminds the early communities that God is with them and will bring results to their efforts. He tells the Corinthians, "I planted, Apollos watered, but God gave the growth" (1 Cor 3:6).

Christ the Reconciler

Paul views Christ as the ultimate beginning and end of all things, the one who reconciles all with God:

> He is the image of the invisible God, the firstborn of all creation; for in him all things in heaven and on earth were created, things visible and invisible, whether thrones or dominions or rulers or powers–all things have been created through him and for him. He himself is before all things, and in him all things hold together. He is the head of the body, the church; he is the beginning, the firstborn from the dead, so that he might come to have first place in everything. For in him all the fullness of God was pleased to dwell, and through him God was pleased to reconcile to himself all things, whether on earth or in heaven, by making peace through the blood of his cross. —Colossians 1:15-20

One of Paul's disciples, who most likely authored the letter to the Ephesians, develops this same theme, pointing out that creation is planned by God and that God's will with regard to Christ is "to gather up all things in him, things in heaven and things on earth" (Eph 1:10). Here the divine plan of redemption is not only for human beings but for all of creation. In the fullness of time there is a plan to bring all of creation to fulfillment. The ultimate goal of this new creation is that "Christ is all and in all" (Col 3:11; see also Col 1:15-16).

The applications of this Pauline theology are obvious. God is the source of all things, dwells within all, and manifests the divine self through all that is visible. God has plans for the fulfillment of all creation, and Jesus Christ plays a central role in bringing this plan to fruition. Disciples of Christ, then, are called to discern God's plan for creation and resist those who would bring destruction to the earth. It is clear that irresponsible destruction of the environment is a moral offense against God's plan and stands as an impediment to Christ's work of bringing all to fulfillment.

SUMMARY

Hebrew theologies of creation are carried forth in the New Testament but are brought to new depths through Christian resurrection faith. Jesus taught and demonstrated that Abba loves, cares for, and heals the earth and all its creatures. Human dignity is brought to new heights through association with Jesus Christ, and the poor and oppressed are shown to have a special blessedness. The dangers of greedy affluence are made clear, and simplicity becomes the badge of those committed to the reign of God.

New Testament creation theology proclaims Christ's conquering of evil in the world and celebrates his salvation of all. Parables teach the closeness of God's reign, and miracles demonstrate that the divine power provides for all. The central mysteries of Jesus Christ—his birth, death, and resurrection—are seen as being integral to creation. He is now the center of all and the herald of a new creation.

Christians concerned about their planet can find strength and hope in this vision. With Jesus Christ they can do all things, especially the actions needed to conserve the earth and assure that its resources are shared justly with those less fortunate.

4.

Jesus the Christ

The hole in the ozone layer that everyone talks about is right over our heads here in Southern Australia. They say that the ultraviolet radiation is pretty bad here and they tell us kids to cover up with silly looking hats that flap over our necks and ears. I feel like a real geek going to school wearing my hat. And at our school they won't even let us go outside for recess. They say that if we do we might get skin cancer and bad eyes when we grow up. We can't go out on the beaches in summer either. It is really a pain and I worry it will even be worse when I have kids.

— Michael Murdoch, Adelaide, Australia

Teilhard de Chardin once pointed out that early Christianity's task was to link the Logos with the incarnation, and that in his era there was a need to link Christology with evolution and cosmos.[1] It would seem that in our own time, we are charged with the task of connecting Christology with environmental concerns. In this chapter we explore the main christological mysteries—incarnation, salvation, resurrection, and the notion of the "Cosmic Christ"—and suggest possible connections with the environment.

THE INCARNATION

The doctrine of the incarnation is central to the Christian tradition. Unique among all religious beliefs, it teaches that God has entered creation as a human being. The author of the gospel of John put it simply: "And the Word was made flesh, and lived among us" (Jn 1:14). Here the biblical writer witnesses to the belief that the creative principle of the divinity indeed became part of creation itself. The Logos, which was always with God, and through whom all creation came about, became one with the physical and material world.

Not an Afterthought

Contemporary theology places the incarnation in continuity with creation, as part of the ongoing creative process. In other words, the incarnation is not

98

simply an afterthought decided upon to repair the damage done through the fall. Taking their lead from Scotus rather than Aquinas, some contemporary theologians propose that the incarnation was in God's plan from the very beginning of creation and represents a climactic stage of creation.[2] From the beginning, the divine goal for creation was to culminate in the birth of Jesus and then move toward an ongoing re-creation of all reality.

Jesus Christ, from this theological point of view, is integral to the creative process and, as we shall see toward the end of this chapter, continues to direct and save the world as the Cosmic Christ. Jesus Christ here is the creative force behind a new creation, which is taking place now and will come to fulfillment in the end time. He is the power within an ongoing creation, a process wherein humans and indeed all creatures play unique roles. Speaking from the Orthodox perspective, which has traditionally understood the incarnation in this fashion, the Russian Patriarch Alexy writes:

> The Incarnation of the Lord Jesus has originated the renewal not only of humans, but of the whole of nature as well. The mystery of the future glorified state of the Universe was opened to us in the Transfiguration of the Lord. The created world is called to become a "new heaven and a new earth" (Rev 21:1) in which God, the Source of Life, will be "everything to everyone" (1 Cor 15:28).[3]

New Dignity to Humans

The incarnation obviously brings a new dignity to all of creation, but especially to human beings. Walter Kasper points out that the incarnation is "the unique and supreme realization of the human essence."[4] The incarnation serves to reveal not only the pristine dignity of one human individual, Jesus Christ, but also the singular value of all humans. Human beings are images of God and manifest the presence of God in the world. In Jesus Christ humanity is seen at its best, fully and perfectly expressing divinity. The incarnation proclaims that God is not isolated somewhere in a transcendental realm as a remote "sky god," but rather is intimately present to the world. The God of Jesus Christ has been intimately involved in creation from the beginning, and will remain so until the end of time.

A Unique Dignity for Materiality

The incarnation gives a unique dignity not only to humans but to all living and material things. Jesus, like all humans, experienced a physical life with all its appetites, desires, pleasures, and limitations. Jesus took children in his strong arms and embraced them (Mk 10:16). He enjoyed food and drink and was known for his active table ministry with people of all kinds. He had a power that enabled him to reach out with healing hands to crippled and diseased bodies and to bring them healing and wholeness. He knew joy, pain, laughter, loneliness, love, and rejection. The coming of Jesus Christ is the apex of the creative process, the revelation of where matter had been heading from the very beginning as it evolved toward the spiritual. Human beings are a singular integration of the spiritual with the material, and the incarnation adds distinction to both dimensions of reality. Jesus Christ became the locus wherein the destiny of humanity and all of creation is revealed. He is the revelation of God's solidarity with all of creation.

Belief in the incarnation offers vision and purpose to those who are concerned about the future of the earth. The coming of Christ raises the physical and material to renewed dignity and sacredness and calls for respect and reverence toward all things. The world will never be the same now that Jesus Christ has come into it, lived a full human life here, and showed a willingness to give himself completely for its salvation. There can be no doubt now but that the Creator is within the world, drawing it toward its purpose and goal. The incarnation reveals also the wickedness of those who abuse and waste the resources made available to all creatures by the Creator.

The integration of matter and spirit, which is epitomized in human beings, has been intended from the beginning. Spirit seems to have gradually evolved within matter. There is a certain "withinness" in all things, which uniquely exists in humans because we have the power to reflect. We are the conscious, thinking, and deliberate climax of material evolution. Teilhard called us the "reflective species," the spearhead of all creation. Humans are unparalleled in that not only can we know but we can reflect or "know that [we] know."[5] We are the only creatures who can plan with deliberation and either enhance or destroy creation through free choice. Thomas Berry has insightfully observed that humans have evolved to the point where we might indeed be called the "conscious universe."[6] Hence our responsibility for sustaining creation is enormous.

Both matter and spirit share a common history and find their ultimate source in the same Creator. Rahner has pointed out that matter is oriented to spirit and develops toward spirit by virtue of its own inner being and potential. He is insistent that if we refuse to see ourselves as products of nature, then nature will become our opponent.[7] We shall then either feel helpless in the face of nature or fight to overcome it. But it is unlikely that we will be inclined to reverence and care for nature.

For Rahner, Christ is the perfect union of the material and the spiritual. His person and life reveal how completely God has communicated God's self to creation and embraced it in all its dimensions. This is also Teilhard's vision: "You are the Center at which all things meet and which stretches out over all things so as to draw them back into itself: I love you for the extensions of your body and soul to the farthest corners of creation through grace, through life, and through matter."[8]

Incarnation and Dualism

Early on, the Christian theology of the incarnation was challenged by those who were dualistic and thereby demeaned materiality. The Docetists rejected the value of matter and held that Jesus only *appeared* to be human, that he wore his humanity superficially as a kind of cloak. The Gnostics also viewed matter as evil and were repelled by the thought that God would become united to the physical. Such views were confronted and condemned by the early councils which defined that God had indeed become truly human in Jesus Christ. Since then, one of the central doctrines of Christianity has been that Jesus Christ truly entered the material and physical world of the human. The theology of the incarnation acknowledges that all the creatures on earth are somehow interrelated and interdependent. The incarnation provides a firm foundation for the much-needed recognition that all things are connected in a web of life and also linked with the Creator.

Dualism has taken new forms in our times. Contemporary materialism and consumerism often separate the spiritual from the "real world" and value material things in terms of profit and usefulness. The spiritual dimension of the world is thus excluded and materiality loses its ultimate source and its participation in ultimate goals. Material things are to be used up and then discarded. This mentality is partially responsible for many of the environmental problems the world now faces. John Carmody, one of the earliest Catholic theologians to acknowledge the connection between religion and the environment, pointed out that the Christian tradition should challenge abuse toward material things with a theology where creation, the incarnation, and the continuing saving activity of Jesus Christ are in continuity and reveal the dignity of all things.[9]

Connectedness

Many in the environmental movement today maintain that there is an essential connection between the material and spiritual, between the earth and the human. Bernard Häring calls for a "chastened anthropocentrism" in which people recognize that they are one family with other creatures and are truly connected to and dependent on all of nature. He calls for interaction, solidarity, and renewal of the covenant with nature. Häring also urges people to undergo a conversion to a "renewed relationship with God-given nature, but always with and through renewed relationships within humankind. . . . Our ecological responsibility, then, is a central act of justice and love for God and our fellowman."[10]

Teilhard's Vision

No one has been able to offer a better vision of the dignity of matter than Pierre Teilhard de Chardin. His was a vision that came both from his lifelong study of rocks and fossils and from his passionate love for Jesus Christ. Teilhard speaks of "the Divine radiating from the depths of blazing matter."[11] For Teilhard, matter should not be celebrated as an end-all and be-all in the manner of the "pontiffs of science." Nor does he think that matter should be debased, as it often is by moralizing preachers. Teilhard embraced nature and felt immersed in God when he was studying it. For him, the earth was the ambiance where God revealed the divine will and purpose for all things.[12]

For Teilhard, matter was blessed, and through faith he could see Christ in the heart of the world. He recognized and loved Jesus Christ as the center of all things, and he could experience Jesus extending himself and revealing himself through matter. He saw Jesus hidden in the forces that give increase to the earth and observed that as evolution moves on, the incarnation triumphs even more in the world. Teilhard was not, as some of his critics portray him, a naive idealist. He was a realistic and professional scientist, who intensely contemplated matter in its pain as well as its beauty, its destructiveness as well as its creativity. Yet Teilhard embraced matter and found it charged with creative power, stirred by the Spirit, and "infused with life by the incarnate Word."[13]

Even during his years in the trenches of World War I, surrounded by death and suffering, Teilhard could look for a new earth, a new creation. Teilhard was a citizen of the earth, who perceived that there was a spiritual power in matter. It was his conviction that, through the incarnation, God reached into all the elements of the world.

> Now the earth can certainly clasp me in her giant arms. She can swell me with her life, or take me back in her dust. She can deck herself out for me with every charm, with every horror, with every mystery. She can intoxicate me with her perfume of tangibility and unity. She can cast me to my knees in expectation of what is maturing in her breast. . . . But her enchantments can no longer do me harm since she has become for me, over and above herself, the body of Him who is and of Him who is coming.[14]

For Teilhard, Christ is re-creating the "soul of the earth," and this gave the priest-scientist solid grounds for having faith in the world. Prophetically, he proclaimed that now was the time to build the earth, and he was willing to face opposition from his own church in order to link Christianity with the material world. His message is indeed relevant to us as we attempt to rebuild so much of the planet that has been damaged.

Earlier in the twentieth century Teilhard spoke of the "malady of space-time," or a loss of nerve, which he sensed was prevalent in modern times. He described this as a feeling of anxiety and futility, a sense of being crushed by the enormities of the cosmos. In our time, with so many ecological dangers, such feelings can become even more intense. As Christopher Mooney, an expert on Teilhard, has pointed out: "We have a new dimension of this with ecology today and we must be like him and be hopeful."[15]

Hope is an essential virtue for facing the environmental crisis of today. Little can be accomplished by reciting frightening apocalyptic warnings and rendering people helpless. Nor is a posture of denial useful in these perilous times. Jacques Cousteau once observed that the computer projections about our environmental future are quite alarming and often predict ecological disaster. And yet Cousteau remained hopeful until his death because he firmly believed in the goodness of the human spirit and in its capacity to meet any challenge and overcome any crisis. The coming of Christ gives a powerful witness to the dignity and power of this same human spirit.

Rahner's Holistic Approach

Karl Rahner offered a vision of creation as a whole, with one Creator bringing forth one system of being and acting as the ongoing creative force that sustains, empowers, and draws all toward fulfillment. For Rahner, the world has from the beginning been completely "graced" with the life of God. This perspective pervades Rahner's theology of the incarnation. His views have had a profound influence on Catholic thinking in the twentieth century and are profoundly relevant to our concerns for the future of our environment.[16]

The World as the Home of God

In the Rahnerian perspective God has come to the earth and its people in the person of Jesus Christ and continues to be present to all of creation. In the incarnation God has revealed a self that is immanent in all things and yet at the same time transcends all as the Creator. The incarnation is a "radical affirmation that God is at the heart of humanity and all creation in Jesus Christ."[17]

Through the incarnation, God somehow changes into "Other." The immutable actually "becomes" in the humanity of Jesus. The self-emptying of God, which has always been present in the creative process, culminates in the incarnation. Creation and incarnation are here seen in continuity, and Christ is acknowledged to be the apex of the creative process.[18] At the same time, the incarnation is a new stage in creation, an unrepeatable event, by which God has entered into a radical nearness with the world. In Jesus we see that all things material and spiritual are linked intimately; they come from the same origin and are moving toward the same ultimate completion.

For Rahner, Jesus is the culmination of the gradual movement of materiality toward conscious spirit. Humans represent nature arriving at reflective consciousness. Though humans are products of nature, we are uniquely able to give meaning to nature. In Christ the authentic meaning of all things is revealed. We see that nature is not our enemy but our family and the place where God is a continual presence and power in the person of Jesus Christ.

Rahner maintained that human beings have been graced with the capacity to experience God's becoming in the world. He characterized human beings as a living openness to infinite Mystery, which is both the ground and goal of all things. As we saw earlier, one of Rahner's major contributions to theology was the insight that human experience is a valuable resource for understanding the divine. He was convinced that God could be encountered in the entire range of human experience.

For Rahner, Jesus' own human experience is the model for our struggle to discover God in the world. Jesus was so completely open to the experience of God in the world that his life was one with the divine. In Christ we find the way to respond to our world with a new sensitivity. Jesus of Nazareth, a man of earth, can teach us that this is indeed God's world, God's home. He is the teacher from whom we can learn to reverence our world and care for it. The incarnation, then, is not simply an event of the past but an ongoing process that is both personal and cosmic. The renowned scholar on Christian mysticism Evelyn Underhill understood the incarnation in this fashion: "It is an everlasting bringing forth, in the universe and also in the individual ascending soul, of the divine and perfect life, the pure character of God, of which the one historical life dramatized the essential constituents."[19]

Christ amid Brokenness

Henri Nouwen, one of the most profound spiritual writers of our times, was able to bring such abstract theology on incarnation down to an everyday level. He often said that he discovered the depth of the meaning of the incarnation at L'Arche, a community of persons with physical and mental disabilities. Nouwen's own complicated search for Jesus ended here, among wounded bodies and minds, where feeding, cleaning, touching, and holding were so much a part of life. Nouwen said that the incarnation of Jesus confronts us with a Word that can be seen, heard, and touched, and reveals that the body is the way to get to know the Word. Before going to L'Arche, Nouwen gave material concerns minimal attention. But at L'Arche he learned that the body is the place where the Word is encountered. "It is in relationship to the wounded body of the handicapped person that I must learn to discover God. . . . I wonder when and how I will learn fully to live the Incarnation. I suppose that only the handicapped people themselves will be able to show me the way."[20]

Nouwen's deep sensitivity toward the brokenness in our world has much to teach us. He was able to find Christ among the "little ones" of the world and saw that the healing of the world began in a "change of heart" toward the world. At Nouwen's funeral many of his "little ones" gathered around a home-made casket on which they had painted trees, the sun, rainbows, and people. Slowly they danced around the altar, gesturing to each other's hearts and to the coffin. This learned priest had been their friend and had helped them find Jesus in the midst of their brokenness. They would always remember his words to them: "Jesus' appearance in our midst has made it clear that changing the human heart and changing human society are not separate tasks, but are as interconnected as the two beams of the cross."[21]

The Coming of the Word

The theology of the Word, or Logos, was central in the early Christian interpretation of the incarnation. Threatened by heretical denials of the incarnation, early theologians turned to the notion of Logos to explain how Jesus could be both human and divine. The Logos theology was especially effective in defeating the ancient dualisms of Gnosticism and Docetism, both of which disdained the notion of God entering into materiality.

Many scholars think that the Logos theology of the New Testament was in part derived from the Wisdom literature.[22] For the Jews, the Logos or Word was the reality through which God was active in history as a creative, prophetic, and saving power. The Logos was the creative principle in God, so the early theologians used this notion to explain how God could enter into creation as Jesus Christ. The notion also appeared in Greek philosophy to designate the rational and ordering principle that was in God. When the concept appeared in Christian thinking, it was sometimes a blend of Jewish and Greek thinking. Early Christian thinkers taught that the Logos was the aspect of God that entered into history in the creative process and ultimately came in the person of Jesus Christ. Here the Son of God becomes identified with the Logos and enters creation and humanity. The divine creative principle becomes human in a "new creation."

The ancient Logos theology uniquely links creation with incarnation. This theology highlights the extraordinary dignity of all created things by showing that all of reality is born from God. The coming of Jesus Christ becomes a creation event that bring a newness to the earth. Since the Word and world are now one, it becomes clear that the world must be reverenced and treasured.[23]

Recapitulation by the Word

Irenaeus's approach to the Logos in incarnation has been a significant influence in the development of modern incarnational theology. Incarnational theology helps us realize that God is within all things. Much of what Irenaeus taught is also useful in environmental theology. For Irenaeus, there was a continuity between matter and spirit. He also believed that creation, incarnation, and redemption were all part of one continual process.[24] Irenaeus is traditional in viewing the Logos as the creative aspect of God, the means whereby God externally communicates the divine self. God lovingly shared God's self at first in creation and then even more dramatically in the incarnation. For Irenaeus, the incarnation of the Word is the climax of creation, because it sums up or "recapitulates" what God intended from the beginning—the union of the divine and the human.

Irenaeus stressed the realness of Jesus' physical humanity. He struggled against the Docetists and Gnostics, with their negative views of matter, and showed that Jesus was truly born as a human, with true human flesh, and thus recapitulated or renewed the birth of humankind. It was as though God pointed to the Son, Jesus Christ, and said to humankind: "This is how I meant humans to be from the beginning." For Irenaeus, Jesus was a Second Adam, a new creation of humanity. The world, then, is God's world, a place where God continues to create and redeem. In the magnificent and "worldly" theology of Irenaeus, God's saving plan is to "gather up all things in him [Christ], things in heaven and things on earth" (Eph 1:10).[25]

The recapitulation notion of Irenaeus recognizes that the incarnation sanctifies every aspect of human life. Common among the Fathers was the notion that God became human so that the human could become godly. Jesus is seen as representative of all humanity and all are invited then to be one with their Creator. Jesus' victory over evil becomes the "victory of all that belong to him."[26] As Gregory of Nazianzen remarked: "What has not been assumed has not been healed." Christ assumed human nature in its entirety and brought to it the healing power of God.

Incarnation theology can be extended beyond the human to all of creation. If creation, incarnation, and redemption are all of a piece, then creation has been transformed by the coming of Christ, and the benefits of redemption are shared by all of creation. This vision of the world is clearly needed for ecology. If the plan of God is to be one with creation, to save the world, and to bring it to fruition, then abuse of creation is reprehensible. Conversely, those who reverence creation are called to expose such exploitation of God's gifts.

WISDOM

The Hebrew notion of Logos seems to be linked with the rich biblical tradition concerning Wisdom. Denis Edwards has done pioneering work in exploring this tradition and linking it with the environment. He has observed that "Wisdom is always closely associated with God's work of creation. Wisdom is concerned with the whole of creation, and with the interrelationships among human beings, the rest of creation and God."[27] In Jesus Christ, Logos and Wisdom become one.

In Hebrew literature Wisdom is identified with the self-revealing and creative principle of God. The Creator establishes the earth on the foundation of Wisdom, and so it is through Wisdom that the mysteries of life can be learned from "the point of view of the Creator." For the Hebrew, Wisdom dwelt within the natural things of creation, so it is in this context that people could learn of God's self-revelation.

Wisdom is portrayed by the Hebrews as a feminine figure who was present before creation and who stands playfully at the Creator's side, linking the human with the divine. She delights in creation, and she stands as a friend, teacher, even lover to human beings, revealing to them the mysteries of God and creation. Feminist theologians stress the importance of this and many other feminine images of God for better understanding the dignity of creation.

Jesus as the Wisdom of God

The Christian scriptures link the Wisdom tradition to Jesus Christ in what may be one of the oldest themes of Christology. When Jesus invites his followers to take up his yoke, he echoes a similar invitation in the Book of Sirach. Similarly, John's famous passage on the Word becoming flesh and entering the world finds parallels in the Book of Wisdom and the Book of Sirach. Likewise, the author of Hebrews' reference to the Son being the radiance of God's glory is paralleled in the Wisdom literature.[28]

Paul, in his early letter to the Corinthians, links Christ with the Wisdom of God, and shows Christ to be the source of life and redemption:

> Has not God made foolish the wisdom of the world? For since, in the wisdom of God, the world did not know God through wisdom, God decided, through the foolishness of our proclamation, to save those who believe. For Jews demand signs and Greeks desire wisdom, but we proclaim Christ crucified, a stumbling block to Jews and foolishness to Gentiles, but to those who are the called, both Jews and Greeks, Christ the power of God and the wisdom of God. For God's foolishness is wiser than human wisdom, and God's weakness is stronger than human strength.   —1 Corinthians 1:20-25

A number of other passages in Paul's letters also resonate with themes from Wisdom. In Colossians, Paul writes lyrically about Jesus, calling him the "image of the invisible God" and "the firstborn of all creation," and proclaiming that all things were created through and for Christ, who reconciles all things with God (Col 1:15-19). The author of Hebrews also uses Wisdom themes in describing Christ as "the exact" image of God, through whom God made all of creation (Heb 1:1-30).

Wisdom in the Gospels

In the gospels Jesus is associated with Wisdom images. In Luke's gospel Jesus proclaims his message in the name of Wisdom and his cures are said to be the deeds of Wisdom (Lk 7:35; 11:49). In Matthew's gospel Jesus is the teacher of Wisdom, sharing his learning and his yoke with his people and urging them to listen to his prophetic warnings. In John's gospel Jesus is the Word of Wisdom made flesh. He exists with God from the beginning and is both the source and sustainer of all things (Jn 1). Throughout John's gospel Jesus' role of Wisdom-bearer is described with images similar to those in the Wisdom tradition. Jesus is the bread of life, the light of the world, the good shepherd, and the true vine. Like Wisdom, Jesus walks with his people, converses with them, and enters into all areas of their lives.

This Wisdom tradition is fundamentally another form of creation theology; it attempts to explore more deeply the mysteries of creation. The Christian sources link Christ with this tradition and thus see creation and incarnation as one ongoing process. The writer of Ephesians makes this connection powerfully:

> Blessed be the God and Father of our Lord Jesus Christ, who has blessed us in Christ with every spiritual blessing in the heavenly places, just as he chose us in Christ before the foundation of the world to be holy and blameless before him in love. He destined us for adoption as his children through Jesus Christ, according to the good pleasure of his will, to the praise of his glorious grace that he freely bestowed on us in the Beloved. In him we have redemption through his blood, the forgiveness of our trespasses, according to the riches of his grace that he lavished on us. With all wisdom and insight he has made known to us the mystery of his will, according to his good pleasure that he set forth in Christ, as a plan for the fullness of time, to gather up all things in him, things in heaven and things on earth. —Ephesians 1:3-10

Here Christ is active in the creation and redemption. He is the revealer of God's secret and mysterious plans, the one who gathers all creation for salvation and then continues to carry out his mission of bringing about the new creation.[29] The disciple of Christ, Lord of the Universe, shares in this mission to re-create the earth and help bring it to completion. It is a daunting mission in light of the enormous obstacles standing in the way of peace, justice, and the integrity of the earth in our time. Still, a promise accompanies every disciple taking on such a task: "I am with you always, to the end of the age" (Mt 28:20).

JESUS THE SAVIOR

From gospel times Jesus Christ has been acknowledged as the Savior. Reginald Fuller points out that the message of salvation remains normative for Christianity, but that it must constantly "be translated into the contemporary context."[30] The theology surrounding Jesus' saving role has always been culturally conditioned and expressed in a wide range of approaches, including salvation, redemption, liberation and the theology of the Cosmic Christ. In the following, we will discuss these notions and suggest connections with ecology.

A Need for Integration

The contemporary theology of salvation is becoming more integrated and holistic. Traditional approaches to salvation have focused on salvation through the death of Jesus but said little about the saving powers of his life and resurrection. In the past, salvation often focused on souls or spirits; it did not sufficiently include the physical and material, the things "of this world." The classical debates about salvation dealt with such areas as faith, good works, and orthodoxy but said little about the political, social, and ecological dimensions of salvation.

Even today salvation often becomes disconnected from life itself, applied more to an otherworldly existence rather than to everyday problems. As a result, for many people today, especially the young, salvation does not seem to be relevant to life. Once such a central element of tradition as salvation loses its meaning, the entire tradition can lose its meaning and purpose for people.

If salvation is to regain centrality in the Christian tradition, it will have to broaden its scope beyond private salvation and address the pressing issues of public life. People want to know how they can be "saved" from violence, nuclear threat, economic insecurity, oppression, and environmental hazards. If the theology of salvation cannot address these issues, the churches will find it increasingly difficult to hold the interest of the people of today.

Salvation as Protection

The Hebrew notion of salvation developed out of the belief that they as a people were uniquely chosen by God and were thus safe and protected by this same God. Their experience of God's protection reached its climax when the Hebrews were *saved* from slavery in Egypt. This Exodus event is still at the center of Jewish salvation history. The saving process continued as Yahweh rescued his people throughout a long history of exile and persecution. No matter what the difficulty or suffering, even the horrible Holocaust of recent times, people faithful to Judaism have placed their trust in God for the strength to survive and the courage to begin again after their lives have been shattered.

A prophetic tradition gradually built up among the Jews that condemned injustice and looked forward to a future time of complete salvation. A prayerful tradition also developed around the Jewish beliefs in salvation: confidence in God's saving power, as well as an attitude of thanksgiving for God's many saving actions. Psalms and the Book of Daniel carry many passages that express trust that the just person, the person who is meek and poor in spirit, will be saved by God.

Salvation in Judaism, then, has many facets. It celebrates a covenanted relationship with God, a deliverance from demonic and evil forces, a faith in being rescued from whatever horrors come in life, and a complete trust in the forgiveness and fidelity of the Creator. At its best, Jewish faith in salvation is broad and inclusive, touching every facet of creation and life.

This Jewish notion of salvation is useful today as many face violence, deprivation, and enslavements of all kinds. It can offer hope at a time when the very air people breathe or the water they drink can jeopardize their health, when many are left with only an arid scrap of land to farm while a few wealthy families control huge tracts of property.

Salvation for All

Jesus attempted to restore the best of the Jewish tradition of salvation. In his life and teaching he revealed a loving and caring Abba, one who protected all of creation. Jesus lived and died in utter self-sacrifice so that everyone could receive forgiveness. Jesus reached out to his own people and also beyond Judaism to show that God's saving powers were accessible to all.

The gospel stories reflect Jesus' constant efforts to bring salvation to all people. He saved the sick from the despair of mental and physical illness. He rescued the disabled from isolation and rejection. Jesus delivered sinners from self-hatred and despair with his acceptance, compassion, and forgiveness. God's desire that creation be whole and that all be saved was manifested in Jesus. This was proclaimed later by the Johannine community: "Indeed, God did not send the Son into the world to condemn the world, but in order that the world might be saved through him" (Jn 3:17).

It has always been a struggle for the Christian community to keep such an inclusive notion of salvation. The early Christians confronted Gnosticism, which saw no reason to save the body or material things. But Irenaeus in the second century spoke of God gathering all of creation and restoring it through Christ. Monika Hellwig notes that Athanasius, in his battle against Arianism, proclaimed that the Word became human so that the human might become divine, and suffered death so that all might receive immortality.[31] Such an inclusive and universal notion of salvation is essential for an environmental theology. God's love and saving power leave no one and no thing behind. The Creator's protection and care for all things become the standard for how believers are to relate to the earth.

Conquering Evil

The gospel stories reflect the early Christian understanding that Jesus saved his people from the powers of Satan. Often in the gospels Jesus exorcised evil spirits from those who were possessed and restored these people to wholeness and peace. Jesus did not fear evil, nor was it able to destroy him. The stories of his temptations in the desert reveal his victory over Satan, and his many victories over evil throughout his life demonstrate that sin had no power over him.

One of the early Fathers, Justin, understood Jesus as a conqueror of the demonic in the world. He pointed to the gospels' common usage of the demonic in the exorcism stories of Jesus. For Justin, Jesus, as the fullness of the Logos, was a teacher and conqueror who had the power to overcome evil. Jesus brought truth where there had been lies, goodness where there had been evil. Jesus was a liberator who freed his people from the bondage of past and present sins. Central images for Justin were the cross and blood, images that powerfully connect Jesus' suffering with our redemption.[32]

Justin's theology of salvation is applicable today. We still need to be freed of past sins that hold us in bondage. Slavery as a legal institution has been eliminated from many cultures, but it still grips many people through prejudice, racial hatred, and domination. The Holocaust event in Europe is over, yet it continues in places like Bosnia, Sudan, and Rwanda. Political colonialism is passing away but is being replaced by economic colonialism. And, most important to our task here, the many "sins" of our past toward the environment will continue to be upon us for many generations. Our children and grandchildren will receive a legacy of pollution, stripped forests, and depleted resources. They will have much to be saved from, and they will need a strong faith in the saving power of Jesus if they are to meet the challenges ahead responsibly.

There are new and practical needs for salvation today. Technology, while it has benefited humanity greatly, has a dark side. It has resulted in weapons that can devastate the environment and destroy untold numbers. Growing global industry and development threaten to exhaust many resources and damage the environment. Much industry is being transplanted to underdeveloped countries, where wages can be kept at a minimum and environmental laws are lax. Many political situations in Africa, the Middle East, Ireland, Bosnia, Russia, Eastern Europe, and other places are unstable and project a murky and dangerous future. Monika Hellwig has commented that the battlefield where salvation meets destruction is not only within the consciousness and private lives of the individual but also in those very structures of human society that shape our futures. The salvation of God will have to be made relevant to these social, political, and environmental structures if it is to be believable.

Pauline Themes of Redemption

Paul was the architect of much of Christian redemption theology. Many of his themes, as we shall see, are easily adaptable to an environmental theology. Paul often linked creation with redemption, viewing the latter as a "new creation," wherein God's intentions for the cosmos are revealed and humans are restored to the divine image.[33] Paul tells the Corinthians that they can find true freedom in the Lord. They can be led by his Spirit to discover their authentic selves and once again be true images of God. He writes: "Now the Lord is the Spirit, and where the Spirit of the Lord is, there is freedom. And all of us, with unveiled faces, seeing the glory of the Lord as though reflected in a mirror, are being transformed into the same image from one degree of glory to another; for this comes from the Lord, the Spirit" (2 Cor 3:17-18).

For Paul, it is in the materiality of our bodies that we make Jesus Christ visible. It is the visible that manifests the invisible. In a well-known passage Paul writes:

> But we have this treasure in clay jars, so that it may be made clear that this extraordinary power belongs to God and does not come from us. We are afflicted in every way, but not crushed; perplexed, but not driven to despair; persecuted, but not forsaken; struck down, but not destroyed; always carrying in the body the death of Jesus, so that the life of Jesus may also be made visible in our bodies. For while we live, we are always being given up to death for Jesus' sake, so that the life of Jesus may be made visible in our mortal flesh. So death is at work in us, but life in you.
> —2 Corinthians 4:7-12

Paul is convinced that the physical in creation is liberated by the power of the Lord. Jesus Christ sets free all of creation from its bondage to decay and gives freedom to God's children. Jesus' redemption also looks toward the ultimate liberation of all creation. In an oft-quoted passage Paul writes to the Romans about the longing that is in all things for redemption:

We know that the whole creation has been groaning in labor pains until now; and not only the creation, but we ourselves, who have the first fruits of the Spirit, groan inwardly while we wait for adoption, the redemption of our bodies. For in hope we were saved. Now hope that is seen is not hope. For who hopes for what is seen? But if we hope for what we do not see, we wait for it with patience.   —Romans 8:22-25

For Paul, the death of Jesus destroyed forever the solidarity in sin that humans share with Adam. In Jesus' resurrection a new creation was revealed, a renewed solidarity in grace between God and humans. This new creation came about in resurrection and is communicated in baptism. The cross of Jesus transforms humans and provides them with new possibilities and a new future. For Paul, there is now a new world and we are new creatures; we can hope to put the sins of the past behind us and to rebuild the earth. Paul is convinced that the earth is tremendously resilient and through the power of Jesus, the new Light of creation, can rebound from any catastrophe. Jesus can overcome chaos and free his people to enter a new order of being.

A new era begins with Christ, and for those who are "in Christ" there is a new life, free from the evils of the past. In Christ we can overcome all things, and Paul is convinced that "neither death, nor life, nor angels, nor rulers, nor things present, nor things to come, nor powers, nor height, nor depth, nor anything else in all creation, will be able to separate us from the love of God in Christ Jesus our Lord" (Rom 8:38-39).

Jesus in his new creative role again overcomes chaos and restores humans to be once again "images of God." Paul calls upon the Philippians to take on the mind of Christ, to learn how to "empty themselves" of all tendencies to be god-like. He encourages them to dedicate themselves to a life of self-sacrificing service and to desist from the perennial urge to dominate others. Like Jesus, they should be servants.

The new creation involves humans being remade in the image of God, which is now the image of Christ, the image of the man of heaven. In this new image we can once again represent the Creator as servants of the earth rather than as masters. We are to share in Christ's mission to save the entire cosmos:

For in him all the fullness of God was pleased to dwell, and through him God was pleased to reconcile to himself all things, whether on earth or in heaven, by making peace through the blood of his cross.
—Colossians 1:19-20

Paul could have been writing for us. He acknowledges how creation is groaning, and yet he has faith that Christ has liberated all of creation and is bringing about a new creation. Disciples of Jesus come to realize that on their own they cannot deal with many of our overwhelming ecological challenges. But with the creative power of Christ we can restore the earth and help bring about the new creation that is so desperately needed. Paul's themes on redemption offer us much hope.

Teilhard de Chardin understood and was influenced by Paul's theology of redemption, and he linked it with a contemporary evolutionary view of the earth. For Teilhard, redemption was not the restoration of a past perfection but the bringing to fulfillment of a humanity and an earth that have been evolving over eons. Redemption was primarily bringing creation to a fullness that God had intended all along.[34]

SALVATION AS LIBERATION

In our era countless people cry out to be saved from oppression and injustice. Many people throughout the world need to be saved from the political and economic forces that are destroying their earth and their lives along with it. Many people lack clean air and water, food, a decent place to live, and proper health care. They call upon Christ and his followers to save them from the horrible conditions in which they are forced to live. They cry out for justice for themselves as well as for the environment that surrounds them. As one man poignantly lamenting the destruction of the rainforests in British Columbia has said: "They are crucifying the trees!"

Liberation is at the heart of the Judeo-Christian tradition. The central saving act in Judaism was God's liberating the Hebrews from slavery. Yahweh then saved them from sin by giving them a covenant and a law of love for God and neighbor that would keep them protected from sin. The "poor of Yahweh" always received special protection from their Creator, and God's prophets often spoke up for these "little ones" and chastised their persecutors.

Jesus attempted to restore Judaism to its best traditions of liberation. Early in his ministry Jesus identified himself with the prophetic ministry of freeing prisoners and liberating the oppressed (Lk 4:18). Jesus' mission focused on freeing others from sin, disabilities, rejection, or even physical hunger. Jesus' many miracles—when he fed others, healed them, and brought them forgiveness—all witnessed to the power of a Creator who wanted people to be whole and free. In John's gospel Jesus tells his disciples: "The truth will make you free. . . . If the Son makes you free, you will be free indeed" (Jn 8:32-36). Paul proclaimed this good news of freedom to the churches of Galatia when he wrote, "Christ has set us free" (Gal 5:1).

There was a "dangerous element" to Jesus' teachings; otherwise he would not have come to such a horrible and unjust ending on a cross. Jesus was not an anarchist or a political revolutionary, but in his life and teachings he cried out for justice and social change. Jesus revealed that freedom is an inward gift from God and that liberation cannot be accomplished by political systems or imperial edicts. He proclaimed a universal freedom that could be gained by following his teaching and example.

Archbishop Oscar Romero, who gave his life for the freedom of his people, once pointed out that the fullness of life which Jesus brings begins here in history with bread, a roof, a job.[35] Those engaged in providing food for the hungry of the world or building homes for the needy teach the same lesson. Here salvation comes to everyday life and is supported by a church whose mission is to be in solidarity with those who are dehumanized and oppressed. Here action for justice is seen as integral to the preaching of the gospel and to the church's mission of redemption. As Gustavo Gutiérrez, one of the founders of liberation theology, has observed, our understanding of salvation must see a relationship between "the construction of this world and salvation."[36]

Salvation here is not simply of souls but of lives. John Paul II has often preached this message throughout the world. In his touching address to the Indians of Oaxaca and Chiapas in Mexico he spoke of salvation in concrete terms:

> The disheartened world of field work, the laborers whose sweat waters their disheartened state cannot wait any longer for their dignity to be recognized really and fully. . . . They have a right to be respected. They have a right not to be deprived of the little they have by maneuvers that sometimes amount to real plunder. They have a right not to be blocked in their desire to take part in their own advancement. They have a right to have the barriers of exploitation removed. They have a right to effective help, which is neither a handout nor a few crumbs of justice, so that they may have access to the development that their dignity as human beings and as children of God merits.[37]

When salvation is viewed as liberation, religion goes beyond piety and good works and begins to struggle against sinful structures that deprive countless people of their rights. People need to be liberated not only from personal sin but from structures that oppress, whether these structures exist in government, prisons, the military, health care, or industry. People also need to be liberated from sinful structures that inflict abuse and degradation upon the earth. Concerns for liberation must address people's rights to breathe fresh air, drink clean water, own land suitable for growing food, and live in areas protected from pollution and uncontrolled development.

Liberation theology is gradually giving its attention to ecological issues. As early as 1979, at their historic meeting in Puebla, the Latin American bishops showed the beginnings of such awareness. They recognized that the depletion of natural resources and pollution were critical problems for their people. In the name of freedom the bishops urged developing countries to restrict over-consumption and take into consideration the elementary needs of the poor, who constitute the majority of the world's population. More recently Leonardo Boff has observed:

> Worldwide society is becoming more conscious of the implication of ecological disaster on a planetary level. An ecological culture is slowly growing with forms of behavior and practices that embody a vision of the world as a whole and thus lead to greater concentration and concern in our confrontations with nature. The notion is growing that any attack on the earth is aggression against the sons and daughters of the earth.[38]

As we shall see in a later chapter, many feminist theologians from the Third World are exposing environmental abuses in their areas. They seek liberation for women, the poor, and the earth.

RESURRECTION

In the last four decades the resurrection of Jesus has moved from being an anticlimax to the crucifixion, to becoming once again a central doctrine of the Christian faith. The resurrection is now viewed as part of the much larger story of God's new covenant with Israel. It is once again understood as an action of God that validated Jesus and his teaching, promised eternal life, renewed creation, and revealed both the present and future of the reign of God. There is much in contemporary resurrection theology's concern for the cosmic, the material, and the physical dimensions of life that are applicable to ecology.

The cosmic implications of resurrection have been again recognized, especially in the language of epiphany and apocalypse that often surrounds it in the gospels. In his glorified state Jesus Christ manifested the ultimate destiny of creation and the restoration of harmony amid the chaos of sin.[39] Scripture scholar Reginald Fuller observes that in the gospel "vision" stories, Jesus appears in "end-time" images that harken back to stories of God's victory over chaos and evil in the Hebrew scriptures.[40]

The accounts of resurrection in the gospels also echo the stories of physical survival in the Hebrew scriptures. Genesis tells of Enoch, who walked with God and then was taken by God (Gn 5:24). Elijah, who had been accompanying his disciple Elisha, was suddenly taken amid a whirlwind in a chariot of fire to heaven (2 Kgs 2:11-12). The Book of Daniel proclaims that some who sleep in the dust will awake to everlasting life and shine "like the stars forever" (Dn 12:3). And the first Book of Enoch describes not only the resurrection of the dead but the ultimate transformation of the earth.

The New Testament theology of resurrection stresses the transformation of the materiality of Jesus. Paul speaks of Jesus' coming "in human likeness" and "taking the form of a slave" and then shows how in resurrection Jesus is "highly exalted" by God (Phil 2:6-11). In the resurrection God transformed and glorified the physical body of Jesus and in so doing manifested the ultimate fulfillment destined for humans as well as for all of creation.

The resurrection stories in the gospels stress the physical transformation of Jesus. The empty-tomb stories demonstrate that the body of Jesus no longer existed as a corpse in the tomb but had been raised and transformed by God. Jesus' transformed body is integral to all the appearance stories. His physical body is now part of a "new creation" and thus no longer subject to time or space. Jesus can appear and disappear, come through locked doors, and be present without being recognized. At the same time Jesus' presence is portrayed as "real." He can walk with his disciples, be embraced by a friend, be touched by a believer, share meals with friends, and even cook a breakfast of fish. There is a "seeing" here that is real and yet transcends physical seeing. It is a "seeing" accessible only to those with faith. A new dimension to reality is revealed in the resurrection, one that is promised to all those who accept Jesus' promise of eternal life.

The appearance stories attempt to describe the indescribable! Jesus has been raised by God, and though he was experienced in a manner similar to the way he was before his death, Jesus is now in a new and transformed state. He was now the "firstborn" of a new creation and will be present in this glorified condition as he continues to create all of reality. As theologian Gerald O'Collins has observed, the transformation of the risen Lord reveals the future destiny of all of creation.[41]

The Risen Body

Paul developed a theology of resurrection that is somewhat less graphic than that of the gospels and yet is realistic. Paul sees Jesus' resurrection as a pledge of what all the faithful can anticipate after death. He writes about the perishable body being buried like a "seed" that is sown. He teaches that a new and unperishable body will be given to us. Paul observes that the dead are sown as physical bodies and raised as spiritual bodies. He proclaims that "God raised the Lord and will also raise us by his power" (1 Cor 6:14).

A New Creation

Paul believed that the resurrection was truly a new creation. He described Jesus as the "firstborn" and the "first fruits" of this new creation. In his first letter to the Corinthians, Paul uses the imagery of Genesis:

But in fact Christ has been raised from the dead, the first fruits of those who have died. For since death came through a human being, the resurrection of the dead has also come through a human being; for as all die in Adam, so all will be made alive in Christ. But each in his own order: Christ the first fruits, then at his coming those who belong to Christ.

−1 Corinthians 15:20-23

Resurrection is an affirmation that creation is destined to continue on toward newness. Ours is not a world destined for destruction, but a world that has a future of fulfillment. As Monika Hellwig observes:

In resurrection, God proclaims that creation will not be destroyed but will be transformed. Love and life will prevail over death and destruction. It discloses that in the end time those who have suffered unjustly will be vindicated. The resurrection is a unique breaking through of divine power, and it ignites a new age of the kingdom.[42]

This transformation was prefigured in the transfiguration of Jesus, which is described in Matthew's gospel. Jesus' countenance is described with magnificent natural imagery:

Six days later, Jesus took with him Peter and James and his brother John and led them up a high mountain, by themselves. And he was transfigured before them, and his face shone like the sun, and his clothes became dazzling white. Suddenly there appeared to them Moses and Elijah, talking with him.

−Matthew 17:1-3

A similar transformation is described in Luke's account of the ascension of Christ. Jesus blessed his disciples and then withdrew from them and was "carried up into heaven." The disciples then worship Jesus and return to Jerusalem with great joy (Lk 24:51-52). Here the glorified body of Jesus seems to be once again united with creation, and thereby the destiny of all of creation is revealed.[43]

The Heart of the Cosmos

Two great theologians of our time, Karl Rahner and Pierre Teilhard de Chardin, have described the risen Christ as the "heart of the cosmos." In Rahner's reflections on death he describes death as the fulfillment of our very being, the event when we become our true selves and enter into an intimate union with the material cosmos as a whole. In death the individual is rendered "pancosmic" and enters into an ontological relationship with the whole cosmos. This has been made possible by the resurrection of Christ. Rahner writes: "When the vessel of his body was shattered in death, Christ was poured out over all the cosmos; he became actually, in his very humanity, what he had always been according to his dignity, the heart of the universe, an innermost center of creation."[44] In a rather astounding statement Rahner indicates that the resurrection is the divinization and transfiguration of Christ, and at the same time is the "final beginning of the glorification and divinization of the whole of reality."[45]

Teilhard in similar fashion described the risen Christ as "the Personal Heart of the Cosmos." The risen and glorified Lord will now be continually part of the ongoing creative process. In his usual mystical fashion Teilhard says that Christ "inspires and releases the basic energy of love which progressively carries both humanity and the universe toward its future goal."[46]

The possible connections here with ecology are many indeed. The raising of Jesus, the transformation of his body, and his role as "heart of the cosmos" all give new dignity to the material world and reveal its ultimate destiny. The resurrection also manifests how closely human destiny is linked with the destiny of the cosmos. If God's plan is that all of creation is to be transformed ultimately into a new creation, it is clear that we are integral to that plan and have a central role to play in its accomplishment. In a sense resurrection guarantees the accomplishment of God's plan for creation. And yet we know that humans significantly obstruct God's plan for the earth. The resurrection is grounds for hope but not for presumption. It is now in our hands to build the earth. Should we fail, the cosmos can go on as it did for billions of years—without us.

THE COSMIC CHRIST

The term *Cosmic Christ,* has roots in patristic writing but was first used in modern times by John Denney in 1894 and then adopted by German theologians and biblical scholars at the turn of the century. Since then the notion has become integrated into contemporary Christology and, as we shall see, has special relevance to environmental theology.

New Testament Views

There are a number of New Testament passages that place Christ in the context of the cosmos. The author of Ephesians writes of God's plan ultimately to fulfill all things in Christ: "He set forth in Christ, as a plan for the fullness of time, to gather up all things in him, things in heaven and things on earth" (Eph 1:9-10).

The author of Colossians develops the notion of the Cosmic Christ with more sweep and power than anyone else:

He is the image of the invisible God, the firstborn of all creation; for in him all things in heaven and on earth were created, things visible and invisible, whether thrones or dominions or rulers or powers—all things have been created through him and for him. He himself is before all things, and in him all things hold together. He is the head of the body, the church; he is the beginning, the firstborn from the dead, so that he might come to have first place in everything. For in him all the fullness of God was pleased to dwell, and through him God was pleased to reconcile to himself all things, whether on earth or in heaven, by making peace through the blood of his cross.   —Colossians 1:15-20

John McCarthy has written a seminal article on this passage and has explicitly related it to ecology. McCarthy believes that exegesis should have the liberty to go beyond the original meaning of the texts and to place the text in dialogue with new situations. It is McCarthy's view that Teilhard was correct in linking this text with evolution, and he maintains that in our time it legitimately can be linked with ecological concerns.

McCarthy points out that this passage from Colossians is derived from Semitic thought and is not Gnostic or Hellenistic in origin.[47] Semitic thought is holistic and perceives salvation to come about within history, culture, and nature itself. As Roland Murphy points out, the Hebrew canonical scriptures do not separate creation from redemption.[48] Creation is but the beginning stage of the redeeming process and participates in it fully. In this passage Christ is integral to the entire process of creation and redemption.

McCarthy points out that the church must read each new "sign of the times" in order to discern how Christ is calling it to serve in the world. At present many people are deeply troubled about the future of the earth. We have unleashed forces on our earth that seem to be doing irreparable damage. McCarthy maintains that the image of the Cosmic Christ can be a powerful image to move Christians to share the Lord's ongoing mission to save the earth from exploitation and destruction.[49]

Teilhard's View

The Cosmic Christ was a favorite image of Teilhard's, and he used it as a unifying factor in his own thinking about how evolution could be linked with Christianity. For Teilhard, the Cosmic Christ was a third dimension of Christ and served to link Christ with both the beginning and goal of creation.

Teilhard sees the Cosmic Christ as a creative and sustaining energy that is now within the cosmos. This dimension of the Christ, which is linked to the historical Jesus as well as to the risen Lord, exercises a divine power within the universe and draws it toward its ultimate completion and fulfillment.[50]

Teilhard's vision is based on a model of ascent and convergence, with all things in the cosmos gathering into the "Cosmic Christ." The Cosmic Christ is the fullness of Jesus united with all creation transformed and brought to completion. For Teilhard, this ultimate converging of all reality is brought about by the power of love. Teilhard prophetically anticipated the "global village," which he believed could be brought about by both love and progress.

Teilhard's vision, as we've seen, included an interconnection among all things, especially through a "withinness" that exists in all reality. He pointed out that humans are born and then develop in relation to and dependent upon the whole of matter and life.[51] At the same time, Teilhard's vision is of a sweeping upward drive, with humans at the peak of creation and with the Cosmic Christ as the ultimate goal.

Our notion of the Cosmic Christ today differs from Paul's or even Teilhard's. We no longer live in the fixed universe of Paul, with the earth at its center and a sphere above to house the divine and attending angels. We have moved beyond the older hierarchical models that dominated medieval science, political structures, and even ecclesiology. And space travel and the Hubble telescope have taken us beyond the imaginative visions of Teilhard. Modern astrophysics, evolutionary studies, and quantum physics describe a different world. We live in a complex, relativized, and somehow interconnected cosmos wherein humans are of recent and modest significance. It is a cosmos that humans will never dominate or even understand completely. And yet in the infinitesimally small area of the universe in which humans reside, they are having enormously significant effects on their planet. Some of these effects endanger the very continuation of life.

The image of the Cosmic Christ, then, can be extremely useful for an environmental theology. It is important, however, that we don't see the Cosmic Christ as some sort of "galactic Christ" somewhere in outer space and reduced to the notion to a poetic nicety. If the notion of the Cosmic Christ is to be helpful to ecology, this Christ must be identical to the historical Jesus and the risen Lord, who continues to be friend and companion in everyday life. Creation, the incarnation, and the redemption must all be seen to continue in his Person. German theologian Bernard Häring has observed that Jesus Christ lives on among his followers and offers us the vision, energy, and grace to meet two of the most important challenges of our time: sustaining the earth and sharing its resources.[52]

An effective environmental movement also will have to understand precisely the operations of the environment, be sharply aware of the real problems and dangers in question, and be engaged in effective actions in facing these challenges. If faith in Christ can be joined to such expertise, the environmental movement will be all that much more effective.

CONCLUSION

Some have said that the Christian tradition has little to offer the environmental movement and has in fact been largely responsible for much of the damage to the earth. Our survey of Christology belies that position. Christianity is an extraordinary religion in that it professes that the Creator has actually become one with the world in the person of Jesus Christ. What could be a more convincing argument that the world is to be reverenced and cared for? Moreover, Christians believe that Christ is the Savior of the world and has brought redemption, reconciliation, and a new creation. What could be a source of more hope and encouragement for the future of the earth? The resurrection of Jesus is central to the Christian tradition and proclaims that Jesus' body was transformed into new life, the same life he promised his followers. What promise could be more assuring? And Jesus is now the Cosmic Christ, a presence and power of divine grace in the world. Does one need more to be convinced that Christians can play important roles in restoring the earth for future generations?

5.

Sacraments

Fishing has been a way of life for Newfoundlanders for centuries. The old storytellers tell tales of the fish being so plentiful that one could take them out of the sea with baskets. I remember my grandfather and father going down to the harbor as soon as the snow melted to get the boats and nets ready. The men would fish all summer and late into the fall, bringing in tons of cod.

But that all seems to be over now. The boats sit rotting on the shores, the fish plants sit idle, and in some areas unemployment is up to 80 percent. Our young usually have to go elsewhere for work. Many are concerned that we will lose our island culture, with its grand traditions and values. We aren't sure why all this came about: maybe big floating fish factories run by people who were greedy and short-sighted.

—Sean Walsh, Bay de Verde, Newfoundland

All religions depend on rituals and symbols. Theologian David Tracy has pointed out that rituals and symbols can help us escape the nightmares and terrors which surround us and enter "true time, the time of the repetition of the actions of the whole at the origin of the cosmos."[1] He explains that the power of the whole was first disclosed as sacred and that the realm of the sacred can once again be disclosed to us when we participate in sacred rituals and symbols. It is through ritualistic experiences that water, rocks, trees, or mountains can serve as media through which we can experience the sacred.[2]

Sacraments are essential to the Christian tradition. It is through symbolic rituals that disciples are initiated and confirmed into the life with Christ and the church, and are nourished by the Lord's presence in communal liturgy. It is through these ancient sacramental signs that people are joined in marriage and designated to serve in clerical ministry. Through sacraments disciples are forgiven their sins, healed of their infirmities, and prepared for death.

Indeed, sacraments can put us in touch with the sacred dimensions of the cosmos itself. They transform us so that we no longer abuse nature and the cosmos but become committed to their preservation.[3] Sacraments can help us see the world as a graced reality that has its origin in and is loved by the

Creator. Through sacramental rituals we can experience that the immediacy of God is "embedded in this world."[4] Unfortunately, the rich sacramental life of the church has seldom been linked with environmental concerns. In this chapter we will touch on some of the central notions of sacramental theology and then look at a selection of the sacraments in terms of ecology.

SACRAMENTAL THEOLOGY

Theological reflection on the sacraments was slow in developing. Sacramental theology has a complicated and stormy history. Though the community possessed its own treasured symbols and rituals, it took centuries before theories about them emerged. In the early third century Tertullian compared the baptismal vows to the *sacramentum* or oath of loyalty taken by Roman soldiers. Augustine (d. 430) set the foundations for future sacramental theology with his writings about outward signs of God's grace. Medieval specialists devised intricate arguments about how sacraments caused grace and were related to salvation. An explosion of controversy came at the time of the Reformation. The Protestant traditions tended to set sacramental theology aside, while post-Reformation Catholicism established rigid sacramental notions that lasted until the mid-twentieth century.

Each sacrament has a unique history. It was not until the Middle Ages that *seven* sacraments were designated, with marriage being the last added to the list. The Reformation raised serious controversies, with the Protestants finding biblical grounds for only two sacraments (baptism and eucharist), and the Catholics holding strong for the seven that it considered to have been instituted by Jesus Christ.

The modern period has seen enormous sacramental reforms. Vatican II mainstreamed historical and theological research on the sacraments and directed that each sacrament be renewed in its understanding and practice. Many Catholics moved from a rather mechanical and legalistic approach to sacraments to one that is more personal and relational. Theologians like Otto Semmelroth, Karl Rahner, and Edward Schillebeeckx restored Jesus Christ to the center of sacramental theology and demonstrated how the church itself functions as a sign of God's presence and power. The work of Schillebeeckx also brought the personal and relational model of "encounter" to sacraments. Sacraments began to be placed in the context of human life and experience, and not viewed simply as "things that bring grace." The theology of grace, especially through the efforts of Piet Franzen, was linked to its biblical roots and once again understood as sharing in the very life of God.

Sacraments have in the contemporary era been linked with Jesus Christ, the church, human experience, communal life, and social issues. Here I attempt to connect all these facets of sacramental thinking with environmental concerns. My method is to establish a contemporary theological context for the sacraments in general, as well as for some individual sacraments, and then suggest implications for the environment.

Jewish-Christian Roots

In chapter 2 we saw that the biblical tradition reflects the "sacramental" mentality of the Israelites, who often experienced God's presence and power in symbolic fashion. The chosen people spoke of the food they found in the desert as "manna" from Yahweh. God guided them to the promised land with "pillars of clouds," and Yahweh nurtured his people by giving them water from a rock struck by Moses. The psalmist joined with the stars and other "heavenly bodies" to praise the Creator, who was the source and sustainer of all things, the Lord to whom the earth belonged.

The Hebrews did not live in the split level world of the Greeks. The spiritual and the material were two dimensions of one reality: creation. The Hebrews gradually came to understand that the human being was an embodied spirit, who lived in a "good" world, which through its creatures, resources, and history could reveal the Spirit of God. All things had come into existence by a simple word from God; life had come from the Creator's breath. Yahweh was a cosmic divinity beyond all naming and understanding, and yet God walked among the people as mother, father, and spouse. God's presence and power could be felt in the wind, the animals, and the star-studded night sky. This was the sacramental world of the Hebrews. It was a world the Hebrews felt connected to, dependent upon, vulnerable to, and responsible for. Human beings were perceived to be unique creatures, made "in the image" of the Creator and commissioned to represent God's care of the earth and to reproduce more "images of God." This faith needs to be recaptured in this time of environmental crisis.

In chapter 3 we saw that this same sacramental perspective existed in the New Testament. Jesus taught that the reign of God is within. The birds of the air and the lilies of the field were symbols of God's care for all of creation. The harvesting of fish and of the crops demonstrated God's desire to draw people to salvation. The healing of the sick and disabled spoke of God's compassionate drive to have the wholeness and goodness of creation restored. Jesus's Hebrew faith taught him that Abba forgave, healed, and saved all people, especially outcasts. Divine power could be felt in the cool evening breeze and in the generous rays of an afternoon sun. Abba could be encountered in the face of an innocent child or in the silent stretch of the gnarled hand of a leper. The touch of Jesus' hand, the anointing with mud made with spittle, even the brush of his robe could be occasions for someone to experience the power of God's love. Jesus left no doubt but that we are called to cherish creation as our home, as a good place where God saves and continues to create. Jesus knew well of the dark and sinful side of life, but it was his faith-filled conviction that darkness and evil are no match for the power of God. Jesus gave us sacraments that we might be assured that God's presence and power is with us "all days," and that God's creative plan will ultimately prevail.

The Hebrews' sensitivity in finding God in the created world as well as their sense of responsibility for caring for the earth need to be reclaimed by those concerned for the earth. Jesus' notions that God's reign is at hand and that Abba extends love and care to all creation also need to be stressed in our approaches to ecology. As John Haught points out:

> Ever since the Stone Age aspects of nature such as clean water, fresh air, fertile soil, clear skies, bright light, thunder and rain, living trees, plants and animals, human fertility, etc., have symbolically mediated to religious people something of the reality of the sacred. Sacramentalism recognizes the transparency of nature to the divine, and it therefore gives to the natural world a status that should evoke our reverence and protectiveness. The sacramental perspective reads in nature an importance or inherent value that a purely utilitarian or naturalist point of view cannot discern. Nature, then, is not primarily something to be used for human purposes or for technical projects. It is essentially the showing forth of an ultimate goodness and generosity.[5]

Jesus as Sacrament

The center of each Christian sacrament is a unique and singular experience of Jesus Christ. Jesus is the quintessential sacrament in that he is the most complete sign of God's presence and power. This must have been most evident during his life two thousand years ago. People could see the love of God in his eyes, hear the joy of God in his laughter. The touch of his warm and comforting hand brought the healing power of God into many lives. When he cried at the grave of his friend, people could feel the compassion of their God. And when Jesus grew angry at hypocrisy and oppression of the poor, his followers could experience divine outrage over evil.

When Jesus spoke, some of those present must have heard the ring of God's revelation. He enjoyed such an intimacy with the Creator that perhaps some suspected that he had been there "in the beginning." Jesus had such respect for all of creation that some might have an inkling that he was closely related to the Creator. To others, Jesus may have seemed to be the embodiment of the Creator. Encountering him was encountering both Creator and creature as one. When he taught that the presence and power of God (the reign of God) was in their midst, some of his disciples must have felt that they were experiencing all this firsthand in the Lord himself. For many, Jesus must have been a living and dynamic symbol that God was somehow with them. Indeed, there was something sacramental about Jesus throughout his life. He said, "Who has seen me has seen the Father" (Jn 14:9).

Jesus invited people to be visibly, audibly and tangibly in touch with the Creator. He revealed to them the precious and eternal value of their own lives as well as God's presence in all things. He taught them the interrelatedness of all things in the kingdom and promised them that he would be with them until the end.

The intimate encounter with the risen Lord in the sacraments certainly can be a means to becoming more aware of the ongoing creative activity of God. Sacraments can undoubtedly awaken us to the sacredness of the earth and provide us with motivation to care for it. The Jesuit environmentalist Al Fritsch writes eloquently of this sacramental sense: "The Good News is that the earth gently teaches us to sense simple things as the conduits of our Creator. Creatures, tabernacles of mystery, invigorate us, beckon us to change, draw us to adoration."[6]

Post-resurrection Faith

After the resurrection and the coming of the Spirit the inklings and suspicions about the identity of Jesus exploded into faithful conviction. The New Testament is filled with testimony of deep faith that Jesus is the Christ, the Savior, the Son of God. He is now recognized to be Emmanuel (God with us), Messiah, and Lord. John's gospel proclaims that Jesus is indeed the Word of God and that "he was in the beginning with God. All things came to be through him and without him nothing came to be. What came to be through him was life" (Jn 1:3). Jesus was seen by his disciples to be the "firstborn" of a new creation and the initiator of a new covenant. He was worshiped as the Lord of creation.

After the resurrection Jesus could no longer be seen or touched in the same manner as he could before. Understandably, there must have been nostalgia among those who knew him "in the flesh," a longing for the times when he was physically present. One can hear that in the plaintive prayer so popular among the early Christians, "Lord, come again." At the same time, there was among his disciples a vivid sense of his presence and his power in their midst, as well as a hope for his return.

Sacraments as Symbols

Sacraments are derived from the unique human capacity to fashion symbols and attach meaning to them. The human person is an embodied spirit—a combination of the material and spiritual—and needs visible things in order to experience the invisible. We use written and verbal symbols to communicate thoughts and feelings. We use symbols to express our love, material things like gifts, rings, and flowers, or physical actions like kisses, hugs, or sexual contacts. Our lives are filled with symbols that put us in touch with reality and meaning on many different levels.

Sacraments are dynamic symbols by which we contact the Spirit of God and experience the presence and power of the Creator. The *sacramental principle* maintains that we can meet God in natural symbols and experience the "amazing grace" of God. Paul expressed this principle to the Romans: "Ever since the creation of the world his eternal power and divine nature, invisible though they are, have been understood and seen through the things he has made" (Rom 1:20).

Sacraments are not, however, simply symbols that point to God. They have a unique dynamism that manifests and reveals the presence and the power of God.[7] Sacraments have the capacity to connect, link, and bind people of faith to the Creator and creation. They reveal God as the ultimate maker, sustainer, and goal of all things. Sacraments can open us to a new awareness that we are integrally related to the earth, its resources, and all living things; thus we are responsible for respecting and sustaining all of this as "creation." As Dieter Hessel observes: "God is actively throughout the creation, generating and sustaining life, reconciling varied forms of being. God has a continuing role as a creator-sustainer and expects human creatures to be respectful cooperators."[8]

Sacraments are part of the phenomenon whereby the things of creation can communicate the divine to us. Sacraments tell us of the sacred dimension of our world and can thus give us enormous motivation for caring for the earth and for preserving its beauty and goodness. Shannon Jung writes, "Caring for the earth and its future will emerge out of a sense of nature as a sacrament."[9]

Sacraments and Mystery

Sacraments are often associated with the word *mystery,* a word with many meanings. The dictionary definition is "a matter that remains unexplained."[10] We read mystery stories in which a crime is eventually solved. We are fascinated with "unsolved mysteries." Science endlessly attempts to understand the mysteries underlying everything from the galaxies to the tiniest particle. The religious notion of mystery is somewhat different.

The Greek word *mysterion* comes from the root meaning "to close one's mouth," that is, "to be secretive." The Hebrew scriptures use the word *sod* to refer to God's hidden plan for salvation, which is gradually revealed through history. The prophets were often caught up with revealing the divine secrets to the people, and apocalyptic writers have struggled to unveil God's secret plans for the future. Pagan religions are often spoken of as *mystery cults* because their rituals and symbols attempt to explore the hidden secrets of the gods.

In the gospels Jesus speaks of entrusting the secret *(mysterion)* of the kingdom of God to his disciples (Mk 4:11). In his preaching Jesus discloses divine secrets that were "hidden from the foundation of the world" (Mt 13:35). Many of his parables are concerned with using creation itself to reveal the mysteries concerning the Father's care for all things and desire to save the world.

Paul also wrote of God's hidden plan of salvation; he held that this secret was revealed in Jesus Christ and was proclaimed by the apostles (1 Cor 4:1). The mystery of salvation was also at work among believers in their struggles with the "mystery of iniquity" (2 Thes 2:7). Secrets hidden for many years were now disclosed in the gospels. Paul preached that the secrets of creation are revealed in Christ and that everything on heaven and earth will be unified and reconciled in Christ, the firstborn of creation (Col 1:15ff.).

The events of Jesus' life also have been referred to as mysteries. They are the means through which God's hidden plan for salvation was achieved. The central Christian belief is that all are saved through the mysteries of Jesus' life, death, and resurrection. His risen presence continues to give these events enduring power.

Finally, the word *Mystery* is used to refer to the ultimate Reality, God. Rahner described God as Mystery to show that God transcends all naming and understanding. Rahner also explained how Mystery gifted the world and all people with divine revelation and grace.[11]

From this vantage point of Mystery environmentalists can approach the earth with new regard. As Hessel points out, "Faith affirms spirit, God's loving presence in nature. Creation—the whole community of being, animated by divine Spirit—is the context for reality. All of the earth community matters, and has intrinsic value to the one who continues to create, sustain and redeem the whole."[12]

Meeting Mystery in Sacraments

Sacraments are symbolic events that draw us into God as Mystery and allow us to glimpse the secrets of our world, of life, and of ourselves. Sacraments have at their center the person of the risen Jesus Christ, who bears in himself the mysteries of his life, death and resurrection. Through Jesus, the Word, the secrets of creation are revealed. Sacraments can give us occasion to learn of our place in creation, why we were put here, and what we are called to do.

Clearly, sacraments can open us to better appreciate the presence of Mystery in our world and thus move us toward a reverence for created things. Sacraments reveal the ultimate secrets of our reality and enable us to understand better the purpose and goals of our world and to take action to sustain it.

Sacraments Involve Material Things

Sacraments are grounded in materiality, whether water, bread, wine, oil, a healing hand, or people united in marriage. Sacraments proclaim that the divine can be experienced through substantial things. Jesus Christ in the incarnation is the epitome of God entering into materiality and is the fundamental sacrament. It is in his humanity that people see God in action and experience the healing, forgiving, and saving powers of the Creator. In the materiality of the seven sacraments we again see and experience these same powers in our own lives. Created things—like water, olives for oil, grapes for wine, and wheat for bread—donate their deepest meanings so that we can better understand our Creator and creation.

Our world is often oblivious of the sacramental dimension. We live in a materialistic world that is cut off from the spiritual. It is largely a consumer society, in which things are accumulated, used, and discarded. It is often a world in which even people are cast aside; where millions are pushed to the margins in poverty and want. The strong secular bent in our society often excludes God and any notion of creation. As a result, many people take for granted the abundance that is theirs while others go wanting. The wealthy also can be oblivious of the destruction their accumulation and waste bring about.

Sacraments are celebrations of the dignity of material things. Sacraments reveal that all things find their source in God and can therefore put us in contact with the power of God. Sacraments hold up the elements of earth and disclose the preciousness of our resources and food. As Rahner has pointed out, we should bring our world to the sacraments and discover what is "really real," what is sacred, and our responsibilities for caring for and sharing material things.

It is clear that sacraments can indeed help us to understand and revere the giftedness and dignity of material things. This view was expressed powerfully by John Damascene:

> I honor all matter and venerate it. Through it, filled as it were with a divine power and grace, my salvation has come to me. . . . Is not the blessed table matter which gives us the bread of life? Are not the gold and silver matter out of which crosses and altarplates and chalices are made? And before all these things is not the body and blood of our Lord matter?[13]

This same sacramental awareness can also serve as a motivation to care for material things and to share them with others, in particular with those who are in dire need.

The Emergence of Sacraments

After Jesus' ascension the disciples needed symbolic rituals wherein they could celebrate Christ's presence among them. The first two that emerged were baptism and eucharist. Jewish purification and initiation baths, memories of Jesus' baptism by John, and Jesus' commissioning of his disciples were the foundation of the Christian initiation rite of baptism. The waters of baptism powerfully symbolize and effect the washing away of converts' sins and "plunge" their lives into the life, death, and resurrection of Christ. In the breaking of the bread they do as he commanded them and allow their spirits to be nourished with the bread of life.

For the new Christians the world would never be the same. In faith, the Christians were now creatures of God, part of creation, and yet share new life in Christ. A oneness with Christ means a oneness with all things. Paul put it this way to the Corinthians, "So whoever is in Christ is a new creation: the old things have passed away; behold new things have come. And all this is from God, who has reconciled us to himself through Christ and given us the ministry of reconciliation, namely God has reconciled the world to himself in Christ" (2 Cor 5:17-19).

This same awareness of Christ's risen presence in the world, of a new creation in his Spirit, and of Christ's ministry of reconciliation have relevance to today's concerns about the deterioration of our world and the growing disparity between the rich and the poor. As the Irish priest-environmentalist Sean McDonagh observes:

> The resurrection is the cosmic sign of hope. All creation is united in Christ. This hope for wholeness or redemption is anchored in the presence in the world of the spirit, who despite human failures and sins can bring forth things. . . . This is a profoundly liberating experience for the believer and can release new energies to work to bring about a healing of creation.[14]

The Community as Sacrament

We mentioned earlier that modern theology now perceives the church as having sacramentality. Christian communities are called to make Christ visibly present in the world. The early communities knew that wherever they established themselves, whether in Jerusalem, Antioch, Corinth, or Rome, they would attract new members only if they somehow reflected Christ's love. In John's gospel Jesus says: "As I have loved you, so you also should love one another. This is how all will know that you are my disciples, if you have love for one another" (Jn 13:34-35). Communities of loving and caring people can be concrete signs that this is God's world and that Jesus' love is operative in the world. These communities can be sacraments.

Jesus ties the sacramental nature of his followers with creation itself. In John's version of the last supper Jesus prays that the unity, glory, and love of his communities will reveal a Creator who loved his son "before the foundation" of the world. Jesus prays that his followers "may all be one" and thus reflect the oneness in God (Jn 17:20-24). The "community of the beloved disciple" witnesses to its belief that its members make Jesus present in the world. Jesus prays: "As you sent me into the world, so I sent them into the world" (Jn 17:18).

Today Christians number well over a billion people. Gathered in communities in every nation of the world, they are commissioned to stand as living symbols of God, whose creative love existed before the foundation of creation. This creative love eventually overflowed in the creation of our world, peaked with the coming of Jesus, and is now carried forth by his disciples. Whether through young Irish lay missionaries caring for the orphaned children of AIDS victims in Uganda, Peace Corp volunteers, a community of sisters risking their lives to teach people how to grow food in Sudan, or a parish in the Congo providing clean water to children to prevent cholera, Christ is visibly present in Africa. Christ is made present in Appalachia in communities resisting the dumping of toxic waste in their treasured hollows. Christ becomes visible in groups of disciples in Lithuania who try to restore lands that were degraded by Communist regimes. Wherever people become one with their Creator through Jesus Christ, they become sensitive to the living things around them and intent upon conserving the resources available to them. Moreover, their bond with Jesus gives them a power that can overcome enormous difficulties. Paul reminded the Romans that no power in the universe is stronger than that which comes from being one with Christ: "For I am convinced that neither death, nor life, nor angels, nor principalities, nor present things, nor future things, nor powers, nor height, nor depth, nor any other creature will be able to separate us from the love of God in Christ Jesus our Lord" (Rom 8:38-39).

Seven Privileged Signs

There are many ways to experience the power and presence of God in our world. A sunset on a summer evening, a walk on a beach, holding a newborn, or working in a garden can bring us in contact with the Lord. Sacraments are privileged symbols that have been designated by the church to be uniquely intimate meetings with the Creator. They are all linked with creation and can help us see ourselves interrelated with all things. Since the Middle Ages these unique symbols have been numbered as seven, a mystical number that denotes fullness. Each of these seven sacraments is designated for a significant phase or need in our relationship with our Creator.

Edward Schillebeeckx reclaimed a relational understanding of sacraments when he called them "encounters with Christ." But sacraments are not simply chance encounters. Rather, they are gifted opportunities to be up close and personal with the Creator and Redeemer. These are times of "amazing grace," when believers can enter more deeply into the life, death, and resurrection of Christ. Sacraments are celebrations of life shared with God as well as with all living things. From this perspective sacraments can be opportunities for coming to a deeper appreciation of the beauty and value of the earth. An intimate encounter with the Creator can at the same time be an intimate encounter with creation and a graced opportunity to better appreciate the intricacy and integrity of nature and to move us to care for it. Fritsch writes, "By touching the earth and being close to the earth we feel the connectedness which actually exists, our nearness to our relative, our mother Earth, who gives us birth and life."[15]

THE WATERS OF BAPTISM

Christian baptism is a sacrament of initiation into Christ and his community. Its central symbol is water, one of the most basic elements in creation. Science indicates that life on earth began in water. A good portion of the earth, its elements, and living things is made up of water. Water is life-giving and necessary for the sustenance of all living things. Humans grow and are nurtured in water before birth; we need water for drinking, washing, and cooking. But water can be also death-dealing in storms, floods, and drownings. Polluted water can carry disease and death to humans and other living things.

Water is a central symbol in scripture. Both creation stories begin with water. In Genesis 1 creation begins with the Spirit of God sweeping over the primordial ocean and separating waters above the sky from those below the earth. In Genesis 2 a stream wells up out of the earth, waters the ground, and produces the clay from which the first human is formed. In the epic flood story God's judgment is brought upon the earth, and creation is begun again and a new covenant is sealed by God with the earth and all living things (Gn 9:12-17). Water stands as the context for both creation and salvation in the Hebrew scriptures. The Lord pollutes the waters of Egypt, changing them into blood in order to persuade Pharaoh to free the Israelites; the Lord miraculously brings his people across the Red Sea; Moses is empowered to bring water from a rock to save his people from thirst in the desert; and the Israelites cross over the Jordan River into the promised land. Thus the constant concern among the Hebrews for water purification and initiation rites. As the rabbis said, "With the washing of the bodies must go the washing of hearts."[16]

Accounts of water's creative and saving features continue in the New Testament. Mark opens his gospel with John the Baptist calling people to repentance and baptizing them in the Jordan. Then Jesus comes from Nazareth and submits to baptism by John. A new creation scene is drawn with the Spirit of God once again hovering over the waters and the Creator's voice approving Jesus from the heavens: "You are my beloved Son; with you I am well pleased" (Mk 1:11).

In the gospels the Sea of Galilee is a significant place for Jesus' teaching and miracles. Jesus teaches his disciples about faith in the gospel stories when he manifests divine power over creation by calming a storm, walking upon the waters, and catching great quantities of fish.

John's gospel also alludes to Jesus' creative powers by using water symbolism. Jesus' first miracle is described as a conversion of water into wine; Jesus teaches the Pharisee Nicodemus that to enter the kingdom of God one must be born of water and the Spirit; and Jesus offers to give the Samaritan woman "living water." Jesus invites those who are thirsty to come to him for drink, and he heals the man born blind in the waters of Siloam. Jesus washes the feet of his disciples at his last supper. And blood and water flow from Jesus' pierced side after his death. The final resurrection story in John's gospel occurs at the Sea of Galilee, where Jesus once again manifests creative powers in assisting in a miraculous catch. Jesus then cooks breakfast for his followers on the shore of the lake.

Christian Initiation

It is clear that from the beginning the disciples of Jesus Christ continued to sacramentalize water; they made baptism an integral part of their initiation rite. Matthew's gospel, which seems to have come from the community in Antioch, reflects this custom in Jesus' commission, "Go, therefore, and make disciples of all nations, baptizing them in the name of the Father, and of the Son, and of the Holy Spirit" (Mt 28:19). Acts tells numerous stories of conversions followed by baptism. Much of early Christian theology describes baptism as a new creation, a source of unity, and a conquest of sin. All of these emphases can be useful in our development of an environmental theology.

A New Creation

Paul develops the notion of a new creation in his theology of baptism. Paul teaches that baptism brings people "into Christ," and that anyone in Christ "is a new creation; everything old has passed away; see everything has become new!" (2 Cor 5:17). Paul shows how being plunged into the waters of baptism symbolizes how we are buried into Jesus' death and then are raised into the newness of life (Rom 6:4).[17]

The extensive water symbolism in scripture and the theology of baptism can be helpful in reminding us that our waterways and oceans are gifts from God and can be means of encountering God. Anne Morrow Lindbergh, who had a deep sensitivity for the sea, writes beautifully of this sacredness of water:

> The waves echo behind me. Patience–Faith–Openness, is what the sea has to teach. Simplicity–Solitude–Intermittency. . . . When we start at the center of ourselves, we discover something worthwhile extending toward the periphery of the circle. We find again some of the joy in the now, some of the peace in the here, some of the love in me and thee, which go to make up the kingdom of heaven.[18]

This same awareness can help us to realize the damage we have inflicted on the waters of the earth and to strengthen our resolve to work toward a restoration of our waters to their original purity.

The baptismal promises hold out the hope and possibility of healing the earth. Those who have been baptized into the Lord can become aware of the possibility of new creation in themselves and in their world. There is much reason for hope, especially as we see many of the faithful young concerned about the environment and engaged in doing something about the damage that has been done to it. There are many reasons to believe that many young people are committed in faith and hope to a new creation of the earth.

Oneness

For Paul, joining with Christ through baptism achieved a deep unity among all things. In baptism the same Spirit of God who created the world remained the life principle of the world and of the followers of Christ. Baptism clothed the disciples with love, which can restore harmony to a broken world (1 Cor 13:4-7; Col 3:14). To be clothed in Christ is to be clothed in one who embodies all creation. Old divisions among people no longer hold, "for all are one in Christ Jesus" (Gal 3:27-29).

Christians, according to Paul, are baptized into the "body of Christ," or the total Christ, which is all of creation united in him and redeemed by him. In Christ, "God was reconciling the world to himself" (2 Cor 5:18-19). It is this oneness in Christ that binds all things together: "For us there is one God, the Father, from whom are all things and for whom we exist, and one Lord, Jesus Christ, through whom are all things and through whom we exist" (1 Cor 8:6).

The ancient Semites had a sense of corporate personality, a strong solidarity among the people. One member of a family or tribe could affect the entire group by his or her actions. Whole communities could be affected by the destiny of one person, especially significant figures like Adam, Abraham, or

Jesus. The Hebrews also held for solidarity in atonement. The death of the righteous man gained merit from God for those who stood in community with him. Thus Christ's life, death, and resurrection brought a new creation, a new humanity, a new image and likeness of God, which could now affect the entire world. Jesus was "the firstborn of a large family" and all things work toward good for those who are joined with Christ in the new creation (Rom 8:28).

Words commonly read in current environment literature include *connectedness* and *interrelatedness*. Ecology is in itself the study of the links among things, the investigation of ecosystems and how they connect within one web of nature. Those attempting to connect religious faith with ecology emphasize that all of creation is indeed connected. Chief Standing Bear wrote from the Native American perspective many years ago: "The man who sat on the ground in his tepee meditating on life and its meaning, accepting the kinship of all creatures and acknowledging unity with the universe of things, was infusing into his being the true essence of civilization."[19] Only when people regain such awareness of their interdependence with all things will they recognize their responsibilities toward the earth. When we acknowledge the links among the Creator, humans, and the rest of nature, we will grasp the ethical aspects of ecology. The baptized are uniquely able to act as *Christoi,* the anointed ones of the Creator, who serve as mediators between God and all of creation.[20]

The Hebrew notion of corporate personality can also strengthen Christians' sense of community with all things. *Neighbor* can be extended to include all living things and to the earth itself. Moreover, corporate atonement is called for in ecological matters. Many Christians have returned to a more simple way of living and have sacrificed luxury, comfort, lucrative jobs, and even their lives to prevent environmental abuse.

A New Dominion

There has been much discussion in environmental writings about the concept of dominion and how it has been distorted by those who have abused nature. Paul, in his letter to the Romans, expressed the nature of authentic dominion. He pointed out that just as sin and death came into the world in the beginning and have exercised dominion, now through Jesus an abundance of grace and the gift of righteousness have dominion.[21] Paul is convinced that the creative life of God now has dominion in the world and not sin (Rom 6:1-11). Christ has defeated sin, which brings death, and has brought new life to the world. Through Christ we receive God's grace, which brings us salvation and hope for the future (Rom 6:23; Eph 4:4-7).

True dominion is not destructive or selfish. It does not view the earth as a mechanism to be harnessed, or resources as things to be accumulated, used, and then discarded. Dominion finds its source and meaning in the Creator, a gracious, loving, and creative God. Authentic dominion attempts to save, preserve, and sustain the integrity of all things. True dominion arises out of sharing God's own life and extending that graciousness to all of creation. Here one is also concerned about the future of coming generations. According to Paul, that is the victory that has been made possible by the life, death, and resurrection of Jesus Christ. It is a hopeful and encouraging perspective for anyone concerned about ecological issues.

Washing Away Sin

Baptism is a symbolic washing away of sin. Here water donates its meaning of cleansing and refreshing. I live near the Ohio River and know that this water is not fit for washing or drinking. It has lost its basic meaning as water–freshness and the quality of being life-giving. The waters of the Ohio have also lost their sacramentality. To baptize someone in the Ohio River would be counter to the symbol of bringing new life and new creation.

For water to be sacramental it must be pure. The Didache (c. A.D. 100) speaks of baptizing in "running water," seemingly in an era when streams and bodies of water were cleaner than today.[22] Consideration of this sacramental dimension of water can remind us of how much of our water has been polluted; it has to be bombarded with chemicals in order to "purify" it. Few streams or bodies of water today are in pristine condition. Candidates washed of sin in the waters of baptism might be reminded of the sinful fouling of the earth's waters. As Sean McDonagh comments: "If the purity of water continues to deteriorate, will it still retain the power to symbolize new life and purification? This fear of destroying the symbolic power of water and other natural symbols can act as another spur to Christians to be particularly concerned about what is happening to our most precious resources."[23]

Thomas Berry recommends that in baptism we should not simply "use" water but should try to appreciate and to relate to water and allow it to give us a relationship with the divine. He points to the blessing of the water in the Easter Vigil, which carries this appreciation for water as it is taken into the world of the sacred. He also recommends the initiation rite of the Omaha Indians–in which infants are presented to the four regions of the universe–as a model which could better relate baptism to the earth.[24]

The Baptismal Anointing

The candidate for baptism is anointed with oil. In the ancient world oil had many uses. It was an important food in the Middle East, where olive trees were plentiful. It was used as a soap in the baths, and often athletes were anointed before exercise or athletic games. Oil was also used for cooking, medicinal uses, lamp fuel, and, when mixed with spices like frankincense or myrrh, as perfume. Oil for the ancient world carried many meanings: cleansing, strengthening, healing, lighting, and friendship.

Oil also was used as a natural symbol for God's blessings. The Hebrews saw oil as a food whereby God blessed and saved his people. The flourishing olive tree was often used as a symbol of the person blessed by God. The Hebrew scriptures speak of anointing oneself with perfumed oil as a sign of love and friendship (Prv 27:9; Ps 133:2). To pour oil on someone's head was to pay that person honor and wish him or her joy and happiness. Mary of Bethany poured oil on Jesus' head at the home of Simon the leper (Mt 26:6-13) and the repentant woman anointed Jesus' head and feet at the home of Simon the Pharisee (Lk 7:36-50).

Oil was commonly used in Hebrew religious rites as a sign of consecration. Chrism was a blessed oil, and the anointed person was considered to be anointed by God. The word *Christ* applied to Jesus literally means "chrismed one," the one anointed by God to be the messiah.

Early Christian writing speaks of oil as a natural symbol used to signify the presence of Jesus Christ. Cyril of Alexandria refers to this symbolic use of oil in his description of the anointing of catechumens: "Then when you were stripped you were anointed with exorcised oil from the very hairs of your head to your feet and were made partaker of the good olive tree, Jesus Christ. For you were cut off from the wild olive tree and grafted into the good one and were made to share the fatness of the true olive tree."[25] Here the natural image of the olive tree and the oil from the olive "donate" their meaning to the sacramental event of being joined to Christ.

The anointing at baptism has multiple levels of meaning. It cleanses of sin, consecrates, strengthens, and joins the candidate more closely to the Lord. The anointing acknowledges that the candidate is now linked to Christ, the Lord of creation, and can participate in his mission of service to the world. This comes through in the prayer of the chrism Mass each year when the chrism oil is blessed: "Father, by the power of the Holy Spirit you anointed your only Son Messiah and Lord of creation; you have given us a share in his consecration to priestly service in your church. Help us to be faithful witnesses in the world to the salvation Christ won for all humankind." Certainly this call to be witnesses includes the vocation to appreciate all of creation, to nurture it, and to make sure that no one is deprived of rights to the earth's resources.

Baptism and Original Sin

Since Augustine, baptism has been closely associated with original sin. His battle with Pelagius's optimistic view of human nature led Augustine to emphasize the necessity of grace for salvation. Since baptism was the only way to gain grace, Augustine concluded that infants who died without baptism would be deprived forever of eternal life. This was softened in the Middle Ages to the idea of *limbo,* wherein unbaptized infants would enjoy natural happiness but not the vision of God. For centuries this motivated Christians to have their infants baptized as soon as possible and caused much anxiety for parents whose child was miscarried and the fetus not baptized. Today the church has set aside the notion of limbo and relies on the mercy of God to bring salvation to unbaptized babies.

Biblical criticism has moved away from a literal interpretation of the fall and has given theology the resources for developing new interpretations of original sin. Contemporary theologians interpret original sin as the human inclination to sin as well as the "sin of the world" into which all people are born. Here both nature and nurture contribute to the evil that has been always characteristic of humans, the only creatures with the freedom to choose to sin.

Original sin certainly can be recognized in the destruction humans have brought to the environment. Human ignorance, greed, wars, and selfishness have eliminated countless species, destroyed vast acres of arable land, leveled irreplaceable forests, polluted the oceans and waterways, fouled the air, and even altered weather patterns. As a result, there are sinful structures now set in place that seem to have a life of their own and are capable of massive destruction. In addition, economic systems increasingly funnel money to the top of the social pyramid and deprive those on the bottom. Resources are accumulated by the few, while the masses live in poverty and hunger. The wealthy and powerful own most of the good land and often have the legal and military power to protect it and do whatever they want with it. Meanwhile, the majority of people live in depressed, unhealthy areas. In their desperation many of these "environmental refugees" are forced to debase the areas given them even more.

Baptism into Christ and the Christian community might well take into consideration these facets of original sin. As candidates are prepared to enter the church they should be catechized about the sinfulness of doing damage to the environment. The baptismal and confirmation promises ought to include a commitment to imitate Jesus' respect for nature, desire for unity, and commitment to care for the poor of the world. Baptism links disciples with Christ, who is the Word through whom all things were created. By their very connection with Jesus, Christians are uniquely bonded with all of creation.

The sacrament of baptism is about new creation, regeneration, enlightenment, and rebirth. Baptism relates disciples intimately with Jesus Christ, the Lord of the universe. It gives a new identity to the baptized so that they now are uniquely related to both the Creator and creation. Baptism brings new vision with regard to self, other people, and the world. The baptized live within a larger process of creation and salvation that is universal and ongoing.

So baptism is not world-denying but rather world-affirming. Christians are baptized into the great ongoing mysteries of creation as well as into the mysteries of the Christ event. Faith moves them to see that all things can be tangible signs of God's loving, creative, and saving presence.

Many parents approach the baptism of their infant with confusion, possibly even apprehension. For them, baptism needs to be connected to everyday life. Let's listen to Pete, a former student of mine who recently had his infant daughter baptized. "I was uncomfortable when we brought Kara to be baptized. I had not been to church for years and felt like a fake as I promised to share my faith with her. Then the priest spoke about things that are important to me. He talked about reaching out to those in need, and I could relate to that because I help Habitat for Humanity build houses. He spoke of caring for the earth, and I am a real outdoorsman and love nature. I suddenly realized that I had lots to share with my little girl. Baptism is about my way of life, and I really do try to live a good life. Maybe someday going to church will be a part of all this for me." The preparation of parents for the baptism of their children is an opportune time to discuss with them their own faith life as well as ways in which they can teach their children to care for the earth.

In the many parishes that have catechumenates, the Easter Vigil has taken on new meaning and excitement and can be linked easily to environmental concerns. The vigil itself focuses on creation, with the new fire, lighting of the Paschal candle, singing of the Exultet, and the reading of the creation story. The liturgy commemorates the saving presence of the risen Lord in all of creation and in the midst of the community. It celebrates new life in the spring of the year. The vigil is an appropriate liturgy not only to celebrate the beauty of creation but also to focus on the Christian responsibility to preserve and sustain the earth. The vigil is a good time to continue teaching the catechumens, as well as the community, how the Christian faith relates to caring for the world in which we live. Christian initiation is not a private matter but a public statement of commitment to serve others. Those "others" include the poor, all living things, and the earth itself.[26]

EUCHARIST

Christians have often been so preoccupied with debates on "how" Jesus is present that they have too often lost sight of the central meanings of eucharist. The word *eucharist* means "gratitude," and it is gratitude that moves people to thanksgiving. Eucharist is rooted in ancient Hebrew meals where God's people gathered to thank their Creator for gifting them with all the blessings of creation. The Hebrew word for "blessing" *(brk)* is related to the knee and thus to the posture of adoration. The Hebrew scriptures describe the great harvest feasts celebrated in Jerusalem wherein Yahweh was adored, praised, and thanked for all the gifts given the chosen people. The scripture tells of the offering up and then eating of the first fruits and the spring lamb in meals of thanksgiving. The Hebrews also developed fellowship meals, where they would gather to share bread and wine, strengthen their community bonds, and thank God for the blessings of creation and their covenant with God.

Even before the Exodus, the nomadic Semites seemed to have a family meal that they celebrated on the night of the full moon of the spring equinox. At this meal a new lamb or kid was eaten and its blood was placed over the entrance of the dwelling as a sign of God's blessing and protection. This meal might well have been the basis for the later Passover meal, which the Jews celebrated to commemorate their liberation from slavery in Egypt. (The last supper as well as the later Christian "breaking of the bread," "Lord's Supper," and other eucharistic rituals were also linked with Passover.) Praise and thanksgiving for the gifts of the Creator, as well as for Yahweh's covenant with his people, were characteristic of these Jewish meals. In these celebrations there was a profound sense of unity with the Creator and creation, as well as a deep gratitude for all blessings. Many of the psalms are testimonies of gratitude to Yahweh for protecting and nourishing his people.

Jesus' Table Ministry

The gospels describe a number of meals that seem to be based on memories of Jesus' fellowship meals and that also echo early Christian eucharists. In each of these stories Jesus gave his friends reason for thanksgiving to God. At Matthew's house he revealed the mercy of the Creator by eating with tax collectors and sinners (Mt 9:9-13). At the table of Simon the Pharisee, Jesus proclaimed the love and forgiveness of the Creator by raising up the repentant woman (Lk 7:36-50). At table with Martha and Mary, Jesus revealed the priority to be given God's treasured revelation, and at Cana he spared a wedding party embarrassment and manifested the creative and compassionate powers of God (Lk 10:38-42; Jn 2:1-11). Jesus dined with Zacchaeus and transformed him from a corrupt miser to a repentant, generous disciple (Lk 19:1-10). Jesus brought blessings to his friends and to outcasts and fed their hunger, both physical and spiritual.

The story of the multiplication of the loaves is another example of God's bounty on an even grander scale. The story is framed appropriately "near the time of Passover" on a mountain overlooking the Sea of Galilee. Jesus sees the hunger of the people. The story echoes eucharist as it recounts that "Jesus took the loaves, gave thanks, and distributed them to those who were reclining, and also as much of the fish as they wanted." All had their fill, and there was an abundance left over (Jn 6:11-15). The story captures the true meaning of eucharist—thanksgiving for the abundant gifts of God and the call to share them.[27]

Jesus' last supper with his disciples is also depicted as a meal of thanksgiving and blessing. Matthew's version speaks of a blessing with the bread and thanksgiving with the cup. Jesus refers to "my blood of the covenant" and looks to the end time when he will drink it anew with his disciples in the kingdom. Mark's version is rather similar to this, but Luke's version has Jesus telling the disciples to "do this in memory of me"; Luke also places the remark about "the new covenant in my blood" and the cup after the meal (Lk 22:14-20).

Thanksgiving shows up also in Paul's description of the Lord's Supper in Corinth. He reminds the Corinthians of the night before Jesus died when he gave thanks, broke bread, and said, "This is my body that is for you. Do this in memory of me." He also reminds them of the cup and then characterizes the ritual as a proclamation of "the Lord's death until he comes" (1 Cor 11:23-26).

The Didache contains prayers that seem to have been recited before eucharist.[28] One of these prayers indicates how eucharist was related to creation in the early church: "Lord Almighty, you have created all things for the sake of your name, and have given food and drink to people to enjoy, that they may give thanks to you; but to us you have bestowed spiritual food and drink and eternal life through Jesus your servant. Above all, we give you thanks because you are mighty. To you be glory forevermore" (10:1-4).[29]

Justin, writing in the middle of the second century, also gives an example of a eucharistic prayer that is thankful for creation: "And for all that we eat we thank the Maker of all through his Son Jesus Christ and the Holy Spirit."[30] Athenagoras of Athens, another apologist writing toward the end of the second century, describes the connection between creation and the eucharistic sacrifice. In explaining to the Roman emperor why Christians do not offer sacrifices to the gods, he writes:

> First, as to our not offering sacrifices: the Fashioner and Father of the universe has no need of blood, nor of the savor of fat, nor of the fragrance of flowers or incense. . . . Instead the best sacrifice to Him is that we know who it was who stretched out the heavens, gathered them into a sphere, and fixed the earth as a center, who brought together water into the seas, and divided light from darkness, who adorned the sky with stars and made the earth to cause every seed to spring up, who made animals and fashioned men. But what to me are whole burnt offerings of which God has no need? Indeed, to offer sacrifices is necessary, but to offer an unbloody sacrifice, a spiritual worship.[31]

Christian eucharist raised the Jewish notion of thanksgiving to a new level. Christians continued to be thankful to the Maker for all their blessings, but now they included their gratitude and praise that God's Son was one of them and had saved them through his life, death, and resurrection. Their Creator had come in a form beyond their wildest imaginings, as a human person. The early Christians celebrated his coming and thanked God for their salvation in Christ. They believed that the risen Lord was uniquely present in eucharist, transforming their lives and continuing the creative and saving power of God in their world.

The Eucharist and Ecology

The eucharist has many levels of meaning, and a number of them can be readily connected to environmental concerns. The eucharistic symbols are rooted in matter: bread made from wheat, and wine made from grapes. The eucharist symbolizes concern with the flesh and blood of the Lord. In light of this, Christian orthodoxy rejects the disparagement of material things. It views matter as a gifted part of creation and is strongly committed to the reality of the incarnation and the sacramental principle. Jesus was truly human and comes to us through the things of creation. Eucharist thus is a thanksgiving for the gifts of creation, a time to worship and commune with the Creator God now manifested in the risen Lord. It is a meal wherein Christians share God's bounty and commemorate the starving and deprived of the world, who reach out for their rightful share.

Eucharist celebrates the renewal of the covenant that God made with the earth and all living things. A new covenant is now made with a "new creation" by Jesus, the firstborn. Hence, eucharist can be an occasion to deepen the covenant the faithful share with the earth, with others, and with the Creator. In the liturgy it is proclaimed that the Word of God became one with the earth and its people and died to restore all things. Here we worship the Lord of creation, who comes to the faithful in created things. As Fritsch observes: "The earth beckons and calls us to hear, smell, taste, see. Let's never go to a new place without tasting the land's fruit, root, herb, berry or nut. That's part of our Earth-communion, our openness, love, respect and compassion."[32] Eucharist celebrates this same union with creation and with the Lord.

Eucharist symbolizes the transformation of created elements into the risen Lord. Eucharist also signifies the transformation of the community as it repents its complicity in harming creation and examines its responsibilities toward the earth. The eucharistic celebration should be a time when the faithful resolve to live more simply, to share with those less fortunate, and to take action to sustain the earth.

This sacrament is also about the future. The ancient liturgies looked forward to the heavenly banquet and called for the Lord to come again. Eucharist can alert the community to the hopes and expectations of future generations. It can move the community to sacrifice for those to come. As McDonagh observes: "In partaking of the Eucharist we are challenged to live not merely justly but also in a way that will not injure the fruitfulness of the earth and impair the lives of creatures for all time. The Eucharistic dimension reminds us that in caring for the earth we must act as a community."[33]

The eucharist reflects on suffering in that it recalls Calvary. Thanksgiving is given God for blessing the tragic death of Jesus and giving it the power to bring forgiveness and salvation. Eucharist also lifts up the suffering of the world's needy and hungry and joins it to the Lord. Liturgy brings the agony of orphaned children, the anguish of those suffering without health care, the desolation of refugees, and the loneliness of the homeless to the table of the Lord and asks the community to bring nourishment to those in need. From the earliest "breaking of the bread" there has been concern at the table of the Lord for the poor and the outcast. In our own time we think of the countless people in the world suffering from malnutrition and hunger. As Sean McDonagh observes, "One cannot celebrate Eucharist today without being challenged to do something about this appalling reality."[34]

Since the time of Paul the eucharistic bread has symbolized unity, with one bread standing for one body. In today's world that must translate not only into parish unity but into a unified global perspective. The global issues of poverty, hunger, and environmental destruction need to be "on the table" of the Lord and addressed. As David Power points out, liturgical reform needs to address the postmodern disillusionment many in the community feel with progress: "Technological advances have not brought progress and prosperity to the world, and indeed have caused much environmental damage."[35] It is his conviction that liturgical reform must address this and other critical issues of our society.

The eucharist is about not only remembering the saving events of the past but also seeing how these events are operative in the present. Liturgy brings into the midst of the community the risen Lord, the Lord of creation, with all his compassion and self-giving. Teilhard understood this when he wrote his Mass on the World. Here are some selections from his "liturgy":

Since I have neither bread, nor wine, nor altar, I will raise myself beyond these symbols, up to the pure majesty of the real itself; I, your priest, will make the whole earth my altar and on it will offer you all the labors and sufferings of the world.

My paten and my chalice are the depths of a soul laid widely open to all the forces which in a moment will rise up from every corner of the earth and converge upon the Spirit.

And again one by one . . . I call before me that vast anonymous army of living humanity.

But the offering you really want . . . is nothing less than the growth of the world borne onwards in the stream of universal becoming.

Because, my God, though I lack the soul-zeal and the sublime integrity of your saints, I yet have received from you an overwhelming sympathy for all that stirs within the dark mass of matter; because I know myself to be irremediably less a child of heaven than a son of earth.

Do you now therefore, speaking through my lips, pronounce over this earthly travail your twofold efficacious word. . . . Over every living thing which is to spring up, to grow, to flower, to ripen during this day say again the words: This is my Body. And over every death force which waits in readiness to corrode, to wither, to cut down, speak again your commanding words which express the supreme mystery of faith: This is my Blood.[36]

If Teilhard were alive today, he would be aware of the urgency of environmental problems, and he would be passionately involved in solutions. Teilhard was sensitive to the human relationship with creation and realized how God could be experienced in our world. Most certainly his vision of eucharist is applicable to our present-day concerns about the environment.

A more contemporary environmentalist, Wendell Berry, also speaks of creation in eucharistic images and applies these images to ecology: "To live we must break the body and shed the blood of creation. When we do this lovingly, skillfully and reverently it is a sacrament. When we do it ignorantly, greedily, clumsily and destructively, it is a desecration. In such a desecration we condemn ourselves to spiritual moral loneliness and others to want."[37]

PENANCE

The sacrament of penance is concerned with repentance for sin, forgiveness, and reconciliation. Jesus called his disciples to imitate the love that he had shown all, yet he knew well the sinful side of humanity. Jesus called his disciples to repentance, which means to stop in one's tracks, turn around, and allow God to lead one in the right direction. He urged all who would listen to turn from their sinful ways and walk with him toward life eternal. Jesus' reason for such repentance was clear—the reign of God is at hand. In other words, the presence and power of the Creator brought the world into existence, sus-

tains it, and is its ultimate goal. To be allied with the Creator's reign of goodness, love, and creativity is the "narrow path" to salvation. It is the path of
reverence toward life and authentic stewardship. It is the way where love and
justice prevail, not destruction and oppression.

The heart of Jesus' mission was to call sinners to conversion. He was em-
phatic about the outcome if repentance is refused: "But I tell you, if you do
not repent, you will all perish" (Lk 13:5). Jesus was also adamant that conversion was not a turning to material things, self-righteousness, or even family
relationships as the ultimate reality. Authentic conversion is the setting aside
of all things and opening the heart to the divine mercy and love. In a proclamation that must have been disconcerting to those who felt spiritually secure,
Jesus said, "There is more joy in heaven over a sinner who repents than over
the ninety-nine just who have no need of repentance" (Lk 15:7). His commission to his disciples was to preach such repentance to the world. After the
resurrection he said to his disciples in Jerusalem, "Thus it is written that the
Messiah would suffer and rise from the dead on the third day and that repentance for the forgiveness of sins would be preached in his name to all the
nations" (Lk 24:47).

The celebration of the sacrament of penance should include conversion in
the area of environmental responsibilities. New directions are called for in
the way we treat nature, relate to other living things, and share resources. The
danger of "perishing" can take on a whole new meaning if we consider the
damage that has been done to our air, waterways, and other natural resources.
Humans have for centuries seen themselves as masters of the universe rather
than servants of the Creator. Material things have become idols for many,
and there has been a hardening of hearts toward the dispossessed. Attitudes
of use and abuse, accumulation, consumerism, and runaway debt are creating
social, political, and natural threats to life on the planet. These are now being
recognized as moral issues. As we shall see in chapter 10, an environmental
ethic is being developed that will address these issues.

Sin

The Hebrew scriptures describe the origin of sin in terms of the human
inclination to submit to temptation to disobey God's law. The biblical notion
of sin is the refusal to trust in God, a stiff-necked and proud refusal to submit
to God's truth. Sin is infidelity to friendship with the Creator. It brings alienation and violence into families and nations and cuts off humans from their
Maker. Sin is a rupture in the sacred covenant between the Creator and creation. It is exemplified in attempts on the part of humans to make material
things into idols or even themselves into gods. Sin is denounced throughout
the scriptures as the cause of social and natural disorders. Sin scorns Yahweh,

abandons the divine plan of love and creativity, disturbs the harmony of creation, and brings devastation and destruction to humankind.

The gospels portray Jesus as one sent to save sinners. John's gospel describes the mission of Jesus "to take away the sins of the world" (Jn 1:29). He comes as the "light" to those who hate the light; he comes to defeat the powers of evil in the world (Jn 3:20; 16:33). Jesus is seen often in the midst of those who are "possessed" by evil, those whose lives have somehow come under the power of evil.

The sacrament of penance is in part concerned with sin. It provides an occasion for disciples to examine their consciences with regard to evil. We have passed through an era when sins were lists of infractions against the commandments. Now sins of omission have been added to the examination of conscience, and much emphasis is given to sins against peace and justice. Our examination of conscience will now include sins against the earth, whether they are done out of ignorance, apathy, or malice. We will now have to consider corporate sin, whereby our industries pollute the earth and manufacture products that endanger the public health.

Creation is of a piece, and offense against any part of it is an offense against the Creator. Disobedience to God's law—infidelity to God's friendship—must include offenses against the planet and against any creatures who live here. As Hessel observes:

> Human activity affects the future of earth community, even though the planet's destiny is God's responsibility. On the one hand, the creation is being threatened with disintegration because of human sin and injustice, which result in oppression of both people and nature. We experience collective consequences that are understood biblically in terms of divine judgment and sorrow.[38]

Forgiveness

Jesus did not come to bring judgment but to extend the power of forgiveness. He said, "The Son of man has the power to forgive sins" (Mt 9:6). Jesus extended forgiveness to anyone open to it and turned his anger only on self-righteous hypocrites who thought they had no need of forgiveness. Jesus made it clear that even the most rejected were welcome to repent, seek forgiveness, and walk with him in friendship. He preached the amazing belief that God is so loving that he is open to forgive people their sins even before they repent!

Jesus' teaching about forgiveness and his amazing freedom in extending it to even the most wretched sinner was received by many as "good news." Jesus depicted the Creator as a gentle, loving Abba who, like the father of the prodigal son, would come running down the road to embrace a returning sinner. He showed God to be a shepherd who would go to any extreme to save one stray sheep, a God who turned no one away. In his parables Jesus compared God to a ruler who invited the unworthy to feasts and to an employer who lavished pay on those who had done little work in the vineyard.

Jesus' teaching on God's mercy was not acceptable to many of the religious teachers of his time. His opponents had a different view of the Creator and creation. Theirs was often a God of vengeance and punishment, who sent storms, plagues, disabilities, and poverty to those who sinned. Yahweh thus was more often feared for his punishments than praised for his gifts. Consequently, many felt cursed, rejected by their own religion, and even cast aside by God. Fear, anguish, guilt, and despair characterized the spiritual lives of such people. In the gospels one can hear this desperation in the cries of lepers, paralytics, the blind, and the mentally disturbed as they reached out to Jesus for mercy and healing. In Luke's Calvary scene we hear the plaintive request for salvation from the criminal next to Jesus on the cross.

Forgiveness certainly needs to be linked to the environmental crisis. We have learned a dramatic lesson about forgiveness from the Reconciliation Committee chaired by Archbishop Tutu in South Africa. Although horrible atrocities have been inflicted upon the black majority in the country for centuries, healing and forgiveness seem possible if the guilty persons come forward, confess their evils, and show signs of remorse. The truth in itself, even without justice, has the power to free people of hatred, guilt, and the desire for vengeance. Healing and forgiveness can come to our planet, if we all face the truth of how the earth has been damaged, leaving millions afflicted and impoverished. All churches and religions must confess their complicity and apathy with regard to this destruction and seek forgiveness. The same confession must be made on the part of nations, especially the wealthy nations, and they must resolve to repair the environment and to share its resources more equitably.

Reconciliation

The word *reconciliation* is often used for this sacrament. *Reconciliation* means "to walk with again," implying that there has been a break in relationship. Sin, as we mentioned earlier, is a severing of the covenant with God. We discussed in chapter 2 how important the covenant was in the biblical perspective, and how God generously made covenants with his people. There were singular covenants made with Noah, Abraham, and Moses. Yahweh's covenant with Noah was with the earth and every living creature; Abraham's was a promise that his descendants would be a chosen people; and Moses' was the covenant of the Law. In all of these covenants God offers irrevocable bonds between the divine and creation. The scriptures repeatedly recount the infidelity of God's people and yet reveal God's constant willingness to forgive them and accept them back.

There is an ongoing "newness" added to the covenant throughout the scripture. The prophet Jeremiah speaks of a new covenant with Israel: "But this is the covenant which I will make with the house of Israel after those days says the Lord: I will place my law within them, and write upon their hearts; I will be their God, and they shall be my people" (Jer 31:33). Ezekiel also speaks of a new covenant in which Yahweh promises to "give you a new heart and place a new spirit within you, taking from your bodies your stony hearts and giving you natural hearts. I will put my spirit within you and make you live by my statutes" (Ez 36:26-27).

Jesus also promises a new covenant "in his blood," and the early Christians viewed this new covenant as the fulfillment of all that had been promised by the Creator. In Christ, God made his people a royal priesthood and appointed them to be unique mediators between creation and the Creator. This privilege is extended to every nation, for all people are called to be reconciled with God.

Paul describes reconciliation as an action of God: "Everything comes from God who reconciles us to himself through Christ" (2 Cor 5:18). Through Christ, God has brought about a "new creation" and has given the disciples a "ministry of reconciliation" (2 Cor 5:17-18). Paul speaks of a universal reconciliation in Christ: "For in him the fullness was pleased to dwell, and through him to reconcile all things for him, making peace by the blood of his cross whether those on earth or those in heaven" (Col 1:19-20). Paul writes to the Romans that just as the material world once shared in the fall, it now shares in the resurrection:

> For creation awaits with eager expectation the revelation of the children of God; for creation was made subject to futility, not of its own accord but because of the one who subjected it, in hope that creation itself would be set free from slavery to corruption and share in the glorious freedom of the children of God. We know that all creation is groaning in labor pains even until now.   —Romans 8:19-22

In the sacrament of reconciliation sinners walk again with their Creator. In the 1920s a Carmelite, Fr. Xiberta, retrieved the notion that the sacrament of penance also reconciles us with the church, in that sin has social implications. That idea was developed more by theologians Karl Rahner and Edward Schillebeeckx, and it is now integral to our understanding of the sacrament of reconciliation. Reconciliation is now broadening to include the poor, who are oppressed by sin, as well as the earth and all living things that have been ravaged by human greed and violence.

The reconciliation sought from this sacrament, then, is not only with the Creator but also with creation. There is a need to be reconnected to the earth and to other living things—to respect and sustain the "web of life." This sacrament needs to be linked with the human alienation from nature, so that it can help people walk once again not only with God, the church, and their fellow human beings, but also with the earth. As McDonagh observes:

> The stance men and women take toward the earth is of a piece with their stance toward their fellow human being. . . . If, through a conversion of heart, they seek a harmonious relationship with nature and show respect, love and gratitude for all of creation, this will also spill over into their human affairs and transform their relationships.[39]

MARRIAGE

Marriage is an earthy institution, born out of human desires for intimacy and procreation as well as a range of cultural needs. From the beginning it was concerned with tribal identity, blood lines, inheritance, maintaining a stable home base, and raising offspring. For the Jews, marriage was a family matter; it was not associated with synagogue, temple, or priesthood. Like all created things, marriage was from the hand of God and therefore was deemed "good." It was a place where one could experience God's blessing and follow the divine command to increase and multiply "images of God" and participate in the creative process. The Hebrew scriptures often paralleled the covenant in marriage and the covenant God had made with the Israelites. From the beginning there was a sacramental dimension to marriage, in that it was viewed as a created reality in which the fidelity of God could be experienced. This is beautifully expressed in the Song of Songs, where love and sexuality are lyrically celebrated as gifts from the Creator. Many passages in this piece closely link the wonders of nature with human love and ascribe a sacramental quality to the union between a woman and a man.

In the gospels Jesus carries forth the positive Hebrew concept of marriage as an intimate union and takes the position that once God has joined a woman and man in such a bond their commitment has permanence. The New Testament highlights the dignity of marriage in such stories as the birth of Jesus, the finding in the Temple, and the first miracle performed at a wedding feast at Cana. The nativity stories accentuate the blessedness of conception and birth and the need for parents to be faithful to the will of the Creator, and they surround the extraordinary birth of Jesus with rich images from creation. It is clear in the gospels that Jesus' life was shaped by parents who were faithfully devoted to the will of the Creator.

Christian Ambiguity toward Marriage

Even though many early Christian writers struggled to defend these blessed elements of marriage against Gnostics and other sects that viewed the flesh and sex as evil, a certain ambiguity toward marriage and a preference for virginity persisted in the early church. The sexual excesses of the pagan world led many early Christian writers to perceive a lower law of lust within sexuality, so they cautioned their readers with regard to the use of sex. Augustine was the most influential of these patristic writers. He opposed the Manichean view that sex and marriage were darker realities, but he still had a limited—even at times negative—view of sex. Augustine taught that sex was tainted by the fall and thus concluded that only procreation could justify its use.

Negative views on sexuality and other factors held back the church from naming marriage as one of its sacraments for over a thousand years. Marriage was accepted as a good thing, especially needed for the procreation and education of children as well as a means of keeping concupiscence (the sinful desires of sex) in check. But church theologians struggled for centuries with the questions of how marriage could be a sacred sign of God's grace. Marriage was finally defined as one of the seven sacraments in 1439, but ambiguity toward the holiness of marriage and its status as an authentic vocation remained and still affects the church's attitudes toward sexuality and marriage today. Such ambiguity toward the physical and natural is certainly not helpful at present, when there is such need for families to value nature and to be concerned about its preservation.

New Directions

In modern times the theology of marriage has shown considerable development.[40] Vatican II placed marital love at the center of marriage and recognized that sex is important for the nurturing of marital love as well as for procreating. The council stressed the sacramentality of marriage and spoke of married life in terms of partnership, mutuality, and vocation. John Paul II has carried forth this positive development and has pointed out that marriage is a living sign of the creative love to which all humans are called. Thus married couples are able to express authentic love in sexual relations, and the children of such unions become the incarnation or embodiment of the mutual love of the spouses. Obviously, such constructive views about creative love can be easily carried over into a deeper appreciation of creation as a whole.

Today's theology of marriage acknowledges that the bride and groom are indeed the ministers of the sacrament, the ones who in their exchange of vows seal a sacred covenant. The marriage covenant is recognized as a living sign of God's covenant with all of creation. As Walter Kasper has observed:

"Marriage, then, is the grammar that God uses to express his love and faithfulness."[41] The marital union also can be a dynamic symbol of the presence and power of Jesus Christ in the world. The married couple becomes a new creation, a unique union in which the Lord's love can be revealed in many ways. Marriage then becomes a "school" that can teach those within it about the love of God for all things. It becomes a context in which people can learn to value all life and to revere and preserve the earth from which life comes and returns. The family can be a creative world where new love comes forth and is nurtured; it can indeed be a metaphor for the large creative processes within all of creation. It is this kind of vision of marriage and family that is needed to sustain the environmental movement and to motivate people to pass a better world on to future generations.

Sacramental marriage is also a "place" where people choose to join their faith in the Lord and work out their salvation together. Marriage is a relationship in which people are uniquely faced with the realities of sin, forgiveness, and reconciliation. It is a context for singularly experiencing the saving graces of the Lord, without which one cannot make the sacrifices, overcome the challenges, or survive the setbacks and losses so common in marriage. It is within this sacrament that one can learn of God's saving will for all things and experience the unfailing power of God, which is extended to all of creation. Those who experience marriage and family in such a fashion can be better disposed to reverence all life and to participate actively in bringing reconciliation and salvation to the earth.

The growing appreciation for both the creative and the nurturing values of sex in marriage among Christians also has implications for better appreciation of nature. Spouses who have learned to be comfortable with their bodies, with sex, with the physical closeness of their children can more easily recognize the value of nature. Most who have given birth or held a newborn know in a special way what the words *new creation* mean. It is a small step from the intimate experiences of married life to an appreciation of all living things and of the natural world. The sacramental dimension of marriage can help Christians better appreciate their call to be co-creators and nurturers of living things. As Evelyn and James Whitehead put it: "To be married in the Lord is to have eyes to come to a deeper meaning and presence in our love. It is also to respond to this presence–a presence which calls us, together, beyond 'just ourselves,' into an awareness of our involvement in the work of God in the world. As believers, we participate in the mission of Jesus."[42]

The newer notions of partnership, friendship, and equality now included in the discussion of marriage can also be helpful in linking marriage with concern for nature. As we have seen throughout our discussion, the awareness of interrelatedness and interdependence among all things is essential for the restoration and preservation of the environment. It is in family that one can learn to respect the value of others and to build and sustain relationships. Connectedness and intimacy are essential elements in healthy marriages and families, and coming to understand the dynamics of achieving these elements can help one relate not only to people outside the home but to other living things and to the earth itself. Jesus taught that the reign of God was at hand and within all things. Christian marriage should be an experience of the reign of God in one's loved ones as well as in the larger world outside the home.

The family has been called the *domestic church,* meaning that the family is a church in miniature, where the gospel life dedicated to love and justice can be lived out daily. The family can be a community where the "Priestly people" pray together, celebrate, and serve one another and the larger world. Most certainly it can be a place where people learn appreciation of the beauty and integrity of nature, a sensitivity to all living things, and how to work for a better environment. In the family children can learn to avoid waste, resist consumerism, and share with others. Here the basic values of simple living can be learned by all the members of the family. And, without a doubt, families can become powerful advocates for a sustained environment.

It is in the intimacy of marriage that the discussion of family planning must take place. Education, increased resources, broader employment opportunities, and better health care can all be factors in helping couples decide upon the size of their families. It is obvious that the growing population has been and will remain a major factor in the demand for food and resources. This is an area that urgently needs to be addressed, an area in which the churches could play a significant role in assisting couples in responsible family planning.

Many families who are oppressed, impoverished, without resources, and forced to live in degraded environments are adapting the teaching of liberation theology to work toward freedom for themselves. Women who experience abuse in the home often see parallels with the abuse of the nature around them. They are vigorously opposing the subjugation of themselves and the environment by patriarchal structures, and they are calling for equality in the family, in society, and in the churches. These women cry out for clean water for their families, nourishing food, and a healthy place to live.

SUMMARY

The sacramental principle is central to the understanding of sacred symbols and rituals. This principle, which holds that God's presence and power can be celebrated and experienced through natural symbols, can be connected easily with the environmental crisis today. In sacraments the faithful encounter God in the person of Jesus Christ and are thus put into an intimate union with the Creator of all things. Sacraments can help the faithful come to an appreciation of the integrity and beauty of all things and can empower them to work for the betterment of creation. Each sacrament in its own way has the power to enable Christians to come into closer contact both with God and with the natural world. Each sacramental celebration can bond individuals and communities with the earth and the earth's poor, gracing them to be of service in Christ's name

6.

The Churches Speak Out

My heart is heavy these days. My little one, Gitanjali, is quite ill and we have no way to get medicine or care for him. We think it is the water in this area that has made him feverish and weak.

Each morning at sunrise I go with the other women with our brass pots balanced on our heads to try to get water from the Nandira River. It used to be a beautiful river and gave us fresh water and fish each day and a place to wash our clothes. Now the river is gray, covered with a thick coat of ash. We have to dig holes in the beach and hope to get some decent water. There are no longer fish in the river. All this comes from the new coal-fired power plant upstream. It has ruined our river and our lives with its toxic waste. We have tried to protest but the police beat us with canes and drove us away. We are not sure where to turn.

—Calemba Sivarramurti, Orissa, India

The Christian churches are gradually awakening to the urgency of the environmental crisis and are starting to search their beliefs and values for solutions. The churches are also beginning to acknowledge their own complicity in this crisis. As the Conference of European Churches stated in 1995:

> Although many churches have recently taken a clear stand on the ecological crisis, we are aware that the churches have generally been slow in responding to the threats to the environment. . . . Even today many churches do not recognize the urgency of a Christian response to the dangers and risks humanity faces. . . . Christians should proclaim a sustainable lifestyle with great humility in the awareness that for a long time they themselves have been part of the predominant destructive way of living. As we face the present ecological crisis we realize that we have sinned.[1]

Since this awakening on the part of the churches, a number of significant documents have been issued that provide windows into recent Christian concerns about the environment. We have selected key ideas and hope to offer here a panoramic overview of these statements. These wide-ranging documents from churches of different faiths and from places around the globe offer a snapshot of many ecological problems specific to each region as well as a global picture of the crisis. In addition, one gains from these documents a glimpse of the efforts the churches are making to reclaim and revise biblical teachings, doctrines, and moral values that are applicable to the environmental crisis. These statements reflect the concerns the churches have about the millions whose oppression comes from the misuse of the earth and its resources. They provide "seeds of contemplation" that hopefully will flourish and provide Christians with the vision and the motivation to be more active players in the movement to sustain the environment.

The documents considered here represent a broad range of churches. We will look at statements from the Vatican as well as from Catholic bishops' conferences from both first-world and third-world countries. We will also consider messages written by Evangelicals and Protestants, as well as documents from large ecumenical organizations, such as the World Council of Churches and the Conference of European Churches.

JOHN PAUL II

Although John Paul addressed environmental issues briefly in some of his addresses and encyclicals, his first substantial statement on ecology, *The Ecological Crisis: A Common Responsibility*, did not appear until 1990, in his message for the World Peace Day.[2] John Paul begins his historic message by pointing out that a lack of respect for nature should be added to the arms race, local wars, and injustices as a threat to world peace. He warns that the ecological situation today surrounds us with a sense of danger and insecurity, and that it is a "seedbed" for selfishness, dishonesty, and disregard for others.

The document expresses alarm at the widespread destruction of the environment and warns that we cannot continue to use our resources irresponsibly. The pontiff is encouraged by the newly emerging ecological awareness and urges a deepening of this consciousness, especially because ecology is so closely related to world peace.

The pope cites biblical teachings on creation and shows how these are applicable to ecology. He recalls that creation has been deemed "good" by the Creator and has been entrusted to humans. Humans are uniquely made in the image of God among creatures and are related to all of creation. Hence the dominion that humans have over the earth is to be carried out by them with wisdom and love rather than abuse or manipulation. John Paul is clear that it is sinful to destroy the harmony of God's plan and cause alienation between humans and the earth. At the same time he stresses the Christian belief that evil will not prevail; ultimately the liberation for which all creation awaits will come about. For Christians, it is the death and resurrection of Christ that reconcile all of creation with the Father and make all things new.

John Paul makes it clear that human behavior has a definite impact on creation and that the destruction of the environment is only one aspect of a broader moral crisis. This moral crisis includes a lack of discrimination in scientific and technological advances, especially in industry and agriculture. The breakdown in morals also involves a lack of respect for life, whether human, animal, or plant. The pope insists that respect for life is the ultimate norm for progress and an essential factor in the building of a peaceful society.

The pontiff suggests specific solutions for today's environmental crises: a respect for the order and harmony of the cosmos; elimination of the glaring inequities in sharing resources brought on by greed; and a coordinated global approach to ecology with each state accepting its own responsibilities. Solutions also demand a new solidarity among the industrialized world and developing nations. There is an urgency to addressing the problems of widespread poverty, unjust land distribution, the dislocation of peoples, and indebted countries being forced to pillage their environments in order to pay their debts. The menace of war, both global and local, is also addressed by the pontiff, and he warns that the use of chemical, bacterial, and biological weapons can devastate human life and all other aspects of the environment.

The pope also urges people to value simplicity and moderation in their lifestyles. He promotes a widespread educational effort in ecological responsibility, especially in the churches and in families. People are challenged to appreciate the aesthetic value of nature, especially in the growing development of urban areas.

The message ends with a plea that everyone responsibly face the ecological crisis, not only for the sake of this present generation but for generations to come. Those who do not have religious beliefs are urged to act out of a sense of the common good, and people of faith are asked to act out of their belief in creation. All Christians are invited by the pontiff to act in cooperation with other churches and religions, and Catholics in particular are reminded of their serious obligation to care for creation, motivated by their belief in God the Creator and Christ the redeemer.

Francis of Assisi is cited as the patron of those who promote ecology. He is one who stands out as an example of love of creation and devotion to peace. The pope is hopeful that Francis can inspire people to be one with all of creation and to take care of all things, especially our human sisters and brothers.

This document is a good beginning for consideration of the environmental crisis. It sketches out the problems and points out where Catholic teaching might be connected with the environment, particularly through creation theology and ethics. It is significant that the environmental crisis is recognized as a breakdown in morality, and that conversion and a moral renewal are needed to solve this crisis. Especially valuable is the insight that the environmental crisis is closely related to issues of poverty, justice, and world peace. The document will be foundational for future studies of ecology.

One might hope that as future church documents are developed, more time will be given to specific environmental problems around the globe. The church will only gain credibility with the world community if it is seen to grasp clearly the scientific, social, and political dimensions of ecology. Future teachings will also have to include broader development of scriptural and doctrinal perspectives, using a wider range of contemporary biblical scholars and theologians as resources. The incorporation of contemporary liberation and feminist views will also be crucial in the development of future documents.

The church with all its members must eventually confess its past apathy toward the environment and also its complicity in much of the degradation of the earth and its creatures. Before there can be reconciliation among peoples and between people and the earth, there must be confession of sin and a request for forgiveness. As we have seen in the recent process of reconciliation in South Africa, only when people admit their sins and ask forgiveness of those offended can true healing and reconciliation come about.

THE U.S. BISHOPS

The bishops of the United States issued their "beginning reflections" in a statement on ecology in 1991.[3] They begin by echoing Vatican II's call to read the "signs of the times" in order to see what God is calling us to do. They stress that the environmental crisis, both local and global, is a serious moral challenge that Catholics must both come to understand and work to solve.

The bishops see environmental blight to be a justice question facing the whole human race, with profound implications for the poor and powerless, who suffer the most from abuses of the environment. They call for government policies for sustaining natural systems and for the establishment of a world economy that will include the hundreds of millions of poor around the globe.

The U.S. prelates note that the church community is gaining a new awareness of how the faith relates to environmental problems, and that research into many other ethical and religious dimensions of ecology is increasing. They acknowledge the efforts of other Christian churches and faiths toward ecology. They accept a responsibility to work with these churches, and indeed all religions, to shape a new ethic for care of the earth and to develop a just and sustainable economy in this country.

The Biblical Vision

The U.S. bishops use traditional arguments from the Hebrew scriptures for establishing a Christian responsibility toward the environment. They point out that creation is good, and that though creation belongs to the Lord, it has been offered as gift to all creatures with whom God shares a covenant. The Hebrew prophetic tradition is cited to show how humanity's sinfulness has brought about estrangement between humans and nature, and how injustice to the earth brings judgment to the people.

Jesus had a countryman's understanding of the land, which enabled him to use natural images to demonstrate God's loving and saving care. The bishops demonstrate that the new covenant, wherein Jesus restores harmony between humans and nature and renews the earth, is relevant to ecology. They also recall Jesus' proclamation of a Jubilee in which all creation would be liberated.

Catholic Social Teaching

The bishops search the church's social teaching for themes applicable to environmental issues. They begin by pointing to the Christian belief that God dwells within the universe, the earth, and all people. This awareness of God's presence has been foundational in the church's teaching on human dignity and is now applicable to teaching the dignity of all creation. Since all life somehow reflects divinity and enjoys a covenant with the Creator, every creature has value in itself and is worthy of respect and care. This recognition of the integrity of all things is crucial in forming an environmental theology.

The Common Good

The church's social teaching on the common good is central to the development of an environmental ethic. The American bishops recall John XXIII's prophetic emphasis on global interdependence in the 1960s and point out that ecological issues should be added to the concerns of today's community of nations. They also echo John Paul II's frequent emphasis on the common good, indicating that an environmental ethic should begin with concern for the common good and then move toward a sense of solidarity with others, as well as a commitment to sharing, sacrifice, and equitable and sustainable development.

The U.S. bishops point out that although God intends the earth's resources to be for all, a great many people today are deprived of the means of livelihood. Economic systems need to be more equitable, with significantly more concern given to the poor, especially the urban poor and indigenous people. The bishops' concern for workers is evident when they observe that solutions to environmental problems are often unfairly made at the expense of workers' rights.

These social teachings are clearly in opposition to excessive accumulation and consumption. Applying these teachings to ecology, the bishops call for moderation, even austerity in the use of resources; a balanced view of progress; reduction of use of resources by affluent nations; and avoidance of development for its own sake.

Consumption and Population

The bishops oppose efforts by first-world countries to attribute the lack of resources in developing countries to growing populations. They also disapprove of programs that try to curb third-world births rather than restrain the consumerism of the developed world. The bishops maintain that the payment of foreign debt is a more serious cause of poverty and degradation of land than population growth is. They point out that the key factors in dealing with population problems are the equitable distribution of resources, prenatal care, education, good nutrition, and health care.

While the bishops acknowledge that rapid population growth is related to environmental depletion, they insist that the population issues be kept within the larger context of the church's teachings on human life, just development, care for the environment, and respect for married couples' right to decide voluntarily the number and spacing of their children. The bishops oppose coercive methods of population control or incentive programs that oppose cultural or religious norms and church teaching. They encourage the use of natural family planning as well as responsible parenting, and they insist that all life be protected, including that of the unborn, the elderly, and the disabled. The bishops are convinced that environmental problems are best dealt with in the context of other peace and justice issues, such as war and just economic systems.

Theological and Pastoral Concerns

The prelates assert that belief in the goodness of the natural world and in God's presence and power in created things has been the foundation of the church's sacramental and mystical traditions. At the same time, they point out that created things have limits. They are concerned that the environmental movement will become too earth-centered, and even raise the earth to be an ultimate object of devotion. (It seems here that they are wary of a return to some of the beliefs of indigenous or so-called pagan religions.)

God's Stewards and Co-creators

The American bishops warn that the environmental crisis has brought the world community to a crossroads and calls it to conversion. Besides the central Christian virtue of love for all things, there is a need for new attitudes and virtues, such as prudence, humility and temperance. There has to be a recognition of sins against the environment and a desire for forgiveness and reconciliation. The bishops recognize that saving the planet will demand long and sometimes sacrificial commitment. They express their hopes that public concern for the environment will grow and that lifestyles will change accordingly.

The prelates encourage new actions in the areas of ecology: an increase in the scientific study of the environment; more emphasis on such issues in education in schools and parishes; intense study by theologians; efforts by business leaders; and new efforts to change lifestyle. They also encourage the use of environmental themes in worship and prayers. They call upon environmental advocates to connect peace and justice with ecology.

The American bishops rightly link the environmental crisis with peace and justice and have properly begun to integrate social teaching with these issues. They are in sympathy with the poor and recognize over-consumption and the imposition of foreign debt as major factors of both poverty and environmental abuse.

Hopefully, future documents will make more extensive use of available scientific and theological expertise, as in the two historic documents on nuclear arms and the American economy. The 1991 document on ecology reflects the modern church's comfort with modern science and technology, but it does not reflect extensive consultation in these areas; the arguments often seem to be too "in house" or ecclesiastical.

Future statements might also include the history of the oppression of the Native Americans and their land, accounts of other major periods of environmental devastation in this country, and more specifics on the environmental crisis in the United States today. They will need to review the church's own complicity in the past and present environmental abuse and to resolve to be more part of the solution than the problem.

The bishops place the population question rightly in the context of larger issues. However, the absolute position to which they are bound with regard to artificial birth control makes dialogue with other churches and organizations extremely difficult. Is it possible that the questions surrounding the official teaching on birth control can be once again opened for discussion, as they were in the 1960s? Only then can productive dialogue on population issues go on among the churches and among the peoples of developing nations.

VOICES FROM APPALACHIA

One of the most extraordinary documents on religion and the environment has come from the Catholic mountain churches in Appalachia.[4] Appalachia includes parts of Georgia, Ohio, New York, the Carolinas, Kentucky, Pennsylvania, Mississippi, West Virginia, Maryland, Alabama, Tennessee, and Virginia. The purpose of the document was to create and defend sustainable communities; that is, communities where people and the rest of nature live together in harmony and do not rob future generations. Much of the Appalachian region has been badly scarred by the industrial and mining era. Now that this era is ending, the new technological period threatens the area with large-scale unemployment, the death of small businesses, the clear-cutting of forests, strip mining, dumping out-of-state garbage including radioactive materials, and the warehousing of prisoners. The document expresses the fear that all this could reduce Appalachia to a wasteland.

In this "culture of death" the people remain hopeful and are determined to build a sustainable future. They envision a life where their forests will once again rise up like "sacred cathedrals" and be the holy dwelling place of abundant life-forms. They hope to preserve their life-giving aquifers and keep them filled with pure water. They want to be God's co-creators and live in creative communion with land and forest and water and air, indeed with all earth's holy creatures.

The writers use the phrase also used by the American bishops—"the web of life"; they see that the ecological crisis involves not only nature but also people, especially the poor. Both nature and people are victims of the consumer society and are wasted by it. This text proposes a vision wherein all are united in a "single and precious ecosystem" created by God in whom "we live and move and have our being" (Acts 17:28).

The authors point to the past, when native peoples as well as settlers loved the hills and hollows, cherished the clean streams and air, cared for each other, and worshiped the God of creation. They turn to the humble people to teach them these lessons once again. The theology here is one of liberation, a "listening" theology that gives ear to the people, especially the poor. It is a theology "from below," which chooses life rather than death. This theology is a faith seeking understanding, a deep and sincere reflection on the land and its people, the teachings of the Bible and church, and the present call of the Spirit.

The Land and Its People

The writers proclaim their belief that all things come from God and are expressions and revelations of God's word. For them, all nature speaks of

God's beauty and goodness and reveals God's love. The mountain ridges and valleys, the forests, soil, rivers, and all the plants and animals show God's glory and tell of God's presence. Humans, then, are not viewed as superior but as "special" because they are images of God, called to care lovingly for the precious earth. These are people who are deeply in touch with nature, descendants of the great mountain people who lived freely and simply, close to land and kin.

The writers lament the devastation of the peaceful mountain lifestyle by the industrial age of the late 1800s. Giant corporations came in for lumber and coal and in the process ravaged the land. Cheap outside labor was brought in and many had to leave the area to find employment in crowded urban areas. Those who stayed and found jobs in the factories and mines were overworked, underpaid, and forced to work in dangerous and unhealthy conditions.

Now a new post-industrial period is developing. An aging community, large-scale unemployment, and highly mechanized removal of natural resources threaten the vast Appalachian area. These rural Americans fear that their area will become a social and natural dumping ground, exploited by outside forces. There are numerous concerns in the text, including the lack of jobs, violence, and the contamination of the land and water and air. The Appalachian people have come to a crossroads. One path leads to devastation, the other to building a sustainable community. The authors clearly have chosen the latter path, and they turn to the Word of God for guidance in their commitment.

The Theological Framework

The theological framework in this document is well integrated. It links the two processes of creation and redemption, and it relates both to Jesus Christ through whom all things were created and through whom the world is saved (Jn 1:3-10). The authors remind their people that they are earth creatures, and that God has made a covenant with the earth and all living things. Sin is discussed as an attack on creation. This attack is both social and ecological; it is brought against the poor as well as the earth. Nonetheless, the authors place their hope in the reconciliation offered in Jesus Christ, who is the revelation of God's healing will (Jn 3:16). They call all Christians to work for justice, peace, and the integrity of creation.

The Principles of Catholic Social Teaching

Catholic social teaching is used in this text as an effective and rich resource for developing sustainable communities. The writers offer a valuable list of the main principles of this social teaching and show how they are connected with ecology.

One: All people have human dignity by virtue of being images of God and are called to be co-creators.

Two: Each member of the human community needs to recognize the value of the common good. Humans are linked with each other as well as with the rest of creation. Jesus taught that salvation depends on how we treat others, especially the needy (Mt 25:37-40).

Human dignity and community are based on spiritual values. These values challenge both socialism and capitalism, which are both based on materialism and economic determinism.

Three: Individualistic competition should not undermine community solidarity or individual creativity. Economies, then, must be rooted in the plan of God and the web of life and designed to sustain this web.

Four: The principle of subsidiarity demands that larger organizations should help smaller ones rather than undermine them. This applies to multinational corporations and political bureaucracies, which have so often victimized Appalachia.

Five: Everyone has the right to own property, but private property also has to serve the community. Ultimately creation belongs to God, so everyone has the right to created goods.

Six: The natural order of creation or web of life includes both natural and social ecology. If we fail to care for the earth, it rebels against us. Moreover, the undermining of nature and of the poor is a rejection of God's will. Materialism is deep within the ecological crisis. Materialism reveres things rather than creation, and it abuses nature. Jesus himself taught against such idolatry, stating that we cannot serve God and mammon (Lk 16:13).

Seven: The principle of sustainability requires that we replace what we take out of the earth, lest we steal from our children and destroy ourselves.

Eight: The government must serve the common good and support human dignity, community, and the entire web of life.[5]

The Call of the Spirit

The Appalachian churches believe that at this time the Spirit of God calls them to find new ways to live together. They look for creative options to conserve, live more simply, and develop themselves spiritually so that they can create sustainable communities. The churches recommend that more emphasis be placed on local economies and on home-based businesses, many of which can be run by women. They promote the use of methods of agriculture that protect both humans and nature. They call for the preservation of forests and for the halting of clear-cutting and other destructive practices. The authors also seek just and legal land reform, whereby the local people could own their land for housing and farming. Technologies are sought that will serve the human community and care for ecosystems. Especially precious to the mountain people is the fostering of local artists, craft people, storytellers, and historians. Kin is also most important in Appalachia, so the churches point out that families need to be nourished as well as protected from hardship, domestic violence, and addictions. The healing of families and the empowerment of women, the development of men's spirituality, and the support of creative marriages are also strongly encouraged.

There is a vivid awareness here that our churches need to become centers of regeneration and creativity. Churches are encouraged to experiment with new technology in energy, new farming methods, and creative financing; and to become centers of communication, places where basic Christian communities flourish, and settings for prayer, scripture reading, and catechesis. Such church communities can be effective evangelizers for a sustainable world.

This Appalachian document is extraordinary and could well be the model for documents from other areas. It reflects people deeply in touch with their history and environment. These are men and women who have experienced hard times and yet remain hopeful that they can overcome adversity and rebuild their beloved mountain forests and rivers. These are disciples who are filled with the Spirit and committed to gospel living, people uniquely linked with nature and longing for the inner conversion so needed to sustain the earth.

The theological approach here is a fine example of how liberation views can be adapted to different cultures. There is much theology "from below," much "listening" to the experience and the faith of the folks. The biblical and doctrinal positions are linked with life and not merely discussed abstractly. The social teachings of the church are applied concretely and lived out. There is also clear evidence that feminine voices have been listened to in the process of developing this document.

THE BISHOPS OF NORTHERN ITALY

The Italian bishops strongly support the human right to live in an environment suitable for health and well-being.[6] They are distressed by the acuteness of the present ecological crisis and are convinced that this crisis must be of universal concern. They call for theological reflection, a sensitivity on the part of the church, and dedicated pastoral activity.

The document speaks with a certain air of sophistication, avoiding religious platitudes. The bishops realize that the environmental situation calls for a reevaluation of the very structures of Western civilization, a critique of science, and a search for alternate ways of living. They offer no simple solutions. The bishops have a single goal: conscience formation in the area of ecology.

They propose that such formation integrate a thorough knowledge of environmental issues with a consistent understanding of the Christian faith tradition:

> The ecological problem does not require immediate political solutions. Neither are theological theses necessary on the relationship between man and nature. What is needed is to strengthen the conscience of Christians to develop personal reflection, while at the same time maintaining a historically and socially grounded understanding of our region, and maintaining a consistent tradition of faith.[7]

A Threatened Environment—Symptoms and Causes

The bishops attempt to analyze the ecological situation, especially in northern Italy. They point to a common but false belief that natural resources are unlimited and point out how arrogantly nature is exploited in their area. Such exploitation has brought threats of impoverishment, depletion of resources and the loss of numerous species. The pollution problems in their part of Italy are many. The rivers that border Lombardy, beginning with the Po, are degraded, largely by growing demands for agricultural, industrial, and energy production. Increased population, especially through growing immigration, has intensified the need for food and housing and has generated new business and increased traffic. All of these factors translate into greater pollution.

The bishops see that the central question in ecology today is this: How can human activity alter ecological balances and yet still guarantee the survival of the biosphere and the resources essential for human life? They maintain that the crisis is not simply over the use of resources but is also a crisis of spiritual values. Our culture has become materialistic and has seriously neglected the spiritual dimension of life.

Scriptural Views

The Italian bishops develop a Christian view of nature from the Bible. They contrast the greatness of creation expressed in the psalms with the notion in Genesis that the earth is cursed. They point out that technology has the same ambiguity–it can bring great benefits and yet can also be destructive.

The bishops ask rhetorically: "Is the world a God-given dwelling place or just an inventory of material things to use?" For an answer they look to the Sermon on the Mount, which teaches that the concern for food and the body should not be placed over the concern for life. Jesus taught that worry about material things brings anxiety, stress, and unending toil, thus concern for the kingdom and its righteousness is of greater importance. He taught that if we seek first the kingdom, we will receive a way to take care of food and clothing that is in accord with the transcendence of life and respect for all things. The prelates attempt to put material wealth in its proper context: "The so-called material wealth must be recognized as real wealth only on the condition that it becomes for man's conscience a symbol and token of hoped for spiritual wealth."[8]

The bishops point out that dominion easily can be misunderstood. For them, "dominion" should be translated as "stewardship," whereby we are blessed to harvest and share our food. Dominion, they insist, does not give a license to be scientific and technological masters of our world. Rather, dominion proposes an ethical dimension through which we live in relationship with nature. Stewardship consists in the promise of salvation that is inscribed in the earth. God entrusts us with the earth, and stewardship must be carried out according to the laws of nature and morality.

Ethics and Development

The prelates are refreshing in their realism. They understand that we should not go to either of two extremes: a romantic return to nature, or a sweeping condemnation of progress. They call their people to search deeply for the reasons we are in peril and ask them to see the environmental situation as an extremely complex crisis of conscience and of moral values.

Any approach to development, according to the Italian bishops, must be "ethically qualified." There must be respect for our natural environment, and all our advances must be evaluated not only with economic criteria but also with the risks to the environment in mind. The document stresses the importance of moderation, a virtue that considers the common good, the value of sharing, and the importance of passing on a healthy earth to future generations. Finally, the bishops recommend that attention be given to quality of life, especially in issues that involve growth in urban development, industrialization, and new forms of energy.

Listen to the Earth

The prelates have an appreciation for their natural surroundings as well as the advancement of civilization. They challenge their people to discover ways to keep a balance whereby nature is preserved and yet civilization can still advance. They call upon their people to listen to the earth, so that they can discover the delicate balances in nature and act responsibly to preserve these balances. Listening to the earth puts us in touch with a voice that reechoes the Word of God. It follows, then, that how we treat the earth affects both how the earth relates to us and how we relate to God. To demonstrate this, the bishops quote the Book of Wisdom, "For creation, serving you who made it, exerts itself to punish the unrighteous, and in kindness relaxes on behalf of those who trust in you" (Wis 16:24).

This document is straightforward in its approach, and it avoids the stock biblical arguments and simplistic solutions that have become so common in literature on ecology and religion. The bishops recognize the complexity of the environmental crisis and attempt no easy answers. Their accent on the need for conscience formation and their suggestions for the ethical values needed to balance development and the preservation of nature are useful.

The bishops' argument for good stewardship has its limitations, however, for stewardship is still a type of dominion and does not sufficiently recognize the unique integrity of each thing. One hopes that future documents will be more global in perspective and more sensitive to the plight of the poor both in Italy and throughout the world. It would also be useful for these bishops to formulate specific political strategies to move their government toward environmental reform.

THE GUATEMALAN BISHOPS

The Guatemalan bishops point to the desperate "cry for land" from millions of their people.[9] They speak for "people of corn," poor farmers who were expelled from the land and are now strangers in a place that belonged to them for thousands of years. The bishops strongly urge that there be land reform in their country.

The bishops point to the dehumanizing poverty of the peasants and to the glaring inequities in their country. The majority of the land is in the hands of a privileged few, who live luxuriously, while the poor have little and work very hard just to feed their families. The bishops condemn such margination as sinful; they are convinced that such dispossession of the land is the nucleus of the social problems in Guatemala.

They review the history of the land problem, which goes back to colonial times, when large land grants were given to colonials by the Spanish crown, which exploited an unpaid Indian labor force. Even after independence the laws left the land in the hands of a few. In 1871 coffee production discouraged communal lands and gave control to a powerful class of exporters. A revolutionary government in 1950-54 began a land reform, but that was abruptly ended after just a few years.

Now the exporters own huge, fertile tracts of land and bring in enormous profits, while the *campesinos* barely subsist on mini-plots where they grow only corn and beans. Often these workers are exploited by those who own the land. They have neither credit for loans nor the technology needed to sustain the land. Bad weather can bring them to the brink of starvation. The *campesinos* are forced to live with few resources, poor education, unsanitary conditions, and poor housing. Many have only rags to wear and are often ridiculed and exploited as tourist attractions. Tiny children are sent to work in the fields, and thousands of workers are transported to coastal plantations in trucks.

The bishops strongly state that their national constitution on equality is dishonored by these situations. They courageously review some of the abuses. Public funds are not available for the *campesinos,* even though they pay their taxes, do obligatory military service, and work on Civil Defense patrols. The peasants are an exploited work force, laboring in unhealthy conditions for small pay. Some officials want to make the plight of the poor even worse by eradicating the older traditions that allow people to work on the plantation where their family worked for generations. Those who ask that these rights be honored are driven off, sometimes by armed violence, and other work crews are brought in in their place. The dispossessed peasants are forced to flee to urban areas where they live in misery and often lose everything, even their faith. Those who stay in the rural areas live in tense and desperate conditions.

The bishops, perhaps fearing reprisals against their people, are reluctant to point an accusing finger at particular individuals or even at groups of agitators or leaders. They prefer to say that the social situation is to blame for all the misery. Whatever the cause, they believe that the cry of the poor is legitimate, and that, if it is not heeded, the situation could turn violent.

The prelates acknowledge that many Indians already have been killed for their resistance. They point out that as the peasants become more aware of their rights, they are brutally repressed. Again, perhaps fearing reprisals, the bishops do not expose the magnitude of atrocities that have been thrust upon the poor, especially the indigenous poor in Guatemala. Nor do they make mention of the complicity in all of this by the United States, which has provided enormous funds to the repressive governments of Guatemala for many years. Perhaps in the present situation, when reform has been promised and when many of those who have lived in exile for so long are returning, the bishops will be able to get redress for the atrocities which have been done to their people for so many years.

A Theology of Land Ownership

The Guatemalan bishops attempt to build a theology of land ownership by retrieving the Hebrew belief that the Creator gave humans the earth for their home. Humans belong to the earth, and the earth belongs to them because God charged the first people with tilling and caring for the earth. Reflecting an agrarian perspective, the bishops observe that "farmwork appears as the essential task defining and situating the human person in the world and before God."[10] They point to the Bible, where the fruits of labor bring joy and blessing. The bishops recall the prophets' cry against those who hoarded the land, wrongly coveted the land of another, and paid unjust wages.

The prelates point to Jesus Christ and his teaching as the way to environmental reform. Jesus is described as a man of poverty who came to bring the good news to the poor. He taught that wealth is not of great significance and can be a serious obstacle to entering the reign of God. The document lays the foundation for linking Christology with ecology. The incarnation gives a new dignity to creation, in that the Word through whom all things were created became flesh in Jesus. Jesus is the firstborn of the new creation, and his redeeming work reconciled "everything on earth and in the heavens" (Col 1:15-20). This is the fulfillment looked forward to in the Book of Revelation: "At that time there will be a new heaven and a new earth where there shall be no death nor tears, nor cries nor fatigue, because the old world shall have passed away" (Rv 21:1-4).

The Fathers and the Magisterium

The Guatemalan bishops build their case for the right to own property from the church's tradition on social justice. They point out that the right to property is not an absolute right, and that ownership for some has exceeded personal needs while others lack the essentials for living. The bishops also cite the teaching of Vatican II that God has destined the earth for the use of all human beings.[11] They also cite some interesting patristic resources. Ambrose commented that when we give goods to the poor we are only giving them what belongs to them, because the things of the earth belong to everyone. John Chrysostom said that God did not make some people rich and others poor. The earth belongs to the Lord, and its fruits should be available to all.

John Paul II's teachings on sharing resources are also relevant. In Cuilapan, Mexico, the pope pointed out that it is unjust for the rich to hold uncultivated land when so many are without food. In Brazil the pontiff stressed that the earth is a gift from God to every human being, and that all people belong to God's family. It is not the divine plan that the earth benefits just a few and excludes others.

The bishops reiterate that the Guatemalan *campesinos* live in undeserved misery. They demand urgent reforms and a sharing of goods in equity, justice, and charity.

Pastoral Conclusions

The bishops of Guatemala strongly denounced the inequities in land ownership in their country and reiterated that such injustice is at the root of the dehumanizing poverty among the *campesinos*. They call upon all Christians to make themselves aware of the situation. Along with John Paul II, they decry how millions in the developing countries, including many of their own people, are exploited as they are forced to cultivate land that belongs to the wealthy.

The bishops protest the killing of the thousands among their own people and strongly object to the suppression of organizations by the Civil Defense patrols. They censure the silencing of the poor with guns when they cry out for justice, and they condemn the hunting down and disappearance of many *campesinos*. The prelates also criticize their government for having strict legislation to preserve rights of landowners while doing little to protect the poor. They make an impassioned plea to Christians not to remain passive but to respond out of their belief in the redemption of Christ. Church leaders call for solidarity among Guatemalans and entreat their people to view each other as children of God and as sisters and brothers who share the same dignity and rights.

The bishops strongly seek economic and social development for their entire people. Courageously, the bishops point out that if any should be privileged it should be the Indians, not just because they are the majority but because out of justice they should be compensated for centuries of abuse. They warn that the huge population of *campesinos* is a sleeping giant, and if there are not serious reforms, it will awaken embittered passions and there will be violent conflict.

This document ends with an urgent call to change sinful and obsolete social structures in Guatemala. The bishops turn to John XXIII's classic *Mater et Magistra,* which they view as the "magna carta" for *campesinos,* and they reiterate its call for reform in public policies, especially in the area of farming. Desperately needed reforms are listed, including land reforms, legal defense of *campesinos* and refugees, the availability of education, better salaries, open markets for *campesinos,* and a halt to the violent oppression.

The bishops close by defending their right to get involved in all these secular matters as part of their mission as pastors. They call for radical conversion from the goals of wealth and power to ideals that promote human dignity, the common good and Christian love.

This is a powerful document. The Guatemalan bishops present a clear case for much needed land reform and strong arguments for such change from the church's teachings on social justice. The bishops exhibit deep compassion for their people. Their courageous stand in solidarity with the poor against oppression and injustice is much more evident than that of many bishops in the developed countries.

There is much hope in Guatemala today, as many of its people return from exile in Mexico and continue in their struggle for social and political reform. More than ever the poor need the church to be in solidarity with them and actively to assist them to achieve freedom and an equal share of the land and its resources.

THE BISHOPS OF THE PHILIPPINES

The bishops of the Philippines have written one of the most significant church documents on environmental issues.[12] They see their country at a critical point in its history. Political instability, economic decline, and armed conflict have characterized its recent history. The bishops maintain that their nation is in peril, and that the root of the problems is the ruthless exploitation of the living systems of the land and seas. The damage is extensive and often irreversible. In just a few short years luxuriant forests have been replaced by brown, eroded hillsides; river beds have dried up; and the land is dangerously eroding and being poisoned by chemicals. In addition, fish catches are rapidly shrinking due to the destruction of coral reefs and mangrove forests.

The bishops denounce this attack on the natural world as sinful and contrary to Christian beliefs in creation and stewardship. Such degradation of the earth is also declared to be against God's will that we have life, as well as contrary to the purpose of Jesus' mission: "I have come that you may have life and have it to the full" (Jn 10:10). The bishops call their people to reflect on the beauty of their land, to develop an appreciation for the fragility of the islands' life-systems, and to take action to protect them for present and future generations. They urge the people in the barrios to admire the beauty of the rice paddies, coconut groves, and the rich grasses. They ask their people to remember the islands' original beauty, which their tribal forebears respected and preserved. The bishops lament that the huge plantations of today have pitted humans against nature for short-term profits. The bishops challenge their people to restore their land to its original beauty.

Tragic Losses Reviewed

With great sensitivity to their own history, the bishops recall that their country was covered with lush trees, thousands of flowering plants, and many species of animals, birds, and insects when their ancestors arrived. Tropical rains came in from the seas to water soil and vegetation and to form clear rivers and lakes. The islands, born out of volcanos and earthquakes, brought forth a bounty of riches. They were surrounded by blue seas and wonderful coral reefs, with fish of every shape and color. This was how God shaped their land, and it took millions of years to develop such a magnificent place.

The bishops point out that tragically much has been lost. Only 3 percent of the forests are left, and many of the animal species have had their habitats destroyed and have been hunted down relentlessly. Most of the birds are gone, even the great eagle and the colorful hornbill, and in many areas one hears only the cocks crowing. The chocolate-colored rivers carry the life-blood of the land to the sea and then become cloaks of death, killing the coral reefs. The precious land so desperately needed to produce food has been lost, while some of the rivers have become running sewers where no one can fish. Only 5 percent of the coral reefs are in their pristine state, and dynamite blasting and relentless fishing methods endanger the remaining coral reefs. Mining companies use the sea for a dump, while chemicals poison the lands and rivers and threaten the people with dreaded diseases. Life-systems that took millions of years to develop have been laid waste. The air in the cities is noxious, and the forests and rivers are devastated. Flash floods have destroyed towns and cities, and the lakes have grown heavy with silt. With deep emotion the bishops cry out: "We have sinned against God and his creation." They call for immediate action to protect their country and its resources, action that will be difficult to implement in view of the prevailing greed and the drive of an economic system based on plundering the earth.

Signs of Hope

In spite of the desperate ecological situation in their country, the bishops have hope for the future. They see their tribal brothers and sisters still trying to live in harmony with nature, still sensitive to the presence of the Divine Spirit in the living world, and respectful of nature in their prayers and offerings. The prelates point to many signs of vitality among the Filipino people. Many are dedicated to their families, especially mothers working quietly in the home to create an atmosphere of acceptance and love. The bishops applaud women's role in environmental reform and point out that some of the women in India and Kenya have been leaders in the environmental movement.

Other signs of hope are enumerated: there is still a sensitivity toward the beauty of nature and flowers among the people; small efforts are being made in farming methods and tree planting; protests have brought about the suspension of projects like the Chico dam and the Bataan nuclear plant; reforestation is beginning, and some have defended the forests with their own bodies; one diocese of Pagadian has chosen eucharist and ecology as the pastoral focus for a whole year. The bishops see all these as signs that the Spirit of God is with the people, helping them at this crucial time.

A New Vision

The bishops propose a new vision for the environment in the Philippines, one grounded in creation theology, stewardship, and the covenant that binds all creation together. The goal here is the restoration of the land to the way God intended it to be, a perspective where nature is linked with justice. The bishops write: "More and more we must recognize that the commitment to work for justice and to preserve the integrity of creation are two inseparable dimensions of our Christian vocation to work for the coming of the kingdom of God in our times."[13] They derive their vision for the future of their country from Jesus Christ, who "lived lightly on the earth and warned his disciples against hoarding material possessions and allowing their hearts to be enticed by the lure of wealth and power."[14] They believe that Jesus Christ is the center point of human history and creation, and they proclaim that destruction of the environment defaces that image of Christ which is etched in creation. They also call upon Jesus' mother, Mary, whom they see as the mother of life and an advocate for the poor, for help and protection in the achievement of this profound renewal of their people and their land.

A number of recommendations are made to make this vision a reality: more education concerning damage in each local area, and efforts to organize and take action against environmental destruction. Conversion is urged on the part of the church, which has been slow to respond to this crisis. There is a call for the development of a creation theology; an incorporation of ecological concerns into preaching, catechetics, liturgies, and school programs; and the development of an earth ministry within the various levels of the church. The bishops ask that ecological concerns be incorporated into all areas of life. They urge the government to support ecological research, to perform ongoing evaluation and "watch-dogging" of the environment, and to formulate legislation for conservation.

The bishops close by reiterating that the exploitative mentality so prevalent in their country is at variance with the gospel of Jesus. Grave violence has been done to the people, the land, and the waters. Nature cries out, and the bishops have listened to this cry and have called their people to choose life rather than death.

This moving document gives a clear picture of the local environmental problems and makes an impassioned plea for reform. In spite of the seriousness of the situation, the bishops remain hopeful and provide religious vision for their people. They make a real contribution by showing their people how to link their beliefs with their concerns for the betterment of their environment. Their willingness to listen to feminine voices and to see women activists as role models for their people is unusual in such church documents.

THE EVANGELICAL LUTHERAN CHURCH OF AMERICA

The Lutherans begin by expressing their faith that the world is created, redeemed, and sustained by God.[15] They proclaim that the Creator attends to creation faithfully, justly, and lovingly through his Son, Jesus, through whom all things were made. Many biblical passages are cited to support this belief.

God is here seen as linked to creation through a covenant with all the earth and all living things. The Lutherans are quick to note that while creation is good, it is *not* God and may not be worshiped. God is wholly "Other," a reality that transcends and stands above all creation as judge. At the same time, they believe that God is very near, and deeply and passionately involved in what happens to the planet.

The Incarnation and Creation

The authors rightfully link the incarnation with creation. They believe that God is "intimately and irreversibly connected to all creation through the incarnation, where infinite grace is brought to finite creation. In Christ God takes on the earthly material of human life. Through Christ, God is reconciled to 'all things whether on earth or in heaven' (Col 1:20). Thus the incarnation has a saving significance for a creation which longs for fulfillment."[16]

The Lutheran leaders point out that the eternal Word became flesh and dwelled among us, teaching us of the divine presence in the world. Many of Jesus' parables teach us to understand the land. Jesus presents the world as a theater of God's grace and glory.

Sacraments

The Lutheran leaders link sacramental theology and ecology. They observe that the eternal Word lives as part of earthly creation and comes to us in the elements of bread and wine. The sacraments underscore the intimate relationship between God and a nature that is neither unclean nor unspiritual. In a variety of sacramental ways nature imparts God's faithfulness and loving kindness.[17]

Science

The authors seem comfortable with the findings of modern science and are able to integrate them with their beliefs. They recall the first photos of earth relayed from space about thirty years ago, which showed a shimmering blue planet glowing in the light of the sun. For people of faith this was a portrait of the planet God had made. Over five billion years this planet has survived continental drift, ice ages, volcanic eruptions, and the appearance and disappearance of various forms of life. In the midst of all this the earth still finds its ultimate meaning in God.

The link between the earth and its creatures is related to the biblical notion that we were all formed from the same dust as trees and animals. Bears, cows, children, and serpents are all a part of a united world, which blesses and praises the lordship and power of the Creator. The Lutherans recognize the importance of interdependence. They extend the concept of neighbor to all creatures: "We cannot be persons without other persons; we cannot be humans apart from other creatures."[18]

Called to Live according to God's Wisdom

The authors believe that Wisdom has much to teach us about creation and that Wisdom themes can be valuable for addressing environmental concerns. They point out that Jesus himself has been portrayed as the Wisdom of God, sent to reveal the mysteries of creation. They observe that modern science can be for us the counterpart of the Wisdom of Israel. God gives humans the faculty for science so that they might learn the complexity of the earth's systems and the interdependence of all things.

For the Lutherans, the true meaning of dominion is to stand in the place of a gracious God. They concede that in ancient times, because of human's vulnerability to nature, dominion might well have meant overcoming nature. Today, however, in the midst of an environmental crisis, dominion should be viewed as acting in the image of a forgiving and self-giving God.

Sin against the Earth

There is a clear link here between sin and doing harm to the environment. Sin is described as placing one's loyalty and trust in something other than God, looking to the self and to things for ultimate security. Sin resides in humans attempting to be masters of the universe, in humans losing sight of the fact that they are creatures, in humans attempting to be God.

The Lutheran leaders point to extensive destruction of humanity and creation as signs of today's sinfulness. As sinners we threaten creation and oppress other humans in the name of nation, race, gender, or ideology. We bring social injustice and environmental degradation to the earth. Through sloth and cowardice we neglect to defend the creation. The writers of the document are willing to grant that some environmental destruction is done out of ignorance, but they also believe that there is a great deal of wrongful "denial" among people about the damage to our world. They maintain that comfort, convenience, and greed too often are given priority over caring for the earth.

The Lutherans candidly admit that the churches have often mistaken domination for dominion and have taken part in lifestyles and structures that have exploited the environment. They boldly tell their members that by leaving unchallenged such distorted ideas of God's will for creation, or by actively promoting them, they have contributed to a sinful state of affairs.

Christians and Hope

The Lutherans find grounds for hope in the midst of present-day sinfulness toward the earth. They have faith that God will help people overcome their failures and will ultimately bring the universe to its intended destiny. God is the savior of the world: "Through the death and resurrection of Christ, God does not save us *from* the world, but saves us *and* the world."[19] The authors resolve to answer the call to the cross of Christ and thereby give up their pursuit of security and their arrogance toward the rest of creation. They ask God to enable them to see what they have done to one another and to the earth. Freed by forgiveness from guilt, regret, and remorse, they resolve to serve and protect the victims of environmental abuse.

As one might expect from the Lutheran tradition, there is a strong emphasis on faith, a realistic recognition of the power of sin, and hope in the saving power of Christ to save the world from environmental destruction. More specifics on the environmental problems in this country and concrete suggestions for solutions would strengthen their position considerably. Again, a listening theology that consults the poor in the country and throughout the world could add to what is already an extremely enlightened theological perspective.

THE PRESBYTERIANS

The Presbyterians published an initial document in 1971, and then, after more years of study and discussion, published a thorough and powerful document in 1990. In this document there is a strong biblical awareness of the value of creation and the radical relatedness among all things. Creation is seen as a living reality that cries out for justice for both humankind and the earth. The authors acknowledge a major new insight of our time: justice and peace among human beings are inseparable from right relationships with and within the natural order.

The authors recognize the unprecedented dangers to the environment in our time and call for an immediate response. The biblical command to till and keep the gardens is interpreted to mean not merely using resources but also maintaining creation's capacity to sustain us. The perspective of the document is initially human-centered, but later this view is critiqued and the integrity of all things is recognized.

Many shocking statistics are given with regard to the global distribution of resources. Here are some examples:

- 25 million people, three-fifths of them children, die each year from diseases in or spread by water.
- Americans produce 230 millions tons of garbage per year, which is twice as much as either France or West Germany produces, and far

exceeds the production of China, which has *four times* the population of
the United States.

• The United States generates 250 million tons of hazardous waste each
year.

Useful statistics are also given on population growth and its relation to environmental problems, although not much attention is given to this crucial problem in this document. It does offer extremely well-informed treatments of
such problems as global warming and ozone depletion.

An important principle of ecology is cited: "The individual of whatever
species depends upon the healthy functioning of its community, and the human community depends upon the vitality and stability of the biotic community."[20] The authors agree with the 1989 warning of the Worldwatch Institute
that the community of nations will soon have to turn back the threatening
trends, or else environmental deterioration and social disintegration will begin to feed on each other.

The Presbyterians acknowledge that God is the leading player in the creation story, and will disclose God's self also in this present crisis. God's coming to restore creation to righteousness begins with divine judgment. They
predict that this judgment will bring to light the truth that we have been unfaithful to the covenant. It will reveal that we have not "kept" creation, or
shared its benefits, but have pursued "competitive individualism" and prosperity. God's judgment will bring humans to humility and shatter their as-
sumption that nature is strictly for human use.

The Presbyterian leaders make a touching confession that their church has
been "too uncritical, too unbiblical, too self-serving in going along with our
culture's abuse of nature and pursuit of affluence."[21] The authors ask God's
grace in this crisis and seek to receive judgment and forgiveness so that they
can make a new beginning.

A Biblical and Theological Basis

The Presbyterians establish a solid biblical and theological basis for restoring
creation. They view God as Creator-Redeemer, who continues to be active in
saving creation and reconciling all things. Here the world is depicted as an
arena for God's creating-liberating activity, where Christ is a "new creation."
They also point to the connectedness between human and nonhuman creation
and express their belief that redemptive justice applies to all of creation.

Norms for Healing the Earth

The authors list norms for bringing about the healing of the earth. The first
norm is of paramount importance: sustainability. Sustainability is the capac-

ity for things, in this case the ecosystems of the earth, to continue on. Earth-keeping assures that social systems and natural systems are properly sustained. This precludes undermining the self-renewing capacity of natural systems and demanding unreasonable yields of resources. Proper care and management of all human and natural resources is essential. Creation is a gift and should be cherished. "As each has received a gift, employ it for one another, as good stewards of God's varied grace" (1 Pt 4:10).

Another norm for healing the earth is that of the common good, wherein all humans, especially the weak and the vulnerable, get their fair share. The Presbyterian leaders point out that on a global scale there is presently a massive inequality in the distribution of resources, especially in the Third World. Justice demands that all obtain sufficient sustenance but that excess and waste must be stopped.

The Presbyterians call for radical changes in lifestyle and ask their members to learn to live well on less. They maintain that the "good life" must be characterized by frugality. They submit that the principle of the common good calls for greater sharing and must also include protection of all living things. The document calls upon the church to address the resistance to change that exists among rich and powerful individuals, corporations, and nations. It urges the church to respond with a prophetic word, pastoral concern, and support for the actions of its members.

The final norm proposed for the healing of the earth is solidarity. Solidarity calls for a strong, vibrant community, with commitment and fidelity, in which there is a fundamental interdependence and unity among all creation. Noting the ever-widening gap between rich and poor, humans and nature, the authors call for reconciliation and community. They strongly urge all their members to be deeply concerned about the liberation of the earth.

The document has many practical strategies for dealing with improvements in agriculture, water purification, waste disposal, preservation of wild life and wild lands, and even for solving problems as complicated as ozone depletion and global warming. These authors have done their homework scientifically, politically, and theologically, and they are prepared to lead their people to make a difference in the area of ecojustice. This document is a model for what can be produced by the churches if they are willing to spend a great deal of time and effort in consultation with experts in both secular and religious fields.

THE WORLD COUNCIL OF CHURCHES

In its historic statement on ecology the World Council of Churches (WCC) pursued the theme of liberation.[22] The WCC points out how in our times life in all its forms cries out for liberation. People all over the world want to be freed from oppression due to poverty, race, gender, handicapped conditions, and many other causes. Uniquely, the WCC includes the cries for liberation on the part of animals, plants, and the earth itself. Singular attention is given to the care of animals in this document.

There is a global perspective here and striking examples are given of environmental destruction around the world. For instance, the authors turn their attention to South Africa and observe that in 1988 the Afrikaners celebrated the 150th anniversary of the white man's trek into the north. The white man came to a beautiful country teeming with game, grass as high as humans, where many silver streams flowed. Although there was some tribal conflict, the indigenous people lived in community with nature. The people felt the presence of Modimo, the source and presence of life, which penetrated all.

Soon the land was confiscated by the white man, and the minerals, coal, gold, diamonds, and uranium were taken. Many animals were killed for sport, so that numerous species are now on the point of extinction. Indigenous people were forced into tribal "homelands," where they have to live in squalor. Families were divided, as the men had to go to work in the cities in factories.

Korea is given as another example of exploitation. It had been a land with people united to the soil, a "land of morning calm." In 1910 Japan colonized Korea, recruited the women into the military, then forced them to be prostitutes for the soldiers. Over 200,000 women died of sexual abuse. After liberation in 1945 the peninsula was divided by the United States and the Soviet Union, and many family members were separated. Eighty thousand of the Cheju islanders, mostly men, were killed by Korean soldiers under the command of the United States. Now the island, which was so beautiful, is famous for three things: strong winds, volcanic rocks, and women. It is the center for international sex tourism, with many houses of prostitution, some with three- to five-hundred women. There is also much heavy industry, so that the land, rivers, and air have been polluted. It is now a land of violence, division, and exploitation.

Division Theologies

The WCC points out that throughout the world communities of people, land, animals, and plants have been neglected and destroyed. Western development and technology have not been accompanied by an enlightened Christian theology. Too often the perspectives available were "division theologies," which took an arrogant approach to nature. In such theologies nature has no value in itself but is merely a tool for human use. People also are reduced to "cogs" in the labor force or military. These theologies were generally male-centered and tolerated exploitation of women and the poor.

A New Liberating Theology

The WCC calls for a new theology that liberates life and moves beyond arrogant human-centered views. It searches for a theology that will promote respect for all communities of life in their diversity and advance connectedness among all things and with God. This should be a "listening" theology, which hears the voices of the oppressed. It should seek to liberate those who are oppressed and also the privileged, who often live in complacent isolation. The WCC calls for a theology of peace, justice, and respect for the integrity of creation. Its members hope that such a Christian theology will integrate a thorough understanding of the Christian tradition with a sound knowledge of the environmental sciences.

The authors turn to biblical witness in attempting to develop such a theology. They admit that Christians have often been shaped by interpretations of the creation story that have been human-centered, occupied with dominion, and concerned about salvation from a sinful and fallen world. They admit that too often this perspective has been used for the exploitation and destruction of the earth.

The WCC points out the need for a new reading of the creation story, one that sees a cosmic world that is good and that engenders a loving care of the world. It calls for a rediscovery of the Noahic covenant, which God made with all things. Here all things in creation have intrinsic value, are interconnected, and are included in God's salvation. This covenant bears with it a responsibility to restore the things we have violated and to bring peace and justice to our earth. Jesus' words about the "least" among us have now been extended to all living things (Mt 25:40).

The Role of Science

The theological approach in the WCC document is open to science and appreciative of the way science has opened up many of the mysteries of the cosmos. Recent discoveries in physics, biology, and other sciences are applauded for offering a new understanding about the formation of the universe and the evolution of life. The churches are not threatened by these findings and can remark with amazement, "We are made of the same stuff as the stars. Our existence is deeply embedded in the existence of the universe itself."[23] They are also grateful for what the sciences have revealed about the uniqueness of human nature, the range of human sensibilities, and the human capacities to understand and freely to make decisions. The authors are convinced that the sciences can be partners with religion and can be of great value in helping the faithful better understand their responsibilities toward their environment.

A New Sensibility

The World Council of Churches signals some innovative directions in theology. New readings of scripture have revealed an interrelatedness of all creatures to each other and with their Creator. There is now a new awareness that everything that exists is part of everything else. In addition, alternate images of God are being retrieved that are more appropriate to ecology than some past images. For example, the more dominative images of lord and king are being replaced with the images of potter and mother. The image of *church* has also been broadened to include all things, and there is a renewed awareness that everything "lives and moves and has its very being in God" (Acts 17:28). All things are perceived as one with the Cosmic Christ, who has saved all things and has bound them together with the Creator.

An Ethic for Liberation

The WCC observes the emergence of a new ethic that is concerned with the liberation of life. This ethic honors and respects the integrity of all things. It sees humans as part of a larger community and strongly links peace with justice. The arms race and military destruction are now recognized as related to the waste of resources. This ethic also challenges the unjust power over people and resources exerted by the wealthier and more powerful nations. It exposes abuses of the world's ecosystems and urges action for peace and justice among all peoples. The ultimate goal of this ethic is to provide sustainable communities; that is, ecological communities that will continue to exist indefinitely into the future.

The churches warn of the severity of global soil problems. Modern agricultural practices have not always taken into consideration proper care of the land. Much land that was once arable has become arid as corporate agriculture accelerates a process of desertification. Many nations have to import their food, while millions of poor farmers leave the land for overcrowded cities. Chemicals and pesticides that kill the microorganisms that maintain soil structure are being used on the soil. The authors proclaim that such violence to the soil violates the dignity of people as well as the integrity of creation itself.

The Integrity of All Things

The WCC sees the urgent need to shift from an ethic of conquest to one that has "reverence for" nature. Such reverence is essential in order to save the rainforests, with all their great diversity of plants and animals; preserve the soil; and give dignity to the poor and indigenous peoples, who are still being driven from their lands. There is also an appeal here for respect for marine communities. Greed and mismanagement in the fishing industry are causing a sharp decline in yields, which in turn brings hardship to the poor who depend on the fish for food and income.

This document pays extraordinary attention to cruelty to animals. It expresses concern over the pain and death inflicted on animals by testing laboratories, the fur industry, industrial farming, the entertainment business, and biological and medical education. The WCC reminds its members that animals are to be included in "the least of the brethren" and should be given the respect and care that their dignity merits. It calls for education in this area of animal abuse and encourages conferences, dialogues among scientists and theologians, and boycotts of industries that abuse animals. The authors also ask that church organizations and agencies be formed to protest and take action against the abuse of animals.

The WCC should be applauded for the contemporary tone of its document. The perspective is global, ecumenical, and open to science. The churches confess the limitations of past Christian theologies and admit that these often contributed to harming the environment. At the same time, they make insightful suggestions for how the Christian tradition might be revised to meet the ecological challenges of today. The authors seem especially sympathetic to the indigenous people of the world and encourage their liberation. The commitment these churches have to animals is singular and merits serious consideration.

SECOND CONFERENCE OF EUROPEAN CHURCHES

We will close with a brief consideration of some views on the environmental crisis by the Second European Ecumenical Assembly, which gathered in 1997 in Graz, Austria.[24] These views are of special significance in that they represent the concerns and theological insights of the Protestant and Catholic churches in both Eastern and Western Europe. The gathering of these churches is truly historical and was only made possible by the recent collapse of Communism in Eastern Europe and the breakup of the Soviet Union.

The religious leaders begin by observing that the spiritual or sacramental dimension of the world has been appreciated by all religions. They point out that only in recent centuries has the Creator been blotted out and nature subjected to domination. They add that a distortion of the Jewish-Christian creation faith often justified such domination and the destruction of the wisdom of other religions and cultures.

The document recognizes modern science for its multiple discoveries and achievements. At the same time, it acknowledges that scientific and technical progress has led us to the nuclear threat and to environmental devastation. The authors also accept cultural advancement but warn that cultural progress brings dangers beyond our control. For the sake of future generations of all living things, therefore, we must reverse direction and attempt to avoid putting the environment in peril.

The churches opt to begin with themselves and call for more ecumenical dialogue on how elements of the Christian tradition might help them understand and carry out their responsibilities toward creation. They ask their people to be less centered on the human and to give more emphasis to the holiness of everything, the close relationship between human beings and nature, and the interdependence of all things in creation.

Special attention is given here to the importance of maintaining the bio-diversity of species, which reflects the generosity of God. Strong emphasis is given to the need to respect the uniqueness and integrity of all things. They do not accept the position that the dying out of species is simply natural and beneficial. While willing to grant that there is a certain natural process of elimination, they point out that much of the extinction of species in modern times has come from irresponsible human activity.

The religious leaders pay special attention to issues involving the weather. They point out that human activity is actually changing the climactic conditions of the planet and posing disastrous consequences. Hence humans can no longer foster the delusion that they can do anything they wish. Limits must be established and there must be respect for the conditions necessary for maintaining life on earth.

The document acknowledges a new ecological awareness in society and in the churches yet expresses the fear that this often does not translate into real conversion or change in behavior. It recognizes that economic pressures in Europe could push ecological issues into the background. Therefore the churches call for a change in the entire system of values that govern decisions in politics, economics, industry, agriculture, and transport, as well as habits or lifestyle. They end with many specific recommendations for action and a powerful plea to their people in all parts of Europe: "This calls for a new orientation of our self-understanding as human beings, in which we acknowledge the other creatures with which we share this world in their own right, which, equally with our right to life, is founded in the will of the Creator."[25]

SUMMARY

This collection of church documents from many parts of the globe reveals the many environmental problems that are unique to individual areas and at the same time shows that the environmental crisis is indeed global. It is quite remarkable to see how the Christian churches worldwide have awakened in the last decade both to their own complicity in environmental destruction and to their responsibility to become involved in solving these problems. There is still more room here on the part of the churches, however, for a broader recognition of guilt, sincere confession, and repentance.

It is evident that third-world countries are experiencing more critical environmental hazards than are the developed countries. In the developing countries, especially, church leaders generally seem to recognize their contextual problems and are able to relate environmental problems to issues of poverty, peace, and justice. Religious leaders in the developing countries are also in solidarity with the poor and the oppressed, and in some cases are strident in their condemnation of abuses of the earth and its people.

One would hope that the church leaders in the developing countries would be more vocal against the wealthier countries, who often manipulate them with foreign debt, world market monopolies, and arms sales. These factors and others are integral to the degradation of the environment in poorer countries. The invasion of these poor countries by foreign industries that often have little regard for environmental protection or living wages is also a serious problem.

Religious leaders from the wealthier countries need to be aware of the complicity their countries and their churches might have in damaging the environments of poorer countries. Ecumenical dialogue between wealthy and poor countries could help church leaders from both sides locate these abuses and jointly pressure governments and international organizations for protective legislation.

These documents show that religious leaders throughout the world are coming to understand the complexity of both local and global environmental issues. Nonetheless, there seems to be room here for much more in-depth consultation with scientists, politicians, economists, and other experts. Only then will the churches be able to gain respect from secular leaders and be effective players in the environmental movement.

Religious leaders obviously have begun to link many areas of the Christian tradition with ecology. There have been many applications of biblical teachings, and some progress has been made in relating doctrinal and ethical teachings. Catholics have begun to integrate their social-justice teachings with ecology. Surprisingly, however, they have done little to link their rich sacramental and spiritual traditions with their concern for the earth. (Suggestions for such connections are made in chapters 5 and 9.) Nor has sufficient attention been given to the integration of the valuable insights of liberation theology or feminist theology with environmental concerns.

The churches need to give much more attention to the role that overpopulation plays in the shortage of resources and in further endangering the environment. Population control is an extremely complex issue; it involves cultural values, education, religious beliefs, and many other factors. The Catholic church, numbering a billion worldwide, can play an important role in this discussion, but it will first have to listen more carefully to women's views and give further study and discussion to its positions on family planning.

7.

The God Question

My Mayan people and their ancestors have lived in this tropical rainforest for thousands of years. We have everything we need and we live at one with nature here. Now our government is selling off our sacred place to Asian people for logging. We have no deeds to this land, even though we have been here long before the white man came. So they tell us we must leave. They expect us to simply scatter and disappear so that they can tear this place apart for profit. The great green forests, the palm that we use for our houses, the animals, the medicines, and all that we have held to be gifts from God will be gone forever.

—Leonardo Acala, Santa Anna, Belize

Walter Kasper points out that God "is the sole and unifying theme of theology."[1] God has been described as the ultimate ground of all reality, the mysterious source, sustainer, and goal of all things. God has been depicted as the greatest reality that we can possibly reflect upon, the One from whom we can expect support in every aspect of life.

If all this is true, then to dislodge faith in God is to destroy the very center of faith, decisively changing the worldview of human beings and drastically altering the meaning of life on our planet. That is precisely what happened in the nineteenth century, when modern atheists, in their efforts to critique the dangers of religion, ended up denying the very existence of God. God was reduced to a mere human projection, an illusion arising from poverty or weakness.

Two of the major social and political movements of the twentieth century, Nazism and Communism, were deeply influenced by this rejection of religion. These two movements alone have been responsible for the loss of countless lives in the Western hemisphere, an inestimable waste of resources, and incalculable destruction to the environment. No doubt this is why Vatican II pointed out that atheism is one of the most serious problems of our era, one of the "signs of the times" that the church must consider in designing the church's mission in the modern world.

We now examine the development of modern atheism and its role in the degradation of the environment. We will then look at some of the main theological approaches to God and discuss how these might affect ecological concerns.

THE DEVELOPMENT OF ATHEISM

It was common among the ancients to identify their world with their gods, so to deny the existence of the gods would have been to deny the existence of the world itself. Gods were often identified with the animals, birds, rivers, stars, and other elements of nature. When such an identification existed, as in the case of many of the Native American religions, nature was usually held in high esteem and considered to be the sacred dwelling place of the Great Spirit. Ohiyesa, the Santee Dakota physician, puts it this way:

> Whenever, in the course of the daily hunt the red hunter comes upon a scene that is strikingly beautiful or sublime—a black thundercloud with the rainbow's glowing arch above the mountain; a white waterfall in the heart of a green gorge; a vast prairie tinged with the blood-red of sunset—he pauses for an instant in the attitude of worship. He sees no need for setting apart one day in seven as a holy day, since to him all days are God's.[2]

In ancient times there were many disputes over the nature and the activities of God but never an outright denial of the existence of God. Certain heresies regarding the divinity were at various times condemned, but these were departures from established traditions and not denials of the divinity itself. Individuals like Socrates were actually put to death because of their unacceptable views on the divinity, but no one was accused of denying the existence of the gods.

It was only in the nineteenth century that a new brand of atheism emerged: one that brought a severe critique to religion and denied outright the very existence of God. This modern atheism was a product of some of the most influential thinkers of the century. They were "masters of suspicion," who, in various ways, challenged the classical truths of the past, shattered time-honored principles, and debunked the prevailing social, political and religious structures.[3] Generally their main agendum was not atheism but the search to redefine the human person and society. In the process each thinker brought to his work a critique of the falseness and even duplicity of religion and denied the existence of God. The thoughts of these intellectual giants are foundational to the modern worldview. They have provided us with many cautions with regard to the possible distortions and pain that religion can bring to people. At the same time these thinkers have been instrumental in fostering an atheism—and even a nihilism—that in the hands of demagogues has helped bring about massive destruction of human life and of the environment.

Feuerbach's Projection Theory

One of the pioneers of modern atheism is the nineteenth-century German philosopher Ludwig Feuerbach (d. 1872). Feuerbach maintained that the idea of God was a projection of all that humans want to be and can be. In other words the characteristics of God—love, justice, compassion, power, freedom— are really human characteristics. The idea of God is nothing other than the human projection of these characteristics and the formulation of a fictitious image. Feuerbach concluded that in creating this God, we alienate the best of the human from ourselves. As a result, religion reduces the self-esteem of humans and prevents them from exercising their full potential. Feuerbach believed that this denigration of the self was at the root of human conflict and hostility. Feuerbach believed that for true humanity to be achieved, religion must be rejected.[4]

Frederick Engels, a close associate of Karl Marx, reflects the enthusiasm with which many in the nineteenth century greeted Feuerbach's *Essence of Christianity:*

> The spell was broken. The "system" was exploded and cast aside and the contradiction, shown to exist only in our imagination was dissolved. One must himself have experienced the liberating effect of this book to get an idea of it. Enthusiasm was general: we all became at once Feuerbachians. How enthusiastically Marx greeted the new conception and how much— in spite of all critical reservations—he was influenced by it.[5]

One can sense the feeling of liberation in Engel's remarks. With God reduced to nothing other than a mental projection, humans could now take center stage and material reality could be recognized as the absolute. Reason and will were free to be exercised as infinite capacities, and humans could be liberated to chart their own destinies. While such views generated tremendous human energy and hope, they also cut away the ultimate source and goal of all things and dismissed thousands of years of religious tradition. As John Courtney Murray once observed about atheists, talk about God would now become talk about themselves.

Marxist Atheism

Karl Marx was the mastermind behind the communist ideology that has until recently dominated the Soviet Union, and which is still a powerful force in China and other parts of the world. He was deeply influenced by Feuerbach's notion that God is a human projection. But Marx was not interested so much in the human consciousness or in philosophy; he was a practical materialist whose main concerns were economic and social reform. For Marx, the human person was a social reality, and his focus was on the working class, which he thought had become enslaved by industrialization.

For Marx, the notion of God was not so much a projection of human possibilities as it was a phenomenon that arose out of the suffering of the oppressed, offering them consolation and hope:

> Religious suffering is at the same time an expression of real suffering and a protest against real suffering. Religion is the sigh of the oppressed creature, the sentiment of a heartless world, and the soul of soulless conditions. It is the opium of the people.[6]

Marx also believed that much oppression comes from the fact that religions sanction state authorities as ordained by God, whether they are just or unjust.[7] Moreover, religion distracts people from actively being involved in freeing themselves or others because religion teaches that the true home for people is in heaven. Marx believed that religion lacked moral substance, because it did not empower people to work for justice and freedom. Instead, religion promoted an escapist mentality.

Lenin, who led the Russian Revolution, went beyond Marx in his alienation from religion. For him, religion did not arise out of human suffering but rather was a "drug" handed to people by corrupt rulers of church and state in order to keep them enslaved. In a much more sardonic tone than Marx's, he writes:

> Those who toil and live in want all their lives are taught to be submissive and patient while here on earth, and to take comfort in the hope of a heavenly reward. But those who live by the labor of others are taught by religion to practice charity while on earth, thus offering them a very cheap way of justifying their entire existence as exploiters and selling them at a moderate price tickets to well-being in heaven. Religion is opium for the people. Religion is a sort of spiritual booze, in which the slaves of capital drown their human image, their demand for a life more or less worthy of man.[8]

Lenin rejoiced that Darwinism had forever put to rest the notion of creation by God. He hoped that now science would continue to help socialism battle "against the fog of religion, and free the workers from their belief in life after death, by welding them together to fight in the present for a better life on earth."[9] He demanded the complete disestablishment of the church and encouraged a widespread propaganda of atheism. The unity of the people in revolution was Lenin's prime goal, so that they could have a paradise on earth rather than vainly aspire to a paradise in heaven.

Lenin believed that the duplicity of religion had to be eliminated and so he set in motion forces that would destroy religion. Numerous believers, both lay and clergy, were killed or sent off to the gulags to languish in hard labor, starvation, and exposure to the harsh Siberian winters. Socialists were expected to be atheists. The "Party" was now considered to be the absolute authority and the "classless society" the ultimate goal. Stalin, in his craven reach for power, carried forth Lenin's thinking and proceeded to destroy millions of people who opposed him. One of the most monstrous and violent people of the twentieth century, Stalin had many of his own people executed simply to terrorize the Russian people and keep them in line.

The atheistic materialism that began in the work of Feuerbach and then deeply influenced the worldviews of Marx, Lenin, and Stalin has challenged religion to become more authentic. The churches have come to realize that they should not project images onto God that generate fear, apathy, or helplessness. Religion's true purpose is not to harm the self-esteem of its people or to keep them preoccupied with heavenly goals while there is so much violence and injustice in the world. Authentic religion does not mesmerize people, so that they do not see the injustice and oppression that is in their own lives and the lives of others. Religion should not blind people to enslavement, nor should it be an escape from engagement in everyday problems. Authentic religion does not promote submissiveness and blind patience.

Authentic religion, however, is not based on imaginary projections or ephemeral urges arising out of human fears and suffering. Religion links God with humans in a commitment to love and serve all of creation. Religion engenders an awareness of the sacredness of all things. It is committed in faith to the belief that God is in all and that all is in God.

Genuine religion empowers people to discover their own gifts and to stand in solidarity with other people, all living things, and the earth itself. It should not drug but inspire. It should not blind but enlighten. Religion should be a stimulant toward engagement in work for peace, justice, and a healthy environment.

At the end of the twentieth century the world stood amazed as the Berlin Wall came down, Western communism collapsed, and the Soviet Union disintegrated. It has become apparent to most of the people of Eastern Europe that atheistic communism has failed politically, economically, and culturally. Absolutizing the state and setting the ultimate goal of life to be a classless society have not liberated people; rather, they have stifled human freedom and brought economic ruin to Russia.

Communism has devastated the environment of Eastern Europe. A recent report from Russia pointed out that its negative influence upon the environment is much greater than that of other technologically developed countries.[10] Chernobyl stands as a symbol of the apocalyptic destruction that can come to people and to the earth from the irresponsible use of technology. Materialism and atheism have for generations moved people to lose sight of the values of human dignity and environmental integrity. This is particularly evidenced in the environment devastation the Soviet Union has left in its former satellites in Eastern Europe, most notably, the Czech Republic, the Slovak Republic, the Ukraine, and Lithuania.

The euphoria over the collapse of communism has now subsided, and the world has become more realistic about how long it will take to rebuild Eastern Europe. The old problems attached to communism have been replaced with new ones. There are enormous economic barriers to overcome as nations move into the unfamiliar waters of market economies. Many deadly ethnic and religious memories smoldering under the surface have erupted, as in Bosnia, to further de-stabilize that part of the world. The removal of rigid legal standards leaves the way open for lawlessness and chaos. Some have warned of the danger of a new "ruthless freedom," which promotes consumerism, instant wealth, and progress at any price.[11] These drives often leave little time or interest for the environment, and so there is a grave danger that as these countries of Eastern Europe move to develop industrially, there will be a lack of concern for clean air, land, or water.

Gradually the churches of Eastern Europe are beginning to awaken to the environmental crisis left in the wake of the breakup of the Soviet Union. There is now a new sense of religious revival in these countries and a new commitment to rebuilding the earth. This was expressed recently by Patriarch Alexy of Moscow and all Russia:

> The Christian Church has a moral view on the problem of preserving the Creation in its integrity. Human concern for the environment should be inseparably linked with moral responsibility for the results of human activities. Overcoming the present ecological crisis is possible only when the relations between humans and nature are built upon harmonious interaction based on human morality. . . . The reconstruction of the integrity of Creation can be accomplished with revival of the spiritual wholeness of people and with restoration of peace in our hearts.[12]

Ironically, the very religious impulses that Marxists complained drugged people into passivity and indifference are now acting as stimulants for action on behalf of justice, including ecojustice. The churches seem to be rising again in Eastern Europe and are regaining their influence on the political, social, and environmental future of Europe.

Communist China

One of the last strongholds of atheistic communism is mainland China. With a population of 1.2 billion, and a breath-taking pace of economic expansion, China could "push demands on some of the earth's natural support systems beyond their sustainable yields."[13] China's escalating demand for food could also de-stabilize the world's grain market and further aggravate desperate shortages in Africa, India, and Mexico. China's need for water for farming and drinking has placed tremendous burdens on its waterways. China is also undergoing a construction boom and yet has only 3 percent of the world's forests. This will put significant pressure on rainforest markets to supply China's demands. As for replacing trees, there is a saying in China: One hoe making forests, but several axes cutting them down. Rapid industrial growth is also affecting the quality of the air in the big cities, and the Chinese speak of the "Beijing cough." The tremendous demand for energy is being met by nineteenth-century coal-burning systems, and the production of chlorofluorocarbons (CFCs) has doubled in the last ten years. This stands in stark contrast to much of the rest of the world, which is attempting to phase out such pollutants in order to protect the ozone layer.[14]

One wonders what chance religious values concerning the earth and its resources have in modern-day China. Much of what is being done is controlled by an aging communist regime in an economy that seems driven by pragmatism and the profit motive. One sees few signs that conservation or sustainability are operative values in China today.

Nietzsche's Eulogy for God

The thought of Friedrich Nietzsche (d. 1900) also contributed significantly to the development of modern atheism and has been revived today in some of postmodern thought. Nietzsche rejected both the Judeo-Christian tradition that had been the foundation of Western civilization and the modern progress of science, technology, and industrialization. He declared that in fact the traditional notion of God was dead in the hearts and minds of modern society. If that is in fact the case, then Nietzsche proposed that we live accordingly and not go on with traditional values and lifestyle. Nietzsche proposed a nihilism that would reduce all philosophy and theology of the past to nothing, and he hoped to replace it all with his own thought. It was his conviction that culture is now in a position to make a fresh beginning and to build a "higher" history than the archaic history of the past.

Latching on to Darwinism, Nietzsche held that the discovery of evolution revealed that the human goal was not to achieve some spiritual reward but rather to become Supermen and have dominion over everything. These superior humans would be able to transcend traditional values and norms and build a new humanity. Ultimately, these powerful warriors and the aristocratic few would gain supremacy through their superior "will to power."

One can readily see how such nihilism and advocacy for the violent domination by the elite would serve as one of the foundations of the notorious movement of National Socialism in Germany. Adolf Hitler became the leader of "Supermen" and proclaimed the beginning of a thousand-year Reich wherein the Aryan race would dominate the world.

In its wake Nazism left inestimable destruction of human life and the earth's resources. Twelve million people were not considered suitable for membership in the future Reich and were exterminated in camps. Many more millions died during the years of brutal conflict. Enormous quantities of irreplaceable resources went into war machines on all sides, and enormous amounts of pollutants were dumped into the atmosphere. The sinking of ships seriously damaged areas of the oceans, and the dropping of countless bombs did serious damage to many ecosystems in Asia and Europe. In the end the "Supermen" perished, fled to other continents, or hid for the rest of their lives in anonymity.

There are lessons to be learned from Nietzsche's position that we should be able to live free of traditional values if God is truly dead. Many in contemporary society often seem to want to have it both ways: they want to live secular lives and be free of traditional religious values, and yet they cling to traditional beliefs in God and religion. As a result, religion often seems to have little relevance to real-life situations where sexual morality, social justice, or honesty are in question.

The dichotomy between life as it is lived today and religious beliefs and values takes its toll in environmental issues. Many today maintain belief in the Creator and the sacredness of creation, and yet these beliefs are often not operative in their attitudes toward the environment. Decisions with regard to resources, species preservation, conservation, and lifestyle are often based on usefulness, profit, or enjoyment. These standards seldom work for the benefit of the environment. We need an authentic integration of religious beliefs and values with the crucial decisions that we face regarding the earth. In an ironic twist, Nietzsche's views can hold the secular person's feet to the fire and demand a realistic acceptance of the void he or she must face if God is truly dead. It is a world without the holy, without revelation, without a source, without an ultimate purpose.

Postmoderns and God's Absence

The nihilism of Nietzsche has been recovered today in some of the postmodern deconstructionists. God, the self, history, and scripture are viewed as no longer relevant to our times. Since God is dead, so too is the meaning of self, history, and any foundation for scripture or religious tradition. As we wander in this land of nothingness, only the absence of God and "mazing grace" accompany us.[15] In this view, there is no creative source, nor final goal, just purposeless process. There is a complete loss of meaning as we struggle to move ahead in the darkness.

Obviously, such a nihilism proffers little appreciation for a world created by God, who is the source, sustainer, and ultimate goal of everything. The deconstructionist approach to theology often sounds like a revival of Sartre's pessimism. It places humans in a world devoid of meaning and purpose. Given such a fate, why cherish the world in which we live? Why sustain our world for a future that is so bleak and uncertain? Why share our resources with others less fortunate, when in fact there are no clear norms for doing so? Since the universe and the world are no longer acknowledged to be God's, what reasons are there to believe that the elements of the world are somehow interconnected and engaged in a meaningful movement toward a time of ultimate fulfillment?

Sigmund Freud's Illusion Theory

Sigmund Freud, the great pioneer in the study of the unconscious, sustained a fascination for religion even though he found it to be illusionary. Freud was raised a Jew and was well instructed in the tenets of Judaism. In his early years and his old age he carried out extensive studies of the origin and purpose of religion but was never able to resolve his many ambiguities about religion.

Freud held that the religious impulse arose in primitive times out of fear and the need to be secure and protected. It was his conviction that religious faith was an illusion, and that it was often related to neurotic and obsessive tendencies. His work in psychoanalysis convinced him that religious faith was a sign of human inadequacy and dependency. His forays into fragments of religious history taught him that religion had its origins among primitive peoples, who needed gods to provide ultimate answers to their questions and to protect them from the many dangers that threatened them in nature. He also ascribed special significance to a primitive event wherein the sons of a tribe killed and ate their father. Out of guilt for this Oedipal original sin, they established a totem meal that marked the beginning of religion as a social and ethical organization.[16]

> Religion would thus be the universal obsessional neurosis of humanity; like the obsessional neurosis of children, it arose out of the Oedipus complex, out of the relation to the father. If this view is right, it is to be supposed that a turning-away from religion is bound to occur with the fatal inevitability of a process of growth, and that we find

ourselves at this very juncture in the middle of that phase of development.[17]

Freud discredited religion because it lacked evidence and was based on the testimony of forefathers who were locked in primitive ignorance. It was his position that the testimony of these ancient people is untrustworthy and often full of contradictions. Their beliefs are nothing other than the material of dreams, wish fulfillment and the deepest desires of humanity. They also served to fortify these primitive people against the superpowers of nature and fate:

> I have tried to show that religious ideas have arisen from the same need as have all the other achievements of civilization: from the necessity of defending oneself against the crushingly superior force of nature.[18]

Freud held that in a modern era, when science can explain the forces of nature, religion is no longer necessary. If we need the moral values religion once supplied, we can come to these by our own reason. In his later years Freud thought that religion was needed to stand off the chaos of Nazism, but he would not concede that religion was anything other than illusion and wish fulfillment.

Freud's critique of religion, though flawed in its historical and social data, can provide correctives for religion. It is true that religions in the past often have promoted false and repressive images of God that generated fear and the feeling of helplessness among people. In addition, religion can distract people from the real problems of everyday life by providing them with beliefs that are mere illusions—and even at times delusions. Religion also can provide an escape from dealing with the difficult realities of the world by promising rewards in another life. The strict laws and absolute authority of some religious groups have led some followers to be scrupulous, legalistic, and even obsessive. Moreover, church authority has at times been exercised with such a spirit of dominance that members have lost their sense of freedom and autonomy. Churches can be elitist and exclusive, and ignore the needs of the poor, women, and the oppressed. And finally, religion can get caught up in taboos about sexuality, nature, and gender, and as a result inhibit the growth of its believers.[19]

Religions need to respond to these critiques, especially if they wish to address the environmental crisis effectively. Fearful images of God need to be replaced with positive images of a loving and caring Creator, who shares responsibilities for nurturing creation with all people. Nature needs to be viewed as God's creation, in which all things have their own integrity and are interrelated, and not as an enemy to be mastered. Rather than provide dreamlike escapes from reality, religions are called to empower people to struggle for justice for living things as well as for the earth. Religions should liberate, not control; they should be dedicated to healthy growth, not to repression; they should bring about healing, not hurting. Authentic religion is inclusive and attentive to individual and collective needs. It bonds its people with each other and with the world community to deal with the pressing global issues such as injustice, oppression, and environmental destruction.

Freud's perspective itself deserves critique. Freud was a materialist, and his medical training was from the mechanistic school of medicine. Scientifically, he was trained to view the universe, the earth, and the human body as machines to be mastered. For Freud, the human psyche was a kind of appliance hooked up to the body. Its defects could only be repaired through manipulation of the subconscious. Thus Freud gave little credence to the spiritual aspect of human beings and discounted the possibility of leading a spiritual life. Furthermore, he viewed primitive societies as having little to offer but harmful taboos and myths.

Freud's highly influential views also have ecological implications. We have seen that such an anthropocentric outlook generally has little appreciation for the environment; it sees it only as a useful resource and pleasurable place to be. Freud's mechanistic approach to the world and to the human species tends to objectify the world and people, and then subjects both to considerable manipulation. Without a notion of the spiritual, it becomes impossible to appreciate a creation theology that gives meaning to the material world. Without religious traditions the many values derived from religions can be dismissed along with the illusions religions are thought to generate. Finally, the negative attitude toward primitive peoples devalues the treasured religious beliefs that are now being recovered from these indigenous cultures. Moreover, the dismissal of religious rituals as neurotic actions undercuts the value of religious symbols and sacraments, as well as the efficacy of prayer. Much of religious tradition arises out of an appreciation of nature and is essential for helping believers come to a better appreciation of their connectedness with and responsibility for the world around them.

CONTEMPORARY FORMS OF ATHEISM

Rather than the alienated and destructive atheism of the past, one often finds forms of contemporary atheism more benign. Yet they are equally dangerous to the environment.

The Atheism of the Academy

Today's atheism of the academy strives to keep all mention of God out of educational disciplines, except perhaps as an element of myth or magic. A dualistic mentality ignores talk of God as arcane to matters of science, politics, and culture. As a result, biblical beliefs in God as creator, sustainer, savior, and goal of all reality are set aside as irrelevant to current affairs. Only the observable, measurable, and programmatic sides of reality need be addressed. Consequently, students can receive extensive education and yet never be taught to see any connection between classic religious teachings and contemporary issues.

One example of this is the attitude of the late astrophysicist Carl Sagan, who scoffed at the notion of a Designer-Creator.[20] In his television programs and popular books Sagan was patronizing toward creation myths and the notion of a Creator God. He considered them to be products of ancient minds that had no access to modern science. He considered such notions simplistic and failed to appreciate the great depth of religious experience and meaning that underlies these myths. Nor did he seem to acknowledge that we cannot expect ancient myth-makers to be concerned with scientific questions.

Another contemporary example of the atheism of the academy is the work of Monod, who holds that both the microcosm and macrocosm have come about strictly through a process of chance. Such scientific positivism leaves no room for a creator, a designer, a sustainer, or an ultimate goal toward which everything is moving. In this context there seems to be no design and therefore little possibility for either restoring or sustaining natural processes.[21]

The Atheism of the Marketplace

There is also an atheism of the marketplace, which excludes God and biblical values from commerce and business. In business, the profit margin can become the ultimate goal. Greed and dominance can emerge as the prevailing norms. From this perspective resources are for speculation and use; they do not have sufficient intrinsic value to motivate us to preserve or sustain them. Ethical norms easily can become circumstantial and relativized–far removed from the gospel values of justice, charity, and compassion so central to Christian revelation.

Modern Secularism

The modern drive for the autonomy of the human subject (which was given great impetus by Descartes and the Enlightenment), as well as the modern urge for freedom (as evident in modern revolutions, the rise of nationalism and democracy), moved the West to a secularism that is still dominant today. This secularism rejects any notion of God that might inhibit human freedom or cultural progress. Many believe that if humans are to be independent and free, the reality of God must be denied or at least excluded from much of human life.

Secularism takes the position that religious beliefs should remain private; they should not be allowed to enter into education, science, industry, technology, politics, or any other aspects of culture. In the public educational system of the United States, for instance, consideration of God and any prayerful activity are excluded. Public universities generally pay only token attention to religion in their curriculum and often exclude the study of religion altogether. Moreover, religious values are often suspect in the transaction of business, in the formulation of plans for development, and in the proper use of technology. Secularism moves all levels of society beyond religious influence and insists that every aspect of life develop its own autonomous principles and values. It often rejects the Bible as a source of values and insists that God be keep out of all institutions.

Since secularism separates religion and God from everyday life, it also separates religious perspectives from environmental concerns. Once the theology of creation is removed from life, a kind of utilitarianism takes over. Usefulness, profitability, and enjoyment become the prominent norms for sustaining resources and caring for the earth. From this perspective the earth and living things are not acknowledged to have value in themselves.

Atheism and Religion

Modern atheism provides correctives to religion. To be authentic, religions must resist being instruments of fear, guilt, low self-esteem, and helplessness. Religions should not deal in illusions and simplistic dreams that offer people escape from the pressing issues of the day. They are in the world for service, not domination.

Authentic religion holds firm to belief in the existence of God as source, sustainer, and goal of all of creation. Religion should bring freedom and empowerment. It should engender healthy self-esteem, a spirit of bondedness among all things, and a serious commitment to peace. True religion gathers people and all things into unity with the Creator. It stands for the dignity of all life and all persons, and it is willing to live in solidarity with everything that is deprived of such dignity.

POSITIVE APPROACHES TO GOD

We have so far looked at atheism, the negative side of the God question, and examined its implications for ecology. Now we will discuss some positive approaches to God and reflect on how these might affect attitudes toward creation. We will briefly deal with what might be called the outside God, and then more extensively examine perspectives on the inside God.

The Outside God

Today many view God as a distant reality, far removed from everyday life: a divine force that dwells in the heavens and watches "from a distance." In early centuries this perspective was espoused by Deists, who described God as a kind of "old man in the sky," one who was indifferent to what was happening in the world. God's power was often relegated to some creative event in the distant past and not seen as operative in present creative processes.

Deism has often been a companion to the modern scientific movement. As science systematically studied reality and provided answers on the nature of things, divine explanations were no longer necessary. Even the so-called "gaps" left for God were gradually filled with scientific explanations, and the reality of God seemed to have less and less relevance to world affairs and everyday issues.

Bacon, Newton, and other thinkers of the Enlightenment thought of the world as a giant machine, which God designed and equipped with natural laws. Science's task was to discover this divine design and come to understand the laws of nature. Some viewed God as a master builder or clockmaker who set all things in motion and then sat back in benign and inactive transcendence.

With the appearance of the theory of evolution in the nineteenth century and the development of astrophysics in the twentieth century, science moved from seeing the world as a machine to conceiving of it as a dynamic process. Scientists who denied the existence of God could simply dismiss any notion of there being a Creator. The Deist, however, could still keep faith in the notion of a divinity as a remote "sky god."

Albert Einstein (d. 1955), a scientific giant of the modern era, seemed to take a deistic approach to God. Einstein always considered himself to be a religious man, but for him religion implied being open to the mysteriousness of the cosmos rather than belonging to an organized religious group.

> [There is] a knowledge of the existence of something we cannot penetrate, of the manifestations of the profoundest reason and most radiant beauty, which are only accessible to our reason in their most elementary forms. . . . It is this knowledge and this emotion that constitute the truly religious attitude; in this sense and in this alone, I am a deeply religious man.[22]

Einstein, in his relentless search to unlock the mystery of how the universe was constructed, often had the feeling that he was attempting to look into the mind of the Creator and decipher how God had put the world together. Einstein felt that a mysterious master design existed and hoped to do his share to unlock some of its secrets. He once remarked that the scientist is "like a child trying to understand the superior actions of grown-ups."[23] He spent years trying to explain the deep questions surrounding light, time, and gravity, and in the end often seemed to achieve his incredible insights not so much through calculation as through a kind of inspiration and intuition. Einstein refused to accept that there were any incongruities in the plan of the universe. He was fond of saying that the "Old Man" does not roll dice. Einstein maintained that the search to understand the universe is eternal.

Stephen Hawking, the Cambridge astrophysicist who in many ways is Einstein's successor in attempting to solve some of the most difficult questions about the cosmos, seems to have a similar religiosity. In attempting to bridge the puzzling gap between the theory of relativity and quantum theory, between the macrocosm and the microcosm, he suggests that in so doing we will discover "the mind of God."[24] Whether this reflects a religious naivete or is said with tongue in cheek, there does seem to be a notion here of a God remote in time and distance, one who has left traces in the cosmos for science to gradually unveil.

The notion of a distant, outside God can have varying implications for environmental concerns. On the one hand, there can be a deep respect for the mystery and complexity of the universe, yet at the same time science can become the ultimate source of truth about the universe as well as the most reliable guide for practical decision making. Since God is not perceived as being involved in the process, it is up to humans to gain mastery over the environment and to use its resources to expand national interests and economies. The motto here might be: What can be done, should be done. Norms from divine revelation and law can be dismissed. From the deistic point of view humans possess the world and are in charge of it, so it is up to them to make the rules and the decisions. There can be a certain moral sense, but the Creator is not involved or concerned enough to set standards for moral decisions, including those involving the environment. Human needs for comfort, convenience, profit, pleasure, and progress become the standards for dealing with the environment. Insufficient thought is given to sustaining the earth for its own sake, and even less consideration is offered to those who languish in hunger and squalor for lack of resources. The "old man in the sky" is praised and paid due reverence but has little relevance to the issues of everyday life.

The outside God can also be perceived as allied with one particular person, nation, gender, or class. Hitler is said to have thought of himself as a prophet appointed by God to purify the human race and to establish a new kingdom that would last for a millennium. The Conquistadors commonly thought of the New World as a new Garden of Eden to which they had been led to be masters of its indigenous peoples and resources. The United States' expansion over the lands and lives of Native Americans was justified by the notion of "manifest destiny." A remote and indifferent God can be perceived as giving his blessing to racial supremacy, gender discrimination, or militaristic and economic domination. Needless to say, such an approach to God is of little value to those who want to turn to the Creator as a dynamic presence and source for the norms, guidance, and assistance needed to deal with the environmental challenges of today.

The Inside God

Even though the "old man in the sky" is still somewhat prevalent as an image of God, theology in the last few decades has shifted to an inside God. In this section we examine a number of approaches to God's immanence, including the theory that the world is in God and the proposal that God is in the world as the power of freedom, the depth of all reality, the source of beauty, and the lure of the future. We discuss God as a personal presence in the universe, as a feminine presence that is the source of life and nurturance, and as a driving force within all of history. Naturally, we look for important implications for environmental theology.

The World in God

The process philosophy of Alfred North Whitehead has been most influential in the development of *panentheism,* the theory that all creation is *in* God. Whitehead attempted to understand God in relationship to the contemporary world, which is no longer considered to be static but rather changing and evolving. Whitehead proposes a God who is compatible with such a world, a God who is dynamic and constantly interacting with the universe. This is a "becoming God" of infinite potentials and possibilities. Whitehead describes this God as a "fellow sufferer," a "poet of the world," who patiently continues to create and at the same time is affected by the changes in the world.[25] This is a God in whom all exists, evolves, and develops. One thinks of Paul's statement to the Athenians in Acts: "Yet God is actually not far from any one of us; as someone has said: 'In him we live and move and have our very being'" (Acts 17:27-28).

The process view sees the world and its history as an "essential moment of divine life."[26] This perspective reaches back to Hegel, who saw God (the Absolute Spirit) manifested through the world. In this view God constituted the world as different from the Divine but nonetheless entered into a relationship with it. God is the basis of freedom and now suffers along with the world. For Whitehead, God also must be somehow temporal and spatial. Process thought "posits a real relation of God to the world, as well as a real relation of the world to God. Hence it is as true to say that God needs the world as it is to say the world needs God."[27]

For Whitehead, God and the world exist for each other, and both operate as forces of creativity. Many theologians think that the process model of a dynamic God can be compatible with trinitarian theology as well as incarnational theology. Its emphasis on the suffering aspect of God also seems compatible with the theology of the cross. The downside of the process approach to God is that it seems to neglect the transcendent and personal characteristics of God so evident in the biblical tradition.

Panentheism, or the existence of all things in God, has been adopted by process theologians such as John Cobb, A. R. Peacocke, Thomas Berry, and others. It does not equate God with creation, as pantheism does. Rather, panentheism sees God as intimately connected with and related to all things. Jay McDaniel describes panentheism as "the view that the creation and all its processes are somehow 'in' God, even though God is 'more than' creation. If God is the Sacred Whole, then the whole is more than the sum of the parts."[28] God is the reality to which all creatures belong. All have an interiority that ultimately is derived from God, and by virtue of such interiority are within the Source. God is the fullness of life and is thus closely allied with all living things and gently lures all things toward further creativity. The Jewish-Christian notion of neighbor is broadened to include all of creation.

Much of process thinking is valuable for ecology, for it sees all of the world in God, with *both* caught up in a process of creativity. Unfortunately, Whitehead does not clearly place goals for this process, so Christian process theologians often have had to introduce their own ultimate goals. But the very fact that the world is in God gives the world a certain value and dignity and recognizes that abuses of the world are moral issues. Whitehead's notion that God is a compassionate fellow-sufferer can serve as a source of meaning in the midst of so much futile destruction and offer hope that God accompanies people as they "create anew."[29]

Process theologians tend to work outside of the biblical sources and prefer to use philosophical or scientific terminology. If their description of the process and how it is in God could be better integrated into the biblical theologies, the process perspective would be more widely acceptable to mainstream Christian theologians. An integration of the biblical perspective with panentheism could enable environmental theology to hold onto biblical wisdom about creation and at the same time be able to speak to people living in a scientific age. Environmental theology, as we have seen, must be rooted in biblical revelation, but at the same time this revelation has to address contemporary issues and problems.

God in the World

Theologians have often reflected on the belief that God is in the world, not only as creator and sustainer but as an absolute Being who communicates God's self to the world. Aquinas linked humans with God through "being," which then became the bridge through which God communicated God's self.

Aquinas held that God, the Infinite Being, shared God's self with humans and has given them a share in being, albeit in a finite manner.[30]

Karl Rahner, using a more dynamic notion of being that he learned from Heidegger and Maréchal, says that every reality is based and grounded on divine reality and is thus somehow related to its transcendent origins. What God has in absolute fullness, reality has in its own limited fashion. This view has many possibilities for restoring the integrity of all things and thus for developing a theology concerned with all of nature.

Rahner points out that at first sight it would seem that if God entered our world, God would somehow seem to be an object alongside other objects and would thus no longer be the divine self. Yet, Rahner points out, religions insist that God is everywhere present in reality. How can this be? Rahner attempts to answer with the position that God freely chooses to grace reality with the divine presence. Such self-communication of the Divine to reality is pure gift. As Rahner says: "What is given in grace and incarnation is not something distinct from God, but God himself."[31] It is as though God is "embedded" in reality and has given all finite matter an openness to receive the Divine, just as humans have been given the capacity to be open to the Spirit of God. Somehow God can come to our world without becoming an element of our world. God remains absolute and yet enjoys communing with creation.

In order to have a theology of God that is appropriate for ecology, we must walk the fine line between two positions: one where God actually becomes finite things, and the other where God is considered to be far removed or even absent from reality. The first position easily slips into idolatry, which of course is not compatible with the Jewish-Christian tradition. The other ends in the kind of Deism we discussed earlier, whereby God seems irrelevant to environmental concerns.

Rahner's view, which preserves the transcendence of God and at the same time keeps God as our "horizon," freely and lovingly "in touch" with cre- ation, is indeed useful for ecology. Here the world is linked with the Creator ontologically as well as personally, and this offers abundant reason to treasure all of creation and see it as a link with the Creator.

The God of Freedom

Rahner also stresses freedom as uniquely characteristic of God and maintains that human freedom is derived from God. God *is* freedom, in that the Creator is One who must be (*Yahweh*, or "I am who I will be"). Rahner observes that we are not permitted to make God into what we want through inappropriate projections and rationalizations. God must be free to be God.

Rahner maintains that God freely chooses out of love of creation to communicate God's self to the finite world. God does not have to do this, but "he has bound himself: he has taken up a position with regard to man and the finite which he himself freely declares to be definitive, and of which he himself says that he will never go beyond it again, and never withdraw from it."[32]

To be free is one of our deepest urges, perhaps the area in which humans best image the Creator. Vatican Council II stated that "authentic freedom is an exceptional sign of the divine image within the human person."[33] Freedom is about choices, and the ultimate choice for humans is to be in union with the Creator. To achieve this requires being free from sin, attachments, addictions, and other obstacles. Authentic freedom, however, is not only freedom *from,* it is also freedom *for.* In the area of the environment, freedom means choosing to serve the earth and all living things out of regard for the Creator of all things.

Karl Rahner taught that to discover ourselves freely is the way to find the God within us. For Rahner, anthropology was theology, and he gave the people of today direction in how to look into the self and others when searching for God. This is no "sky god" but the divine presence who dwells in all things. For Rahner, true freedom is discovering the truth about God, self, and others.

Thomas Merton had similar views. He was convinced that if people choose to discover their true selves, they will be able to find God within. Merton learned from years of monastic discipline and contemplation that in the innermost darkness of the self one can find the "I am" of the almighty Being. Getting in touch with the authentic "self" seemed to bring Merton a great sense of inner freedom, as well as a deep awareness of his connection with his fellow human beings and with nature. Concretely, this awareness came out in Merton's later passionate commitment to peace and justice. We will discuss his views on this in more detail in chapter 9.[34]

We can move one more step further and say that to find the truth of any reality, including the earth, is to meet the Creator who shaped all things. True freedom is choosing the good, whether in people or in nature, and all good in creation finds its ultimate source in God. Just as we can discover the Creator within ourselves, we can encounter the Divine in creation. Once we have done that, the reasons for caring for creation become manifest.

God as the Depth Reality

John Haught has suggested that "depth" can be useful in the search for God.[35] Whether looking into the depths of ourselves or others, the microcosm or macrocosm, it is possible to discover the presence of the Creator. Abbot Sertillanges, the great scholar on the intellectual life, held that the scholar can use study, reflection, and the pursuit of truth as a path to God. He maintained that since God is the source of truth, God often can be discovered in the pursuit of intellectual knowledge.

The mysteries we strive to understand with regard to our own identity or the identity of loved ones, and the mysteries with which we grapple in our studies of science, literature, philosophy, and other disciplines are somehow related to God, the ultimate mystery. As we plunge into these depths, meaning always seems to elude us, to recede from us, and at times to remain incomprehensible. There is something that seems to be almost within our reach, and on occasion there is only darkness and the abyss. At other times there is the comforting satisfaction of gaining understanding. There can be great joy in discovering a "new" idea, a fresh insight. The same applies in our search for the Divine. God often seems to be hidden and seemingly inaccessible, and then suddenly in a flash of graced insight there is a presence that touches the spirit.

For many, exploring the depths of music can be a context for the experience of the Divine. Great theologians like Karl Barth, Hans Küng, and Hans Urs von Balthasar have described how the music of Mozart brings them an undefinable "bliss," even "traces of transcendence." Mozart, sometimes elfish and childlike, seems to have been profoundly in touch with both the harmonies and discords of creation. In the sweeping variations of his music he connected with the "mysterious order" that exists in the depth of reality. He could make audible both the light and dark sides of life and put his listeners in touch with the spiritual and the Divine. Hans Küng puts it this way:

> If I allow myself to be open, then precisely in this event of music that speaks without words I can be touched by an inexpressible, unspeakable mystery. In this overwhelming, liberating experience of music, which brings such bliss, I can myself trace, feel and experience the presence of a deepest depth or a highest height—pure presence, silent joy, happiness. To describe such experience and revelation of transcendence religious language still needs the word of God, the nature of which . . . makes up the reconciliation of all opposites, which is also characteristic of Mozart's music.[36]

For many, the same "traces of transcendence" can be found in the depths of natural experiences. Pierre Teilhard de Chardin, the great Jesuit scientist who pioneered the Catholic acceptance of modern science, began as a child to sense "the Divine radiating from the depths of blazing matter." His contact with the earth, whether it be in touching rocks or admiring flowers and plants, taught him about God. These experiences led him to follow a vocation "to chart the history of the cosmos and the rise of human life on earth." It was in the context of matter that he would find his spiritual destiny.[37]

The depths of reality are accessible to all of us, and it is in the depths of knowledge, art, music, nature, and personal intimacy that we can meet the Creator of all. There is much to be learned and experienced about the earth and the universe in which we dwell. Note the great excitement that was generated in the summer of 1997 by *Sojourner*'s exploration of Mars. The late

Jacques Cousteau, one of the environmental giants of the twentieth century, was thrilled by so many elements of nature. Shortly before he died, he wrote about the return of the butterflies that had for years been absent from his Normandy garden:

> The butterflies are back! They zigzag like motes of dust, alighting on a flower here and there, drinking so deeply of the nectar that for a moment they are too dizzy to fly. The spontaneity which enchants us in the butterfly is something I've been struck with throughout my life, and that I've seen in ladybugs, hummingbirds, sea otters, and even the most enormous whales. May humans be inspired to delight in life with the same sort of simplicity.[38]

For the person of faith this can be a way to also experience the Creator, better appreciate the gifts of the earth, and resolve to better tend to them with care.

The God of Beauty

John Keats wrote that "a thing of beauty is a joy forever." As humans, we have an aesthetic sense whereby we recognize beauty and are drawn to it. The beauty of a face, a body, a painting, a poem, a song, or a natural scene can lift us out of ourselves and fill us with delight. Humans are the only creatures who have this aesthetic capacity to appreciate the harmony, variety, and contrasting elements that merge to create that mysterious element we call beauty.

Beauty is considered to be *transcendental,* a dimension of reality that goes beyond definition or time-space location. Beauty transcends all things as a metaphysical aspect of reality. It is, in a sense, godlike, in that we constantly reach for beauty, and yet it continues to evade us. Experiences of beauty are temporary, momentary, but they point to a Beauty that is lasting, eternal.

The person of faith can commune with God through watching the magnificence of a sunrise, sitting on a beach listening to the waves lap the shore, or holding a newborn baby. There is a rich treasure of beauty to be found in nature, people, art, music, architecture, and many other aspects of life. These experiences of beauty can also be ways to experience God, the source and Creator of all that is beautiful.

Those who have difficulty discovering the experience of God in traditional church rituals are sometimes able to encounter God in aesthetic experiences. Bernard Meland calls this approach to faith "appreciative awareness."[39] The experience of the beautiful, whether in art, music, dance, or athletics can move us beyond the ordinary and touch us with the powerful and creative presence of the Divine. Meland holds that appreciation for the beauty in life can move us to an appreciation of the Author of such beauty.

Recognition and valuing of the aesthetic dimension of our earth in all its facets are essential for the kind of ecological consciousness we have been discussing. If one is able to appreciate the beauty of people and nature—and really believe that all of this is somehow a reflection of the Creator—commitment to sustaining the earth will follow.

The God of the Future

Some theologians have suggested a change in time in the search for God. Instead of the tradition notion, which places the Creator in the past, perhaps God might be found ahead of us, drawing us to a hopeful future. The God ahead is a God of hope, inviting people to be fulfilled and to share in God's ultimate goals for all of reality.[40] The Christian tradition has an eschatology—a future that God is bringing about, a creative ordering of chaos, a healing of wounds. People of faith look to an ultimate future when pain and suffering will be gone. For the Christian, that ultimate future is being with God, an experience of divine presence and power for all eternity.

Religious eschatology or concern with the end time arises out of concern for the future. The future symbolizes the fulfillment of dreams and the accomplishment of goals. In times of crisis—whether the Babylonian Captivity for the Hebrews, the persecution of Christians in the early church, or the Holocaust—people have turned to God for a more hopeful future. Here God is a future horizon of peace and happiness, a way out of suffering and chaos.

Unfortunately, this desire for a better future often makes people vulnerable to deception by those who offer false futures. Hitler promised the German people a millennium of racial superiority and world domination but brought them only despair, destruction, and a burden of guilt for atrocities. Communism offered the people of the Soviet Union a "classless society," where there would be equality and a mutual sharing of material things. In fact, this vision turned out to be false, because it attempted to replace God with material things, the state and the party.

Environmentalists are passionately concerned with the future of the earth and all living things. Many point to signs of a threatened if not catastrophic future. As Norman Myers has pointed out, we are coming to a turning point comparable to the great geological and climactic upheavals of primeval periods. He foresees a future that might produce "the greatest single setback to life's abundance and diversity since the first flickerings of life almost four billion years ago."[41] Others warn that the consequences of our environmental destruction might be similar to a "nuclear winter." Cousteau laments over what our children may never see: "I pitied today's children . . . who might never see a robin or a thrush! And year after year, even the swallows grew rarer and rarer."[42]

Geologian Thomas Berry warns:

If there is to be any acceptable future for the variety of living forms that constitute in great part the splendor of the earth, or if there is to be any acceptable human future, the grandeur of the planet must continue to flourish. This can only come about by a transformation of patriarchal dominion to a more nurturing attitude, both toward the natural world and all its living creatures, and of humans toward each other.[43]

There are many other prophetic warnings today that if we do not radically change our behavior toward the environment, its future is in jeopardy.

A Personal God

The God of the Christian tradition is a personal God. This is not to say that God is a person alongside other persons, but that the human personal capacities that come from the Creator are apt metaphors for exploring the mystery of God. To be personal implies the capacity to understand, reach out, and be in relation with. The personal denotes concern, intimacy, a "standing with"– all aspects of the experience of God. Christian spirituality has always been concerned with experiencing God as personal in everyday life as well as in prayer. Ours is a God who acts and cares, a God who "walks with" and challenges. A personal God is a God who is compassionately engaged with creation, not a deity who merely watches from afar.

This God, though often hidden, is present in life as love, power, freedom, and forgiveness. For Christians, God is not only the God of the cosmos or the Yahweh of Israel but also the Abba of Jesus Christ. God is a Trinity of distinct individualities in community. The Christian God is not a distant impersonal force but a subjective reality that shares God's self with creation, communicates in revelation, and ultimately becomes one with creation through the incarnation.

The personal metaphor helps us understand the self-consciousness of God, the dynamic "becoming" aspect of God. People of faith seek to relate to and be at one with the unique individuality of God. For the Hebrews, God could be jealous, angry, forgiving, and welcoming; a God who acts, saves, feeds, protects, and guides; a God who is the source of personal freedom. As Piet Schoonenberg puts it: "We cannot as Christians abandon the personal image of God."[44] For Christians, the one who makes God ultimately personal is Jesus Christ.

The importance of a personal God for ecology is evident. If we see God as impersonal, there is scant reason God should care about or sustain a covenant with creation. If God is not personally involved with creation, what motivation is there to consider the earth sacred? A God outside of our realm of experience can hardly be a source of inspiration or guidance.

In contrast, a personal God who is in a constant relationship with creation is deeply concerned about creation and vigorously active in its conservation. Humans are a part of that creation, are interconnected with it, and are in covenant with its Creator. God's laws for creation become our laws, and our relationship with God rises or falls to the degree that we are faithful to these laws. A personal God accompanies us, offering the vision and power we need to share in the process of creation.

A Feminine Life-giving Presence

The images of mother, midwife, and spouse have been applied to God with depth and insightfulness in the scriptures. The feminine energy experienced in God is also described in the rich terms of Spirit and Wisdom. This model has been sustained in the Syriac and Eastern traditions and is now being reclaimed in Western theology. In the gospels Jesus used the image of the mother hen for himself and in one parable depicted God as a woman searching for a coin. Jesus' treatment of women and his unprecedented selection of women for disciples were also instances of his conviction that women were indeed created in the image and likeness of God. Paul's recognition of the value of women leaders in the first communities and his statement on equality between the sexes show the influence of Jesus' respectful regard for women. Paul writes: "There is no longer Jew or Greek, there is no longer slave or free, there is no longer male and female; for all of you are one in Christ Jesus" (Gal 3:28). Both women and men can stand in the world as effective images of the presence of Christ.

Trinitarian theology also has been an arena for considering feminine images for God. Life within God is now described in terms of equality, partnership, interaction, and relationship. These values offer women many possibilities for exploring the mystery of God from the feminine perspective. Needless to say, these same values offer new possibilities for regaining the connections that both women and men need to have with each other, with their God, and with all of creation.

Discoveries in the ancient cultures of Europe and in the belief and value systems of indigenous cultures have also enkindled new interest in the great worth in applying feminine images to God. So-called pagan traditions are now being revisited as rich sources for God imagery. Notions of God from Native American religions seem to have special appeal to young people today and are most appropriate for gaining a renewed appreciation for nature.

All of this emphasis on feminine imagery for God has allowed theologians to become better aware of the life-giving, nurturing, and communal dimensions of God. This perspective also has enabled theologians to link God more closely with issues involving the sustaining of creation.

The God within History

As we saw earlier in our considerations on the Hebrew scriptures, one of the predominant Hebrew beliefs was that Yahweh was a God of history. Yahweh was not only the Creator of all things but the director of all things, including storms, floods, and even battles. Yahweh even punished his people with natural disasters, exiles, and other calamities. For the Hebrews, history consisted of events that happened between God and his people. As Claus Westermann puts it: "The Old Testament reports what happens from God towards people and from people toward God."[45] For the Hebrews, writing salvation history meant proclaiming events of experienced faith, saving encounters with God, and not the recording of factual happenings. The key question for the Jews was: What does this event *mean?*, not What happened?

This is quite a contrast to our modern notion of history, which focuses on what happened and is concerned with the causes and secular interpretations of the events. The modern Western mind is not as expansive in its portrayal of God acting in the world. Scientific explanations for such phenomena as disease and weather leave little room for ancient notions of providence. Few today see natural disasters as anything other than the results of natural forces or human negligence. Such happenings are seldom considered punishments from the hand of God. Moreover, the Western scientific mind generally sees wars as political actions, not as holy wars or crusades in which God takes sides.

The contemporary generation has much more control of events, both natural and historical, than did generations of the past. The control of waterways, the modernization of farming, and the development of land is much more in the hands of technology. Genes can be manipulated, life can be controlled and extended, animals can be cloned, and species of plants and animals can be altered in ways that would have not been imagined in the past. Even wars, which in the past could have gone on for years, can now be fought in the span of a few days, as was demonstrated in Desert Storm. At times it seems that life itself is programmed and tailored by the media. Thus the notion of God acting in history means something much different today than it did in ancient times. Even though Christians still believe that God acts in the world, history is perceived as the result of human choices.

Liberation theology has offered fresh interpretations of the God of history. In former times the poor were told to accept their sufferings as the "will of God." Now they are told by liberation theology to seek out those who are responsible for their oppression and take a stand for justice and freedom. Faith here is not in a God who permits evil but in a Creator who is in solidarity with the oppressed and involved with them in their struggle for justice. This is a God of liberation rather than a God who tests and punishes people with adversity. This is a God of empowerment rather than a God of resignation. The will of this God is that his children be saved, not that they suffer or be punished. As Gustavo Gutiérrez has written: "God is present in the cosmos, but God is also present in the midst of history. The living God is present and active in the historical movement of human society. God has decided that it should be so."[46]

The future of our planet is in some ways in our hands. Though we do not control evolution and all the natural processes, much of what we do in our industrial, technological era deeply affects the environment as well as history. We are altering weather patterns, disturbing ecosystems, and eliminating species. We could ultimately make it difficult for our rapidly growing population to survive on this planet. Future wars may be fought over water and other resources. Future conflicts might arise out of the desperation of the majority of people who have been deprived and oppressed while their fellow humans live in luxury and comfort. Generations to come look to us to restore the earth to health and to discover ways for sustainable development. The God of the future beckons us to a wiser and more careful use of the things of earth, as well as to a more equitable sharing with the millions who are deprived of even the basic necessities.

CONCLUSION

How contemporary society settles the God question is of crucial importance for the environmental crisis. Two world wars in the twentieth century have demonstrated the enormous destruction that can result from political movements rooted in atheism. Industrialization, often carried forth without a moral compass, has devastated many areas of the environment. Materialism, secularism, and consumerism threaten to exhaust the earth's resources, spread contamination and pollution, and leave millions deprived, undernourished, and without the basics of life. Revivals of Nietzsche's nihilism among postmoderns and political extremists threaten an already unstable world. Some approach the coming millennium with warnings that sound apocalyptic.

Yet there are many reasons for hope. Believers throughout the world are beginning to link their faith in the Creator with their concerns for the future of the planet. Churches and religions everywhere are awakening to this most threatening "sign of the times" and are calling for a renewal of faith. Catholics, after centuries of neglecting the Bible, are returning to the scriptures as a primary resource for God's self-revelation and as a guide for their lives. Older images of a patriarchal divinity far removed from the world are being set aside as no longer relevant to our times. Other images of God that have been long ignored, especially feminine images, are being reclaimed and given new richness.

Many Christians today discover God in their midst: in personal experience, in nature, in the poor and oppressed. This is a God who enlightens people to see both the immorality and the hazards of environmental degradation, a God who empowers people to be a part of a growing movement to conserve this planet for both present and future generations.

8.

Women's Views on the Ecological Crisis

I am only nine years old, but I feel so much older than that. I am in the hospital with a sickness they name to be cholera. My mother, who died last month, had the same sickness. This was such a beautiful place on the shore of the lake I love, the lake called Tanganyika. Just a few years ago we used to play in its waters and swim. But then the rains came, rains that the old people say were never like this. The rains washed all the filth from the village into our drinking water. After that the war came and the soldiers took everything we owned and left us without food, electricity, or running water. My friends and I lived in the woods for a while until I got sick. It was scary at night. My only food now comes from a bottle hanging over my rusty old bed. I don't think that will last much longer.

—Msembenge, Kalemie, Zaire

In this chapter we look at a cross-section of women's views on environmental issues, discuss the gradual evolution of ecofeminism from the larger feminist movement, and consider feminist theories on the link between women and nature. We also examine feminist reconstructions of how patriarchy, hierarchy, and dualistic thinking have brought abuse to both women and to nature. We close with some suggestions by Christian women theologians for revising the Christian tradition so that it can be used to nurture both women and the earth.

THE EVOLUTION OF ECOFEMINIST THEOLOGY

It is not easy to sort out the evolution of ecofeminism. It seems linked to the secular movement of feminism, which only in the last several decades became linked with ecology. In 1972 Francoise d'Eaubonne coined the term "ecological feminism." She argued that the destruction of the planet was due to the profit motive inherent in male power and that only women could bring about an ecological revolution. As women thinkers began to turn their attention to the environment, women theologians in this movement began to look also at the religious dimensions of the ecological issues.

Ivone Gebara, a Brazilian theologian, maintains that feminist theology went through several stages before it began to link theology with ecology.[1] In the first stage women became conscious that they were oppressed. Poor women are often the most deeply affected by environmental degradation. In third-world countries it is usually the women who have to get up before dawn, travel long distances on foot, and wait in lines to collect water suitable for cooking and drinking. Likewise, it is usually women's task to gather wood for cooking and heating, often in areas stripped nearly bare by loggers and developers. In many areas mothers attempt to nurture and feed children who are suffering from malnutrition and disease brought on by the devastation of arable lands and the pollution of air and water.[2]

The voice of Carmelita, a Mayan mother who lives in the rainforests of Belize, describes such oppression:

> My people have been here in the forest for thousands of years. My husband, two children and I live in a tiny grass hut in a village of about 1200 inhabitants. We have been a happy community and live with the forest as a friend. It supplies us with food, material for our houses, medicine and cedar wood for our canoes. The forest has been our church, a place where we praise and thank the Creator. All that is changing now. The government is selling our forest to Asian governments and they are coming in and stripping the wonderful forests. We are losing everything and they don't care what we think. The land is growing bare and dry, the air is different, and the streams are clogged with logs, broken plants and dead animals. The authorities tell us that we are not important and that our way of life is a thing of the past. We do not know what will become of us. We pray to the Creator to protect us and guide us in our resistance to this destruction.[3]

Environmental poverty often goes hand in hand with severe economic need. One of the pioneers of ecofeminism, Vandana Shiva, points out:

> The poverty crisis of the South arises from the growing scarcity of water, food, fodder and fuel associated with increasing maldevelopment and ecological destruction. This poverty touches women most severely because they are the poorest among the poor, and then because with nature they are the prime sustainers of society.[4]

Often women have to watch the homes they have so carefully made for their families be destroyed by bulldozers. Often women stand by and watch their husbands become frustrated by not being able to find animals to hunt or fish to catch for family sustenance. Some have to watch helplessly as their children die from malnutrition or disease.

It is out of this unique pain and suffering of women in the midst of the environmental crisis that the movement of ecofeminism was born. Many women point to a strong link between the abuse of the environment and the exploitation of women. As we shall see in more detail later in this chapter, many women have also observed that patriarchal and hierarchical structures have been responsible for the domination and exploitation of both nature and women.

Rosemary Radford Ruether describes some of the trends among women ecofeminists.[5] She observes that some Northern scholars tend to begin with an analysis of how patriarchal structures have linked women with nature and then placed male-dominated cultures over both women and nature. Others explore the socioeconomic aspects of the domination of women's bodies and work and then demonstrate how this interconnects with environmental exploitation. Some propose that hierarchies of race and class are at the root of gender suppression, while others move to become defenders or mediators, resisting with both theory and action the impoverishment of women and the environment. As the work goes on, it becomes apparent that much has been done by privileged women who are often as much a part of the domination of the earth as they are a part of the critique. Ruether proposes that we need to hear "from below," from women who are suffering firsthand from the environmental crisis.

Many religious women also began to suspect that their oppression was linked with the Bible churches and theology. This realization often brought about anger, a desire to "get even," and at times engendered feelings of superiority over the men who had been responsible for the abuse. Gebara points to the second stage of this evolution as one where feminine images for God and feminine theological insights were rediscovered in the scriptures and tradition. During this phase women also began to gain a voice in their churches and universities, and started grassroots organizations to promote feminine perspectives. At the same time liberation theology stimulated many women's desire for freedom.

In the next stage in the development of feminist theology, according to Gebara, a link was made among the degradation of the environment, the oppression of women, and some traditional religious beliefs. Once this connection was made, a new challenge was raised against any notions of God, redemption, and church that in any way contributed to abusive activity. In this phase some began to reject the image of God as an almighty and all-powerful Creator. The anthropology that viewed humans as fallen beings who could only be saved if God sent his Son to rescue them from original sin also came under scrutiny. Many feminist theologians challenged the image of a patriarchal God, as well as the messianic triumphalism that image engendered in the church. A holistic ecofeminism began to develop, one which viewed God as an immanent presence who fosters an egalitarian spirit among people and nurtures new relationships among humans, the earth, and the entire cosmos. The ultimate goal here is to put an end to patriarchy in all its forms; to liberate all people, especially women and the poor; and to cease environmental degradation, which so often has been aimed primarily at women and the earth.

In its beginning stages feminine perspectives on ecology worked out of the European framework and studied how the Hebrew and Christian traditions were linked with the oppression of women and nature. Strong ties between women and nature were exposed as key elements in the degradation of the earth and women.[6] The theology of creation in the Hebrew scriptures was often challenged as a factor in human alienation from the earth. In traditional creation theology creation is "fallen" and the earth excluded from redemption. Here, according to Heather Eaton, the human-male creature was given central position and was divinely commissioned to dominate the earth and women.[7] Many women scholars moved beyond this ancient cosmology and began to work out of contemporary scientific perspectives. Others preferred to return to the ancient cosmologies of the so-called pagan cultures of the past.

As the feminist movement began to diverge, various schools of ecofeminist theology emerged. Voices were heard from all points of the globe, as well as from many religions and churches. At present feminists offer a diversity of historical and cultural analyses of ecology, submit new interpretations of religious traditions, and challenge their religious leaders to take action against the abuse of women and the earth. Many call for a reconstruction of their religious traditions so that the dignity and integrity of women and nature might be restored. Among Christian women suggestions range from radically abandoning the biblical and doctrinal traditions of the past to the retrieval of more holistic and egalitarian elements of the tradition. Many search for new theological interpretations that would promote good ecology.

WOMEN LINKED WITH NATURE

It is common among ecofeminists to view the link between women and nature as a key for understanding the abuse of the environment. This identification of women with nature, and conversely of men with culture, seems to go back millennia. On a physiological level the woman's body often is thought to be closer to nature, while the man's prowess is directed more toward culture. The woman's body, of course, is designed to reproduce and nurture new life. While women nurture their children and perform the tasks of homemaking, men have the leisure to carry on the artistic, social, and political tasks that are integral to culture. These latter activities often have been given more importance. Male activity also has been more public, whether hunting or going to war, and therefore much more likely to be recorded and given historical significance. Women's activity in homemaking and raising children has been private and has not been given much notice in history. Thus women often have lived silent and hidden lives that have been given little significance and have gone unrecorded. Many women scholars maintain that male-dominated cultural activities eventually gained precedence. Women, it is proposed, became associated with nature, and once there was a demand to use the resources of nature for progress, both women and the environment were abused.

Many early social attitudes grew out of the reasoning that because women brought forth life, they should be associated with work associated with child care, the gathering and preparation of food, cleaning, and the production of clothing and other artifacts needed for daily life. Men, on the other hand, took over the work of hunting animals, clearing trees, and warring–and these were seen as more prestigious. Women's work was ongoing and time-consuming, while men's work was occasional, more adventurous, and more the material for myth-making. Feminists suggest that the male world tended to demean the work of women while glorifying men's work. Men had the leisure and the power for politics and commerce, while women were preoccupied in the material and natural world of food-growing and children. According to Rosemary Ruether, both nature and the material world became closely associated with women, and both were reduced to things to be owned, dominated, and used.[8]

Women's social standing also seems to have been affected by their close link with nature. Perhaps women's life-giving and life-nurturing tasks limited their mobility in society and culture. Moreover, a contrast might have developed between the home and the "real world," between domestic life and public life. Homemaking over time became trivialized, and women were often perceived as preparing others for cultural life but not as actively taking part in culture.

Other factors might have led to linking women and nature, and to their ultimate abuse. The shift from hunting and gathering to agriculture could have been an important factor in feminine subjugation. With the development of farming and the ownership of land, a need for slaves arose in the ancient world. In many cultures women, who had become linked to nature, were enslaved. Their work was usually confined to the domestic scene. When rival tribes were conquered, the males often were killed and the women enslaved. Women's work easily could be identified with slave work, and by law animals, slaves, women, and land were linked as property to be dominated.

The Denigration of Matter

Some suggest that in early cultures matter became identified with women, and that matter at the same time was devalued. This denigration of matter could also have been a factor in the subjugation of both women and the earth. Platonic thought, which had a tremendous influence on ancient Christianity, sharply separated matter from the eternal ideas that were the loci for reality. The soul matters, not the body, and a hierarchy was established that moved from male down to female and then to animal. Matter and spirit were dichotomized, with women being associated with matter and men with spirit. Women also were associated with the lower realm of the sensual.

In the Greco-Roman period an attitude of pessimism toward matter developed in the Middle East. In apocalyptic thinking the material world would be destroyed, and in Gnostic thought material things were looked upon as evil.[9] Heaven consisted of leaving the flesh and returning to the spiritual realm above the cosmos. In Christian asceticism perfection often entailed leaving behind the sexual and the physical and concentrating upon the spiritual. Women who wished to follow the spiritual life would have to forgo their ability to bring forth new life. Male asceticism generally involved avoiding women, who had become associated with the natural rather than supernatural realm.

The medieval world vacillated in its attitude toward nature. On the one hand, a growing sacramental vision held that God nurtured the church through material things. On the other hand, nature was often associated with the demonic powers. Superstitions, preoccupation with witchcraft, and a fear of death often placed nature in a negative context, and women were commonly associated with all of these.

According to some feminist scholars the advent of Protestantism brought on a substantial rejection of sacramental practice. Especially in Calvin's thought, the material world and nature could not be trusted to convey the experience of God. Many Protestants set aside any religious inclination toward the natural and material being sacred and branded such sacramental thinking as "pagan." Some submit that this suspicion of nature resulted in women, who were identified with nature, being kept under tight control, both in their churches and in their homes.

Modern Science and Matter

As modern science developed during the seventeenth and eighteenth centuries, nature came to be viewed by many as "dead matter" to be analyzed and manipulated. As science became secularized, the notion of spirit was either set aside in a dualistic approach to reality—or simply rejected out of hand. Many feminists connect the resulting mechanistic view of the cosmos and the subsequent destruction of the environment.

Many feminists censure Francis Bacon (d. 1626) as a major contributor to the denigration of women. Bacon, one of the founders of the scientific method, used the Christian myth of the fall and the sin of Eve to justify the need for science. He believed that science could regain the dominion over nature that had been lost through the feminine. For Bacon, science was the ability to master nature, which he associated with the feminine. Some feminists point to Bacon's scientific metaphors as evidence of his negative identification of the feminine with nature. He proposes that nature be coerced, penetrated, and forced to yield. He speaks of wresting new knowledge from nature's womb, of grabbing nature by the hair of the head and shaping her into something new through technology. He suggests that nature is a devious woman, similar to those whom he viewed as witches. He compares the scientific method's interrogation of nature to the inquisitional tortures through which nature had to be exposed and robbed of her secrets. He once wrote: "I am come in very truth leading to you nature with all her children to bind her to your service and make her your slave."[10] Bacon is challenged by many feminists for his view that nature is no longer the teacher of man but man's servant. As Vandana Shiva points out: "For Bacon, nature was no longer Mother Nature, but a female nature, conquered by an aggressive masculine mind."[11] Nature was no longer a living and nurturing persona but matter to be exploited. When earth was mother, this belief acted as a constraint on environmental abuse. Once the earth became an objective resource, degradation was acceptable because of the profit motive.

René Descartes (d. 1650), another key figure in the Enlightenment and the Age of Science, is often blamed by feminists for contributing significantly to the separation of nature from spirit. Descartes is accused of placing tremendous emphasis on the importance of the cognitive and of viewing the thinking mind as over and against material nature, which is without spirit. He is also criticized for proposing a mechanistic approach to material nature and for suggesting that the world was somehow so objectified that it was in a different realm from religious truth. Critics charge also that Descartes helped establish dichotomies between the male, who is associated with reason, and the female, who is associated with the less reliable feelings and sensuality. According to Catharine Halkes, it is here we find the beginnings of the tragic separation of religious beliefs from scientific matters, as well as the roots of the uncoupling of religious beliefs from the environment. Descartes indicated that practical philosophy would make men "lords and owners" of nature.[12]

Finally, many feminists maintain that the work of Isaac Newton also tended to objectify matter and portray the universe as a gigantic clock. He is at times blamed for seeing nature as a machine to be controlled by science and for dissociating spiritual dimensions from conceptualization of the earth. His opponents often note that his views on these matters can be closely associated with negative attitudes toward both women and the earth.

It is also proposed that the modern chemical and industrial age further objectified and despiritualized nature. Progress became the watchword, and natural resources were the key to progress. Pollution of the air, land, and water was simply a necessary side effect to moving ahead in a technological age. Some believed that colonialism spread this mentality throughout Asia, Africa, Latin America, and the indigenous cultures, where people had to watch while their own natural environments were systematically obliterated. Indigenous people, who honored natural things and who understood their local ecosystems, were systematically annihilated. Ancient peoples who were close to nature were labeled savages, objects to be denigrated, and they were traded as work animals. Cultures that honored gender equality were quickly "civilized" beyond such outlooks.[13]

Powerful militarized countries prevailed, drained the natural resources from their colonies, and often enslaved the inhabitants of these areas. Exploitation of the land and people was justified under such labels as "manifest destiny" and "the white man's burden." Hand in hand with this degradation of nature went the impoverishment and oppression of women, who had become so closely identified with nature.

Adam Smith is commonly criticized by feminists for even further devaluing both nature and women. For Smith, man's work supplied all the necessities and conveniences of life. In today's terms we would say that man is the "bread winner." Manufactured goods became the source of wealth. Working along with nature, as was done in peasant and tribal societies, was no longer considered to be creative or productive. Their natural foods, customs for nutrition, and herbal medicines were devalued and even ridiculed. Many feminists hold that women, who were the ones generally occupied with these productive and creative activities, were concomitantly reduced to meager stature.

It is quite possible that with all of these advances people were able to step back from nature and come to the conclusion that "humanity was no longer a part of nature. . . . Therefore, when humanity interferes in nature (often aggressively), it interferes in something which has become foreign to it, and to which it is not emotionally tied. Humankind is even less inhibited by trepidation before nature, or by respect for nature's intrinsic, individual meaning."[14] Now humans can dominate nature (and women, who are associated with nature) with a certain cool aloofness and distance. Nature is no longer a home (*eco*) to cherish; it is now a thing to be manipulated and used.

The Mind Masters Matter

The placing of mind over matter, of spirit over material, has obvious consequences both for women and for ecology. Women became "other" and, while needed as a source of life and pleasure, were treated with condescension and even abuse. Aristotle, whose thought still significantly influences Western thinking, maintained that ruling-class Greek males were exemplars of reason, while women and slaves were servile people who were to be subdued. Aristotle also set up opposing elements: femininity/matter *vs.* virility/spirit; passivity *vs.* activity; water *vs.* fire. In each case the feminine was associated with the "weaker" element.[15] Even the Greek notion of conception seems to have honored the male as playing the primary creative role, while the female was viewed as a mere receptacle and supplier of materiality. In Hebrew thought it was the male seed that was of primary importance; the woman provided only the soil in which the seed could grow.

Johnson points out the ecological consequences of placing the male over both nature and the female. Man is the noble and powerful figure, while woman and nature are to be tamed and controlled. Both women and the earth bring forth life, but only in an instrumental and subservient way that meets the needs of men. As Johnson observes: "Women whose bodies mediate physical existence to humanity thus become symbolically the oldest archetype of the connection between social domination and the domination of nature."[16]

Many feminists maintain that the Cartesian male mind stands over and against feminine matter, which can be measured, quantified, and probed. From this perspective it is clear how vulnerable both women and the environment become. In our own time there are those who see nature as something to be dominated, as one might dominate a woman. The phrase *rape of the earth* indicates how the degradation of the earth is related to sexual abuse of women. We use the phrase *virgin forest* to refer to a forest that has been untouched and which awaits "mastering." Mother Earth, at times held in esteem, becomes the mistress of the developer and the exploiter.

Positive Approaches to Women and Nature

Not all feminists see the linking of women and nature as entirely negative. Some suggest that there can be positive effects from the association of women with material things. Maria Mies indicates three ways in which women have a special relationship with nature: (1) women react with nature and conceive of their bodies as being productive in the same way as does nature; (2) women appropriate nature, but not in a way that is dominant; they tend to relate and cooperate with nature the way they do with their own bodies; and (3) as producers of life women are initiators of productivity and subsistence.[17] All of these perspectives can help people better appreciate the life-giving and nurturing qualities of both women and nature.

There also are certain aspects of the feminine psyche that can benefit nature. Women are often more focused on relatedness, the concrete, the practical, the intimate. Women are commonly connected to place and can thus be more sensitive to the natural settings in which they live. They are at times more drawn to the subjective rather than the objective and thus may be in a better place to restore nature as a "thou" rather than an "it." Women are often adept at linking and drawing together. There is an urgent need for these skills in restoring the relationships among humans, other living things, and the earth itself. And, finally, women are often effective mediators and thus can help bring together humans and their earth.

Women, therefore, can be viewed as being able to play a special role in promoting good ecology. Women can empathize with the suffering of the earth; they are often so closely allied with nature that they are in a unique position to be her advocates. Vandana Shiva puts it this way:

> To say that women and nature are intimately associated is not to say anything revolutionary. After all, it was precisely just such an assumption that allowed the domination of both women and nature. The new insight provided by rural women in the Third World is that women and nature are associated not in passivity but in creativity and in the maintenance of life.[18]

Shiva calls for a recovery of the feminine principle as a means of restoring the earth. This principle can stand for the liberation of women and nature, as well as the liberation of men, who have been the primary destroyers of the environment. Liberation of the oppressed must also include liberation of the oppressor.

The recovery of the feminine principle means the restoration of inclusivity, relatedness, and creativity. It can restore the view that nature is living and organic, not dead matter or a machine. It can initiate action that is life-giving not death-dealing. The feminine principle stands for creativity rather than destruction; empowerment rather than domination; and activity rather than passivity on the part of women.[19] The feminine principle calls for a restoration of the dignity of indigenous women, as well as a reclaiming of the indigenous religions that honored the feminine.

PATRIARCHY AS NEMESIS

For most feminist theologians patriarchy is a nemesis. They view patriarchy as a social and religious structure wherein men are held to be superior and more powerful. Feminist theologians hold patriarchy to be largely accountable for the domination and exploitation that have been imposed upon both women and nature. Shiva observes: "Such systems are sustained by and reenforce the dominance of male culture and decision-making 'over,' 'apart from' and 'above' the female. These patriarchal structures programme both men and women to regard themselves as 'in control' of the rest of the world."[20]

The patriarchal worldview is perceived as closed off to other ways of thinking and alternative values, beliefs, or lifestyles. It is seen as absolutist and controlling, and as exerting power that comes from the top level of authority, which is male controlled. Opponents view patriarchal cultures as generally identified with and controlled by males, as well as giving insufficient acknowledgment to the importance of the feminine aspects of culture. Areas associated with the feminine, such as art, feelings, intuition, and relatedness, are commonly relegated to the margins of the culture.

Many feminists maintain that patriarchal structures are usually detrimental to the environment. They point out that values like beauty, connectedness, and immanence, which are essential for appreciating and sustaining the environment, are generally peripheral to patriarchal concerns. The I-Thou relationship, so important to feminine cultures, becomes overshadowed by the I-It posture. Patriarchal systems since the Enlightenment and the birth of science place too much emphasis on the power of the intellect and on materialist progress. Their goals can be to objectify nature, control it, and exploit it for profit. Abuse of the environment is an obvious result of such a pragmatic and dominating view of nature.

Cultural history reveals a cycle of women struggling to overcome patriarchy and claim their rightful place in society as dignified and equal persons. There are numerous instances where women rose to a certain level of equality and prominence only to succumb once again to the control of patriarchal structures. For instance, in the ancient culture of Sumer several millennia before the birth of Jesus, some women had several husbands, owned large tracts of land, received equal pay for their work, and held leadership positions in their culture. Conquests of Sumer, first by Babylonia and later by Assyria, quickly put an end to such gender equality and patriarchy once again prevailed. Similarly, in Egypt around the year 2500 B.C.E., women gained the right to choose their own husbands on the basis of love, were considered equal to their spouses, and gained equal rights. These rights were lost when Egypt was conquered by Greece and later by Rome.[21]

Greek and Roman Patriarchy

Both Plato and Aristotle had a great deal of influence on the development of patriarchy in Greek culture and in other cultures influenced by their philosophies. Plato maintained that women should remain at home and be obedient to their husbands. Aristotle taught that women were by nature inferior to men and should allow their fathers and husbands to rule them. During the Hellenistic period, which followed the conquests of Alexander the Great and lasted until the rise of Rome in the first century B.C.E., women gained extensive rights in the family and in society. Still, these rights were not equal to those of men, and this culture remained predominantly patriarchal. In the Roman culture there were periods, especially in the third century B.C.E., when laws were improved in women's favor. Yet the structures remained largely patriarchal, and women were not able to gain access to the highest positions in government or religion.

Hebrew Patriarchy

The Hebrew scriptures, which were a thousand years in the making, reflect a wide variety of views toward the feminine. Yahweh is generally portrayed as a male figure: a warrior defending his people, a father extending love and care to his children, a husband displeased with the infidelity of his people, a judge passing judgment on sinners. Yet in a number of instances, minor but nonetheless significant, God is described in feminine images: a seamstress clothing her people, a nurse caring for her children, a mistress, a midwife, a loving mother. During the time of the exile in Babylon the Hebrews incorporated devotion to the Goddess into their rituals. Unfortunately, these feminine images were often kept on the margins. There were, however, great women in Israel's history. Sarah and Rebecca were honored as mothers of Israel. Miriam, the sister of Moses, was described as a prophet and one of the leaders of the Exodus. Deborah was both a prophet and a judge; she brought God's word and justice to her people. At different times women ruled as queens of Israel.

But these instances where women gained prominence in Israel were exceptional, and the women in question were of the higher classes. We know little of the life of the poorer classes of Hebrew women, because their voices were seldom heard. Generally, Hebrew women were viewed as property and servants, were subject to divorce laws that favored men, and had few rights in court. A Jewish girl came of age at twelve and a half. Prior to that she did not have the right to possess anything or to receive payment for her work. Fathers often lamented the birth of a daughter and yet used daughters as cheap labor and as property that could bring in money in a marriage arrangement. It was even possible to sell daughters into slavery during times that were financially difficult. In the Hebrew culture a woman's identity was generally derived from her role as wife and mother. Women were expected to marry young, and marriages were arranged by the father. A woman's success hinged on how well she carried out her duties in the home.

In the Hebrew patriarchal system the woman was revered as a source of happiness to the husband and inspiration for the children. Her primary responsibilities were to maintain the home and to nurture the husband and children. The private world of nurturance were hers, not the public life of culture. If a woman did have occasion to appear in public, she was required to cover her face and refrain from speaking to anyone, especially to men. Divorce was largely a privilege for men, and the liberal school of Rabbi Hillel permitted divorce for minor grievances. Widows were not permitted to inherit from their husbands, and their futures lay in the hands of their husband's brothers.

Hebrew religious structures were also patriarchal. Circumcision, the sign of the covenant, was a ritual in which only the male could participate. Men carried out the teaching of the Torah; women were usually exempt from studying Torah. Women were not obligated, as men were, to make pilgrimages to Jerusalem for the feasts, and they were segregated in both Temple and synagogue. Women were generally limited in their participation in public prayer and had to defer to men for leading Sabbath observance.[22]

Many feminists hold that these patriarchal structures have been and remain at the root of much oppression against women and the earth. They point out that patriarchy has set in motion forces of dominance, use, and ownership that still prevail in the way society deals with women and the environment. Most feminists believe that these structures must be replaced with ones that are egalitarian and respectful of life in all its forms.

Jesus Challenges His Tradition

The teachings and activity of Jesus represent a departure from traditional patriarchal attitudes. The gospels portray Jesus teaching women, conversing with and healing them in public, and even choosing them as his disciples. Jesus treated all people as children of God, and he had little regard for the taboos of his tradition with regard to women. He was an advocate for women on many levels of society and had special regard for women who were outcasts, as is indicated in the stories of the woman taken in adultery, the Samaritan woman, and the prostitute who comes to pay Jesus homage at the house of Simon the Pharisee. Jesus commanded his followers to respect both mother and father. When his disciples attempted to send away the mothers and children who intruded upon Jesus, he rebuked the disciples and welcomed the mothers and children into his presence and care. Jesus challenged his religion's unjust divorce laws, defended widows against their oppressors, ignored the taboos regarding the uncleanness of women, and extended his teaching and healing ministry even to Gentile women. Jesus' kingdom is indeed for all!

Jesus' choice of women disciples is perhaps his most significant challenge to patriarchal structures. There are no records of other rabbis choosing women for followers. His commissioning of both women and men to carry forth his message to all nations reflects both the inclusive and global dimensions of Jesus' mission. A woman's place can be on mission, not necessarily in the home. She can derive her identity in other ways besides being mother and wife. In Jesus' community, discipleship and mission take precedence over ties to patriarchal structures and roles.

We see this radical feminine discipleship symbolized in the gospels by women like Mary, Jesus' mother; Joanna; Mary Magdalene; Martha; and Mary. In the early churches we see this tradition carried on. Paul's letters tell of women both founding and holding positions of leadership in the early communities. We see in Acts and the letters of Paul women serving as missionaries, preachers, teachers, healers, leaders of churches, prophets, speakers in tongues, and apostles.[23]

The power of women in the church has continued throughout its history, particularly through offices held by widows and deaconesses, in the religious orders, in outstanding contemporaries like Dorothy Day and Mother Teresa, and in the multitude of women who today carry out the main portion of church ministry.

The official structures of the church, however, have remained largely patriarchal. This might explain why historically the church has often uncritically accompanied male cultures that have devastated so much of the environment, and still today remains far too aloof from the ecological crises facing us. It might also explain why the strongest voices in opposition to ecological abuses and the most vigorous voices for environmental reform are often those of women living in poverty and substandard conditions.

It would seem that reclaiming Jesus' unique attitude toward women and nature could be most useful in developing an environmental theology that honors people of both genders, perceives the presence of the kingdom in all things, and seeks to extend a nourishing and healing touch to the earth and all its people. The love of all things, which was so much at the heart of Jesus' message, certainly rules out the notions of dominance and abuse that often have been characteristic of patriarchy.

The Fall into Patriarchy

Rosemary Radford Ruether, who has been one of the most vocal opponents of patriarchal structures, surveys feminists who propose that the original fall was a fall from original matriarchal structures. Some feminists maintain that there was a time prior to patriarchy when women ruled over men. These feminists harken back to a time of high culture in early Egypt, the Near East, and Old Europe when women were in the ascendancy in family, religion, and society, and the worship of the Mother Goddess often was prominent. Scholars from this perspective lament that these ancient matriarchal cultures were conquered by the patriarchal Jewish and Christian religions.[24] They regret that the matriarchal cultures in Old Europe were overrun by the male-dominated and warlike barbarian tribes. There is also severe criticism of those who have devastated indigenous religions in Africa and Latin America, which also honored the feminine principle.

Many ecofeminists point to the fall into patriarchy as one of the root causes of the environmental crisis. They maintain that patriarchal cultures have destroyed much of the environment and rich resources of the earth through wars and conquests. Patriarchal cultures, they charge, also have been largely responsible for colonialism, industrialization, and militarism, all of which have a direct link with the devastation of the earth.

HIERARCHY AS AN ABUSIVE STRUCTURE

Feminist theologians point out that hierarchical thinking accompanies patriarchal structures. Hierarchy implies a "top down" approach to church, state, and family matters. Hierarchical thinking usually carries an attitude of "higher than" and "better than" on the part of those in positions of ascendancy. There is a chain of being, a chain of command, a pecking order in the hierarchical mode. There are haves and have-nots, insiders and outsiders, the superior and the inferior. It was just such a perspective that Jesus took aim at when he told his disciples that among them "the first shall be last" and the servant of all.

In the hierarchical model one is considered to be superior to another: human superior to nonhuman; male superior to female; white superior to black (or to any other color, for that matter); adult superior to child; royalty superior to commoner; First World superior to Third World; developed nations superior to developing nations; straight superior to gay or lesbian; intelligent superior to slow; handsome or beautiful superior to homely; tall superior to short; thin superior to fat; rich superior to poor; Jew superior to Gentile; Christian superior to non-Christian; Catholic superior to non-Catholic; pope superior to bishop; clergy superior to lay.

The hierarchical model is often the source of bias, oppression, violence and domination. It can be the source of power *over* rather than power *for* and power *with*. It can be the source of aggression, exploitation, and destruction. Many feminists believe that the hierarchical model is at the root of the environmental crisis today.

Spirit over Matter

The hierarchical superiority given spirit over matter is viewed by many ecofeminists as significant in the decline of the environment. In the Greek version of this separation, spirit is the transcendent principle that underlies reason, the soul, and the infinite. Spirit is thus greater than matter, which is associated with passivity, the physical, the body, nature, and the finite. More often than not, in the Christian versions of this hierarchy, spirit is also valued more highly than matter. Thus salvation is for the spirit, for the soul. In Christian spirituality the body is often more a source of temptation than an element of salvation. As Johnson writes: "The essential self is the soul, which is divided from the body. In the resulting hierarchy of the self, the body is less valued and is even given a negative connotation, while the mind is prized as more permanent, closer to the sphere of divinity, and meant to rule over the recalcitrant flesh."[25] In traditional Christianity death causes the soul to leave its imprisonment of the body and migrate to heaven, where the spirit will live eternally. The material body is left behind in the world, which will ultimately be destroyed in a fiery end time.

Feminists point out that the "higher" element of spirit has been equated with the masculine principle, and then men viewed as having ultimate authority over matter. Men become associated with the rational, the transcendent, and action. Women and the earth become associated with the "lower" material principle. This can translate into male domination and mastering of both women and the earth. Men can assume positions of control and then rule over and even enslave women and the earth. "Mind over matter" can be translated into men using, controlling, abusing, and even destroying women and the environment.

Male over Female

The roots of gender inequality run deep. Anne Primavesi suggests that such inequality began the uprooting of the male from the female context and the establishment of a male image that was stereotypically separate from and then higher than the female image.[26] Once the male image was established, men were pressured to prove themselves in terms of these exaggerated male images. For instance, the male image of hunter and warrior established males in roles that were often dominant and aggressive. These roles were then played out in the domestic and social contexts.

Marija Gimbutas, an archeologist who has studied Old Europe, maintains that prior to the rise of the warrior cultures (4500-2800 B.C.E.) the urban agricultural towns in southeastern Europe gave much more prominence to women and were thus more peaceful and egalitarian. She has shown the importance of women in the development of tools, cooking with fire, and the beginnings of agriculture. Gimbutas has also shown the prominence of feminine images in the gods in these cultures. Some are cautious about these studies, but there seems to be growing evidence that early feminine-centered societies were characterized by nonviolence and concern for the earth.

Similar prominence of women has been found in some of the ancient cultures of Africa. For instance, in 1890, when the British entered present-day Zimbabwe, the Shona women were part of a religious worldview in which they were prominent participants and enjoyed equality. The Shona women exercised power and authority in all aspects of tribal life. Tumani Mutasa Nyajeka submits that in this tribal worldview the uniqueness of all entities was celebrated, existing things were seen to be related, and all creatures were given respect and care. Indeed, in many precolonial societies there was a high regard for women as well as for all living things. Colonialism changed all that, lowering women to a state of servitude and reducing the environment to a collection of resources to be exploited.[27]

Some feminists submit that gender inequality is an important factor in the environmental crisis. Primavesi, for example, points out that the domestic tasks of homemaking, reproduction, and nurturing are often viewed as inferior work that is beneath the dignity of men. At the same time the male work of industry, production, and development is viewed as far superior to domestic labor.[28] The very work that can become so detrimental to the environment is held in honor, while labor that can be life-giving and conserving is disenfranchised and even held in contempt.

An example of how oppressive such hierarchical thinking can be was recently expressed by one of my students, Ling, who is from China. She reports:

> One of my personal heroes is a woman journalist back home by the name of Dai Qing. She courageously has stood up to the oppressive government in my country. She has been openly critical of the development that is destroying so much of our natural environment, especially the Three Gorge Dam Project, which will be most destructive. She has exposed how women have little to say against this devastation, which affects them and their families deeply. She has objected to the ways women are often silenced in the cultural, religious, political, artistic, and philosophical realms in many areas of my country. She has tried to rally women to oppose the destruction to the environment that goes on all over China. For her efforts Dai Qing was imprisoned for ten months and now is forbidden to work as a journalist.

There are many other contemporary versions of such hierarchical thinking. Men still hold many of the higher and more dominant positions in the worlds of business, politics, industry, education, and church leadership. Since male is considered to be "higher than" female, women often find themselves working harder at menial jobs, getting paid less, and having less opportunity for advancement.

The hierarchical position plays out also in ecology. Industrial production, military build-up, and the increasing need for resources often allow a male-dominated culture to continue to pollute the air and water, eliminate multiple species forever, and level irreplaceable rainforests in the name of progress. The physical environment can be reduced to mere matter, here to be exploited and used to its limits. Men can be viewed as rulers of the earth, masters of their universe, captains of industry, whose job is to beat the competition, advance progress and development, and maintain a large margin of profit in a dominant economy. Being number one, staying on top, and climbing to the highest rung of the ladder become hierarchical goals. Whoever or whatever gets in the way, people or the environment, is of little consequence. The goal is to win at any cost. Often such progress is made at the cost of the suppression of women or the debasing of the environment.

Ecofeminists call for a rethinking of the traditional hierarchical chain of being and chain of command. They maintain that the hierarchical model has placed human over nonhuman. Furthermore, it has reduced land to property to be owned and has viewed resources as means to gain wealth. Hierarchical thinking also has entered the social realm and placed male over female and owner over laborer in the same exploitative relationship. Some feminists link such thinking to the patriarchal portrayal of God as spiritual source of the chain of being, and they call for a reinterpretation of the Divine so that it can no longer be used to justify a system of male domination. Others call for the retrieval of the feminine principle in God, a restoration of the notion of the divine Matrix, which would rejoin both matter and spirit in a new and holistic sense of being and reality.

Ruether indicates that Teilhard's vision is a partial answer. His contemporary scientific perspective on reality recognized a "withinness" in all things and saw the Divine as the immanent source of all energy. But she cautions that this vision could also be no more than a new version of the chain of being. In Teilhard's evolutionary view of God and reality, there are still higher and lower forms, and the human person still remains the cutting edge of evolution. Teilhard questions neither the superior posture of the West nor the drive for progress that so endangers the environment.[29]

Many feminists advocate that humans find ways to construct their culture so that the lines do not run from top to bottom but are interconnected among both sexes, and among all living things and all elements of the earth. While natural forces and other living things can bring damage to the environment, the human person is the only creature who can sin against nature and deliberately disturb the balances of nature so that it becomes difficult for life to prevail on earth. We can cause destruction to such a degree that the earth could return to a lifeless planet. Ruether's projections are apocalyptic:

> The universe will create inversions, under the weight of human distortion and oppression, that will undermine the whole human life-support system. But we may be able to bring the earth down with us in our downfall. We may destroy much of the work of evolutionary development back to the most primary level of minerals and photosynthesis, and leave even this deeply poisoned against the production of life. We are the rogue elephant of nature.[30]

The Danger of Dualistic Thinking

Many feminist theologians call for the rejection of traditional dualisms and a reclaiming of more holistic approaches to nature. We have already discussed the dichotomies between spirit and matter, soul and body, supernatural and natural, which have set humans apart from the earth, culture from nature. Humans tended to separate from nature and lose their relationship with the nonhuman. With the emergence of science, nature became a separate entity for science to harness and control. As Halkes puts it, "The world becomes split into a 'spiritless nature' and a 'natureless spirit.'"[31] Some fell under the illusion that they were the creators rather than integral parts of creation related to and responsible for the whole. The polarity in this vision tended to de-stabilize the way people related to each other, to other living things, and to the other elements of the earth. Women and men separated and even became alienated from each other. Reason was cut off from feelings, and cold analysis became the method for dealing with reality.

Such polarities can affect spirituality and cut religion off from environmental concerns. The dichotomy between natural and supernatural can produce a spirituality that is separated from the sensual, the physical, and even everyday life. Religion then has little reason to be concerned about such mundane matters as ecology. The separation of immanence and transcendence also distorts spirituality. Overemphasis on the God within can deify things and lose touch with divine Mystery. Conversely, placing too much importance on transcendence can produce a "sky god" who is not involved in earthly affairs.

Dualisms have also significantly influenced the development of Western Christian theology. God has been depicted largely in male imagery, while the feminine images in scripture, including the rich Wisdom tradition, have seldom been mentioned. In addition, the supernatural is often set over and against matter as a higher and commanding power. This tension is often then projected onto gender relations, and men are given authority over women. In addition, God's ultimate power over creation can get translated into man's ultimate authority over nature.[32]

Dualistic thinking has affected other areas of Christian theology. Classical spirituality often called for a leaving of the world and material things in order to seek the spiritual. The body and sexuality were often rejected in order to pursue perfection. In the pre–Vatican II era young people were invited to leave the world and follow callings to the priesthood and religious life. In many schools of Christian spirituality natural things were peripheral to the spiritual life. There was little awareness of the self-possessed integrity of nature, its spiritual nature, or its interconnectedness with human perfection.

In liturgical theology dualisms also tend to cut people away from nature. Men are given the privilege of altar and sacrament through higher offices not available to women. Women are often excluded from the sphere of the sacred and generally given only menial and tangential tasks in the sanctuary. There is an irony here. Natural symbols are foundational to Catholic liturgy and sacraments, yet women, who have for so long been closely associated with nature, are kept to the margins or excluded entirely from these ministries.

The dualism that places God over and against the world might also be the reason why the Holy Spirit, which is a more immanent and even feminine image of God, has been so neglected in Western Christianity. As we shall see in more detail later, some feminists hold that retrieving the theology of the Spirit as the feminine aspect of divinity dwelling within all of reality as a power of re-creation could be extremely effective in the development of an environmental theology.

A CALL FOR HOLISTIC THINKING

Most feminists call for a rejection of dualistic thinking and seek to reclaim the holistic perspectives common among ancient cultures. Halkes points out that women want themselves as well as the rest of nature to be emancipated from stereotypical patterns and to be seen in a more holistic context. She observes that the holistic model

> is intended to open up and keep open the pathways between the sexes, between their way of living, working and responding to Nature. It is hoped that this exchange between them will compensate for the inadequacy of the dominant patriarchal view, for the tendency to value input from men alone.[33]

The holistic vision of reality also engenders respect for the human body. From here it is one small step to have regard also for the bodies of animals, birds, plants, and other living things. As many ecofeminists have observed, it is the separation of spirit and matter, soul and body, male and female that have in part led to the human separation from and subsequent abuse of nature. Elizabeth Johnson writes:

> Within a system of dualism, however, both women and the natural world are separated from the men they bring forth and sustain. Both are assigned instrumental value, with little or no intrinsic worth apart from their potential to serve the needs and desires of men. Women whose bodies mediate physical existence to humanity thus become symbolically the oldest archetype of the connection between social domination and the domination of nature.[34]

A holistic approach perceives reality as one but grants that it has several dimensions. Once one is able to accept that there is somehow a spiritual dimension to all things, a new sense of a dignity can be recognized in the environment. If one can accept in faith that God is in all things and all things are in God, then there is reason to oppose pollution and irresponsible damage to the earth.

Diversity among Ecofeminist Theologians

There is a diversity among feminine theologians who address environmental issues, and among Christians there seem to be three main approaches. The first approach maintains that the Hebrew-Christian tradition, with its patriarchal and hierarchical structures, has been too implicated in the oppression of women and the environment to be of any use.[35] This post-Christian perspective often suggests a return to indigenous religions of the past for beliefs relevant to ecology. Often these religions honored goddesses and were more respectful of nature and life. Caution is called for here, however, because commonly these ancient religious traditions have been romanticized and claims have been made regarding ancient beliefs about the sacredness of nature that were never operative.

A second approach attempts to hold to the classical teachings of scripture and tradition but to reinterpret them from the point of view of contemporary feminist experience. Theologians like Rosemary Radford Ruether and Sallie McFague, willing to work within the framework of the theology of God, Trinity, Christ, and the church, attempt to strip these doctrines of the patriarchal and hierarchical interpretations of the past and to begin anew with fresh feminine interpretations.[36] Often women's experience, especially that of the many oppressed women of the Third World, is the main context for such interpretations. Once Christian doctrines have been revised from the feminine point of view, they are then linked to the contemporary environmental crisis.[37]

Finally, theologians such as Elizabeth Johnson and Anne Clifford wish to work more closely within the tradition and Christian orthodoxy. They are, of course, aware that there are patriarchal and hierarchical distortions in the scriptural and doctrinal tradition, but they are equally conscious that there is much of value that can be retrieved from Christian beliefs that are relevant to ecology. These scholars are willing to revise and interpret Christian beliefs within the boundaries of orthodoxy and link their interpretations with concern for the earth.[38]

Ecofeminist theology seems to be gaining strength in third-world countries, where women often experience oppression against themselves and their environment. In most of their writings there is also a strong political agenda, because the injustices are coming from their governments as well as from economic and even military pressures from the more developed countries. Originally many theologians were influenced by liberation theology, but most now seem to have moved beyond liberation theology as being too male in its perspective. Increasingly, these theologians are engaged in advocacy for justice for women as well as for the earth. There is a down-to-earth dimension to their writings that does not as often exist in the feminist writings of the First World. In fact, at times they are critical of first-world feminists, viewing them as cooperating in the economic and environmental oppression of developing countries.

Ecofeminist theologians work within a variety of worldviews. Some indigenous theologians use cosmologies that are part of their ancient traditions, while Western scholars tend to work with the post-Einstein cosmology. Rosemary Radford Ruether combines modern science with the Gaia theory, which views the earth as a living organism, while Sallie McFague attempts to integrate a modern scientific perspective with metaphorical theology.[39] McFague proposes that the world be perceived of as "God's Body," a notion we will discuss in more detail later. Another ecofeminist theologian, Elizabeth Johnson, accepts the modern scientific perspective on the environment and at the same time attempts to develop a theology of the Spirit that might move Christians to protest the oppression of both women and the earth.

Catholic feminist theologians working in the area of ecology need to maintain a careful balance. It is important to preserve the Catholic tradition and at the same time revise and reinterpret the tradition so that it can be linked to ecology. Christian beliefs have had to face many crises for two thousand years, and yet they have been able to stand up to these challenges. Today the Catholic tradition can be reinterpreted, revised, and linked to our environmental concerns, so that Catholics can be a vital force in the environmental movement.

Some Principles for Theology

Ynestra King suggests several feminist principles that theologians might well find useful for reinterpreting the Christian tradition and challenging church structures. She believes that women should accept their closeness to nature and use that to protest abuse both toward themselves and toward nature. She also urges that all life be viewed as an interconnected web and not as a hierarchical structure. Women are charged to reveal the interconnections of all things and at the same time to expose all forms of domination. Further, King believes that all healthy ecosystems must be allowed to sustain diversity. Women should struggle to sustain global diversity and at the same time work together for peace and nonviolence. Finally, she believes that ecofeminism should be committed to help people understand their own bodies as interrelated to other things in nature.[40] She writes movingly of the role of women at this moment of ecological crisis:

> The ecology movement, in theory and practice, attempts to speak for nature—the "other" that has no voice. . . . Feminism represents the refusal of the original "other" in patriarchal human society to remain silent

or to be the "other" any longer. Its challenge to social domination extends beyond sex to social domination of all kinds, because the domination of sex, race and class and the domination of nature are mutually reenforcing.[41]

Ecofeminist theology seeks to revise the Christian tradition so that Christians can be moved to be advocates for the liberation of both women and nature. It would seem that the most useful approach for Catholics would be one that honors the tradition and carefully reinterprets the doctrines from a theological perspective that is inclusive, egalitarian, and respectful of nature.

Revising Some Beliefs

The feminine perspective on ecology has often called for a retrieval of the Goddess images of the Creator that were common in pre-patriarchal indigenous cultures. Ruether maintains that this Goddess image of a primal Matrix can bring together immanence and transcendence, and break down the dichotomy between spirit and matter.[42] Others point to the fact that in cultures where this feminine image was prominent, there was an emphasis on harmony, community, and peace, all elements needed for an ecological theology. Charlene Spretnak sums up this position as follows:

> The revival of the Goddess has resonated with so many people because she symbolizes the way things really are: All forms of being are One, continually renewing in cyclic rhythms of birth, maturation, death. . . . The Goddess honors union and process, the cosmic dance, the eternally vibrating flux of matter/energy. She expresses the dynamic, rather than static model of the universe. She is immanent in our lives and our world. She contains both male and female in Her womb, as a Male deity cannot; all being are part of Her, not distant creations.[43]

Sallie McFague, one of the most influential ecofeminist theologians, proceeds through a process of deconstruction of traditional symbols of God and reconstruction of new symbols in an age where theology is called to meet the urgent dangers of nuclear and ecological destruction. She calls for a shift from human-centered theology to one that is cosmos-centered. Here a "coming together of God and humans in and on the earth" designs an image of a God concerned for all of creation, a God who is "the source and salvation of all that is."[44] In McFague's metaphorical theology she points out that the traditional monarchical image of God too often has been used by Western Christianity to justify oppression. This is a God who is distant, who rules the world through a combination of domination and benevolence, and who relates exclusively to humans. Even though McFague realizes that it would be simplistic to blame the environmental crisis on the Hebrew and Christian traditions, she does point out that the notion of dominion has been used to control and misuse the nonhuman world. She also maintains that believing that God will somehow take care of the world and that ultimately all will be well no matter what we do to the earth can only bring more damage to our earth.

McFague suggests that the crises on our planet call for reimaging God. She begins with a contemporary, scientific cosmology and suggests that God be seen as in, with, and under the entire process. God here is a continuing Creator who invites humans to work as partners in the ongoing process of creation. McFague suggests that the predominant image should be one prevalent in indigenous religions–"the universe as God's body."[45] In this image the entire universe is seen as a dynamic image, or visible sacrament, of the invisible God. Immanence and transcendence are brought together and the dignity of both Creator and creation is manifested. This image speaks for an embodiment of God that gives matter and the natural world a sacred dimension. It is an image that can move us to appreciate our own bodies as well as the bodies of all things of our earth and universe. Here God bodies forth in the universe and manifests power and concern for all of creation. In this vision we humans find our place in the whole not as dominators but as partners with God in creation. The world becomes our home. We are made for it and from it and called to a key role in sustaining it.

Ivone Gebara, a Catholic ecofeminist theologian who lives with the poor, is also critical of the traditional notions of God. She holds the all-powerful and omnipotent images in part responsible for the superiority and triumphalism in the colonial missionary endeavors. She points out that even though liberation theology challenged the monarchical images of God and proposed a God of life and justice who is concerned for the poor, it did little to confront or attempt to change the patriarchal structures of humanity and the cosmos. In her view liberation theology has not been effective in ecology. She suggests a new image, one of a God who is not separate from, over, and above the earth, but rather a God who is in all things. She proposes a theology wherein both the world and humanity are believed to be in God.[46]

Anne Primavesi observes that the traditional dualistic theology, which set God off from the world and associated God only with spirit, has worked to the disadvantage of material things. Traditional anthropology, which held that only humans were made in the image of God, denigrated all that was nonhuman. Moreover, identifying God and males with the mind and women with the body has brought about the debasement and even enslavement of women. Primavesi recommends that women begin finding God within themselves and within the feminine experience. She calls for an image of God that is inclusive and within all things: "For the Spirit of the one God is not only the crown of the world tree but also its root. It fills both the daughters and the sons of God with power and the earth with knowledge of the divine."[47]

Elizabeth Johnson emphasizes the theology of the Spirit of God and points out that the Spirit has been quite neglected in the Western church.[48] The Spirit is the nurturing, creative, indeed feminine aspect of God. Johnson is convinced that a retrieval of the theology of Spirit can be useful for an environmental theology. She suggests that the Spirit be perceived as present and active in the world, enlightening and giving the earth warmth and energy. The Spirit of God is the creative origin of life and extends life-giving power throughout history. This is the dimension of the Divine that dwells with, encircles, and empowers. It is the Spirit who heals, re-creates, and renews, and our natural symbols for the Spirit reveal how the Spirit is related to the earth. Jesus said that the Spirit moves in the wind and the breeze and in the very breath of all creatures. Fire and water are also powerful natural symbols of the Spirit, who liberates, gives us wings, and protects us.

Johnson reminds us that the Spirit is also a feminine image of God, and that her functions are personified in Lady Wisdom of the Hebrew scriptures. Wisdom is a kindly Spirit who guides, oversees, fashions, and gives life. She shapes the world and restores it to harmony. Wisdom causes us to be reborn with new life, and indeed, she renews the face of the earth. Johnson suggests that with a renewed theology of the Spirit we might reclaim the feminine aspect of God and provide Christianity with images of God that can help us sustain the earth.

Ruether suggests that revisions of the Hebrew tradition might also be beneficial to environmental theology. She believes that the Hebrew covenant tradition, though patriarchal, did not set history against nature. The Jews could find God in all aspects of life. God's reign was absolute and all-embracing, and God's covenant was with all living things on earth. God's blessing was upon both society and nature, and God established laws, including those of Sabbath and Jubilee, so that nonhuman creatures and the land would be protected. Moreover, the messianic future projected by God was one of peace and the restoration of all of creation. Ruether points out that too often the covenant was interpreted to be exclusively for male Jews. Jesus, however, offered a corrective. He proclaimed a new covenant for all nations, especially for the poor and outcasts. Jesus taught that the reign of God was "at hand" and yet was still not established in peace and justice.

Ruether points out that all too often the human, male-centered aspects of the covenant have been used in a narrow sense and have been the source of conflicts between religious sects and nations. It is her position that the covenant should be broadened to include the rights of animals, indeed all life forms: "Each life form has its own purpose, its own right to exist, its own independent relation to God and to other beings. Encompassing our relation to nature as usable things there must remain the larger sensibility, rooted in the encounter with nature as 'thou' as fellow beings each with its own integrity."[49]

Ruether also suggests ways of revising the Christian sacramental tradition. She begins with Christ as the cosmic manifestation of God and sees Christ as the "immanent divine source and ground of creation and healing."[50] In this perspective the cosmos is viewed as sacramental; it mediates the experience of the Divine. The sacraments then are seen as models of the mingling of body and spirit.

Ecofeminists are also searching for an appropriate spirituality for ecology. Most call for an inclusive spirituality wherein God is recognized as loving all things, a spirituality in which nothing is viewed as profane or unclean. Others propose a spirituality where the conversion process is toward the earth and away from sins against the earth; one where there is a kinship, a community among all things. This is an active spirituality, which is committed to transform culture and which stands in advocacy of nature. Johnson calls for the kind of contemplation that is aimed not only at union with God but at union with other people and the earth. She asks that this spirituality be prophetic and that it attempt to move people to speak up for the earth and for those who are forced to live in degraded environments.

Ruether proposes an ecological spirituality that affirms rather than rejects the inner self. She also understands the importance of a sense of mutuality with other persons, an interdependence among all things, and a strong sense of community.[51] Ruether suggests that there are many lessons in the classic schools of spirituality that are useful for ecology.

Ecofeminists also suggest the development of an ethic suitable for ecology. Most seem to search for an ethic of liberation that would free women, the poor, and the earth from oppression. Johnson suggests that such an ethic will extend the concept of neighbor to all things and will help build community with all things. This is an ethic that will include the notion of evil and all oppression, and which will condemn and resist exploitation of any kind.

SUMMARY

Ecofeminist theologians propose a new theological vision. They challenge the abuses that have come to women and nature as a result of the two having been identified. They are often highly critical of patriarchal and hierarchical structures and generally attribute most of the blame for the abuse of women and the environment to these structures. Ecofeminist theologians charge that dualistic thinking has created huge fissures between humans and nature, as well as between genders and even between God and people. Ecofeminist theologians call for a more holistic view of reality and new theological revisions of the Jewish-Christian tradition that are compatible with contemporary concerns for the earth. Here God is within all things and wills to save all things; God is enfleshed in black, yellow, or red skin, the Creator of all people; God is in male, female, animal, fish, and all living things, the Creator of all. The universe, the earth, and all things sacramentally carry forth the presence and power of God in a new creation that is egalitarian, holistic, and nonviolent. This is the vision of a church that works for peace and justice, as well as for care of the environment and the sharing of the earth's resources.

9.

Christian Spirituality

I have lived in this little fishing village all my life, and for sixty years have dived off the coast for seaweed and shellfish. We work hard and have happy lives here in Mikuni. It is such a pretty place that the tourists come here from Tokyo and other cities for vacation. Now we kneel in the oily muck, as it drifts in from a Russian tanker that split and sank off our coast. We struggle with buckets and rakes, but it seems hopeless because they say that a million gallons of oil are headed our way. It is so depressing. This is where we get our food and make our living. We fear that the sea urchins and the seaweed are all lost. I am an old woman and have only a few years left, but I cry for the children.

—Ayaka Konaka, Mikuni, Japan

The ancient traditions of Christian spirituality are filled with rich insights that are applicable to the environmental crisis. In this chapter we briefly discuss the nature of Christian spirituality, look at how its teachings have always been applied to the "signs of the times," and then suggest how our spiritual traditions on self, the world, and God might be useful to those concerned about the earth. The resources are extensive and the insights of many spiritual writers are applicable to the environment. Given the limitations of space, I have chosen to draw largely from three sources: Francis of Assisi, Pierre Teilhard de Chardin, and Thomas Merton.

SPIRITUALITY AS A WAY OF LIFE

Christian spirituality is a way of life. It involves following the example of Jesus, living out his gospel teachings, and applying these teachings to the demands of the period in which one lives. Bernard McGinn describes Christian spirituality in terms of living and practice: "Christian spirituality is the lived experience of the Christian belief. . . . It is possible to distinguish spirituality from doctrine in that it concentrates not on faith itself but on the reaction that faith arouses in religious consciousness and practice."[1]

241

Christian spirituality is rooted in the ancient Hebrew commandment to love God, neighbor, and self. This commandment recognizes that all of creation has its source, sustenance, and goal in a Creator who has made an everlasting and faithful covenant with the earth and all living things. Christians believe that God has entered into creation and has been fully manifested in the person of Jesus Christ. For the Christian, salvation consists of becoming both personally and communally one with Jesus Christ, who lived, died, and was raised so that the world could be saved.

Christian spirituality, then, is a lifestyle wherein disciples of Jesus Christ walk with the Master as friend and brother, attempting to imitate his example. It is a dynamic spirituality, a process of prayerful growth in intimacy with the Lord and a lifetime commitment to serve the world in his name. For two millennia Christians have asked, What would Jesus do in this situation?

We see Christian spirituality in its pristine beginnings in Paul's letter to the Colossians, which was written even before the gospels. This extraordinary passage reflects the spirituality of an early Christian community several decades after Jesus' death, while memories of him were still vividly alive:

> Put on therefore, as God's chosen ones, holy and beloved, a heart of mercy, kindness, humility, meekness, patience. Bear with one another and forgive one another. If anyone has a grievance against one another; even as the Lord has forgiven you, so also do you forgive. But above all these things have charity, which is the bond of perfection. And may the peace of Christ reign in your hearts; unto that peace indeed you are called in one body. Show yourselves thankful. Let the word of Christ dwell in you abundantly: in all wisdom teach and admonish one another by psalms, hymns, and spiritual songs, singing in your hearts by his grace. Whatever you do in word or in work, do all in the name of the Lord Jesus, giving thanks to God the Father through him.
>
> —Colossians 3:12-17

This is the heart of the Christian way, a commitment to follow Jesus' example of compassion, humility, love, and forgiveness. It calls for a disciplined asceticism and a dedication to self-denial, prayer, thanksgiving, and hard work in the Lord's name.

Saints Respond to the Signs of Their Times

The saints of Christianity are those who have been specially graced to live out this gospel spirituality and connect it to the needs of their time. Paul and other early teachers, prophets, and apostles took on the task of initially spreading the gospel and establishing the original Christian communities. During the fourth century, when Christianity was becoming both accepted and inculturated in the Roman Empire, the desert fathers and mothers fled to the barren wastes of Egypt and Syria to preserve the gospel life far from the immorality of the urban areas. Their writings are still foundational to Christian spirituality. During the fifth and sixth centuries, when the Roman Empire was falling into chaos and barbaric brutality, Augustine and Benedict taught Christians to live the gospel life in stable and secure communities. During this same turbulent period the Celtic religious of Ireland provided their people with centers of prayer, learning, and pastoral care. In the Middle Ages, when superstition and church corruption often distorted the gospel, Francis of Assisi called the church back to simple poverty, humility, and love of nature. In his own life Francis provided a renewed image of Jesus of Nazareth. In the midst of post-Reformation divisions, Ignatius reminded Christians that they could find God in all things, especially in their active work for the Lord. During this same period, when monastic traditions were being thrown aside by Protestant reformers, Carmelites Teresa of Avila and John of the Cross and others revived the rich mystical traditions of Christianity. In the seventeenth century Francis de Sales focused on the desperation of the urban poor. He brought spirituality back to the person in the streets and taught that Jesus called his disciples to serve the needy.

In the twentieth century Dorothy Day taught nonviolence, justice, and service to the poor to a generation caught up in war and materialism. Pierre Teilhard de Chardin showed a scientific era how to link science with religion and how to experience the presence of God in the process of evolution and human progress. Thomas Merton taught a postwar secular generation how all Christians can be contemplatives and discover God in themselves and the world. He urged Christians to resist racism and violence and to struggle for peace and justice. Mother Teresa was a dramatic witness to Jesus' love for outcasts and the poorest of the poor in a world where the majority of people still live in substandard conditions. Cardinal Joseph Bernardin most recently gave a powerful witness to the meaning of forgiveness and showed how to die with courage and hope in an era where violence and revenge are prevalent.

Even from this brief sketch we can see that Christian spirituality is a marvelous treasury of ways to link Jesus' teachings to any challenge that might arise. It has been said that all disciples have been called to witness wholly to Christ, but that no *one* Christian witnesses to the whole Christ. The spiritual life of each disciple reflects only one facet of the mystery of Christ's life, only one part of the whole Christ. Each person's spiritual journey to seek the Lord is unique and singular, a combination of divine gift, a humble and open receptivity, and the courage to address the issues of the day. The saints repeatedly have shown the way to relate gospel living to the signs of the times.

A New Kairos

We have come to another crucial period in our history, a time when both individually and communally we are awakening to see that many of the earth's ecosystems, species, and resources are in jeopardy. We have come to a *kairos,* a historic opportunity to change directions in the way we care for our land, water, air, and other resources. If we hope to sustain a growing world population and pass on a healthy environment to coming generations, radical changes have to be made in our lifestyles and in our methods of industry, transportation, and commerce. These ecological problems are not to be seen in isolation but are connected to potential violence, political upheaval, and oppression. The environment is where people live, and its degradation deeply affects human lives, especially the lives of the poor. A world where the majority is hungry, deprived, and forced to live in environmentally depressed areas cannot hope to be stable and peaceful. We have come to a juncture where Christian spirituality, lived out in varied ways by disciples, must address a pressing need: to save the very home where all life dwells.

Lack of Concern in the Past

Why is it that until recently Christian spirituality has been so little concerned with environmental issues? There are a number of possible reasons. Perhaps it is our tendency still to flee to our own personal "deserts" and "cloisters," leaving the world to the devices of others. We still have Platonic notions of God as a "sky god," too far removed from the "real world" to have much relevance to environmental issues. Spirituality and contemplation are often thought to be for those hidden behind monastery walls and not relevant to such earthly issues as sustaining the earth. Possibly we still live in the split-level world of the natural and supernatural, where the principal concerns are for souls rather than bodies, spirit rather than flesh, the afterlife rather than everyday life.

Christian spirituality seems to be persistently tainted with the dualism that has plagued Christian spirituality since the days of the ancient Gnostics. Such dualism takes a dim view of material things, the body, sexuality; thus it has little concern about the physical world in which we live. As a result, spirituality is still affected by the detachment from "mundane" matters that often characterized monastic spirituality. Our world continues to be viewed as a "fallen world," a lost paradise that is really not worth saving.

It is also possible that many of us have become so accommodated to the materialism and consumerism of our age that these have taken the place of spirituality. We may be too busy with the affairs of the day to be concerned with contemplative prayer and biblical spirituality. For some, spirituality has been narrowed to personal prayer and church attendance. For others, such pressing issues as ecology are just too complicated or overwhelming to be related to the spiritual life.

Fragmentation still characterizes the spirituality of many Christians. Their spirituality remains private and devotional, not sufficiently linked with community, scripture, theology, or "worldly" issues of peace and justice. Training for the clergy still focuses on scripture, doctrines, and morality, and fails to give adequate attention to the great spiritual traditions of the church. Moreover, a spirituality cut off from scripture, doctrinal content, and serious interpretive thinking can easily become limited to one's personal life. It is hardly a spirituality that will move disciples into the marketplace or empower them to face the demanding issues of social justice or the environment.

Enlarging the Vision

Christian spirituality needs to enlarge its vision as well as its outreach to the world. It can no longer remain closed to the world, science, or to the spiritual insights of other religious traditions. Christian spirituality needs to concern itself with issues of poverty, violence, injustice, inequality and oppression. A gospel way of life cannot be limited to private piety or to a liturgy more concerned with performance than praxis. The spirituality that is called for today is reflected in the lives and writings of spiritual leaders like Thomas Merton, Henri Nouwen, Dorothy Day, Oscar Romero, Mother Teresa, and John Paul II. Theirs is a spirituality that is deeply contemplative and yet vigorously active in a world plagued with violence, sexual immorality and abuse, inequality, and oppression. It is a spirituality dedicated to serve the millions of innocent and deprived children of the world, the homeless, AIDS victims, and so many others who cry out for help.

Spirituality now needs to include love of the earth and care for all living things that find their home on this planet. Today there is an urgency to reclaim Jesus' teachings that the Creator God cares for all things, even the birds of the air and the lilies of the field, and that God's reign is near at hand and within all things. Christian spirituality must once again focus on the belief that God loves the world and sent the Son to be a part of it and to save it. It must be vigorous spirituality, which seeks union with Christ in his mission to transform the world into a new creation and bring it to wholeness and salvation.

SPIRITUALITY AND THE SEARCH FOR GOD

Christian spirituality has developed over two millennia, and its teachings are extremely extensive and complex. Benedict (d. 550), one of the founders of monastic life and giants of the spiritual life, observed that people came to the monasteries "to seek God."[2] The experience of God is central in the spiritual life, whether it is the awareness of the presence of God in everyday life or the extraordinary in-depth experiences of the mystics.[3] This experience has always been primarily an inner experience, with the self as well as with the world. Humans are embodied spirits living in a dynamic and complex world, and their search for God is best carried out in the context of self and their milieu. The spiritual life, then, involves three dimensions: the self, the world, and God.

The Search for the Self

The search for God is not properly an escape from the inner self, nor should it in any way involve the neglect or isolation of the self. The best of our spiritual traditions describe the search for God in terms of a healthy and authentic self striving to be detached from obstacles to the search for the Divine, a self seeking to be connected to God's creation, and a self with growing awareness and acceptance that it is unconditionally loved by God. Each of these aspects of the self needs to be integral to any formulation of a spirituality concerned about the environment.

Thomas Merton has been one of the twentieth century's best mentors on searching for and experiencing God within the self. His voluminous writing still reaches a broad public with a spirituality that is fundamentally Benedictine, with strong influences from the Carmelite mysticism of St. John of the Cross and Buddhism. Merton often distinguishes between the false or exterior self and the true or inner self. Merton's life was indeed a dynamic and sometimes tempestuous search to find out who the real "Tom" was, and there to meet his God in Jesus Christ.

Merton once wrote that when he left the world to enter a Trappist monastery he had little in the way of material possessions to put aside. He had been a struggling student at Columbia, had worked for a while among the poor in Harlem, and then taught English briefly at St. Bonaventure University. Merton said that he was putting aside the exterior self: the roles he had played, the masks he had worn in order to please or impress others. In his early years in the monastery Merton rejected all this as the false self and took on the new persona of monk. He soon learned that finding his true self did not mean rejecting his past or any part of who he was. Merton learned that God accepted and loved all of him, false and true, inner and outer, and that once he could accept himself, he was ready to accept God. The true "Tom" was the person that God had created as a child of God, an image of God.[4]

Merton often wrote about how elusive this self could be, comparing it to a timid wild animal that lived deep within and was only able to be enticed to appear in an atmosphere of trust and love. Merton's life was a painful search, because he had to face the shadowy sides of himself, the loneliness and isolation of the contemplative monk, the dark nights of his soul, periods when the landscape was barren and stripped of meaning. Through long hours of prayer, writing, and work in his community, Merton waited for moments of encounter with his God. He described these experiences differently. On some occasions he simply rested in the Divine; on others he exuberantly celebrated the presence of God in his inner self. In his contemplation it is as though his personality was somehow remade in the image of Jesus–a personality derived from Jesus and sustained by him. Merton came to know that true humility "consists in being precisely the person you actually are before God. . . . It will not be a matter of mere appearances, or opinions, or tastes, or way of doing things. It is something deep in the soul."[5] It was within this inner core of self that Merton encountered the Lord. He wrote: "If we enter into ourselves, finding our true self, and then passing 'beyond' the inner 'I,' we sail forth into the immense darkness in which we confront the 'I am' of the Almighty. . . . Our inmost 'I' exists in God and God dwells in it."[6]

Merton's notion of the inner self is paralleled in the writings of contemporary theologians. Karl Rahner describes the true self as one that was created and graced by God. Rahner's notion avoids the old dichotomy between the natural self that has to be overcome and the supernatural self that is graced by God. Rahner views the human much more holistically. For him, the whole person has been created to be open to the Divine, to search for God in all things. For this reason Rahner took the position that the contemplative experience of God is possible for anyone who is open to it.[7]

Similar views on contemporary personhood can be found in Bernard Lonergan. His analysis of the person shows that the human psyche is capable of moving through personal understanding, judging, deciding, and action toward the religious experience. Here the self is constituted to move beyond itself, to transcend human limitations. Moreover, the self finds fulfillment when it is grasped in a religious conversion by an otherworldly love, when it is possessed by the love of God.[8]

We find a similar view of the self's capacity to discover the transcendent in the writings of Pierre Teilhard de Chardin. Teilhard was able to take the Ignatian notion of the person finding God in all things and to carry it into a modern scientific perspective. Teilhard viewed the conscious self as the spearhead of evolution, uniquely capable of reflection. The human is singular among creatures in that the human "knows that he knows." Teilhard repeatedly wrote of his encounters with the mystery of God within matter.[9] For Teilhard, the spiritual life did not consist so much in denying the self but in humanizing the self so that it could be more conscious of the God within all things. Teilhard believed with John of the Cross that God is at the center of each person. He was convinced that once humans allowed themselves to be touched by the God within matter, they could enjoy a cosmic view of reality and realize consciously their involvement in the creative process itself.[10] It was his conviction, and he demonstrated this in his own difficult and often tragic journey, that the true self was capable of having such an experience and could achieve it within daily living, personal suffering, and one's work. Teilhard held the conviction, in contrast to much of the spirituality of his time, that the true self could not be found through escaping the world but rather in offering oneself to it.[11] He believed that the world could actually teach us who we truly are.

The True Self and the Earth

It is quite easy to feel overwhelmed and helpless in the face of today's many complicated environmental issues. It is tempting to adopt a spirituality of avoidance or even denial. Privatized faith can quietly withdraw into self-absorption and prayer concerned only with personal needs. Such a spirituality will contribute little to solving environmental problems.

The self living a spirituality that is concerned with ecology is a self that is searching, open, struggling for conversion, and engaged in learning and life. This is a self that strives to understand the facts of environmental issues and has the confidence and courage to confront those who are acting irresponsibly toward the environment. It is a self striving to overcome the feeling of helplessness in the face of so much environmental destruction. It is a repentant self, aware of its own contributions to ecological problems, and sincere about conversion. The authentic self believes that all humans have been created in the image and likeness of God, and that all are called to represent the Creator in restoring the integrity of the earth. This self has a sense of dignity and worth; it honors and respects creation and is holistically committed to a mission for all living things. There is an openness to the experience of God within the self, within people, and nature. There is an awareness of a sacred trust given to each person to honor and care for all living things. This is an inner self that seeks union with the Creator and views God as the true source, sustenance, and goal of all things.

Self-denial

Self-denial is generally considered to be integral to Christian spirituality, but it has various connotations. For example, it can mean the loss of self-esteem. In his desolation, Job proclaims, "I am a worm and no man." The writings of Augustine and Luther portray humans as "sinners" and "masses of damnation." Ascetics of the past have deprived themselves of food, drink, and rest in an effort to "subdue the flesh" and gain control of the sinful self. They allowed themselves few physical pleasures and even beat themselves, hoping to overcome sinful desires. Such asceticism attempted to conquer the self so that it might be free to be one with God. Even the great Buddha is said to have tried such self-deprivation in order to achieve his spiritual goal, but he gave it up because all it did was make him skinny and weak. Francis of

Assisi also is said to have subjected himself to severe penances and drove himself at times to exhaustion. Yet once he was specially graced with the marks of Jesus' crucifixion on his body he came to realize that he was created and loved by God and that the Lord wanted him to be whole. He found self-acceptance and a healthy love of self as a child of God and brother of Christ.[12]

Authentic self-denial is not about self-hatred or extreme self-deprivation. Rather, it is concerned with setting aside those things that are obstacles to union with God. True self-denial is concerned with *disordered* attachments to people or things, addictions and pleasures that so preoccupy us that we have little time for or interest in encountering God. Authentic self-denial does not in fact reject the self; rather, it discards things that stand in the way of leading a good life and searching for the Divine.

Most certainly self-denial involves facing the dark side of the self, the side that can be ugly, mean, and self-serving. Authentic self-denial faces the "dread" that can be experienced when we admit that we are being led on by illusions. Self-denial acknowledges the rationalizations that justify the destruction of ourselves and others. Authentic self-denial renounces all that is false in our lives, so that Jesus Christ can be the center.[13] The self becomes closed to infidelity and opened to a life of the spirit, to the presence and power of God. There is indeed an asceticism, a serious discipline connected with leading a spiritual life. But it does not aim at self-hatred or self-rejection. It is an asceticism concerned with authentically loving the self as a child of God. It is intent on purifying the heart and welcoming the Lord of creation.

Self-denial and Ecology

Environmental concerns bring new light to the discussion of authentic self-denial. No doubt we will all have to live more simply if we wish to share our resources, replenish them, and share them with those in need. We will have to discipline ourselves away from over-shopping and cluttering our lives with things that we don't need. The new asceticism returns to natural foods that are nourishing and healthy, and it sets aside the processed and "fast foods" that are often harmful to health and wasteful in their excess packaging. This spirituality returns to making things, and repairing, patching, and refinishing rather than simply discarding. Such self-denial calls for a detachment from gadgets, faddish items, and luxuries. It is conscientious about adequate exercise and proper health care.

The United States had become renowned for over-consumption. Growth in obesity, alcoholism, drug abuse and waste is startling. Much of this seems to come from lack of self-respect and excessive individualism, both of which are obstacles to any serious search for an understanding and an experience of God. Authentic self-denial avoids such excesses in consumption and the pretense of autonomy. It seeks to let go of addictions and self-centeredness. Authentic self-denial is prepared to sacrifice for the sake of other living things and for the earth itself. It is prepared to share with others and even to deprive the self for those more needy. As the Jesuit environmentalist Albert J. Fritsch observes:

> Through abnegation and fasting we establish our own inner harmony and ecological balance for gaining self-control so that we act more in the spirit of the humble Jesus. We join with others and gradually grow and develop and become one with a community of believers in sharing the blessings of every kind, ranging from the delicate nature of earth to our health, senses, friendships and days of life.[14]

The Self as Connected

In Christian spirituality the true self does not exist in isolation, disconnected from the rest of reality. The saints—who came to know their true identities before God—also experienced a new connection with other people and with the world around them. Once they experienced themselves in the way God saw them, they could also see their world the way God sees it. They could now see their intimate connection to creation. We see this in Francis of Assisi. Once he stripped himself of the outer image of the troubadour knight, he found himself as God had made him, a poor man at the service of Jesus. He discovered his intimate relationship with his fellow humans, especially outcasts and the poor. All people were truly his sisters and brothers. And perhaps more intensely than any other mystic, Francis saw that all of creation was his family. The sun was his brother and the moon his sister. The birds of the air were sacramental signs of God's presence. Francis lived as a "new creation," shaped in the image of the Lord. Of all the human personifications of Jesus we have had throughout the history of Christianity, Francis is perhaps the most vivid.

Merton writes of a similar feeling of connectedness with the surroundings in his hermitage in a beautiful hollow in Kentucky. In the Benedictine tradition he values "place" and "stability." He seems to know the sound of each bird, the name of each tree, and they all speak to him of God. The ebb and flow of day and night and the seasons are part of his prayer and reflection. Something as simple as a shy doe or a scampering rabbit can help bring him to the center of things.

Above all, Merton's contemplation connects him to people. His oft-repeated account of an experience on a corner in Louisville reveals how he came to see himself as one with all humanity:

> In Louisville, at the corner of Fourth and Walnut, in the center of the shopping district, I was suddenly overwhelmed with the realization that

I loved all these people, that they were mine and I theirs, that we could not be alien to one another even though we were total strangers. It was like waking from a dream of separateness, of spurious self-isolation in a special world, the world of renunciation and supposed holiness.[15]

Gradually this sense of community led Merton to concern himself with the issues facing his people, especially those of racism and nuclear war.

We hear the same linkage between self and outside reality in the spirituality of Teilhard. In many of his reflections he speaks of his feeling of oneness with the earth. In a letter to a friend he once said that he wanted to communicate "as faithfully as possible what I hear murmuring in me like a voice or song which are not of me, but of the World in me. I would like to express the thoughts of a man who . . . finds himself a child and citizen of the Earth."[16] For Teilhard, there was a fundamental unity of being among all things.

The Self Connected to the Earth

One of the key notions in much of the literature on ecology and religion is interconnectedness. In order to be adequately concerned about the earth, it is necessary to see how we are related to the earth. We come from the earth, indeed from the very particles that make up the stars, and our human destiny is irrevocably bound to the fate of the earth. As Brian Swimme puts it:

The great news of our time is the evolutionary story in which we come to realize that we humans are all embedded in a living developing universe, and that we are therefore cousins to everything in the universe.[17]

An environmental spirituality, then, will include a belief that as humans we are bound together with each other, with the earth, and with all living things. As humans, we are part of creation and play a unique role on our planet. As self-conscious and free creatures we have the capacity to destroy or to build up more than any other force or living thing. The indigenous people of Latin America have an expression: One must make room in oneself for the immensity of the universe.[18] There is an interdependence between ourselves and our world. To harm or deprive another person is to debase ourselves. To degrade the earth or any living thing is to demean ourselves.

The Self Loved by the Lord

At the very heart of Christian spirituality is the experience of being loved by the Lord. It is said that in the Johannine community this experience of his love was the binding force that held the members together.[19] In the gospel of John this intimacy comes through in the image of the vine, which symbolizes the oneness of Jesus and his followers. The experience of the love of Christ also empowered the early martyrs to undergo horrible sufferings rather than give up their faith. The same love radically changed the lives of saints like Augustine, Francis of Assisi, Dominic, Ignatius, Joan of Arc, Thérèse of Lisieux, as well as countless others. Augustine writes of his deep gratitude in eventually finding this love after years of being oblivious to it: "Late have I loved Thee. You were within me while I had gone outside to see you. I rushed toward all those lovely things you made and you were with me but I was not with you."[20] The charming medieval mystic Julian of Norwich records that the Lord told her he loved her so much that he would have undergone the sufferings on the cross for her alone. For Teilhard, this love from Christ was not only a personal experience but was a blazing fire that welled up through the entire universe as a tremendous cosmic force: "Christ. His Heart. A Fire: a fire with the power to penetrate all things."[21] For Merton, prayer was a celebration of this love from the Lord: "In light of this celebration, what matters most is love itself, thankfulness, assent to the unbounded and overflowing goodness of love which comes from God and reveals Him in His world."[22]

The energy from such divine love can more intimately connect us with the earth. Faith can enable us to see the beauty and abundance of nature as concrete signs of the love of the Creator. Blossoming life each spring, new life born into families, as well as new beginnings after the destruction of war or natural disasters can all be symbols of divine love consistently breaking through in the world. Indeed, the recent global awakening to the environmental crisis after years of unrecognized destruction is for many a symbol of the persistent and renewing power of this divine love.

SEEKING GOD IN THE WORLD

Christian spirituality has often had a tendency to be otherworldly, uncomfortable with the earth and its "temporal" issues. Detachment from material things has too often turned into disdain for them. In addition, Christian spirituality has often focused more on the next world than on the everyday world with all its political, social, and economic concerns.

In the closed spirituality still prevalent in the church, the world is viewed more as an object to be avoided than a subject to which to relate. At best, nature can be a vehicle to remind one of God (as in some Carmelite and Ignatian spiritual writings) but not a subject with its own integrity and its own capacity to reflect in a unique way the beauty, love, and power of the Creator.

It is clear that a world avoided and disdained by people of faith can easily be abandoned to those who would degrade and abuse it. From this perspective environmental degradation is perceived to be a worldly matter and not of concern to the "people of God." A spirituality so cut off from the world understandably is not concerned about harm done to the earth, its resources, or living things. A spirituality that is primarily concerned with "saving souls" will pay little attention to saving the earth, which is thought to be spiritless and without a future in God's plan. The spirituality needed here is one that is decidedly worldly, in that it is intensely concerned about the earth and all living things. Such a spirituality will neither reject nor flee the world but will be actively engaged in reverencing it and caring for it.

Seeing the World as Good

Genesis 1 portrays the Creator as repeatedly seeing the creation as "good." This goodness of creation has been interpreted various ways. For some, the earth is good in that it is useful; that is, it is here to serve the needs of human beings. Humans are seen to be at the center of life, and nature, with its many resources and living creatures, is here solely to sustain, improve, and enrich human life. Unlimited supplies of material resources, as well as animals, birds, fish, plants, and trees exist for human consumption. If nature is to be conserved, it is so that it may be enjoyed and admired, not because it has value in itself.

However, the Creator's refrain in Genesis that creation is "good" does not refer only to usefulness. Creation is primarily good because it reflects the goodness, beauty, and power of the Creator. That which is brought forth by God's creative word comes from the Creator's desire to share divine goodness in a visible manner. Creation is born from a God who is Love, who generously expresses Self in a multitude of visible forms. In a very real sense all creation images the love and saving power of the Creator. For those who can see with the eyes of faith, the entire world is graced and blessed.

Antony of the Desert, even in the barrenness of his environment, believed that nature was a book in which one could read the words of God.[23] In the early Celtic monasteries there was also a deep love of nature.[24] Even though the world was perceived as fallen, there was strong faith that God would protect the people from harm and even work wonders to save them from the dark forces within nature. This is clear in the medieval stories of Brendan, who was moved by his love of the sea to explore the world. This positive view of nature also can be seen in the writing of Basil (d. 379), who maintained that nature provides the tranquility necessary to experience God.[25] This same appreciation for nature moved the early Benedictines to clear the disease-infested swamps and reclaim the land for farming. They created havens where Christians could search for their God and experience the Divine in the environment around them. It was in this same milieu of work and prayer amid nature that Merton was able to carry out his extraordinary search for God in the Benedictine tradition of spirituality.

Francis of Assisi showed us another way to approach the world. His was not the stable agricultural and learned world of the Benedictines. Francis was a wandering troubadour of the gospel. He was not a garden dweller but a wanderer searching the highways and towns for the poor and the needy. Francis combined a detached poverty with a genuine love for all things. Francis was not a sentimental naturalist who preached to birds and tamed wolves. Most of those stories about him are parables to show that Francis viewed the world as a family. Francis, perhaps more so than any other disciples of Jesus, came to understand the human Jesus. He knew Jesus as the son of a loving and caring Abba whose reign was deeply within all things. For Francis, the birds, insects, animals, and fields were symbols that spoke of God's loving kindness. Francis accepted every person, down to the most repulsive leper, and everything in creation as his family. The sun, the birds, even the wind spoke to Francis of the Spirit of God. The world was filled with poetry that praised and thanked Abba for creation. Yet life for Francis was not an idyllic dream. He knew suffering, ridicule, sickness, and failure. But through it all, Francis understood that this was ultimately God's world, and he ardently believed that the Creator would always take care of him and all of creation.

For Francis, the world was a gift from God to be cherished, shared, and cared for. Everything in creation reflected the goodness, love, and kindness of God. Each thing had its own integrity and was called to speak uniquely of the magnificence of God.[26] All creation spoke to him of God, as well as of Christ, whom Francis saw as the perfect image of creation. Francis believed that by looking at the Jesus of the gospels one could learn the truth of creation and how to relate to it. He thus learned from his closeness to Jesus how to love the world, and he was able to join with all of his brothers and sisters in praise and thanksgiving. Francis writes as though he were a medieval psalmist, praising God for the gifts of creation:

> Praised be Thou, my Lord, with all Thy creatures,
> Especially for Sir Brother Sun.
> Through him Thou givest us the light of day,
> And he is fair and radiant with great splendor,
> Of Thee, most High, giving signification.
> Praised be Thou, my Lord, for Sister Water
> Who is very useful and humble, precious and chaste.
> Praised be Thou, my Lord, for Brother Fire
> By whom Thou dost illuminate the night. . . .
> Praised be Thou, my Lord, for our Mother Earth
> Who sustains and rules us
> And brings forth divers fruits and colored flowers and
>   herbs.[27]

The world, then, is a blessed subject to which we are called to relate. It is within this "world" context that God brings all to fulfillment and salvation. Teilhard's spirituality has much to offer here, for he was "madly in love with the divine influence which guides the world."[28] Teilhard actually experienced the universe as animated by God and was able to feel divine energy in all the material things around him. He said it was his calling "to feel with the earth" and to come to union with his God through this same earth.[29] Through the structures of the earth Teilhard seemed to be able to learn of the personality of God. In his scientific work he could be in touch with the love that charged the world. In his now-classic statement Teilhard proclaimed, "Nothing here below is profane for those who know how to see."[30]

Merton's spirituality reflects this same sense of appreciation of the world for its own goodness. In earlier years he fled the world, disdaining its sinfulness. But in later years Merton was able once again to embrace the world as the place where God could be intimately experienced.

> For it is God's love that warms me in the sun and God's love that sends the cold rain. It is God's love that feeds me in the bread I eat and God that feeds me also by hunger and fasting. It is the love of God that sends the winter days when I am cold and sick, and the hot summer when I labor and my clothes are full of sweat. . . . It is God's love that speaks to me in the birds and the streams, but also behind the clamor of the city God speaks to me in His judgments, and all these things are sent to me from his will.[31]

Merton came to see that it was only in embracing the world that the Creator could be found. His was the God who made all things in order to reveal God's self through them. Merton's faith revealed to him not a world to be denied or escaped but a world that was a "new creation" where God still walked with human beings. Merton believed that the contemplative's role was to help the technological person of our time regain a respect for self and for the integrity of the world. Merton came to see that all things have an integrity of their own, indeed a "self," which must stand before God in praise.[32]

An environmental spirituality reclaims the notion that the earth, its resources, and all living things are reflections of God's goodness, and must therefore be treated with respect and care. This spirituality recognizes that nature is a gift from God, a mirror of God's goodness and love, a book in which the revelation of God can be read. All creation is perceived to be charged with divine energy. This spirituality, like the prophets and psalmists, will praise, glorify, and thank the Creator for the earth and all living things. Here humans play a unique role and are called to "seek God, perhaps grope after him and find him, though he is not far from any one of us. For in him we live and move and have our being" (Acts 17:27-28).

A World That Is Dynamic and Changing

Science tells us that the universe is expanding and that the earth is a living reality that is constantly evolving. Change and progression are integral to the contemporary worldview. We live in a time when enormous shifts are taking place socially, politically, and technologically. It is not easy to develop a spirituality to address adequately all the complex issues of our time.

A spirituality concerned about ecology can take a stance on the enormous progress of today. We cannot afford to look at progress uncritically. Some critics of Teilhard's spirituality point out that he was naive with regard to the dangers inherent in progress. Although Teilhard was realistic enough to recognize that there was a downside to progress, he often did seem willing to accept the evils attached to progress as necessary for continuing toward what he described as the Omega Point. When reading Teilhard's reflections, one gets the impression that he could be rather philosophical about two horrible world wars and even the Holocaust as long as the process of building the earth continued. Few spiritual writers today share his optimism about progress.

Thomas Berry is an example of a Teilhardian who does not share his mentor's utopian views on progress. Berry points out that we have

> mastered the deep mysteries of the earth at a level far beyond the capacities of earlier peoples. We can break the mountains apart; we can drain the rivers and flood the valleys. We can turn the most luxuriant forests into throwaway paper products. . . . We can pollute the air with acids, the rivers with sewage, the seas with oil—all this in a kind of intoxification with our power for devastation at an order of magnitude beyond all reckoning.[33]

Berry laments that our managerial skills and computer speeds seem designed to "move natural resources through the consumer economy to the junk pile or the waste heap."[34] He points out that the pace of destruction is so fast that it is difficult to know how to respond. We now have technologies that nature cannot withstand. He laments the price of "progress": the extinction of species, and the pollution of air, land, and water. Berry holds that there is a certain pathology in our culture, our value systems, even in our religious traditions.

Berry says we stand by helplessly while we lose many splendid modes of divine presence. He warns that if we destroy the beauty and magnificence of nature, we destroy the very vehicles through which God makes the Divine present to us. Berry also complains that by destroying life on earth we are lessening the opportunities of future generations to experience God in nature.

Berry points out that the change that is taking place on the earth and within us is perhaps the greatest ever to occur in the history of humankind. We are now able to change the earth within decades on a scale that before would have taken hundreds of millions of years. Berry at times speaks as a modern Jeremiah, warning us of impending doom if we do not radically change our commitments to development.

Berry suggests ways to guide us in formulating technologies that would enhance both the human community and earth processes. He holds that technologies should be developed in an integral relationship with the earth and not in a despotic manner of conquest. There must be a clear knowledge of the magnitude of the changes as well as provision for waste products. Progress must take in the entire earth community, with all its ecosystems, and consideration must be given to both the physical and spiritual elements of the cosmos. Berry writes:

> If there is to be real and sustainable progress it must be a continuing enhancement of life for the entire planetary community. It must be shared by all the living from the plankton in the sea to the birds over the land. It must include the grasses, the trees and the living creatures of the earth. True progress must sustain the purity and life-giving qualities of both the air and the water. The integrity of these life systems must be normative for any progress worthy of the name.[35]

Contemporary spirituality, if it is to have credibility in our era, has to accept change, progress, and development. Nevertheless, Christians need to know and adhere to their timeless spiritual values and be countercultural when ecosystems are threatened. The eye of faith sees all things as God's creation and carefully protects the environment from irresponsible development and the misuse of resources. Faith resists the wanton destruction of creation, which is given to us to reflect the beauty, love, and care of the Creator. Christian spiritual writing today should express shock at the scandalous degradation that is daily being imposed upon the earth by developers bent solely on gaining profit. It should be prophetic and liberating in its statements and actions on behalf of nonhuman creatures as well as for the millions who have been shuffled off to the areas abandoned by the rich.

A World with a Dark Side

Merton teaches that it is destructive for us to attempt to remake our world in our own image and likeness rather than in the image of God. He points to the darkness of our secular age, which ignores or even denies the spiritual dimension of reality and excludes God from the process. Merton labels such useless and painful human labor "the labor of science without wisdom; the mental toil that pieces together fragments that never manage to coalesce in one completely integrated whole: the labor of action without contemplation, that never ends in peace or satisfaction."[36]

The ancient myth of the fall in the garden indicates that though the world is basically good and sustained by a loving and caring Creator, it is finite, fragile, and vulnerable to destructive forces and sinfulness. Natural evils come upon us in violent storms, floods, tornados, fires, volcanic eruptions, earthquakes, and other threats to our environment. Moral evils rising out of greed, hatred, the lust for power, and many other human sinful tendencies bring on widespread destruction of human life and the environment. The human story, besides being one of great creativity, achievement, and heroism, has also been a tragic narrative of carnage and devastation.

The environment has always mirrored this dark side of reality. Present-day deserts in Mesopotamia, Persia, West Pakistan, the Orient, Latin America, and the Middle East once supported powerful and wealthy civilizations. But lands were stripped of timber, the soil was depleted, the water supplies were exhausted, and many areas became wastelands. Present-day Megiddo in Israel stands as a symbol of such destruction. In the midst of a desert area stands a tel, under which lie more than twenty ancient civilizations that at one time or another flourished at that spot.

The condition of the environment in our own day reflects that same shadow side of reality. In many areas of Eastern Europe, where air pollution has killed off the forests that once soaked up the rains, mammoth floods now rage through the villages and leave deadly destruction in their path. In the United States we also see the results of poorly planned development and industrialization. For example, the World Resources Institute in Washington has reported that 99 percent of our original frontier forests have been destroyed or ruined.[37]

Just as spiritual theology has seen the wonders of nature as metaphors for God's grandeur, there are also metaphors aplenty for the evil forces in the world. Ravaged forests, gouged landscapes, polluted waterways, and the poisonous air around some cities tell of human ignorance, greed, and avarice. The menacing nuclear mushroom has now been replaced with the ominous image of the "greenhouse" or the "clouds" of Chernobyl. Merton once observed that the ruin we have brought upon our earth is a metaphor for how we have degraded ourselves.[38]

Spirituality is concerned with conversion. In an ecological age it calls for a deeper awareness of the horrendous damage humans have inflicted on the earth. It stands with firm resolve to not be a party to the many ecological evils and to stand against those who persist in such sinfulness. Our spirituality calls us to a compassion for the millions deprived of essential resources and to a determination to provide them with healthy places to live and raise their young.

The God of Creation

Christian spirituality has often focused on an outside God, one who lives in the realm of heaven, far removed from earth. Such otherworldly spirituality, as we mentioned earlier, often moved disciples to flee the world to find God in a Platonic sphere of existence. Even though spiritual writers like John of the Cross stress that the experience of God is to be gained beyond the senses without negating them, there often has been the inclination to deny the senses and fear beauty and pleasure.[39] "The world, the flesh, and the devil" were all of one piece in such spirituality and were to be avoided. The ultimate reward was perceived to be a heavenly one and not of the earth. In the extreme such spirituality viewed God as a Being so far beyond this earth that the earth was considered to be a godless place, a fallen world, which had to be transcended completely in order to be in union with God. The pilgrim Christian was expected to endure life's trials on earth until God came and took the soul home. Often God was perceived as one who sent "crosses" to test the dwellers of this world in order to see if they were worthy of heaven. This same heavenly God was expected to come ultimately as an avenging Judge to bring a fiery apocalyptic end to the earth and all material things.

These images of God often still prevail in Christian spirituality today. With our contemporary understanding of nature and concern for environmental issues, however, more positive images of God as Creator and Nurturer can better engender a reverence for the earth and motivate Christians to be active as co-creators with a God who is lovingly involved with creation.

An Inside God

Contemporary spirituality is shifting its emphasis to an inside God, a God who dwells within all things as a loving, forgiving, and saving presence. Merton and many other spiritual writers of our time have stressed that this God can be found within the depths of ourselves, in our world, and in our work to build the kingdom. We have retrieved Paul's notion that "we all reflect as in a mirror the splendor of the Lord" (2 Cor 3:18). This is a new awareness that God is imaged not only in people but in *all* things, that God shares divine goodness and love with all of creation. God embraces the world as its Abba, caring for it and commanding that the integrity of all things be respected and protected. God can be discovered in the depths of all reality.

This is the God of Francis of Assisi and Ignatius, who found the presence of the Divine in all things. This is the God of Teilhard, who encountered the Creator in rocks and fossils and who passionately believed that the Divine penetrated and permeated all things. Here God dwells with the noble as well as with the lowly, who struggle to survive. This is a God who touches and transforms all things with the power of love.

In Teilhard's vision God is at the very heart of the universe and thus can be pursued in created things. Teilhard writes lyrically about this God and throughout his life he constantly strove "to undergo God." He wrote: "To cleave to God hidden within the inward and outward forces which animate our being and sustain it in its development, is ultimately to open ourselves to, and put trust in, all the breaths of life."[40] This God of immensity "allows us to seize him everywhere, within us and around us." Here God is hidden within all of reality, a God who can transform all things, even suffering and death, into good. This ever-creative God continues to bring order and goodness out of the chaos around us. Teilhard has given us this prayer: "Lord grant that I may see and feel you present in all things and animating all things." Teilhard often writes of "the Grand Option," that is, the total acceptance of God as the source and goal of all things.[41]

Merton also writes of his experience of God as dwelling within all of reality, the inner and outer, the spiritual and physical. Merton points out that God can be encountered unexpectedly in the world. To illustrate this, Merton uses the image of an ancient Easter custom practiced by Russian peasants:

> The Russian peasants used to carry the blest fire home from Church. The light would scatter and travel in all directions through the darkness, and the desolation of the night would be pierced and dispelled as lamps came on in the windows of the farmhouses one by one. Even so the glory of God sweeps everywhere ready to blaze out unexpectedly in created things. Even so his peace and his order lie hidden in the world, even the world of today, ready to reestablish themselves in his way, in his own time: but never without the instrumentality of free options made by free men.[42]

In this perspective God extends the divine Being to all things and entitles all to be worthy of respect.

Ancient Celtic spirituality reflects this divine immanence in the following prayer: "That I may bless the Lord Who conserves all—Heaven with its countless orders, land, strand, and flood."[43] God creates in love and empowers us to hold all creation in reverence. Thérèse of Lisieux came to this awareness as a young Carmelite nun and exclaimed, "Everything is Grace."[44]

Environmental spirituality will stress the immanence, the "insideness," of God. Thomas Berry observes that our present ecological age

> fosters the deep awareness of the sacred presence within each reality of the universe. There is an awe and reverence due to the stars in the heavens, the sun, and all heavenly bodies; to the seas and the continents; to all living forms of trees and flowers; to the myriad expressions of life in the sea; to the animals of the forests and the birds of the air. To wantonly destroy a living species is to silence forever a divine voice.[45]

Today's spirituality must perceive and experience the presence of God in all people and all things. Such an awareness can provide strong motivation for resisting pollution and waste and for serious efforts to restore the integrity of the earth. A God of *this* world who is the source, sustenance, and goal of all reality is a companion in the daunting task of facing the many ecological challenges of today.

The spirituality needed to sustain the earth must perceive the world primarily as a place where God waits to be experienced. Francis teaches Christians to walk on the earth humbly and lightly, since it is the dwelling place of God. Franciscan spirituality teaches a certain courtesy to all people and all things because they image God, who invites us to experience the Divine within.[46] Francis was able to put his trust in people and indeed in all creatures because he was able to detect the presence of God in everything.

Ignatian spirituality also stresses finding God in all things. In our present scientific age this perspective has been developed by the Jesuit Karl Rahner, who sees the world as a horizon toward which humans move. It was his conviction that human nature is "an openness to God" and can thus gradually reach for and experience God within the world. We have actually been created by God and for God and in our world find the context for experiencing God in everyday human life.[47]

Merton uses the interesting image of the cosmic dance to show how God "plays and diverts himself in the garden of his creation."[48] It is his position that if we stopped taking ourselves so seriously and let go of our obsession with what we think is "the meaning of it all," we could follow God in this dance.

> We do not have to go far to catch echoes of that . . . dancing. When we are alone on a starlit night; when by chance we see the migrating birds in autumn descending on a grove of junipers to rest and eat; when we see children in a moment when they are really children; when we know love in our own hearts; . . . at such times the awakening, the turning inside out of all values, the "newness," the emptiness and the purity of vision that make themselves evident, provide a glimpse of the cosmic dance.[49]

Merton was a gifted listener and visionary of the movements of God in our world.

It was Teilhard who taught many Christians how to be citizens of the modern world. He was one of the first to move with faith into the evolving earth of Darwin and the expanding universe of Einstein and Hubble. Flying in the face of traditional spirituality, which avoided the world, Teilhard believed in the world, embraced it, and found in it an inexhaustible resource for the revelation and experience of God. The God whom Teilhard worshiped was within the universe. Teilhard's God animated the world, transfigured it, and drew it toward final fulfillment. Teilhard felt he could truly learn of the personality of

God by studying the earth. He was convinced that he could hear God speak infallibly from within the earth. He saw the earth charged with the love of God, as well as with the love of Christ.

Teilhard often urged his readers to have a "sense of the earth," a common passion to participate in building the earth along with God.[50] For him, the world was the "divine milieu," a world which had Christ as its heart. The vastness of the universe did not make Teilhard feel either insignificant or lost in awe. Neither did he hide from the grandeur of the world. Instead, Teilhard wished to be one with the God who penetrated and permeated all things. One of Teilhard's charisms was his ability to bring the Ignatian spiritual value of "finding God in all things" into the modern technological and scientific era.[51] Teilhard was devoted to the earth and its progress because he believed that Christ had indeed come to save and consecrate all things.

Teilhard has been accused of being too optimistic, of not being aware enough of the negative side of life. This seems to overlook the enormous amount of pain Teilhard suffered in his life and the lessons he learned from his many losses. He saw the slaughter of World War I from the trenches, and gradually he lost most of his family through illness. He was cruelly suppressed by Vatican officials and by some of his Jesuit superiors for his views on evolution. He was forced to give up his professorship at Institute Catholique, was all but exiled for most of his adult life, and was not permitted to publish any of his religious views.

Yet in the midst of isolation, loneliness, and rejection, Teilhard never lost his loyalty to the church or to his order. He was well aware of pain, suffering, and evil in the world, and yet he had deep faith that the creative and saving power of God's love would ultimately prevail in all things. It was his conviction that God could be found in discovery, growth, and progress. Teilhard never faltered from his position that he could rely on the earth. He once wrote, "The earth can do me no harm since it is the body of Him who is coming."[52]

An ecological spirituality will be committed to finding God in nature, in the change of the seasons, in the many wonders of creation. The earth will be viewed as the divine milieu where God can be experienced as dwelling with his creation and sharing a home with all. Such spirituality can sensitize our eyes to see the beauty, power, and love of God in all things. It can tune our ears to listen for the movement of the Spirit constantly renewing the earth. Even in the midst of disaster, suffering, and death the Spirit can be perceived bringing new life and hope. Such a spirituality needs to understand and appreciate technology, science, and industry, and yet at the same time monitor decisions in these areas to make sure that the environment is given priority. A "preferential option" is extended to the poor, but also to the earth, which feeds and sustains all peoples.

JESUS THE CHRIST

Authentic Christian spirituality is centered on the person of Jesus Christ. Merton points out the importance of the doctrine of the incarnation for spirituality and how it must be linked to the doctrine of creation. It was his belief that the coming of Christ was the eternally planned culmination of the creative process. Merton puts it this way, "The Lord made the world in order that He Himself might descend into the world, and that He Himself might become Man."[53]

Merton also stressed that God entered the world not as a dominating king or a ruler but as a servant and friend. The Son came as "unknown, unremarkable, vulnerable."[54] For Merton, this clearly revealed that humans are called to play this same role of servant and friend. Merton repeatedly looks to the historical Jesus for insight into this role.

Jesus and Nature

Jesus of Nazareth was a rural craftsman who embraced the Hebrew faith that all creation is good, a gift from God. He felt the warmth of Abba's love and protection in the wind, sun, rain, and the harvests, and he learned of Abba's protection of the birds and the flowers. Jesus knew firsthand the forgiving, healing, and nurturing power of the Creator through daily living. In his life and message Jesus exemplified detachment, simplicity, generosity, love, and forgiveness. He preached that compassion and mutual sharing were the ways to God, not violence or oppression. His death was an act of self-sacrifice to save the entire world. Jesus' resurrection proclaimed the power of God to overcome death and re-create the world once again in the likeness of the Christ.

A spirituality that is sensitive to ecology cherishes the belief that God has intimately entered creation in the person of Jesus and has thus given new dignity to all of materiality. The world was created to be the home of Jesus. Jesus himself stands with his disciples, inviting them to reverence creation and empowering them to imitate his life of friendship and service. Jesus promises his presence, his "being with" all of creation until there will one day be a "new creation." The power of his Spirit enables his disciples to take part in saving the earth in a wholly new way–through commitment to working for a healthier environment.

The Role of Christ

We have seen how Teilhard brilliantly developed the notion of Christ's role in the cosmos. Let us briefly examine now how Teilhard was able to integrate this vision into his spirituality.[55] Teilhard's vision of the universe is one of ascent and convergence. Ultimately all things will converge and be in union with the whole Christ.

> Throughout my life and through my life, the world has little by little caught fire in my sight until, aflame all around me, it has become almost completely luminous from within. . . . Such has been my experience in contact with the earth–the diaphany of the divine at the heart of the universe on fire. . . . Christ; a fire; capable of penetrating everywhere and, gradually, spreading everywhere.[56]

For Teilhard, Jesus is a creative force, both in the physical and spiritual elements of cosmic movement. Teilhard was also conscious of the finiteness of the world and of the widespread reality of suffering and death. Yet he never dwelled on the negatives, even those inflicted upon him by his critics. For Teilhard, the cross revealed that ultimately love would conquer suffering and death. He believed that both personal and global suffering were intimately linked with Christ's suffering and could thus be redemptive. Merton shared this perspective when he wrote: "All over the face of the earth the avarice and lust of men breed unceasing divisions among them, and the wounds that tear men from union with one another widen and open out into huge wars. Christ is massacred in his members, torn limb from limb; God is murdered in men."[57]

In Teilhard's spirituality Christ can be experienced in every person and in every thing, for the world is directed by a process of "Christification."[58] The power of the risen Lord permeates the universe and draws all things to himself. For Teilhard, this "universal Christ" permeates every atom of the reality and thus can come to us through both the physical and material:

> Lord, it is you who through the imperceptible goadings of sense-beauty, penetrated my heart in order to make its life flow out into yourself. You came down into me by means of a tiny scrap of created reality; and then, suddenly, you unfurled your immensity before my eyes and displayed yourself to me as Universal Being.[59]

In Teilhard's spirituality salvation is not a matter of working for a reward but of contributing to the growth of unity in Christ. Salvation consists in this: "To love one's brothers and to receive the body of Christ is not simply to obey and merit a reward: it is organically to build up, element by element, the living unity of the pleroma in Christ."[60] Everything has been created for Christ and finds fulfillment in him. Christ was the first thought in the process of creation as well as the ultimate goal of all creation. Christ was the center of all things and extends self through grace, life, and also through matter.

Teilhard insisted that each of us, through our connection with Christ, plays a unique role in the process of development of the world:

> Would not the reconciliation of our age with God be effected, if men were to see themselves and in one another as part of the fullness of Christ? If they were to understand that the universe, with all its natural opulence and all its exciting reality, does not reach its full development save in Christ? And that Christ, for his part, does not reach full stature save through a universe pushed to the very limits of its potentialities.[61]

For Teilhard, to look at Christ is to see the ultimate goal of creation:

> It is impossible for me, Lord, . . . to look on your face without seeing in it the radiance of every reality and every goodness. In the mystery of your mystical body—your cosmic body—you sought to feel the echo of every joy and every fear that moves each single one of all the countless cells that make up mankind.[62]

Teilhard sets out to live what he called a cosmic life, and to see himself as an atom in the Cosmic Christ. Teilhard placed Christ at the beginning, the now, and the future of our expanding universe and the evolving earth. For Teilhard, participating in the creative process was integral to the human mission. Human work, discovery, progress, and suffering were all related to the creative process. Humans were, in Teilhard's view, a deciding factor to the direction of the process. This was Teilhard's gospel, and he preached this "good news" better than anyone else in this century. His sense of mission is expressed in this prayer: "I should wish, Lord, in my very humble way, to be the apostle and, if I may ask so much, the evangelist of your Christ in the universe."[63]

An environmental spirituality must be christocentric; it must view the Lord as present among his followers, empowering them to build his kingdom on earth. Such spirituality sustains a vision wherein the Spirit of the Lord is ever creating, healing, and drawing the universe and the earth toward wholeness. Here God is a "fellow-sufferer"; in Christ, God suffers along with the earth and along with those oppressed by their environment. The Spirit of the Lord is an energy and power for those who resist the degradation of the earth. Jesus' risen and glorified presence offers continual hope that ultimately there can be a new creation. Jesus Christ came to save the world and will continue to assist those who carry out this mission. This is a spirituality of servanthood: to the many who are deprived of food, clean water, and a decent place to live; to the animals that are abused through experimentation or mistreated in captivity or sports; to other living things and species that need to be saved from extinction; and to the earth itself, which is being desecrated in so many places.

AN ACTIVE SPIRITUALITY

Most of the great spiritual writers advocate a spirituality that is both con-templative and active. The Christian way of life follows the Master in strug-gling to make broken people whole and in confronting those who oppress "the little ones." Christian spirituality is based on a faith that is actively en-gaged in praxis for the kingdom.

Ignatius told his followers that they need not spend long hours in prayer but could find God while working for Christ. He initiated a lasting tradition whereby disciples of the Lord could find God in all things and in all activities. Teilhard carried this tradition into the modern world and found God in long years of laborious digging through rocks and fossils to unlock the mysteries of the past. Benedict taught his followers the value of "sacred place" and that work could be an effective way to find God. Merton brought this tradition into modern times in his many writings and in his tireless efforts for peace and justice. Francis of Assisi was a servant to the servants as a way of being a servant to God. He left financial security and spent his life ministering to people, especially the poor. Dorothy Day brought this tradition into our time with her constant dedication to the poor and homeless. John of the Cross and Teresa of Avila both had a strong sense of God's presence in the world and of the dignity of human life. Titus Brandsma carried their teaching into the twen-tieth century in his heroic confrontation with the Nazis in Holland, for which he paid with his life at Dachau. The imitation of Jesus for all of his followers has meant searching for the God within and at the same time sharing the good news of salvation in service to others.

Since Vatican II the Christian faith has become better integrated with peace and justice. The church has begun to be in solidarity with the marginal of the world and has begun to see work for them as constitutive of the gospel life. Rising out of a new and vigorous church "from below," there is a new libera-tion movement that seeks to free all those who are locked into starvation, thirst, violence, discrimination, disease, political intimidation, and so many other "prisons."

Now the debased environments that so many of the world's poor inhabit must be added to the list of injustices. Outrageous inequities in how the re-sources of the world are distributed must be of serious social concern. The scandal of millions dying of malnutrition while obesity and waste abound among the privileged calls for challenge by Christian believers.

A spirituality committed to ecological reform will actively resist pollution and waste. It will confront those who hoard and monopolize resources while so many are desperately in want. It will be committed to the liberation of those whose health is threatened by contaminated living conditions.

CONCLUSION

The Christian reflects on the presence of God in all things. The great Carmelite mystic Teresa of Avila observed: "Let truth dwell in your hearts, as it should through meditation: and you will see clearly the kind of love we are to have for our neighbor."[64] Christian spirituality is contemplative, seeking to experience the Divine within the self, others, and in the world. John of the Cross once described such contemplation as "nothing else than a secret and peaceful and loving inflow of God."[65] Christian spirituality is active, striving to bring love, peace, and justice into a troubled world. It nurtures individuals and binds communities together. Christian spirituality is a journey on the earth that constantly calls for conversion and maturing. It is dedicated to prayer and to liturgical celebration in which the Creator is thanked and praised for the gifts of creation. It is a spirituality centered on Jesus Christ and looks to his Spirit with hope for the restoration of creation. As Paul writes, "If anyone is in Christ, there is a new creation: everything old has passed away; see, everything has become new" (2 Cor 5:17).

Christian spirituality is prophetic, proclaiming the reign of God and challenging the forces that oppress people and the earth.[66] It takes disciples to the wilderness and the desert to find the Spirit and then empowers them to return to the world with hearts afire. It disciplines disciples so that they might find God within themselves and their world. Spirituality calls disciples to risk security and comfort in order to serve those who suffer inequality, deprivation, and violence.

10.

An Environmental Ethic

I work as a secretary in Manaus, a large city in the Amazon area of Brazil. When I step out of my apartment in the morning, I step into a thick haze of smoke. My doctor tells me that I have a serious respiratory infection from breathing all this bad air. The papers tell us that the rainforest is burning this year as it never did before. They say that in some places even the lakes are on fire. We have had the worst drought in twenty-five years, and this has caused many trees to dry out and be vulnerable to fire. In addition, the government continues to pay people to slash and burn their land, cut down the tropical trees, and use the land for farming. The farmers soon find out that the soil lasts only several years, and then they have nothing. But we never seem to learn. Now they tell me that El Niño is going to bring even more droughts and make things even worse. It is very discouraging.

—Selena Casara, Manaus, Brazil

Bernard Häring, one of the great theologians and ethicists of the twentieth century, prophetically placed environmental ethics in the center of his 1981 volume on social ethics, *Free and Faithful in Christ*.[1] Häring observed that environmental issues touch on many areas of social living: health, economics, politics, even genetics. Environmental issues also reveal the interdependence of all realities and thus call humans to serious responsibilities toward the world in which they live. Today the church increasingly recognizes its role in addressing world issues. Christians are beginning to accept an active role in the area of ecology and are in the process of developing an environmental ethic.

In this chapter we discuss the formulation of such an ethic. We begin with a brief discussion of the newness of these moral issues and suggest reasons some past and present positions are resistant to the ethical dimensions of ecology. Then we consider two significant directions in the current formulation of Christian environmental ethics: (1) the reshaping of gospel morality; and (2) the development of new understandings of nature.

A RECENT MORAL QUESTION

Until recently the environment has not been an arena for moral considerations. Lists of "sins" did not include polluting rivers, wasting resources, and the destruction of living things other than humans. Only in the last few decades have Christians begun to see the magnitude of environmental degradation and realize that they have a serious moral responsibility to care for the earth and its resources.

One wonders how in the past we could have not seen the sinfulness in the destruction of our own home? Was it, as Lynn White and others have charged, because the Judeo-Christian tradition has believed that God gave us dominion over creation and that dominion justified the use and abuse of the earth? Certainly there is an element of truth in this charge, but there were many other factors involved in blinding people to their moral responsibilities toward our world's ecology. For instance, Christians have often been rather otherworldly and private in their morality, not concerned about such "mundane" issues as those pertaining to ecology. There also has been a legalistic approach to morality in past traditions, which did not include laws for sustaining the earth. In addition, faith often was not linked to justice questions, and so obviously was not concerned with ecojustice.

There have been many shifts in Christian morality in the latter half of the twentieth century, yet many of these shifts have bypassed ecological issues. The morality of today is often quite human-centered and subjective. It guides us in the care of self and those closest to us, but often does not reach out beyond the home or suburb. It might reject the growing violence in our society, and yet it shows little awareness or concern about the violence that is being done daily to the ecosystems upon which human life depends. It often values comfort, convenience, and pleasure but is unaware of the environmental price paid for such personal advantages. Contemporary morality might guide us in honesty, truthfulness, sexuality, and social behavior, and yet have little concern about the waste of resources or pollution of air, land, and water. This morality might be concerned about paying a fair price for goods in a mega-store, and yet not be aware of what these goods are costing the poorly paid workers who manufacture them or the damage done to the environment in the emerging countries that supply them.

Contemporary morality also can be quite utilitarian in its attitude toward nature. It equates the value of things with their usefulness to people rather than the intrinsic value things may have in themselves. Material things (and even people) can be used, enjoyed, and then discarded. This tends to objectify the earth and its resources and keep them at a distance. A morality that centers on personal comforts and pleasure tends to be little concerned about the conservation of the objects that bring such satisfaction. Resources can be viewed as mere products or possessions, not understood as gifts from God. The knowledge of nature can be sought as a means of mastering and controlling nature rather than as way toward intimacy with nature.[2] Control, not contemplation, then becomes the approach to the earth and its people.

Contemporary morality often stresses progress and profit at any cost. A world economy where the rich nations and individuals live off the labor and environmental devastation of poor nations can be pragmatically justified. Corporate farming, which turns the land into food factories with little thought given to sustainability or the proper treatment of animals, can be justified by profit. Science can be separated from religion, and little heed given to the ethical issues surrounding such procedures as genetic manipulation or cloning.

Christians living in the secular culture of today are significantly influenced by a morality that is individualized, subjective, and utilitarian, a morality that bears little resemblance to the teachings of Jesus in the gospels. Society's drive toward progress, pleasure, and accumulation leaves behind the traditional Christian values of reverence for nature, sharing with others, simplicity, and compassion for outcasts and the suffering. An environmental ethic must somehow reclaim these values.

RESHAPING GOSPEL MORALITY

Many of the spiritual perspectives from the last chapter flow into this chapter on environmental ethics. A Christian environmental ethic will be rooted in the gospels and will derive from them a love of life and all things. It will struggle against self-aggrandizement and self-centeredness. It will resist sloth, greed, and violence and be concerned with building the strength of character that can resist consumerism and live simply. It is an ethic characterized by respect, compassion, forgiveness, and generosity, one which moves people to sacrifice for others and to share with others.

Gospel morality is centered on love of God, self, and others. In an environmental ethic the definition of the "other" or the "neighbor" is extended to all living things, indeed to the earth and the universe. It is not only private and individual but also public and social, concerned with justice and resistance to evil, violence, and oppression in all forms. It sees the self linked to all people as sisters and brothers, and to all things as God's creation. It discovers the presence of the Divine in all of reality and struggles to sustain the goodness, dignity, and integrity of all things. Christian environmental ethics is centered on the example and teachings of Jesus of Nazareth, a man who intimately experienced the creative and healing energy of the reign of Abba in the world, a man who died to save the world and who was raised to reveal the ultimate transformation of all things. It is an ethics that discerns and acts through the power and presence of Christ's Spirit.

Reclaiming Gospel Virtues

One of the most useful approaches to developing environmental ethics involves a consideration of gospel virtues. Attention to virtues appropriate for environmental decisions moves the focus from individual actions to a broader ethical base.

Aquinas's discussion of virtue is a useful beginning. Aquinas held that virtues are qualities of the mind by which a person lives righteously and makes decisions based on what is perceived to be good, with the ultimate good being God. The virtue approach is valuable in our environmental crisis because it provides links among humans, the world, and God. Choices away from environmental degradation toward sustaining the environment become steps along the way to perfection.[3] Individuals are encouraged to develop virtues, or traits of character, that will help them make proper choices with regard to nature. For instance, virtues like tolerance of diversity, mercy, and respect can provide a person with an excellent foundation for his or her approach to the earth and other living things.

Love as the Central Virtue

James A. Nash, in an important study on Christian ecological responsibility, has made a significant contribution to discussion of virtues and the environment.[4] Nash begins with the central Christian virtue, love. He points out the difficulties of using love in this context because of the predatory aspect of life. All creatures, including humans, survive by feeding off other species. Another difficulty is that Christian love has been traditionally focused on humans; nonhuman forms of nature have not been included. Many speak of a love of nature, but aside from a few modern ethicists, few have taken this seriously or developed any serious standard in this regard.

Despite these difficulties Nash proceeds to link love with our responsibilities toward the environment. He first observes how love is identified with God the Creator in John's gospel and is the ground and goal of all being. Creation itself is an act of love, and all creatures are products of love and recipients of God's ongoing love. Since we are all called to love what God loves and value what God values, we are called to love all of creation. The reign of God, so significant in the Hebrew scriptures and so central in Jesus' teachings, means in fact the reign of God's love *in the world.* God's love in the world is inclusive and universal. The Hebrews reveal this reverential love for nature especially in Psalms and the Song of Songs; the teachings of Jesus reveal the divine care for birds, lilies, and sheep. The central commandment in both testaments is love of God, neighbor, and self. Nash maintains that the "neighbor" is anyone or anything loved by God and that this notion can be extended to all of creation.

Common sense tells us that there is going to be a difference between the love we have for humans and nonhumans. Yet we often speak of a love for animals and nature that is quite real. If we can extend our consideration for the well-being of others—a common description of love—to all living things and to the earth itself, this will surely make a difference in our concern for ecology. We also will no doubt be able to sacrifice some of the satisfaction of our own needs and comfort to sustain our environment and pass it on in a healthier condition to the next generation. A balanced and considered reverence for nature would certainly make an enormous difference in how we treat the world around us.

Loving nonhuman reality does not necessarily mean putting everything on an equal plane with humans. Teilhard was correct in his observation that humans represent a "peak" in the evolutionary process. He does, however, seem to have been misguided in his view that humans are now in charge of evolution, for there are often forces much larger than ourselves that move the evolutionary process. Yet humans are undoubtedly unique and unparalleled among creatures. This is not to say that we should see ourselves as masters of the universe, dominating the world around us. Nor is this to deny that there are unique powers among other creatures as well. But humans are the only creatures with intelligence and freedom. We are able to shape our world (and also destroy it) in ways not available to any other creatures. We are the ones who determine what is right and what is wrong, so we bear a personal and communal responsibility in shaping and developing the earth. Only for humans is there an environmental ethic, a standard for guiding actions that affect the earth and all its resources and inhabitants.

Nash points out that some of the many dimensions of Christian love can be applied to ecology, including the following: (1) *beneficence,* which is serving others, looking out for the interests of others, or doing good for others. In ecology this can be expressed in the way one treats animals; in efforts to clean up the air, water, or soil; in the preservation of certain endangered species; and in other acts that benefit the environment; (2) *esteem of others,* which includes a respect for the integrity of all things, the avoidance of abuse of animals, and the avoidance of manipulation or destruction of natural areas; (3) *receptivity,* which includes the recognition of our dependence on nature, an attitude of awe toward the wonders of nature, and a concern to protect and nurture other living things; (4) *humility,* which avoids arrogance and feelings of superiority over nature. This facet of love helps us recognize that we come from and return to the earth, and that we share in the finiteness of all creatures; (5) *understanding,* which moves us to learn of the intricacies of nature, its vulnerabilities and the ways in which the environment can be repaired and sustained; and (6) *communion,* which moves us to be linked with nature, be in solidarity with the earth, and be prepared to take action when damage is being done.[5]

Justice and the Environment

Justice is another virtue that recently has been connected with environmental issues. It is now recognized that the church has a rich tradition of social justice and can be a useful resource. This tradition began in the nineteenth century, with Leo XIII promoting the living wage and the right to form unions. In the twentieth century John XXIII gained the ear of the world when he spoke out against unjust social conditions. Paul VI argued for development as the right for people to "unfold" their own potential and to write their own histories. He also took radical positions on the rights of the poor to lands that the rich monopolize. John Paul II has been tireless in his efforts to speak out for human rights and to defend those who suffer economic, political, or religious oppression.[6]

Church documents have begun to include the environment in their considerations of social justice. In *On Social Concern* John Paul II pointed out the injustices in both Marxism and capitalism, lamented the growing inequity in the world, and spoke strongly for each person's right to be seated at the table of the common banquet.[7] The pope often singles out the environment as a special area of abuse. He challenges the common disrespect for nature and urges that the nature of each being and the mutual connection of all things in the cosmos be taken into consideration. John Paul has pointed out that world peace is threatened by human injustice as well as by lack of respect for nature.[8]

The church's social teaching has consistently stressed the importance of distributive justice—or the more equitable sharing of the world's goods. Limits in resources and the capacity of the environment call for development that benefits the poor. Moreover, the growth and development of the wealthier nations will have to slow to accommodate the progress of other nations. Christiansen writes:

> Questions of distributive justice are always with us, but the ecological crisis raises them in an especially acute way. In the first instance, an ecological sustainable economy must eventually face the limits of growth. . . . For too long, western political systems have relied on the engine of growth to provide greater equity. Faced with the physical limits to growth, the industrial economies, in particular, will face the classic political dilemma of either finding some fair pattern for the distribution of wealth or facing social conflict and political disorder.[9]

At present inequities are increasing between the haves and the have-nots. This is manifested not only in economic matters but also in terms of the substandard environmental conditions in which the poor are often forced to live.

Justice implies a right relation with nature in which we recognize that all living things have a right to life and integrity, that all things have inherent value, although these values differ. As Rasmussen states: "Justice assumes creation's integrity and, against the workings of destructive systems, establishes the *prima facie* right to the life and flourishing of all creatures."[10]

The rights of all beings are intertwined and therefore should be protected. Where we destroy any area of the environment, we not only affect many ecosystems but also the people living in the area. One thinks of the many children who have died from cancer in Tom's River, New Jersey, because of careless disposal of toxic waste. Consider how many young people have had to leave their families in Newfoundland, because of the collapse of the fishing industry due to over-fishing of factory ships from other countries.[11]

Justice calls for sharing resources. It questions the individual and absolute right to private property in areas where the poor can barely get enough to eat. Justice calls for administering creation in ways that are restrained and thoughtful. Justice condemns squandering resources and dumping wastes that pollute and cause health problems to others. The Christian tradition teaches us that the earth is a gift to all people and that it must be shared. Justice, therefore, asks for the sacrificing of time and goods so that the less fortunate can have the things they need. Justice also demands that we preserve nature so that its beauty can be admired and so that it can be a source of contemplation of God's presence.

Nash does extensive reflection on what he calls "ecological justice." Aware of the possibility of extremes when it comes to talking about "rights" of snail darters and spotted owls, Nash takes the position that all things have certain rights and that justice indeed applies to all creation in some way. It is his conviction that such justice toward all is founded on the biblical notion that the God of justice wants all creation to be respected and cared for. God's covenant was extended to the earth and was the basis for Sabbath and Jubilee laws to honor and protect creation.

In the New Testament we find Jesus elaborating the Hebrew notion of justice. Jesus defended the rights of the poor and outcasts; he taught his followers to have a strong sense of moral responsibility toward Abba, who loves and cares for all things. He taught that the reign of God is within the world, moving it to an ultimate destiny of a new heaven and a new earth. Thus the divine plan of redemption includes the entire world. This leads Nash to conclude that "the moral responsibilities that are entailed by that ultimate expectation presumably include justice to all creatures."[12] Jesus himself carried out a ministry characterized by a pursuit of justice, especially for the oppressed, and Nash holds that this justice can be extended to all creatures: "There is no inherent reason, however, why the poor and oppressed cannot be extended to include nonhuman creatures—without implying equality of rights or denying human primacy."[13]

Nash also considers distributive justice and discusses the complexities of attempting to apportion the goods of the earth justly. He points out that millions do not have even their basic needs met. The global economy makes it extremely difficult to discern who is at fault here. But given the sinful side of humans, one can be assured that injustice is at work. Nash comments, "Injustice can be understood as the social form of sin—that self-centered human inclination to defy God's covenant by grasping more than our due and thereby depriving others of their due."[14]

Human rights to the basic necessities are an entitlement, and yet such rights are not always recognized. Think of the millions today who do not have food, shelter, health care, security, or even the opportunity to work. And, of course environment is a factor in such oppression. Often the poor are driven from their land and forced to live in deplorable urban conditions where they are subjected to contaminated water and polluted air; their land is stripped and defiled. John Paul II recognizes this injustice and comments, "The right to a safe environment . . . must be included in an updated charter of human rights."[15]

If people have a right to a healthy environment, then there must be a strong commitment to rebuild environments all over the world so that people can live in places suitable to good health and well-being. To bring this about we will need authoritative structures locally, nationally, and worldwide. There will have to be strict laws to protect valuable ecosystems, maintain biological diversity, prevent exploitation, control pollution, and sustain many other areas of the environment.

We are coming to realize that nonhuman creatures also have certain rights. Some in the "deep ecology" movement would set these rights equal to those of humans, but that does not seem to me to be realistic. Without advocating a dominative hierarchy, there is a certain ladder of existence. Humans are not on a level with cows or bugs. This perspective does not justify abuse, but it does recognize that human life and human rights generally take precedence over the rights of nonhumans. The process of progress and development will often involve a conflict of rights between humans and nonhumans. Each of these conflicts must be dealt with in a spirit of respect, compromise, and care. There are limits attached to all rights, and there are situations where there is a proportionate reason to give one life-form preference over another. There are proportionate reasons for which humans can be killed (self-defense, a just war), and certainly there are similar reasons nonhuman creatures can lose their lives.

The Christian ethic maintains that all conflicts of interests and rights be settled in love and justice, with careful discernment of all the ramifications of the decision. Gospel values, the teachings of Jesus, and the tradition of the church give us ample resources for making such decisions fairly and justly. There is no need for an unrealistic equality to be given to all. Nor is it recommended that nature be approached in a romantic or re-sacralized fashion. Nature is nature, and humanity is humanity. They are related and need each other. Nonetheless, as the human population and the pace of progress increase, there will be more of an endangerment to the earth and other living things. A strong and clear ethic will be needed as a guide for future survival.

The Common Good

An environmental ethic will be characterized by more concern for communal rights than for the rights of human individuals over their property and personal lifestyles. Pollution of the air, land and water affects the health and well-being of the larger community. The "greenhouse" effect and depletion of the ozone layer affect the entire global community. Thus more emphasis needs to be given to the social aspect of human life, and the notion of community needs to be broadened to include all living things and the earth itself. The destruction of a rainforest not only destroys a valuable and irreplaceable resource, but it also displaces the indigenous people who have lived there and wipes out all living creatures and organisms that are part of that ecosystem. An environmental ethic will recognize the rights of both humans and nonhumans to their existence and their place in their home environment. Such an ethic will stress relationship, the integrity of all things, and solidarity with all living things. Here the common good of the larger community of living things should take precedence over the preferences or profits of individuals.

The common good principle has been central in modern Catholic social teaching. Unfortunately, the contemporary emphasis on individualism, free enterprise, and competition has often pushed the common good to the side. The principle of the common good maintains that "all sectors of society have a stake in the welfare and well-being of the polity."[16] It argues that the good of the whole society takes precedence over the good of the individual or a specific group. Until recently, the common good was largely applied to social and human rights, but now it is also being applied to nonhumans.

Community rights are being extended to the entire earth community with all its complex species and resources. When the principle of the common good is applied to environmental ethics, broad communal standards are set when deciding about economic growth or development of any kind. For instance, in cutting back a rainforest, often the profit motive preempts any consideration of devastation to the environment. Factors such as the indigenous inhabitants, the many species found there, the effects on the weather, and long-range ripple effects are seldom taken into consideration. With the principle of the common good, it becomes no longer a question of what we *can* do, but also what we *should* do in light of the repercussions on the environment and the local inhabitants. The common good can also set standards for the distribution of resources, establishing economic parity among nations in such questions as waste disposal and emissions control. It also can be used as a principle in land distribution in developing countries, for establishing norms for environmental responsibility, for allowing developing nations to industrialize, and for placing stricter sanctions on the wealthy nations, which have caused most of the environmental degradation.

John XXIII in his historic document *Pacem in Terris* extended the principle of the common good to global proportions. At that time (1963) the pope was concerned about nuclear weapons, developing nations, and the movements of refugees. Now that we have become aware of the global aspects of environmental problems, the application of the principle of the common good is quite relevant here also. Weather, pollution of the oceans and waterways, fallout from nuclear power disasters, the "greenhouse" effect, and ozone depletion are just some global environmental problems. International efforts and sanctions are certainly called for, and the principle of the common good should be central in making the many crucial decisions connected to these problems. In particular, the plight of the poor, the dispossessed, indigenous peoples, and future generations should be given preferential consideration. The survival of certain species and the preservation of important ecological areas need also to be decided in light of the principle of the common good. Many of these are new questions, and the conflicts of rights will not be easy to resolve.

As moralist Daniel Maquire points out, the common good does not mean the greatest good for the greatest number.[17] If that were the case, the majority would always reap the benefits and minorities would be left empty-handed. The common good principle embraces the entire community and reaches out especially to the have-nots. Charles Murphy puts it this way: "The common good brings with it a notion of community life involving everyone and everything without exception, living in mutual accommodation. It transcends even national boundaries. Its scope is as large as the earth."[18]

Central to Jesus' teaching was concern for the outcast, the lost sheep, the oppressed person. This concern should be given special consideration in making environmental decisions, for often it is the poor who suffer most when the environment is abused or when resources are monopolized by a few. But the notion of the poor can be extended to nonhuman creatures and indeed to the earth itself. All of these are the objects of oppression in so much of our unrestrained development today. The principle of the common good can be effective in saving all that is poor or without advocacy from destruction by humans.

Wendell Berry has set down useful norms for exercising responsibility toward the environment. He proposes that any changes and innovations in the environment take into consideration the entire human and natural community. Berry maintains that priority be given first to local autonomy and needs. He cautions against unsound industrial doctrine; demonstrates the value of developing small-scale and local industries, farms, forests; and stresses the importance of using local energy. He emphasizes the importance and strength of local communities. Berry also believes in learning from the elders, and he advocates a special concern for them as well as for the young. He sees the importance of a close link between rural and urban communities and stresses that cooperation is always more important than competition.[19] Berry's work provides a fine basis for an environmental ethic because it accentuates respect for all things, a strong sense of community, and mutual cooperation.

Social Ethics

Since the environmental crisis affects all areas of public life, social ethics can be a useful resource. An environmental ethic must challenge political parties to incorporate environmental issues into their platforms and actions. Such an ethic will scrutinize national and foreign policies regarding the conservation and the just distribution of resources as well as arms control. It will lobby local, state, and national legislatures to give justice and compassion a place in their law-making and policies with regard to environmental issues. As Häring points out:

> No private person and no economic corporation should consider the human biosphere as his or its domain. The very context of this biosphere and the limitedness of important material resources urges humankind not only to strengthen local responsibilities but also to provide international agreements and organizations to guarantee the security of this, our most precious patrimony.[20]

Corporate law, industrial procedures, and business practices need to be monitored constantly with regard to their ethical approach to environmental concerns. Scientific research has to be critiqued from the ethical point of view with regard to the ecological impact made by new discoveries. As Schumacher has pointed out, technology should not commit society to the kind of giantism, speed, and violence that can only bring exploitation and destruction.[21] The health-care industry also needs an effective ethic in order to alert the public to the many health hazards connected with the degradation of the environment, and also for the proper development of new techniques for dealing with such health problems and extending these services to the poor.

Finally, the ecological education of the populace on all levels must include ethical considerations. Students of all ages need to learn not only all the intricacies of environment but also how to develop their consciences with regard to the care of the earth and the sharing of its resources. Our universities can be centers of interdisciplinary research and teaching about the environment, places where the generations who will be deciding the future of the earth can learn how and why the integrity of created things needs to be honored. Higher education can also provide centers where many religious faiths can share beliefs and values relevant to ecology.

NEW UNDERSTANDINGS OF NATURE

Environmental ethics seems to take a more inclusive and expansive view of nature. Nature is not simply plants and animals but the world in its entirety, with all things sharing the same materiality and with all things integrally interrelated and mutually interdependent. Rather than a chain of being, nature is now perceived as a web of intricate and interconnected ecosystems. Many environmental issues are now understood to have global implications. The world is one, and thus an environmental ethic will have to be holistic in its view of nature, and all-inclusive in its concerns. Precisely where the center of this world is has been a matter of debate.

Where Is the Center?

There are various suggestions as to where the center of nature or reality should be in the development of an environmental ethic. Traditionally, ethics have been human-centered. Since humans are rational, they are acknowledged to be greater than all other things and empowered to use and manipulate them as they see fit. Since the Enlightenment and the beginnings of modern science, knowledge has been equated as power to master nature. Religiously, this was supported in the eighteenth and nineteenth centuries with an interpretation of the notion of *dominion* that allowed humans to control and manipulate nature. Even the more moderate view of *stewardship* placed humans over nature and viewed nature as a resource to be used, albeit carefully and with respect.

The human-centered approach has often led to abusive treatment of the planet. With human progress as the goal, the earth's resources and nonhuman creatures have become expendable. When the Adam Smith theory of economy established consumer demand as the engine of economic growth, the accumulation of goods became the all-important goal.[22] The overuse of resources, pollution from industry, and enormous waste soon accompanied such industrial economies.

Growth and expansion without limits have also been the established goals for industrial leaders of the past, and little consideration has been given to how production affects the environment. In a profit-making economy nature is viewed as a mere product to buy rather than a living reality with an integrity of its own, existing independently from our needs or wants.

The Keynes model of constant growth has contributed to the bigger-is-better mentality. The move toward mega-stores and mega-malls has raised the bar for the accumulation of material things. Marketing and advertising "create" needs for our endless production of material things. As a result, an increasingly heavy strain is placed on the resources of the planet, and there is also a marked increase in pollution and waste. All of this consumption, of course, is reality only for those who have the money. On the other side, among the majority who live in poverty there are long hours working for low wages to produce these goods. The majority also exists in substandard living conditions in "bottom of the barrel" environments.

From either perspective, whether of the haves or the have-nots, a morality centered on the human can seriously jeopardize the environment. When human greed, avarice, or even desperation are parts of the equation, the use and abuse of the earth can be devastating.

Feminists point to ethical standards that are not only human-centered but also male-centered. Feminists describe this situation as hierarchical, patriarchal, and dualistic. They also point out that social, political, and even religious systems that include these three characteristics have been responsible for the abuse of both nature and women.

Christian morality also has been traditionally human-centered, focusing on personal salvation and on sins against other human beings. An environmental ethic must recognize as well sinful offenses against nonhuman creatures and nature in general. It will look at salvation in a much broader sense, in terms of the saving powers of God being extended to all of creation. As Häring writes:

> Redeemed humanity alerts us and calls us to join in a healing solidarity in the struggle between man and the universe. It is as if God himself, through all these ecological insights, calls us to a renewed cooperation with nature, to a "planetary solidarity."[23]

The Earth as the Center

Thomas Berry has suggested that our focus shift from the human to the earth as center. He points out that environmental devastation has brought the human community to a crisis, perhaps the most momentous in the planet's history. Today's generation of humans is experiencing profound changes in the very structure and chemistry of the planet. These changes are of a magnitude that is unparalleled in human history; many of the developments of the past sixty-five million years of the planet's history are being extinguished.

Berry holds that religious traditions, including Christianity, have shaped us into the kind of people we are now, but they cannot now deal with the changes that are now going on:

What is happening now to Christian theology, or any theology or any religious life or any moral code, is the most profound change that has taken place in the past 5000 years. All human affairs are forced to change more than they have changed, certainly since the larger civilizations came into being.[24]

According to Berry, we have been entranced with the "industrial world of wire and wheels, concrete and steel, and our unending highways, where we race back and forth in continual frenzy."[25] He believes that we are now called to return to our native place, the earth community. Berry sees the human community moving into a new era where the main focus will be enhancing the presence of humans and the earth for each other.

It is Berry's conviction that to face the challenges of this new age a new revelation is needed and that this new revelation must come from the universe itself. We must shift our focus to the world and listen to its story. This story will reveal that our world is our primary community, and in the experience of the world we will discover the true meaning of who we are and who our God is. We will come to realize that we are part of our world and that we can only save ourselves by also saving everything of which we are a part. Berry puts it this way:

> In this sense, we are not simply genetically cousin to everything else but we have a certain identity with everything else. We cannot save ourselves without saving everything and everybody else. . . . If we lose the outer world, we lose the inner world.[26]

Berry was a student of Teilhard de Chardin, whom he maintains "gave expression to the greatest transformation of Christian thought since the time of St. Paul."[27] It was Teilhard, as we have said earlier, who linked the Christian story with that of the earth and who maintained that the earth is the revelation of God. Teilhard hoped to shift theology from excessive concern with human salvation to focus on creation and salvation as the ultimate transformation and fulfillment of creation.

Berry assesses Teilhard as one who reflected the human-centered vision of his time and was so enamored of progress that he did not foresee the potential for destruction that attached itself to progress. Still, Teilhard's mystical perception of God's revelation within our physical world is valuable to help us deepen our ecological vision. It is in listening to our world that we can learn the lessons we need to sustain it and preserve it for future generations. Following the lead of Teilhard and Berry, we see ourselves related to creation and thereby responsible for loving care and just treatment of our world. Such a sense of connectedness can also move us to share the earth's vast resources with the millions who live in want. We have to be more than stewards; we have to be part of our world, honor it as our family, and care for it and other people as we would care for ourselves.

For Christians, this will mean shifting from traditional emphasis on human life in moral thinking to a closer study of the earth and nature. Northcott observes that the Catholic view of the natural law traditionally has been drawn exclusively from human experience.[28] He suggests that an environmental ethic need not overact and go the way of "ecological pantheism," which he finds in Teilhard as well as in North American authors like Matthew Fox, Sallie McFague, and John Cobb. Neither is he attracted to the solutions of "deep ecology," which place the human and the nonhuman on the same level. Northcott suggests "natural law," but with a focus that is "not just on human life and human moral goods but on the moral significance and moral goods of the natural created order."[29] His perspective recognizes the value of biblical insights on the dignity of all creation but at the same time accepts contemporary scientific perspectives on the universe. It seems that a new environmental ethic might find a way to integrate both scientific and religious understandings of nature, and come to a new view of natural law that might aid us in dealing with environmental issues.

God as the Center

There have been attempts to develop an environmental ethic with God as the center. Protestant theologian Jürgen Moltmann begins his study of ecology with a new reading of the doctrine of God and moves to propose a new understanding of nature. The accent here is on immanence, and it is pursued down to the smallest virus. Again, this is a version of panentheism that blurs the distinction between the Mystery of God and the mystery of creation. Using this approach in constructing an environmental ethic is problematic. It resacralizes nature, so that decisions even for well-considered and justifiable future development and progress at the expense of ecosystems become indefensible. This perspective also places such an emphasis on the "big picture" and the future of the creation that it becomes difficult to construct a practical ethic that would be a useful guide in making environmental decisions.

Ethicist Charles Murphy indicates that an ethic for the earth might well start with the vision of God given us by Christ. It is Murphy's view that the biblical vision presents God as one who loves the world so much that he sent his Son to save it, and presents Christ as one who came to signal the proximity of the kingdom and to call all to repentance. He maintains that such an ethic goes beyond what can be found in a natural law embedded in the world and beyond reason's capability functioning on its own. This is a moral vision based on divine intervention and teaching, a higher and unique morality.[30] It is morality based on imitation of the teacher and prophet Jesus Christ. Murphy suggests that such a Christ-centered environmental ethic would involve interpreting the gospel teachings and applying them to the pressing ecological issues we face today.

James Gustafson has contributed significantly to the God-centered approach to environmental ethics. In his view God is to be found as the presence somehow responsible for both the order and the disorder in creation:

> We meet God as the power that brings all things into being, that bears down on them and threatens and limits them, that sustains them and is the condition of possibility for their change. But we do not meet that power in the abstract; we meet it in the details. . . . We *experience* the reality of God.[31]

Because God is ultimately responsible, Gustafson is thrust into a sense of ultimate dependence upon the power of God when he confronts the contingencies, conflicts, chaos, and harmony in the natural world. He acknowledges that nature is not always in equilibrium and that the source and power and order of nature are not always beneficent to humans and other living things. For him, "God is the source of human good but does not guarantee it."[32] He proposes that such a God-centered position moves us to a sense of dependence and an awareness of the ambiguities in nature. It helps us become aware of the benefits that can come about when we intervene in nature, but at the same time it keeps us conscious of our limits in controlling the outcomes. Since God is the ultimate power and orderer of things, and since nature has no clear ultimate end, we make our choices in ambiguity. Yet we make our choices intentionally and are therefore answerable for our actions. He summarizes his position as follows:

> I have stressed that the theocentric perspective not only provides a framework for making conscious moral choices, but also it is an attitudinal, dispositional, affective stance. It is a sense of dependence, a sense of gratitude, a sense of accountability which properly on occasions evokes a sense of remorse and even guilt, and a sense of the possibility to intervene for justifiable ends.[33]

Gustafson points out that with regard to our position with nature we are not gods, or even delegates of the gods, so we cannot do what we will with our environment. We are neither sovereigns who master nature nor the center for which all of nature exists. Therefore we should not usurp divine prerogatives and act as despots toward nature.

It is Gustafson's conviction, therefore, that we must carefully discern what God is enabling and requiring us to do regarding our world.

We are to relate all things to each other in ways that concur with their relations to God, again, insofar as this can be discerned. But God will be God. As intentional participants we have responsibility, and the destiny of the natural environment and our part in it is heavily in our hands, but the ultimate destiny of all that exists is beyond our human control.

In contrast to Teilhard, who maintained that evolution is now in the hands of humans, Gustafson asserts that God has a mysterious plan that humans have to discern in dealing with the environment. It seems to me that environmental ethics will have to take a middle position, whereby we work with the facts before us and apply gospel values and our tradition in making ecological decisions.

The Integrity of Nature

An effective environmental ethic has to recognize the integrity of nature. Each creature and resource has its own inner character and plays a distinct role in its ecological system. These unique qualities need to be recognized and sustained. This precludes, of course, the view that natural things are available solely to be used, manipulated, and enjoyed.

It is useful to note that nature has been on this planet long before human life ever appeared and had value and purpose exclusive of human use. From the point of view of faith, God created each and every unique aspect of creation to reflect the divine goodness and glory. Therefore, the integrity of each creature and element of the earth has to be recognized. Our primary motive, then, for sustaining the things of the natural world is not for human use and enjoyment but rather for the preservation of the purpose and integrity that each thing has in the web of life.[34] The church's tradition can make a unique contribution here. Revelation teaches that all things emanate from God and that God has placed a value on all of creation. As Christiansen puts it: "A Catholic environmental ethic will appeal to God as valuer of nature and will thus have a resource for attributing intrinsic value to it independently of mere human evaluation."[35]

The Uniqueness of Human and Nonhuman

The recognition of the integrity of nonhuman creatures does not imply that all creatures are on the same level with humans. Human beings have a level of consciousness, reflection, and spirituality that is simply not found in nonhuman creatures. Freedom, self-reflection, contemplation, humor, aesthetic experience, creativity, and many other traits are uniquely human. This does not make us superior to or dominant over other creatures. Humans are part of nature and dependent on nature, and yet we also have a unique responsibility to care for nature. We are the only ones who can "figure out" ways to better sustain our environment, for we are intentional beings who act out of purpose and design. We can correct our mistakes and think of creative new ways to enhance our environment. Unlike other creatures, we need not be subject to the aberrations of nature. We can protect ourselves with shelters; we can choose our homes so that they are not subject to floods; we can put out forest fires and replant and recultivate after their destruction. We can devise ways to improve and enhance the environment. Though we as a species can be most destructive of our environment, we are also gifted with powers to sustain and rebuild that are not available to other creatures.

At the same time, it must be acknowledged that nonhuman creatures often have powers that humans do not possess. Some have speed, agility, or a sense of smell or sight that far exceeds that of humans. Some have a sense of direction or survival techniques that causes humans to stand in wonder. Understanding and respecting the unique integrity of each creature is key for developing an environmental ethic. Aldo Leopold, a pioneer in land ethics, maintains that morality must extend to all of nature: "A thing is right when it tends to preserve the integrity, stability and beauty of the biotic community. It is wrong when it tends otherwise."[36]

Nature as Gift to Be Shared

The modern sense of absolute ownership seriously challenges the biblical notion that nature is a gift from God. Paul VI in his message to the first-world conference on ecology reminded those attending that the earth belongs to the Lord and has been entrusted to us as gift. He insisted that "the environment in *res omnium,* is the patrimony of humankind."[37] This position radically confronts the greedy land-grabbing that has been part of colonialism, as well as the monopolizing of land by governments and oligarchies, and the absolute notions of property ownership that still prevail today. Häring points out:

> In justice, everyone individually, and private and public agencies, must cooperate in preserving the common heritage. Wrong concepts of property have led to a grave social malaise; but only the present malaise of the biosphere's ecosystems manifests the gravity of the errors that allows a vast abuse of God-given resources and our accumulated capital, to the detriment of whole social classes and, indeed, of all humankind of present and future generations.[38]

Nature as Our Home

The root of the word *ecology* means "home," hence the environment can be viewed as the home or dwelling place of humans and all living things. Each creature has a right to its "place" in this home; each serves a distinct purpose in keeping its own given place in balance. Earth, then, is home for a family of creatures who depend upon one another for their very existence. To harm or destroy the earth is to do damage to all of its inhabitants.

Charles Murphy makes an interesting distinction between a home and a hotel. He points out that a hotel is a temporary place where people stay when they are traveling away from home. Since people feel no connection with hotels, they are simply used, even abused. There is no link with the place, no particular reason for caring for the facilities. Certainly there is no inclination to repair something in a hotel room or to make improvements during our stay. Murphy observes that for many the earth is like a hotel, a place people pass through anonymously and without care.[39] This is particularly true in urban areas, where people are so cut off from nature that they have lost regard for it. Daniel Cowden puts it this way:

> Indeed a huge portion of our ecological degradation is not the result of being self-consciously "at war" with nature, or battling it for our own survival and cultural richness. To be honest: a vast proportion of it stems from a reckless disregard for nature, from a sense that it just does not matter what we do to it or simply from its absence to our consciousness. The impact of our daily urban actions on nature is cut off from our awareness (though that is changing for the better).[40]

For people of faith the earth is a home that has been entrusted to us by God, a place where God lives along with us. As such, it is to be cherished and cared for, kept in good repair, improved and renewed from time to time, and thoughtfully passed on to the next generation.

To say that the earth is our home does not imply that it is a static reality. The earth is always in transition, moving forward, in need of transformation. Moreover, the earth is filled with natural and moral evils, so living in it will always be a challenge. But the earth has within it the reign of God; God's presence and power move within the world, filling it with goodness and healing and drawing it to an ultimate fulfillment. It is to this earth that the Son of God came to become one with its materiality and its people. Here the Spirit of this Lord dwells among the people, constantly renewing the earth and all its inhabitants.

Reconnecting with Nature

Ever since the natural world was reduced to an object to be used and admired, there has been little motive beyond the utilitarian one to sustain nature. A secularized science removed God from the natural world and reduced it to a phenomenon to be studied and conquered. Even the more open and sensitive work of scientists like Albert Einstein and Stephen Hawking portrays God as remote from reality. Einstein viewed God as an old architect whose secret and purposeful plan was being unveiled by science. For Hawking, God is at best a kind of energy field whose laws and designs he hopes to discover through science.[41]

Nature does not consist of broken fragments of a once idyllic world; it is not a collection of dislocated pieces of a fallen paradise now cut off from the Creator. Rather, nature is "being" and "becoming," and as such it manifests and is related to the divine Being who is the source, sustainer, and goal of all reality. This was the view of Aquinas and remains the basis for the theological position that God is present in all things and can be experienced in all things.[42] Aquinas held that God is imaged in all creatures and that the purpose of diversity in creation is that God's richness might be reflected. From this perspective nature remains nature. We need not return to some ancient animism or re-sacralize nature. The world remains what it is, and our scientific understanding of it is crucial. At the same time, the transcendent God, who is beyond all things, can manifest God's self in all things.

The natural world, however, is related to us not only through being and through the divine presence immanent in all things, but it is also related to us materially. We are made from the same particles that make up the rest of the universe. Humans are of the "earth" *(humus)*. Moreover, our bodies return to the earth eventually and once again become part of the earth and its creatures. We are "part of and not greater than nature." Joseph Kitagawa writes:

> In contrast to the contemplation of Western peoples meditation in the East tends to be directed toward Sacred Reality present in Nature. This is due to the fact that unlike their Western counterparts, who believe themselves to be situated somewhere between God and the world of nature, Eastern people have always accepted the humble role of being a part of the world of nature.[43]

There is among all things an interdependence, an interconnection, which once seen helps us to relate to other creatures. Each creature serves its own purpose in this vast web of reality. At present there are millions of species we have not yet discovered, and each of these has a unique role to play in nature. Tragically, many species will be destroyed without our ever knowing what they contributed or what irreparable harm will come about because of their disappearance.

There is a delicate balance in nature. This is not to deny the disruptions in nature, the predatory aspect of nature, or the defects of our world. As Teilhard observed, our world is finite, limited. Yet in spite of the breakdowns, the physical and moral evils, the chance catastrophes, nature seems ultimately to return to harmony and order. Moreover, the cycle of life and death in nature is one with ours; in the end, all living things are born and die. The death of one reality brings new life to another, and this cycle is the same in both the natural and supernatural dimensions of reality. In all of this there is goodness and beauty that reflect the goodness and beauty of the Creator. There is a tranquility in all of reality that can resonate in our inner selves and draw us toward it.

To relate to nature we need to see ourselves as part of an immeasurably large, dynamic process of change and unfolding. The universe, of which we are but an infinitesimal part, is a process that has been taking place for perhaps twelve billion years. It is an infinitely expansive process, which includes many billions of galaxies, ever shifting and changing. Our planet is but a dot-like element of one galaxy, a galaxy which itself has billions of stars. The earth is not an inert planet; it is a living reality. As the Gaia model indicates, the earth is living and organic with its own unique patterns of existence and growth.

The earth existed for billions of years without human life, and presumably it could continue to go on as such. Its unique temperature controls, weather patterns, and tides have a certain equilibrium so that human life can be sustained. If for some reason these patterns are seriously disturbed, either by humans or by nature itself, life may not be able to be sustained on this planet. Human-induced changes in the ozone layer, weather changes brought about by the "greenhouse" effect, and acid rain can do enormous damage to the earth, humans, and other living things. As we become more aware of how much our actions affect the environment and ultimately all that lives here, it becomes more urgent to take serious steps both to repair our environment and to prevent future damage.

The Partnership Model

Some suggest that in developing an environmental ethic we see ourselves as partners with nature. This means, of course, a change from seeing ourselves as being at the center of things. Human needs and considerations have to be put side by side with the needs of other creatures. This does not imply that humans are not unique, free, and bound by singular responsibilities. It does, however, call for a broader field of consideration in making decisions that will affect many levels of nature. It might even call for sacrifice on our part at times when our development and growth will affect the lives of nonhumans. The building of a shipping canal might have to be canceled to save a wildlife habitat. The construction of a dam may have to be stopped to save the salmon runs in a river. The development of a mall or recreational area may have to be set aside to preserve wetlands for waterfowl. The partnership model takes into consideration the needs of creatures other than humans. It develops a respect for the earth and for other living things to the point where all are given serious consideration in every decision that is made for progress and development.[44] This model entails working with nature rather than trying to conquer it.

The partnership model can readily be found in the scriptures. In the Hebrew scriptures God calls humans to see the divine glory manifested in all things and extends a covenant with the earth to all living things. The psalms call us to bless God along with all of nature. The New Testament proclaims that the Son is sent to save all of creation, and it teaches that the reign of God is within all things. Jesus calls his followers to help bring about the fulfillment of God's reign in partnership with his Spirit, with each other, and indeed with all of creation.

The Ethic of Companionship

Some suggest that in the West, especially in the United States, an environmental ethic will have to shift from our characteristic individualistic approach and move toward an ethic of companionship. In the West there is a strong emphasis on individual and property rights. This has worked well for the haves, but poorly for the have-nots. In addition, this focus on individual needs is often characterized by selfishness and greedy accumulation. Little consideration is given to the common good or to the destruction done to the environment in order to satisfy these ever-multiplying needs and desires.

With an ethic that is centered on the individual, even stewardship can shift from participation in the creative activity of God into "cost-benefit analysis."[45] The companion model views nonhuman creatures and the earth in a more relational way. It also shifts the focus from self-interest to the common good. The things of nature are given more of a personal element, and we relate to them in awareness of our mutual interdependence. A tree purifies our air, holds water, bears fruit, provides a home for birds and squirrels, and offers shade and beauty. In turn, we bear a responsibility to care for the tree and attend to its needs. Animals provide us with food, clothing, and many other items. In response, they deserve to have good food, freedom to move about, and proper health care. Here the "other" is extended not only to our human neighbors but to all living things and to all the elements of nature. At the same time, it must be acknowledged that nature is not always "friendly" to humans and can in fact be harmful and even deadly. Not all of nature is in harmony or in balanced equilibrium. In addition, our relationship with nature is sometimes one of conflict. We often have to harness nature to build cultural structures or to avoid natural catastrophes. The companion model, like all others, has its limitations and should not be romanticized to the point where cultural development is brought to a halt.

Revising Natural Law

Since environmental ethics is concerned with nature, it is appropriate that the theology of natural law be applicable. This is not without problems, however, because traditional notions of natural law have tended to look at nature in a prescientific mode as static, a "once and for all time" reality. Ethics proceeding from this notion of nature have traditionally been absolute and legalistic.

If natural law is to be applied in environmental ethics today, it will have to be in a contemporary context. Current science views nature as dynamic, relativistic, and constantly changing. Nature is complex, with multiple interrelated realities forming a whole. From the scientific perspective there are no static essences or predetermined norms that are applicable in all cases. New scientific data are constantly coming in. Therefore, a contemporary natural-law ethic needs to be flexible, open to compromise and exception, and able to use proportionate reasons in order to come to decisions. Moral decisions with regard to development and progress are extremely complicated and require careful discernment as well as the ability to adjust to new situations. It will not be suitable, therefore, simply to propose laws on how to deal with nature as though there were a God-given set of rules. Nature has its own built-in laws and structures, and these need to be honored and discerned in decisions regarding development.

Scripture and tradition also provide useful norms for dealing with nature. Here fidelity to God and to creation become factors in ethical decisions and need to be integrated with the scientific analysis of nature. As we have seen, the virtues of love, humility, and justice as taught in revelation can be powerful forces to help us deal with nature responsibly. The Christian tradition also has laws of spirituality and social concern that add new dimensions to environmental decisions.

Traditional notions of natural law have been human-centered. If the natural-law theory is to be useful to environmental ethics, it will have to be much more aware of the integrity and rights of the nonhuman elements of earth. The framework here will have to be holistic, and decisions must be based on consideration of all the parts of the whole. The rights of nature will have to be considered along with individual, corporate, or state rights.[46] Human comfort, pleasure, ownership, and utility will have to give way to a much larger global and social picture. A concern for justice also will have to apply to the land, animals, all living things, and indeed the planet itself.

To apply natural law to the environment properly, mechanistic notions of nature will have to be set aside. Nature will have to be understood as being organic, dynamic, and interrelated with ourselves, and the unique ecosystems of each locale will have to be honored. Moreover, we will have to understand the limits of nature, as well as our own limits, and proceed with caution and foresight. In view of the environmental crisis we face, we will have to listen to nature and allow it to teach us how to sustain it. As Rasmussen puts it: "The true harvest of on-going evolution is embedded in nature's own designs. Nature is not first of all a big bank of resources standing at the ready; it is the source and model for the very designs we must draw upon in order to address the problems we face."[47]

Such an ethic will have to be more open to a dynamic and changing model of nature. Classical Christian morality was based on a static notion of creation, wherein everything was created as a finished product some time in the distant past. The traditional approach to natural law holds that divinely established norms exist in nature, and that these norms are fixed and final. The task of the church is to preserve and defend these norms and apply them to moral issues. In this classical view of morality there is little room for changes in moral norms or for the development or application of new principles. Moral positions are often absolute and allow for no exceptions, even for proportionate reasons.

In order to address environmental issues one must recognize the open-ended and dynamic character of nature. Science has given us an expansive, dynamic, and relativized vision of the universe, and an evolutionary and ever-changing view of the earth. An appropriate ethic will have to be compromising, adaptive, and open to change. The environment is always in process, and its issues are ever developing. An environmental ethic will have to deal with the complexity and unpredictability of such a process. This ethic will have to be open to revision and dialogue, not imposed in an absolutist manner by rigid authority. And finally, such an ethic will have to be open to compromise as well as to the application of proportionality. The progress of science, economics, and development in general will continue. The church can neither rigidly oppose progress nor ignore its gospel mission of prophetic critique.[48] At times certain concessions will have to be made, and ecosystems will be harmed for the benefit of developing peoples or nations. At other times progress will be halted in order to sustain the environment. For the Christian, this involves a delicate discernment of what actions are compatible with God's law. As Gustafson puts it:

> Humans are to seek to discern what God is enabling and requiring them to be and to do as participants in the patterns and processes of interdependence of life and the world. The divine ordering is perceived, insofar as it is humanly possible, in and through the ordering of nature, culture, history, and personal living. It has no equilibrium which guarantees the realization of all justifiable ends, and our ends as developers of technology and culture infinitely complicate the achievement of even a dynamic one. We are to relate all things to each other in ways that concur with their relations to God, again, insofar as this can be discerned.[49]

SUMMARY

A suitable environmental ethic is still in the making. At this point we can only trace the lines of some of the more promising proposals. We have suggested that such an ethic will have to challenge moral standards that are incompatible with sustaining the earth. Such an ethic, if it is to be Christian, will be centered on Christ, will drink deeply of his gospel values of love and justice, and will courageously apply these values to the many current environmental issues.

An effective evaluation of nature also needs to be integrated into environmental ethics. The notion of nature needs to be extended to all things, human and nonhuman, living and nonliving. In the larger context of nature humans have their own unique integrity, and yet they must not see themselves as superior to or as having dominion over nature. For the person of faith, nature becomes identified with creation and a reflection of the goodness of the Creator. Here nature is viewed as gift that is extended to all to be enjoyed and shared. It is a home to be cared for, repaired, and gratefully sustained. Environmental ethics calls humans to reconnect with nature and to live with it as caring partners and companions. This ethic will continue to study nature and its laws and in so doing formulate moral vision and values that can effectively sustain the earth and all that dwells on it. Such an ethic will call for a "new conscience" in Christians, one that is shaped by tradition, scripture, and the scientific study of the environment. This conscience will be guided not only by reason but also by intuition, the senses, and the imagination. It will have a sense of place and acknowledge the presence of a God who is both beyond and within all of creation.

We close with an ancient Chinese prayer that reflects such an ethic:

Heaven is my father and earth is my mother and even such a small creature as I finds an intimate place in its midst. That which extends throughout the universe, I regard as my body; and that which directs the universe, I regard as my nature. All people are my brothers and sisters and all things are my companions.[50]

Notes

INTRODUCTION

1. James A. Nash, *Loving Nature: Ecological Integrity and Christian Responsibility* (Nashville: Abingdon Press, 1991), 12.

2. Ibid.

3. See Lester Brown et al., eds., *State of the World* [current year] (New York: W. W. Norton) and *Our Common Future: The World Commission on Environment and Development* (Oxford: Oxford University Press, 1987).

4. See Ian Barbour, ed., *Western Man and Environmental Ethics* (Reading, Mass.: Addison-Wesley, 1973). This book contains White's article "The Historical Roots of Our Ecologic Crisis" and a collection of responses.

5. For overviews of these many perspectives, see David and Eileen Spring, eds., *Ecology and Religion in History* (New York: Harper & Row, 1974), Joseph Sheldon, "Twenty-one Years after the Historical Roots of Our Ecological Crisis: How Has the Church Responded?" *Perspectives on Science and Christian Faith* 41, 3 (September 1989), 156ff.

6. See Carolyn Merchant, *The Death of Nature: Women, Ecology, and the Scientific Revolution* (San Francisco: Harper & Row, 1980); Wesley Granberg-Michaelson, *A Worldly Spirituality* (San Francisco: Harper, 1983); Wesley Granberg-Michaelson, ed., *Tending the Garden* (Grand Rapids: Eerdmans, 1987); Douglas Hall, *Imaging God: Dominion as Stewardship* (Grand Rapids: Eerdmans, 1987); Jurgen Moltmann, *God in Creation* (London: SCM Press, 1985); Loren Wilkenson, ed., *Earthkeeping in the '90s* (Grand Rapids: Eerdmans, 1991); Jay McDaniel, *With Roots and Wings* (Maryknoll, N.Y.: Orbis Books, 1995) and *Of God and Pelicans* (Louisville: Westminster/John Knox Press, 1989).

7. For a collection of these documents and others, see *This Sacred Earth: Religion, Nature, and Environment*, ed. Roger S. Gottlieb (New York: Routledge, 1996).

8. See Paul VI's *Call to Action*, paragraph 21, in *Renewing the Earth*, ed. David O'Brien and Thomas Shannon (New York: Doubleday, 1977), 364. John Paul's document can be found in *"And God Saw That It Was Good": Catholic Theology and the Environment*, ed. Drew Christiansen, S.J., and Walter Grazer (Washington, D.C.: USCC, 1996), 215-23.

9. See *Catechism of the Catholic Church* (Washington D.C.: USCC, 1994), nos. 2415-2418, 2456.

10. John Paul II's document as well as the other Catholic episcopal documents are collected in Christiansen and Grazer, *"And God Saw That It Was Good."*

11. The Conference of European Churches, *Environment and Development: A Challenge of our Lifestyles* (Geneva, 1995).

12. Excellent work was done early on by Barbara Ward. See her monograph *A New Creation?: Reflections on Environmental Issues* (Vatican City: Pontifical Commission for Justice and Peace, 1973). For more recent treatments, see Denis Edwards, *Jesus the Wisdom of God: An Ecological Theology* (Maryknoll, N.Y.: Orbis Books, 1995); John R. Haught, *The*

Promise of Nature: Ecology and Cosmic Purpose (New York: Paulist Press, 1993); Christiansen and Grazer, *"And God Saw That It Was Good"*; Kevin W. Irwin and Edmund D. Pellegrino, eds., *Preserving the Creation: Environmental Theology and Ethics* (Washington, D.C.: Georgetown University Press, 1994); Richard Fragomeni and John T. Pawlikowski, eds., *The Ecological Challenge* (Collegeville, Minn.: The Liturgical Press, 1994); Albert J. LaChance and John E. Carroll, eds., *Embracing Earth: Catholic Approaches to Ecology* (Maryknoll, N.Y.: Orbis Books, 1994); Leonardo Boff, *Ecology and Liberation* (Maryknoll, N.Y.: Orbis Books, 1995); Thomas Berry, *The Dream of the Earth* (San Francisco: Sierra Club Books, 1988); Robert Faricy, *Wind and Sea Obey Him* (London: SCM Press, 1982); Bernard Häring, *Free and Faithful in Christ*, vol. 3 (New York: Crossroad, 1981), chap. 5; Sean McDonagh, *To Care for the Earth* (Sante Fe: Bear and Co., 1987); idem, *The Greening of the Church* (Maryknoll, N.Y.: Orbis Books, 1990); idem, *Passion for the Earth* (Maryknoll, N.Y.: Orbis Books, 1994). Some useful "ecumenical" collections, which have included Catholic authors, have also been published. See Charles Birch et al., eds., *Liberating Life: Contemporary Approaches to Ecological Theology* (Maryknoll, N.Y.: Orbis Books, 1990); and David Hallman, ed., *Ecotheology* (Maryknoll, N.Y.: Orbis Books, 1995).

1   TOWARD AN ENVIRONMENTAL THEOLOGY

1. *Dogmatic Constitution on Divine Revelation,* no. 90, in *The Documents of Vatican II,* ed. Walter Abbott (New York: Guild Press, 1966).

2. "Renewing the Earth," in *"And God Saw That It Was Good": Catholic Theology and the Environment,* ed. Drew Christiansen, S.J., and Walter Grazer (Washington, D.C.: USCC, 1996), 225.

3. *Catechism of the Catholic Church* (Washington, D.C.: USCC, 1994), 358.

4. Anne Lonergan and Caroline Richards, eds., *Thomas Berry and the New Cosmology* (Mystic, Conn.: Twenty-Third Publications, 1987), 105.

5. See Michael Tobias, ed., *Deep Ecology,* rev. ed. (San Marcos, Calif.: Avant Books, 1988).

6. See Anne Carr, "Theology and Experience in the Thought of Karl Rahner," *The Journal of Religion* 53, 366; Robert Schreiter, *The Schillebeeckx Reader* (New York: Crossroad, 1984), 28. See also Karl Rahner, *Theological Investigations* (Baltimore: Helicon Press, 1961), 6:211.

7. Schreiter, *The Schillebeeckx Reader,* 69; Denise Lardner Carmody, "The Desire for Transcendence," in *The Desires of the Human Heart: An Introduction to the Theology of Bernard Lonergan,* ed. Vernon Gregson (New York: Paulist Press, 1988), 73.

8. Karl Rahner, *Spirit in the World* (New York: Herder and Herder, 1968), 71.

9. Anne Carr, "Theology and Experience in the Thought of Karl Rahner," 362.

10. Bernard Lonergan, *Method of Theology* (New York: Herder and Herder, 1972), 103.

11. "Declaration of the 'Mission to Washington,'" in *This Sacred Earth: Religion, Nature, Environment,* ed. Roger S. Gottlieb (New York: Routledge, 1996), 641.

12. Karl Rahner, *Hearers of the Word* (New York: Herder and Herder, 1996), 50ff., and *Spirit in the World,* 283ff.

13. David Tracy, *The Achievement of Bernard Lonergan* (New York: Herder and Herder, 1970), 143.

14. Bernard Lonergan, *Method of Theology,* 107.

15. Fred Lawrence, "The Fragility of Consciousness: Lonergan and the Postmodern Concern for the Other," *Theological Studies* 54 (1993), 72.

16. See Brennan Hill, Paul Knitter, and William Madges, *Faith, Religion, and Theology* (Mystic, Conn.: Twenty-Third Publications, 1990), 25.

17. Scheiter, *The Schillebeeckx Reader,* 61.

18. Avery Dulles, S.J., *The Craft of Theology* (New York: Crossroad, 1992), 9.

19. Hans Küng and David Tracy, eds., *Paradigm Shift in Theology* (New York: Crossroad, 1989), 224.

20. See George Vandervelde, "The Grammar of Grace: Karl Rahner as a Watershed in Contemporary Theology," *Theological Studies* 49 (1988), 446. See T. Howland Sanks, S.J., "David Tracy's Theological Project: An Overview and Some Implications," *Theological Studies* 54 (1993), 707.

21. Anne Lonergan and Caroline Richards, *Thomas Berry and the New Cosmology,* 107.

22. Pierre Teilhard de Chardin, *Christianity and Evolution* (New York: Harcourt Brace Jovanich, 1969), 171.

23. Leo O'Donovan, S.J., "Making Heaven and Earth: Catholic Theology's Search for a Unified View on Nature and History," *Catholic Theological Society of America Proceedings* 35, 47-65 (1980), 272.

24. Frans Jozef Van Beeck, S.J., *God Encountered: A Contemporary Catholic Systematic Theology* (New York: Harper & Row, 1989), 39.

25. Tracy, *The Achievement of Bernard Lonergan,* 190.

26. See David Hollenbach, *Claims and Conflict* (New York: Paulist Press, 1979), 43ff.

27. Donal Dorr, *Options for the Poor* (Maryknoll, N.Y.: Orbis Books, 1983), 79ff.

28. See David O'Brien and Thomas Shannon, eds., *Renewing the Earth* (New York: Doubleday, 1977), 115-23.

29. *Pastoral Constitution on the Church in the Modern World,* no. 1, in Abbott, *The Documents of Vatican II.*

30. William J. Kelly, S.J., *Theology and Discovery: Essays in Honor of Karl Rahner, S.J.* (Milwaukee: Marquette University Press, 1980), 1.

31. Paul Tillich, *Theology of Culture* (New York: Oxford University Press, 1964). For commentary, see also James Luther Adams, *Paul Tillich's Philosophy of Culture, Science, and Religion* (New York: Harper & Row, 1965).

32. Paul Tillich, *The Protestant Era* (Chicago: University of Chicago Press, 1957), 56ff., and "On the Idea of a Theology of Culture," in *What Is Religion?*, ed. James Luther Adams (New York: Harper & Row, 1969), 165. The parallel tendency of extreme individualism is studied in Robert Bellah et al., eds., *Habits of the Heart* (Berkeley: University of California Press, 1985).

33. Paul Tillich, *Systematic Theology* (Chicago: University of Chicago Press, 1965), 1:79ff.

34. Tillich, *Systematic Theology,* 1:84.

35. Paul Tillich, *The Religious Situation* (New York: Meridian Books, 1956), 185.

36. Tillich, *The Protestant Era,* 76.

37. David Tracy, *Blessed Rage for Order* (New York: Seabury Press, 1975).

38. See Sanks, S.J., "David Tracy's Theological Project," 701.

39. David Tracy, *On Naming the Present* (Maryknoll, N.Y.: Orbis Books, 1994), 1ff.

40. Ibid., 11.

41. Jurgen Moltmann, "Theology in Transition–to What?" in Küng and Tracy, *Paradigm Shift in Theology,* 224ff.

42. Anne Lonergan and Caroline Richards, *Thomas Berry and the New Cosmology,* 37ff.

2   THE HEBREW SCRIPTURES

1. Roland E. Murphy, O. Carm., *Wisdom Literature* (Grand Rapids: Eerdmans, 1981), 104.

2. Richard J. Clifford, *Creation Accounts in the Ancient Near East and in the Bible*, The Catholic Biblical Quarterly Monograph Series, 26 (1994), 82ff. See also Lawrence Boadt, *Reading the Old Testament* (New York: Paulist Press, 1984), 116.

3. Bernhard W. Anderson, *From Creation to New Creation* (Minneapolis: Fortress Press, 1994), 15.

4. Norbert Lohfink, *Theology of the Pentateuch* (Minneapolis: Fortress Press, 1989), 4ff.

5. See Anderson, *From Creation to New Creation*, 15.

6. Claus Westermann, *Elements of Old Testament Theology* (Atlanta: John Knox Press, 1982), 98. See also Bruce Vawter, *On Genesis: A New Reading* (Garden City, N.Y.: Doubleday, 1977), 58ff.

7. Gerhard Von Rad, *Genesis: A Commentary* (Philadelphia: Westminster Press, 1961), 6. Von Rad indicates that ancient kings would erect images of themselves in the provinces of their empires to indicate their dominion. There is also evidence that Egyptian pharaohs saw themselves as the "living images" of the god Re. See Anderson, *From Creation to New Creation*, 127. See also Claus Westermann, *Genesis* (Grand Rapids: Eerdmans, 1986), 11.

8. Ronald Simkins, *Creator and Creation* (Peabody, Mass.: Hendrickson, 1994), 39.

9. Claus Westermann, *Roots of Wisdom* (Louisville: Westminster/John Knox Press, 1995), 118; also his *Creation* (Philadelphia: Fortress Press, 1974), 55ff. See also Anderson, *From Creation to New Creation*, 33ff.

10. Westermann, *Genesis*, 18-19.

11. Lynn White Jr., "The Historical Roots of Our Ecologic Crisis," *Science* 155 (1967), 1203-7.

12. Anderson, *From Creation to New Creation*, 130. See Westermann, *Creation*, 50ff.

13. Lohfink, *Theology of the Pentateuch*, 7ff.

14. Claus Westermann, *Elements of Old Testament Theology*, 98. See also Bruce Vawter, *On Genesis: A New Reading*, 58ff.

15. See Clifford, *Creation Accounts in the Ancient Near East and in the Bible*, 42.

16. See Jeremy Cohen, "Be Fertile and Increase: Fill the Earth and Master It," in *The Ancient and Medieval Career of a Biblical Text* (Ithaca, N.Y.: Cornell University Press, 1989), 5.

17. Dianne Bergant, *Job Ecclesiastes* (Wilmington, Del.: Michael Glazier, 1982), 232ff.

18. Abraham J. Heschel, *The Prophets* (New York: Harper & Row, 1962), 45ff. See also Bernhard W. Anderson, *Creation versus Chaos* (Philadelphia: Fortress Press, 1987; reprint of 1967 edition with new foreword), 59.

19. Roland Murphy, *Song of Songs* (Minneapolis: Fortress Press, 1990), 68.

20. Ibid., 103.

21. John Paul II, *The Ecological Crisis: A Common Responsibility* (Washington, D.C.: USCC, 1990), 1; see also Catholic Committee of Appalachia, *At Home in the Web of Life* (Webster Springs, W.Va.: 1996), 12ff.

22. See United States Catholic Conference, *Renewing the Earth* (Washington, D.C.: USCC, 1991), 2.

23. Anderson, *From Creation to New Creation*, 150.

24. Westermann, *Roots of Wisdom*, 123ff.

25. Anderson, *From Creation to New Creation*, 35.

26. Ibid., 36.

27. Ibid., 11.

28. Westermann, *Elements of Old Testament Theology*, 92.

29. See Anderson, 13; Westerman, *Genesis*, 10; and Simkins, *Creator and Creation*, 33.

30. Anderson, *Creation versus Chaos*, 64; see also Lohfink, *Theology of the Pentateuch*, 131.

31. Bernhard W. Anderson, *Understanding the Old Testament* (Englewood Cliffs, N.J.: Prentice-Hall, 1966), 494.

32. Gerhard Von Rad, *Wisdom in Israel* (New York: Abingdon Press, 1972), 152.

33. Roland Murphy, *Responses to 101 Questions on the Psalms and Other Writings* (New York: Paulist Press, 1994), 33ff.

34. James Crenshaw, *Gerhard Von Rad* (Waco, Tex.: Word Books, 1978), 147.

35. Roland Murphy, *The Psalms and Job* (Philadelphia: Fortress Press, 1977), 71.

36. Von Rad, *Old Testament Theology*, 136. Von Rad earlier maintained that the Hebrews stressed redemption at the expense of creation. He later moderated that view.

37. In Anderson, *Creation versus Chaos*, 36.

38. Lohfink, *Theology of the Pentateuch*, 128.

39. Von Rad, *Old Testament Theology*, 136ff.

40. Westermann, *Creation*, 116.

41. See Westermann, *Prophetic Oracles*, 22ff.

42. Walter Brueggemann, *The Prophetic Imagination* (Philadelphia: Fortress Press, 1978), 35ff. See also his *Hopeful Imagination* (Philadelphia: Fortress Press, 1986), 68ff.

43. Murphy, *The Psalms*, Job, 30. See also Anderson, *Understanding the Old Testament*, 482.

44. Catholic Committee on Appalachia, *At Home in the Web of Life*, 5.

45. Elizabeth Roberts and Elias Amidon, *Earth Prayers* (New York: Harper Collins, 1991), 158.

46. See Sallie McFague, *Models of God* (Philadelphia: Fortress Press, 1987) and *Body of God* (Minneapolis: Fortress Press, 1993).

47. Jay B. McDaniel, *Of God and Pelicans* (Louisville: Westminster/John Knox, 1989), 48ff.

48. See Thomas Berry, *The Dream of the Earth* (San Francisco: Sierra Club Books, 1988).

49. Grace M. Jantzen, "Healing Our Brokenness: The Spirit and Creation," in *Readings in Ecology and Feminist Theology*, ed. Mary Heather MacKinnon and Moni McIntyre (Kansas City: Sheed and Ward, 1995), 284ff.

50. See Catherine Keller, *From a Broken Web: Separation, Sexism, and Self* (Boston: Beacon Press, 1986).

51. John F. Haught, *The Promise of Nature: Ecology and Cosmic Purpose* (New York: Paulist Press, 1993), 36.

52. See Leonardo Boff, *Ecology and Liberation* (Maryknoll, N.Y.: Orbis Books, 1995).

3 THE CHRISTIAN SCRIPTURES

1. See John P. Meier, *A Marginal Jew* (New York: Doubleday, 1991), 174-75.

2. See Daniel Patte, *The Gospel According to Matthew* (Philadelphia: Fortress Press, 1987), 93.

3. John Paul II, "The Ecological Crisis: A Common Responsibility 1989," in *This Sacred Earth*, ed. Roger Gottlieb (New York: Routledge, 1996), 235.

4. William G. Thompson, *Matthew's Story* (New York: Paulist Press, 1989), 71.

5. Rudolf Schnackenburg, *Jesus in the Gospels* (Louisville: John Knox Press, 1995), 142ff.

6. See Robert J. Karris, *Luke: Artist and Theologian* (New York: Paulist Press, 1985), 98ff.

7. Donald Senior, *Jesus: A Gospel Portrait* (New York: Paulist Press, 1992), 48ff.

8. See Daniel J. Harrington, S.J., *God's People in Christ: New Testament Perspective on the Church and Judaism* (Philadelphia: Fortress Press, 1980).

9. Francis J. Cwiekowski, *The Beginnings of the Church*) (New York: Paulist Press, 1988), 40.

10. Patte, *The Gospel According to Matthew,* 50ff.

11. John F. O'Grady, *The Four Gospels and the Jesus Tradition* (New York: Paulist Press, 1989), 103.

12. Raymond Brown, Joseph Fitzmyer, and Roland Murphy, eds., *The Jerome Biblical Commentary* (Englewood Cliffs, N.J.: Prentice-Hall, 1968), 83, 31.

13. Thompson, *Matthew's Story,* 86ff.

14. Thomas Berry and Thomas Clarke, *Befriending the Earth* (Mystic, Conn.: Twenty-Third Publications, 1991), 33.

15. Schnackenburg, *Jesus in the Gospels,* 29ff.

16. Walter Kasper, *Jesus the Christ* (Mahwah, N.J.: Paulist Press, 1976), 91-106.

17. H. J. Richards, *The Miracle of Jesus* (Mystic, Conn.: Twenty-Third Publications, 1986), 226, 53ff., 89ff.

18. Augustine Stock, *Call to Discipleship* (Wilmington, Del.: Michael Glazier, 1982), 118ff.

19. See Raymond E. Brown, *The Birth of the Messiah* (Garden City, N.Y.: Doubleday, 1977), 138.

20. Ibid.

21. R. A. Rosenberg, "The Star of the Messiah Reconsidered," *Biblica* 53 (1971), 105-9.

22. See Herman Hendrickx, *Infancy Narratives* (London: Geoffrey Chapman, 1975), 37ff.

23. Brown, *The Birth of the Messiah,* 314.

24. Ibid., 40ff.

25. Paul S. Minear, *Christians and the New Creation: Genesis Motifs in the New Testament* (Louisville: Westminster/John Knox Press, 1994), xiff.

26. Paul S. Minear, "Far as the Curse Is Found: The Point of Revelation 12, 15-16," *Novum Testamentum* 33 (1991), 71-77.

27. Ibid., 7.

28. Ibid., 22ff.

29. Ibid., 27ff.

30. See David M. Stanley, *Jesus in Gethsemane* (New York: Paulist Press, 1980).

31. Donald Senior, *The Passion of Jesus in the Gospel of Mark* (Wilmington, Del.: Michael Glazier, 1984).

32. Schnackenburg, *Jesus in the Gospels,* 99-100.

33. Raymond E. Brown, *The Death of the Messiah* (New York: Doubleday, 1994), 2:1120ff.

34. Ibid., 2:1180.

35. Ibid., 2:1260ff.

36. Pheme Perkins, *Resurrection* (Garden City, N.Y.: Doubleday, 1984), 163ff.

37. Ibid., 169ff.

38. Joseph A. Fitzmyer, *According to Paul* (New York: Paulist Press, 1992), 15.

39. E. P. Sanders, *Paul* (New York: Oxford University Press, 1991), 65ff.

40. See Mary Van Possum, *Reinhabiting the Earth: Biblical Perspectives and Eco-Spiritual Reflections* (Liguori, Mo.: Triumph Books, 1994), 55ff.

41. See Fitzmyer, *According to Paul*, 13.

4   JESUS THE CHRIST

1. See J. A. Lyons, *The Cosmic Christ in Origen and Teilhard de Chardin* (New York: Oxford University Press, 1982), 215.

2. John Macquarrie, *Jesus Christ in Modern Thought* (Philadelphia: Trinity Press International, 1990), 170.

3. Patriarch Alexy, "Nature Is a Source of God's Wisdom," in *Christianity and Sustainable Development* (Christian Council of Sweden, 1997), 11.

4. Walter Kasper, "Orientation in Current Christology," *Theology Digest* 31 (Summer 1984), 108.

5. Pierre Teilhard de Chardin, *The Phenomenon of Man* (New York: Harper & Row, 1959), 165.

6. Thomas Berry, *The Dream of the Earth* (San Francisco: Sierra Club Books, 1988), 132.

7. Karl Rahner, "Christology within an Evolutionary View of the World," *Theological Investigations* 5 (New York: Seabury Press, 1975), 159ff.

8. In Ursula King, *Spirit of Fire* (Maryknoll, N.Y.: Orbis Books, 1996), 31.

9. John Carmody, *Ecology and Religion* (New York: Paulist Press, 1983), 76ff.

10. Bernard Häring, *Free and Faithful in Christ* (New York: Crossroad, 1981), 3:181.

11. Pierre Teilhard de Chardin, *The Heart of Matter* (London: Collins, 1978), 16.

12. Pierre Teilhard de Chardin, *Writings in Time of War* (London: Collins, 1968), 168.

13. Pierre Teilhard de Chardin, *Hymn of the Universe* (London: Collins, 1970), 64ff.

14. Pierre Teilhard de Chardin, *Divine Milieu* (London: Collins, 1963), 152.

15. Christopher Mooney, *Teilhard de Chardin and the Mystery of Christ* (New York: Doubleday, 1968), 590.

16. See Karl Rahner, *Foundations of Christian Faith* (New York: Seabury Press, 1978), 181ff., and his "Christology within an Evolutionary View of the World," 161-63; see also Tony Kelly, "Wholeness: Ecological and Catholic? *Pacifia* 3 (June 1990), 201-23.

17. Elizabeth Johnson, "Seminar on Christology" CTSA proceeding 38 (1983), 109.

18. Rahner, *Foundations of Christian Faith*, 177.

19. Evelyn Underhill, *Mysticism: A Study in the Nature and Development of Man's Spiritual Consciousness* (New York: Noonday Press, 1955), 35.

20. Henri Nouwen, "Living the Incarnation at L'Arche: To Meet the Body Is to Meet the Word," *Oxford Review* 54 (April 1987), 4.

21. Ibid.

22. James D. G. Dunn, *Christology in the Making* (Philadelphia: Westminster Press, 1980), 213ff.

23. Other uses of Logos by such thinkers as Tertullian (d. 220), Clement of Alexandria (d. 215), and Origen (c. 253) are more Platonic in their application of the notion and are not as comfortable in approach to the "flesh" or the physicality of Jesus. Indeed, there has been a dualistic tendency in Christianity from the beginning, which has been "world-denying"—uncomfortable with the body and sexuality as well as with material things. It is

this tendency that might be one of the main factors that Catholic theology, even to the present day, has been reluctant to relate to ecological concerns—this and the notion of the fall and that it is a fallen world and fallen flesh.

24. See Monika Hellwig, "Emerging Issues in Soteriology," *Theology Digest* 31 (Winter 1984), 303-13.

25. See Jaroslav Pelican, *The Christian Tradition*, vol. 1, *The Emergence of the Catholic Tradition (100-600)* (Chicago: University of Chicago Press, 1971), 144ff.

26. J. N. D. Kelly, *Early Christian Doctrines* (London: Black, 1968), 376, also 173.

27. Denis Edwards, *Jesus the Wisdom of God: An Ecological Theology* (Maryknoll, N.Y.: Orbis Books, 1995), 19.

28. See Sirach 51:23-27 (Wis 9:9 and Sir 24:8; Wis 7:26); see Dunn, *Christology in the Making*, 165ff.

29. Denis Edwards, *Jesus the Wisdom of God*, 70ff.

30. Reginald Fuller, "Jesus Christ as Savior in the New Testament," *Interpretation* 35 (1981), 156.

31. Hellwig, "Emerging Issues in Soteriology," 304ff.

32. Michael Root, "Images of Liberation: Justin, Jesus, and the Jews," *Thomist* 48 (October 1994), 512-34.

33. Michael Leary, "Creation and Pauline Soteriology," *Irish Theological Quarterly* 50:1 (1983), 1ff.

34. Pierre Teilhard de Chardin, *Christianity and Evolution* (New York: Harcourt Brace Jovanich, 1969), 144ff.

35. Archbishop Oscar Romero, "The Political Dimension of Faith," in *Liberation Theology*, ed. Alfred Hennelly (Maryknoll, N.Y.: Orbis Books, 1990), 300.

36. Gustavo Gutiérrez, "Toward a Theology of Liberation," in Hennelly, *Liberation Theology*, 65.

37. John Paul II, "Address to the Indians of Oaxaca and Chiapas," in Hennelly, *Liberation Theology*, 260-61.

38. Leonardo Boff, *Ecology and Liberation: A New Paradigm* (Maryknoll, N.Y.: Orbis Books, 1995), 19.

39. Pheme Perkins, *Resurrection* (New York: Doubleday, 1984), 22ff.

40. Reginald Fuller, *The Formation of the Resurrection Narrative* (Philadelphia: Fortress Press, 1980), 49ff.

41. See Gerald O'Collins, *Interpreting the Resurrection* (New York: Paulist Press, 1988), 51ff.

42. Monika Hellwig, *Jesus, the Compassion of God* (Wilmington, Del.: Michael Glazier, 1983), 101. See also Brennan Hill, *Jesus the Christ* (Mystic, Conn.: Twenty-Third Publications, 1991), 203ff.

43. See Joseph A. Fitzmyer, S.J., "The Ascension of Christ and Pentecost," *Theological Studies* 45 (1984), 409-39.

44. Rahner, *On the Theology of Death* (New York: Herder and Herder, 1961), 66 and 22ff.

45. Karl Rahner, *Theological Investigations* (Baltimore: Helicon Press, 1961), 6:128ff.

46. See Gerald O'Collins, *Jesus Risen* (New York: Paulist Press, 1987), 192.

47. J. McCarthy, "Le Christ cosmique et l'âge de l'écologie," *Nouvelle Revue Theologique* 16 (1994), 31ff.

48. Roland Murphy, O. Carm., "Wisdom and Creation," *Journal of Biblical Literature* 104 (1985), 5.

49. McCarthy, "Le Christ cosmique et l'âge de l'écologie," 34ff.

50. J. A. Lyons, *The Cosmic Christ in Origen and Teilhard de Chardin*, 215. See also George A. Maloney, *The Cosmic Christ: From Paul to Teilhard* (New York: Sheed and Ward, 1968). See also Michael Day, "Teilhard's Rediscovery of the Cosmic Christ," *The Teilhard Review* [London] 11 (1976), 109-12.

51. Teilhard, *Christianity and Evolution*, 139ff.

52. Bernard Häring, *Free and Faithful in Christ*, 3:179.

5 SACRAMENTS

1. David Tracy, *The Analogical Imagination* (New York: Crossroad, 1981), 205.

2. Ibid., 206.

3. Ibid., 216, 438.

4. Karl Rahner, *Foundations of Christian Faith* (New York: Crossroad, 1987), 87.

5. John Haught, "Christianity and Ecology," in *This Sacred Earth: Religion, Nature, Environment*, ed. Roger S. Gottlieb (New York: Routledge, 1996), 276.

6. Al Fritsch, S.J., *Down to Earth Spirituality* (Kansas City: Sheed and Ward, 1992), 51.

7. Kenan Osborne, *Sacramental Theology* (New York: Paulist Press, 1988), 27ff.

8. Dieter T. Hessel, "Now That Animals Can Be Genetically Engineered," in Gottlieb, *This Sacred Earth*, 622.

9. Shannon Jung, *We Are Home: A Spirituality of the Environment* (New York: Paulist Press, 1993), 3.

10. *Oxford American Dictionary* (New York: Oxford University Press, 1980).

11. Rahner, *Foundations of Christian Faith*, 44ff.

12. Hessel, "Now That Animals Can Be Genetically Engineered," 622.

13. John Damascene, in Scott McCarthy, *Celebrating the Earth* (San Jose: Resource Publication, 1991), 73-74.

14. Sean McDonagh, *The Greening of the Church* (Maryknoll, N.Y.: Orbis Books, 1990), 163.

15. Fritsch, *Down to Earth Spirituality*, 17.

16. Aidan Kavanagh, *The Shape of Baptism* (New York: Pueblo, 1978), 6.

17. Rudolf Schnackenburg, *Baptism in the Thought of St. Paul* (New York: Herder and Herder, 1964), 25. See also Kavanagh, *The Shape of Baptism*, 13ff.

18. Anne Morrow Lindbergh, *Selections from Gift from the Sea* (Kansas City, Mo.: Hallmark, 1967), 61. See also Regis Duffy, "Baptism and Confirmation," in *Systematic Theology*, ed. Francis Schüssler Fiorenza and John Galvin (Minneapolis: Fortress Press, 1991), 2:215.

19. In T. C. McLuhan, *Touch the Earth* (New York: Promontory Press, 1971), 99.

20. Kavanagh, *The Shape of Baptism*, 27.

21. See Jerome Murphy-O'Connor, *Becoming Human Together: The Pastoral Anthropology of St. Paul* (Wilmington, Del.: Michael Glazier, 1982), 98.

22. Kenan Osborne, *The Christian Sacraments of Initiation* (New York: Paulist Press, 1987), 62ff.

23. Sean McDonagh, *To Care for the Earth* (Santa Fe: Bear and Co., 1986), 71.

24. Thomas Berry and Thomas Clarke, *Befriending the Earth* (Mystic, Conn.: Twenty-Third Publications, 1991), 48.

25. Cyril of Alexandria, in Gerard Austin, *The Rite of Confirmation* (New York: Pueblo, 1985), 106.

26. Osborne, *Sacramental Theology*, 17ff.

27. For a discussion of the meal stories, see Philippe Rouillard, "From Human Meal to Christian Eucharist" in *Living Bread, Saving Cup,* ed. Kevin Seasoltz (Collegeville, Minn.: The Liturgical Press, 1982), 141ff.

28. Willy Rordorf et al., *The Eucharist of the Early Christians* (New York: Pueblo, 1978), 1ff.

29. Johannes Quasten, *Patrology* (Utrecht-Antwerp: Spectrum Pub., 1966), 1:32-33.

30. In Rordorf, *The Eucharist of the Early Christians,* 73.

31. In Gary Macy, *The Banquet's Wisdom* (New York: Paulist Press, 1992), 21.

32. Fritsch, *Down to Earth Spirituality,* 41.

33. McDonagh, *The Greening of the Church,* 143.

34. McDonagh, *To Care for the Earth,* 171. See also Monica Hellwig, *Eucharist and Hunger of the World,* 2d ed. (Kansas City: Sheed and Ward, 1994).

35. David Power, *The Eucharistic Mystery* (New York: Crossroad, 1992), 10.

36. Pierre Teilhard de Chardin, *Hymn of the Universe* (New York: Harper & Row, 1965), 19-23. For other liturgies on ecology, see McCarthy, *Celebrating the Earth,* 117ff.

37. Wendell Berry, *The Gift of Good Land* (San Francisco: North Point Press, 1981), 281.

38. Hessel, "Now That Animals Can Be Genetically Engineered," 626.

39. McDonagh, *To Care for the Earth,* 178.

40. See Michael Lawler, "Marriage and the Sacrament of Marriage," in *Christian Marriage and Family,* ed. Michael Lawler and William Roberts (Collegeville, Minn.: The Liturgical Press, 1996), 22-38.

41. Walter Kasper, *Theology of Christian Marriage* (New York: Crossroad, 1981), 27.

42. Evelyn Eaton Whitehead and James D. Whitehead, *Marrying Well* (New York: Doubleday, 1983), 442.

6 THE CHURCHES SPEAK OUT

1. Conference of European Churches, "Environment and Development" (Crete: Europa, 1995), 7, 13.

2. For the complete text, see *"And God Saw That It Was Good": Catholic Theology and the Environment,* ed. Drew Christiansen, S.J., and Walter Grazer (Washington, D.C.: USCC, 1996), 215-23.

3. Ibid., 223-45.

4. Catholic Committee of Appalachia, *At Home in the Web of Life* (Webster Springs, W.Va., 1996). This document was signed by all the bishops in this area.

5. Ibid., 30ff.

6. "Ecology: The Bishops of Lombardy Address the Community," in Christiansen and Grazer, *"And God Saw That It Was Good,"* 295-309.

7. Ibid., 296.

8. Ibid., 302.

9. "The Cry for the Land," in Christiansen and Grazer, *"And God Saw That It Was Good,"* 275-95.

10. Ibid., 282.

11. *Gaudium et spes,* in *The Documents of Vatican II,* ed. Walter Abbott (New York: Guild Press, 1966), 69.

12. "What Is Happening to Our Beautiful Land?" in Christiansen and Grazer, *"And God Saw That It Was Good,"* 309-19. For background and commentary, see Sean McDonagh, *The Greening of the Church* (Maryknoll, N.Y.: Orbis Books, 1990).

13. "What Is Happening to Our Beautiful Land?" 316.

14. Ibid.

15. "Basis for Our Caring," in *This Sacred Earth: Religion, Nature, Environment,* ed. Roger S. Gottlieb (New York: Routledge, 1996), 243-51.

16. Ibid., 244.

17. Ibid., 246.

18. Ibid.

19. Ibid., 250.

20. "Restoring Creation of Ecology and Justice" (Louisville: DMS, 1990), 6.

21. Ibid., 11.

22. "Liberating Life: A Report to the World Council of Churches," in Gottlieb, *This Sacred Earth,* 251-70.

23. Ibid., 256.

24. See *Working Document from the Second European Ecumenical Assembly* (Graz, Austria, 1997).

25. Ibid., 51.

7 THE GOD QUESTION

1. Walter Kasper, *God of Jesus Christ* (New York: Crossroad, 1984), 3.

2. Charles Eastman, *Soul of the Indian* (Boston: Houghton Mifflin, 1911), 59.

3. David Tracy, *The Analogical Imagination* (New York: Crossroad, 1981), 199.

4. John Haught, *What Is Religion?* (New York: Paulist Press, 1990), 217ff.

5. Frederick Engels, "Ludwig Feuerbach," in *Karl Marx Selected Works,* ed. V. Adoratsky (New York: International Publishers, 1933), 85.

6. Karl Marx, "Religion, Philosophy, and the Proletariat," in *Karl Marx: The Essential Writings,* ed. Frederic L. Bender, 2d ed. (London: Westview Press, 1972), 46.

7. Karl Marx, "Religion and Authority," in Bender, *Karl Marx,* 6:22.

8. Vladimir Lenin, "Socialism and Religion," in *Frederick Engels and Vladimir Lenin: On Historical Materialism,* ed. Karl Marx (Moscow: Progress Publishers, 1972), 411.

9. Ibid., 412.

10. Valentin Pessenko, "Sustainable Development from the Russian Perspective," in *Christianity and Sustainable Development in the Baltic Sea Region* (Christian Council of Sweden, 1997), 23ff.

11. Winfried Hohlfeld, "God or Mammon?—A Protestant Perspective," *Christianity and Sustainable Development in the Baltic Sea Region,* 15.

12. Patriarch Alexy, "Nature Is a Friend and Source of God's Wisdom, *Christianity and Sustainable Development in the Baltic Sea Region,* 12.

13. Lester R. Brown, "Nature's Limits," in *State of the World, 1995* (New York: Norton, 1995), 16ff.

14. Megan Ryan and Christopher Flavin, "Facing China's Limits," in *State of the World, 1995,* 113-32.

15. See Peter C. Hodgson, *God in History* (Nashville: Abingdon Press, 1989), 35ff.

16. Sigmund Freud, "An Autobiographical Study," in *Standard Edition of the Complete Psychological Works of Sigmund Freud* (London: Hogarth Press, 1959), 20:68ff.

17. Sigmund Freud, *The Future of an Illusion* (New York: W. W. Norton and Company, 1961), 43.

18. James Strachey, ed., *Works of Sigmund Freud* (London: Hogarth Press, 1973-75), 1:21.

19. Hans Küng, *Freud and the Problem of God* (New Haven, Conn.: Yale University Press, 1990), 96ff.

20. Carl Sagan, *Cosmos* (New York: Random House, 1980), 29, 257ff.

21. For a discussion of Monod, see John Haught, *The Cosmic Adventure* (New York: Paulist Press, 1991).

22. See Gerhard Staguhn, *God's Laughter: Man and His Cosmos* (San Francisco: Harper Collins, 1992), 79.

23. Ibid., 84.

24. Stephen Hawking, *A Short History of Time* (New York: Bantam, 1988), 175ff.

25. See Louis Baldwin, *Portraits of God* (London: McFarland and Co., 1986), 133ff.

26. Hodgson, *God in History*, 44ff.

27. Robert Mellert, "Process Theology and God's Personal Being," in *A Personal God*, ed. Edward Schillebeeckx and Bas van Israel (New York: Seabury Press, 1977), 129.

28. Jay B. McDaniel, *With Roots and Wings* (Maryknoll, N.Y.: Orbis Books, 1995), 97.

29. See A. R. Peacocke, *Creation and the World of Science* (New York: Oxford University Press, 1979), 207.

30. Karl Rahner, "An Investigation of the Incomprehensibility of God in St. Thomas Aquinas," *Theological Investigations* (Baltimore: Helicon Press, 1961-), 16:251-53.

31. Karl Rahner "The Concept of Mystery in Catholic Theology," *Theological Investigations*, 1:66.

32. Karl Rahner, "Theos in the New Testament," *Theological Investigations*, 1:117.

33. *Pastoral Constitution on the Church in the Modern World,* in *The Documents of Vatican II*, ed. Walter Abbott (New York: Guild Press, 1966), 17.

34. Thomas Merton, "The Inner Experience," *Cistercian Studies* 18: 9-10. Quoted in Basil Pennington, *Centered Living* (New York: Doubleday, 1986), 72.

35. John F. Haught, *What Is God* (New York: Paulist Press, 1986), 15ff.

36. Hans Küng, *Mozart: Traces of Transcendence* (Grand Rapids: Eerdmans, 1991), 35.

37. See Ursula King, *Spirit of Fire: The Life and Vision of Teilhard de Chardin* (Maryknoll, N.Y.: Orbis Books, 1996), 70.

38. Jacques Cousteau, *Calypso Log* (August 1996), 3.

39. In Brennan Hill, Paul Knitter, and William Madges, *Faith, Religion, and Theology* (Mystic, Conn.: Twenty-Third Publications, 1990), 25.

40. Denis Carroll, *A Pilgrim God for a Pilgrim People* (Wilmington, Del.: Michael Glazier, 1989), 126ff.

41. Anne Lonergan and Caroline Richards, eds., *Thomas Berry and the New Cosmology* (Mystic, Conn.: Twenty-Third Publications, 1987), 103-4.

42. Cousteau, *Calypso Log*, 3.

43. Lonergan and Richards, *Thomas Berry and the New Cosmology*, 106.

44. Piet Schoonenberg, "God as Person(al)," in Schillebeeckx and van Israel, *A Personal God*, 89ff.

45. Claus Westermann, *What Does the Old Testament Say about God?* (Atlanta: John Knox Press, 1979), 25.

46. Gustavo Gutiérrez, *The God of Life* (Maryknoll, N.Y.: Orbis Books, 1991), 78.

8   WOMEN'S VIEWS

1. Ivone Gebara, "Cosmic Theology: Ecofeminism and Panentheism," in *Readings in Ecology and Feminist Theology,* ed. Mary Heather MacKinnon and Moni McIntyre (Kansas City: Sheed and Ward, 1995), 208ff.

2. Pamela Philipose, "Women Act," *Women and Environmental Protection in India,* in *Healing the Wounds: The Promise of Ecofeminism,* ed. Judith Plant (Philadelphia: New Society Publishers, 1989), 67-73.

3. *National Catholic Reporter* (December 27, 1996), 11.

4. Vandana Shiva, *Staying Alive: Women, Ecology, and Development* (London: Zed Books, 1989), 5.

5. See Rosemary Radford Ruether, ed., *Women Healing Earth: Third-World Women on Ecology, Feminism, and Religion* (Maryknoll, N.Y.: Orbis Books, 1996), 4ff.

6. See Carol Merchant, *The Death of Nature: Women, Ecology, and the Scientific Revolution* (New York: Harper & Row, 1982), 120.

7. Heather Eaton, "Ecological-Feminist Theology," in *Theology for Earth Community,* ed. Dieter T. Hessel (Maryknoll, N.Y.: Orbis Books, 1996), 77ff.

8. Rosemary Radford Ruether, "Ecofeminism," in *Ecofeminism and the Sacred,* ed. Carol Adams (New York: Continuum, 1993), 15ff.

9. Ibid., 18.

10. Quoted in Elizabeth A. Johnson, *Women, Earth, and Creator Spirit* (New York: Paulist Press, 1993), 16. See also Rosemary Radford Ruether, *Gaia and God* (New York: Harper Collins, 1992), 195.

11. Shiva, *Staying Alive,* 17.

12. Catharine J. M. Halkes, *New Creation: Christian Feminism and the Renewal of the Earth* (Louisville: Westminster/John Knox Press, 1991), 36.

13. Ibid., 47.

14. Ibid., 367.

15. Anne Primavesi, *From Apocalypse to Genesis* (Minneapolis: Fortress Press, 1991), 31.

16. Johnson, *Women, Earth, and Creator Spirit,* 13.

17. Maria Mies, *Patriarchy and Accumulation on a World Scale* (London: Zed Books, 1987), 16ff.

18. Shiva, *Staying Alive,* 47.

19. Ibid., 53.

20. Ibid., 26.

21. Elizabeth M. Tetlow, *Women in Ministry in the New Testament* (New York: Paulist Press, 1989), 5ff.

22. Leonard Swidler, *Biblical Affirmations about Women* (Philadelphia: Fortress Press, 1979), 85ff.

23. Elizabeth Johnson, *Consider Jesus* (New York: Crossroad, 1990), 110.

24. Ruether, *Gaia and God,* 144.

25. Johnson, *Woman, Earth, and Creator Spirit,* 12.

26. Primavesi, *From Apocalypse to Genesis,* 27.

27. Tumani Mutasa Nyajeka, "Shona Women and the Mutupo Principle," in Ruether, *Women Healing Earth,* 135-36.

28. Primavesi, *From Apocalypse to Genesis,* 27.

29. Rosemary Radford Ruether, "Toward an Ecological-Feminist Theology of Nature," in Plant, *Healing the Wounds,* 146.

30. Ibid., 146.

31. Halkes, *New Creation*, 37.

32. See Johnson, *Woman, Earth, and Creator Spirit*, 17ff.

33. Halkes, *New Creation*, 48.

34. Johnson, *Woman, Earth, and Creator Spirit*, 13; Ruether, "Ecofeminism," 2.

35. See Carol Christ, "Rethinking Theology and Nature" in *Reweaving the World*, ed. I. Diamond and G. F. Diamond (San Francisco: Sierra Club Books, 1990); and Mary Daly, *Beyond God the Father* (Boston: Beacon Press, 1973).

36. See Ruether, *Gaia and God*; and Sallie McFague, *Models of God* (Philadelphia: Fortress Press, 1987).

37. See Ivone Gebara, "The Trinity and Human Experience," in Ruether, *Women Healing Earth*.

38. See Johnson, *Women, Earth, and Creator Spirit*; and Anne M. Clifford, "Foundations for a Catholic Theology of God," in *"And God Saw That It Was Good": Catholic Theology and the Environment*, ed. Drew Christiansen and Walter Grazer (Washington, D.C.: USCC, 1996).

39. Ruether, *Gaia and God*, 4ff.

40. Ynestra King, in Plant, *Healing the Wounds*, 20.

41. Ibid.

42. Reuther, "Toward an Ecological-Feminist Theology of Nature," in Plant, *Healing the Wounds*, 145.

43. Charlene Spretnak, "Toward an Ecofeminist Spirituality," in Plant, *Healing the Wounds*, 128.

44. Sallie McFague, "An Earthly Theological Agenda," in Adams, *Ecofeminism and the Sacred*, 84ff.

45. Ibid., 95.

46. Ivone Gebara, "Cosmic Theology: Ecofeminism and Panentheism," in MacKinnon and McIntyre, *Readings in Ecology and Feminist Theology*, 212.

47. Primavesi, *From Apocalypse to Genesis*, 140.

48. Johnson, *Women, Earth, and Creator Spirit*, 20ff.

49. Reuther, *Gaia and God*, 228.

50. Ibid., 229.

51. Ibid., 251.

9   CHRISTIAN SPIRITUALITY

1. Bernard McGinn et al., eds., *Christian Spirituality* (New York: Crossroad, 1985), xv-xvi.

2. In Thomas Merton, *The Monastic Life* (New York: Doubleday, 1977), 21.

3. Evelyn Underhill, *The Essentials of Mysticism* (London: Dent, 1920), 2.

4. Thomas Merton, *The New Man* (New York: Farrar, 1961), 139.

5. Thomas Merton, *New Seeds of Contemplation* (New York: New Directions, 1972), 99.

6. Thomas Merton, "The Inner Experience," *Cistercian Studies* 18, 9-10. Quoted in Basil Pennington, *Centered Living* (New York: Doubleday, 1986), 72.

7. Karl J. Rahner, S.J., "The Ignatian Mysticism of Joy in the World," *Theological Investigations* (Baltimore: Helicon Press, 1967), 3:279.

8. Bernard Lonergan, *Method of Theology* (New York: Herder and Herder, 1972), 240.

9. Pierre Teilhard de Chardin, *The Future of Man* (New York: Harper, 1964), 15ff.

10. Pierre Teilhard de Chardin, *Building the Earth* (Wilkes-Barre, Pa.: Dimension, 1965), 110.

11. Pierre Teilhard de Chardin, *The Divine Milieu* (New York: Harper, 1968), 48.

12. Murray Bodo, "The Way of St. Francis," *St. Anthony's Messenger* (1995), 146ff.

13. Thomas Merton, *Contemplative Prayer* (New York: Herder and Herder, 1969), 122.

14. Albert J. Fritsch, S.J., "A Catholic Approach," *The Greening of Faith*, ed. John E. Carrol et al. (Hanover, N.H.: University Press of New England, 1997), 127.

15. Thomas Merton, *Conjectures of a Guilty Bystander* (Garden City, N.Y.: Doubleday, 1966), 140.

16. Pierre Teilhard de Chardin, *Letters to Two Friends, 1926-1952* (London: Collins, 1972), 44.

17. Brian Swimme, *The Hidden Heart of the Cosmos* (Maryknoll, N.Y.: Orbis Books, 1996), 99.

18. Ibid., 108.

19. Raymond E. Brown, *The Community of the Beloved Disciple* (New York: Paulist Press, 1979), 131ff.

20. In Richard Woods, *Christian Spirituality* (Allen, Tex.: Christian Classics, 1996), 116.

21. Pierre Teilhard de Chardin, *The Heart of Matter* (London: Collins, 1978), 47, quoted in Ursula King, *Spirit of Fire* (Maryknoll, N.Y.: Orbis Books, 1996), 204.

22. In Lawrence Cunningham, ed., *Thomas Merton: Spiritual Master* (New York: Paulist Press, 1992), 373.

23. Woods, *Christian Spirituality*, 92ff.

24. Ibid., 129ff.

25. Roger D. Sorrell, *St. Francis of Assisi and Nature* (New York: Oxford University Press, 1988), 19.

26. William J. Short, O.F.M., *The Franciscans* (Collegeville, Minn.: The Liturgical Press, 1990), 105.

27. Quoted in Maisie Ward, *St. Francis of Assisi* (New York: Sheed, 1950), 34.

28. In Henri DeLubac, S.J., *The Faith of Teilhard de Chardin* (London: Burns and Oates, 1964), 74-75.

29. Ibid., 123.

30. Teilhard, *The Divine Milieu*, 35.

31. Merton, *New Seeds of Contemplation*, 17.

32. Ibid., 31.

33. Thomas Berry, *The Dream of the Earth* (San Francisco: Sierra Club Books, 1988), 7.

34. Ibid., 7.

35. In Anne Lonergan and Caroline Richards, *Thomas Berry and the New Cosmology* (Mystic, Conn.: Twenty-Third Publications, 1987), 19.

36. Merton, *The New Man*, 117-18.

37. Gannett News Service (March 5, 1997).

38. Thomas Merton, *No Man Is an Island* (New York: Harcourt, 1978), 39.

39. Thomas Merton, *Contemplative Prayer*, 99.

40. Teilhard, *The Divine Milieu*, 52.

41. In Thomas Corbishley, *The Spirituality of Teilhard de Chardin* (London: Collins, 1971), 41.

42. Merton, *The New Man*, 243.

43. Merton, *Contemplative Prayer*, 36.

44. In Keith Egan, "Carmelite Spirituality," in *The New Dictionary of Catholic Spirituality*, ed. Michael Downey (Collegeville, Minn.: The Liturgical Press, 1993), 123.

45. Berry, *The Dream of the Earth*, 46.

46. Ward, *St. Francis of Assisi*, 29ff.

47. In Harvey D. Egan, S.J., *What Are They Saying about Mysticism?* (New York: Paulist Press, 1982), 99.

48. Merton, *New Seeds of Contemplation*, 296.

49. Ibid., 296-97.

50. Teilhard, *Building the Earth*, 60ff.

51. Teilhard, *The Divine Milieu*, 42.

52. Ibid., 138.

53. Merton, *New Seeds of Contemplation*, 290.

54. In Cunningham, *Thomas Merton: Spiritual Master*, 254.

55. For a thorough treatment of Teilhard's spirituality, see Ursula King, *Christ in All Things: Exploring Spirituality with Teilhard de Chardin* (Maryknoll, N.Y.: Orbis Books, 1997).

56. Teilhard, *The Divine Milieu*, 14.

57. Merton, *New Seeds of Contemplation*, 71.

58. Teilhard, *The Divine Milieu*, 101.

59. Pierre Teilhard de Chardin, *Writings in the Time of War* (New York: Harper, 1968), 120.

60. Pierre Teilhard de Chardin, *Christianity and Evolution* (New York: Harcourt, 1971), 19.

61. In King, *Spirit of Fire*, 64.

62. Ibid., 61.

63. Ibid., 70.

64. "The Way of Perfection," quoted in Lawrence S. Cunningham and Keith J. Egan, *Christian Spirituality* (New York: Paulist Press, 1996), 101.

65. "The Dark Night," quoted in Cunningham and Egan, *Christian Spirituality*, 101.

66. David Tracy, "Recent Catholic Spirituality: Unity and Diversity," in *Christian Spirituality: Post-Reformation and Modern*, ed. Louis Dupré and Don E. Saliers (New York: Crossroad, 1989), 3:143-73.

10   AN ENVIRONMENTAL ETHIC

1. Bernard Häring, *Free and Faithful in Christ*, vol. 3 (New York: Crossroad, 1981).

2. Häring, *Free and Faithful in Christ*, 3:176.

3. Deborah Blake, "Toward a Sustainable Ethic: Virtue and the Environment," in *"And God Saw That It Was Good,"* ed. Drew Christiansen and Walter Grazer (Washington, D.C.: USCC, 1996), 202.

4. James A. Nash, *Loving Nature* (Nashville: Abingdon Press, 1991), 139ff.

5. Ibid., 152ff.

6. For commentary, see Drew Christiansen, "Ecology and the Common Good," in Christiansen and Grazer, *"And God Saw That It Was Good,"* 184ff.

7. John Paul II, "Sollicitude Rei Socialis" (December 30, 1987), no. 32.

8. John Paul II, "The Ecological Crisis: A Common Responsibility" (December 8, 1989), no. 1, in Christiansen and Grazer, *"And God Saw That It Was Good,"* 219.

9. Drew Christiansen, "Ecology and the Common Good," in Christiansen and Grazer, *"And God Saw That It Was Good,"* 189.

10. Larry L. Rasmussen, *Earth Community Earth Ethics* (Maryknoll, N.Y.: Orbis Books, 1996), 260.

11. See "Tom's River Cited as Cancer Hot Spot," *Ocean Co. Observer*, The Associated Press (March 11, 1996), and Rae Corelli, "Fighting for Fish," *MacLean's* (May 19, 1997), 19.

12. Nash, *Loving Nature*, 165.

13. Ibid., 166.

14. Ibid., 168.

15. In Christiansen and Grazer, *"And God Saw That It Was Good,"* 219.

16. Christiansen, "Ecology and the Common Good," 184.

17. Daniel C. Maquire, *A New American Justice* (Minneapolis: Winston Press, 1980), 85ff.

18. Charles Murphy, *At Home on the Earth* (New York: Crossroad, 1989), 12.

19. Wendell Berry, *Another Turn of the Crank* (Washington, D.C.: Counterpoint, 1995), 19-21.

20. Häring, *Free and Faithful in Christ*, 3:182-83.

21. E. F. Schumacher, *Small Is Beautiful* (New York: Harper & Row, 1973), 151ff.

22. Michael S. Northcott, *The Environment and Christian Ethics* (New York: Cambridge University Press, 1996), 73.

23. Häring, *Free and Faithful in Christ*, 3:180.

24. Thomas Berry, *Befriending the Earth* (Mystic, Conn.: Twenty-Third Publications, 1991), 6.

25. Thomas Berry, *The Dream of the Earth* (San Francisco, Sierra Club Books, 1988), 1.

26. Berry, *Befriending the Earth*, 6.

27. Ibid., 1.

28. Northcott, *The Environment and Christian Ethics*, 135ff.

29. Ibid., 137.

30. Murphy, *At Home on the Earth*, 61ff.

31. James Gustafson, *A Sense of the Divine* (Cleveland: Pilgrim Press, 1994), 14.

32. Ibid., 480.

33. Ibid., 73.

34. Roston Holmes III, *Environmental Ethics* (Philadelphia: Temple University Press, 1988), 198.

35. In Kevin W. Irwin and Edmund D. Pellegrino, eds., *Preserving the Creation: Environmental Theology and Ethics* (Washington, D.C.: Georgetown University Press, 1994), 115.

36. Aldo Leopold, *A Sand County Almanac* (New York: Ballantine Books, 1970), 239.

37. In Häring, *Free and Faithful in Christ*, 3:182.

38. Ibid.

39. Murphy, *At Home on the Earth*, xv.

40. Daniel M. Cowden, "Toward an Environmental Ethic," in Irwin and Pellegrino, *Preserving the Creation*, 121.

41. Stephen Hawking, *A Short History of Time* (New York: Bantam, 1988), 175.

42. Northcott, *The Environment and Christian Ethics*, 227.

43. In Gustafson, *A Sense of the Divine*, 77.

44. Rasmussen, *Earth Community, Earth Ethics*, 236.

45. Michael J. Himes and Kenneth R. Himes, "The Sacrament of Creation: Toward an Environmental Theology," in *Readings in Ecology and Feminist Theology*, ed. Mary Heather MacKinnon and Moni McIntyre (Kansas City: Sheed and Ward, 1995), 277-78.

46. Northcott, *The Environment and Christian Ethics*, 237.

47. Rasmussen, *Earth Community Earth Ethics*, 343. See David W. Orr, *Ecological Literacy* (Albany: State University of New York Press, 1992), 29f.

48. Häring, *Free and Faithful in Christ*, 3:178.

49. Gustafson, *A Sense of the Divine*, 148.

50. Elizabeth Roberts and Elias Amidon, eds., *Earth Prayers from around the World: 365 Prayers, Poems, and Invocations for Honoring the Earth* (San Francisco: HarperSanFrancisco, 1991), xxi.

Suggested Readings

Adams, Carol, ed. *Ecofeminism and the Sacred.* New York: Crossroad, 1993.

Berger, Pamela. *The Goddess Obscured: The Transformation of the Grain Protectress from Goddess to Saint.* Boston: Beacon Press, 1985.

Berry, Thomas. *The Dream of the Earth.* San Francisco: Sierra Club Books, 1988.

———, and Brian Swimme. *The Universe Story: From the Primordial Flaring Forth to the Ecozoic Era—A Celebration of the Unfolding of the Cosmos.* San Francisco: Harper-Collins, 1992.

Birch, Charles, William Eakin, and Jay B. McDaniel. *Liberating Life: Contemporary Approaches to Ecological Theology.* Maryknoll, N.Y.: Orbis Books, 1990.

Boff, Leonardo. *Ecology and Liberation: A New Paradigm.* Maryknoll, N.Y.: Orbis Books, 1995.

———. *Cry of the Earth, Cry of the Poor.* Maryknoll, N.Y.: Orbis Books, 1996.

Christ, Carol P., and Judith Plaskow, eds. *Weaving the Visions: New Patterns in Feminist Spirituality.* San Francisco: Harper & Row, 1989.

Christiansen, Drew, and Walter Grazer, eds. *"And God Saw That It Was Good": Catholic Theology and the Environment.* Washington, D.C.: USCC, 1996.

Cobb, John B., Jr. *Is It Too Late? A Theology of Ecology.* Beverly Hills: Bruce, 1972.

De Witt, Calvin B. *The Environment and the Christian: What Does the New Testament Say about the Environment?* Grand Rapids: Baker, 1991.

Dowd, Michael. *Earthspirit: A Handbook for Nurturing Ecological Christianity.* Mystic, Conn.: Twenty-Third Publications, 1991.

Dunn, Stephen, and Anne Lonergan, eds. *Befriending the Earth: A Theology of Reconciliation Between Humans and the Earth.* Mystic, Conn.: Twenty-Third Publications, 1991.

Edwards, Denis, *Jesus the Wisdom of God: An Ecological Theology.* Maryknoll, N.Y.: Orbis Books, 1995.

Fragomeni, Richard N., and John T. Pawlikowski, eds. *The Ecological Challenge.* Collegeville, Minn.: Liturgical Press, 1994.

Fritsch, Al, S.J. *Down to Earth Spirituality.* Kansas City, Mo.: Sheed & Ward, 1992.

Gimbutas, Marija. *The Gods and Goddesses of Old Europe, 7000 to 3500 B.C.: Myths, Legends, and Cult Images.* Berkeley: University of California Press, 1974.

Gottlieb, Roger S., ed. *A New Creation: America's Contemporary Spiritual Voices.* New York: Crossroad, 1990.

Gustafson, James M. *A Sense of the Divine: The Natural Environment from a Theocentric Perspective.* Cleveland: Pilgrim, 1994.

Hall, Douglas John. *Imaging God: Dominion as Stewardship.* Grand Rapids: Eerdmans; New York: Friendship, 1986.

Hallman, David, ed. *Ecotheology.* Maryknoll, N.Y.: Orbis Books, 1995.

Häring, Bernard. *Free and Faithful in Christ,* vol. 3. New York: Crossroad, 1981.

Haught, John R. *The Promise of Nature: Ecology and Cosmic Purpose.* New York: Paulist Press, 1993.

Irwin, Kevin W., and Edmund D. Pellegrino. *Preserving the Creation: Environmental Theology and Ethics.* Washington, D.C.: Georgetown University Press, 1994.

Johnson, Elizabeth A. *Women, Earth, and Creator Spirit.* New York: Paulist Press, 1993.

Jung, Shannon. *We Are Home: A Spirituality of the Environment.* New York: Paulist Press, 1993.

King, Ursula, *Christ in All Things: Exploring Spirituality with Teilhard de Chardin.* Maryknoll, N.Y.: Orbis Books, 1997.

LaChance, Albert J., and John E. Carroll, eds. *Embracing Earth: Catholic Approaches to Ecology.* Maryknoll, N.Y.: Orbis Books, 1994.

McCarthy, Scott. *Creation Liturgy: An Earth-Centered Theology of Worship.* San Jose, Calif.: Resource, 1987.

McDaniel, Jay B. *Of God and Pelicans: A Theology of Reverence for Life.* Louisville, Ky.: Westminster/John Knox, 1989.

——. *Earth, Sky, Gods, and Mortals: Developing an Ecological Christianity.* Mystic, Conn.: Twenty-Third Publications, 1990.

——. *With Roots and Wings: Christianity in an Age of Ecology and Dialogue.* Maryknoll, N.Y.: Orbis Books, 1995.

McDonagh, Sean. *To Care for the Earth: A Call to a New Theology.* Sante Fe, N.M.: Bear, 1986.

——. *The Greening of the Church.* Maryknoll, N.Y.: Orbis Books, 1990.

——. *Passion for the Earth.* Maryknoll, N.Y.: Orbis Books, 1994.

Moltmann, Jurgen. *God in Creation: A New Theology of Creation.* New York: Harper & Row, 1985.

Murphy, Charles M. *At Home on Earth: Foundations for a Catholic Ethic of the Environment.* New York: Crossroad, 1989.

Nash, James A. *Loving Nature: Ecological Integrity and Christian Responsibility.* Nashville: Abingdon, 1991.

Plant, Judith, ed. *Healing the Wounds: The Promise of Ecofeminism.* Philadelphia: New Society, 1989.

Plaskow, Judith. *Standing Again at Sinai: Judaism from a Feminist Perspective.* New York: Harper & Row, 1990.

Rasmussen, Larry L. *Earth Community, Earth Ethics.* Maryknoll, N.Y.: Orbis Books, 1996.

Robb, Carol S., and Carl Casebolt. *Covenant for a New Creation: Ethics, Religion, and Public Policy.* Maryknoll, N.Y.: Orbis Books, 1991.

Roberts, Elizabeth, and Elias Amidon. *Earth Prayers from around the World: 365 Prayers, Poems, and Invocations for Honoring the Earth.* San Francisco: HarperSanFrancisco, 1991.

Ruether, Rosemary Radford. *Gaia and God: An Ecofeminist Theology of Earth Healing.* San Francisco: Harper, 1992.

Scharper, Stephen B., and Hilary Cunningham. *The Green Bible.* Maryknoll, N.Y.: Orbis Books, 1993.

Sheldon, Joseph. *Rediscovery of Creation: A Bibliographical Study of the Church's Response to the Environmental Crisis.* Metuchen, N.Y.: Scarecrow, 1992.

Shiva, Vandana. *Staying Alive: Women, Ecology and Development.* London: Zed, 1989.

Smith, Pamela. *What Are They Saying about Environmental Ethics?* New York: Paulist Press, 1998.

Sorrell, Roger. *St. Francis of Assisi and Nature: Tradition and Innovation in Western Christian Attitudes toward the Environment.* Oxford: Oxford University Press, 1988.

Tucker, Mary Evelyn, and John A. Grim, eds. *Worldviews and Ecology: Religion, Philosophy, and the Environment.* Maryknoll, N.Y.: Orbis Books, 1994.

Index

Also in the Ecology and Justice Series